Good Teaching

Good Teaching

AN INTEGRATED APPROACH TO LANGUAGE, LITERACY, AND LEARNING

Nancy P. Bertrand & Carole F. Stice

Heinemann • Portsmouth, NH

KH

Heinemann
A division of Reed Elsevier Inc.
361 Hanover Street
Portsmouth, NH 03801–3912
www.heinemann.com

Offices and agents throughout the world

First edition, titled *Integrating Reading and the Other Language Arts*, by Carol F. Stice, John E. Bertrand, and Nancy P. Bertrand, published by Wadsworth Publishing Company, 1995.

Library of Congress Cataloging-in-Publication Data
Stice, Carol F.
    Good teaching : an integrated approach to language, literacy, and learning / Nancy P.
  Bertrand & Carole F. Stice.
       p. cm.
    Rev. ed. of: Integrating reading and other language arts. 1995
    Includes bibliographical references (p.) and index.
    ISBN 0-325-00359-9
    1. Language experience approach in education. 2. Language arts (Elementary) 3.
English language—Study and teaching (Elementary) 4. Learning, Psychology of. I.
Bertrand, Nancy Parks, 1949- II. Stice, Carole F. Integrating reading and the other
language arts. III. Title.

    LB1576 .S7986 2002
    372.6—dc21

                      2002017260

Editor: Lois Bridges
Cover design: Catherine Hawkes, Cat & Mouse Design
Cover photo: Loretta Downs
Text design: Darci Mehall, Aureo Design
Manufacturing: Louise Richardson

Printed in the United States of America on acid-free paper
08 07 06 05 04   VP   2 3 4 5 6

8/26/05

In loving memory of my father, James D. Parks, and to my mother, Jean, and my husband, John.

NANCY P. BERTRAND

In loving memory of my parents, Mona V. and Kenneth F. Kirchner, and for Reilly.

CAROLE F. STICE

CONTENTS

FOREWORD

When I read professional books, my mind jumps back and forth from the text to classrooms I've been a part of, and, when I read these books, I always do so with a pencil in hand. The obligatory pencil is for marginalia, that is, for thoughts scribbled or drawn in the margins of the book. I think of these notes as my written conversations with the author, often an affirmation, but sometimes a rebuttal. I've noticed that if I disagree with a writer, the notes are brief, snappish, sometimes rude, and once in a while limited to a single four-letter word. On the other hand, the more I like what I'm reading, the longer the more elaborated the marginalia. If the author addresses my experiences, my issues, my problems, even my dreams, the margins are filled with comments, stars, double stars and *hmmmm*, my shorthand for "need to think about this."

The margins of my copy of *Good Teaching: An Integrated Approach to Language, Literacy, and Learning* are filled! I predict yours will be too. Nancy Bertrand and Carole Stice have poured their lives into this work, lives of two teachers who know how and why it is necessary to address the concerns and dreams of other educators about Good Teaching.

In the musical, "The Wiz," the wiz tells Dorothy that, It ain't enough to know where you're going, you gotta know where you're comin' from. Carole and Nancy follow the wiz's advice. Before presenting experiences suitable for students and teachers, the authors delve into "where we're comin' from," that is, they explore the theory that supports the practices they advocate. For instance, by their own example, they tell us that if we first study how children learn, many of our teaching problems will be resolved. The authors begin their discussion by helping us understand how learning does and does not take place. Building on sound learning theory, they then offer compatible teaching experiences.

Taking their own advice, Nancy and Carole respect and detail diverse points of view. On issues such as the learning process, the function of the brain, how language is gained, reading and writing instruction, and on curriculum planning, the authors describe approaches and opinions that are consistent with their beliefs and those not in keeping with their philosophical base. They attempt to see all sides. And they never fail to include the voices of the most genuine informants: kids. When ten-year-old, Jenny gives her observations on learning, and a six-year-old boy, learning metaphorically, sees the relationship between a pair of pliers and butterfly wings, we gain a deeper perspective on the authors' preferred theories, and on our own beliefs.

At the close of each chapter, the authors link the theoretical foundations that best fit beliefs about learning and teaching to practical classroom experiences; there's no mismatch of theory and practice. They suggest readings and activities that expand and enrich our thinking. Here's where my marginalia becomes dense; Carole and Nancy cause me to reflect (lots of *hmmmms* on the margins of these pages). They invite us all to wonder about learning-teaching experiences that we might want to try and, just as important, they ask us to ponder our pedagogical decisions. For example, the authors thoughtfully build a case for why learning to read and write must be natural, holistic processes. They explore the nature of learning, the function of the brain and how language emerges, all leading to experiences that can help kids become literate. We then are presented with suggestions that cause us to reflect even more on these experiences. In other words, the authors present us with texts of consequence, that is, their ideas initiate what Paulo Freire terms "praxis": hard thinking, intense reflecting, and significant action.

Good Teaching provides new understandings and classroom suggestions, but it also gives some old ideas and familiar classroom experiences new life:

■ We are called on to reflect on significant issues: "If natural learning is defined as the extraction of meaningful patterns from complex input, it follows that in schools, learners require rich, plentiful content that is both meaningful and interesting to them."

■ We are reminded that being a child's teacher is an awesome task in which we must be just and fair: "Teacher expectation plays a part in children's success or failure in school, and teachers may be influenced by dialects to form low expectations for some children. Lowered expectations operate against low-income children."

■ We are asked to avoid empty exercises and wasteful goals: "The main focus is, and remains, on meaning."

■ "The ultimate goal is to instill a love of reading."

■ Parents are given food for thought: "Attention span is learned, so if parents begin reading to their children when they are infants, they will learn to attend."

■ Complex issues are put in perspective: ". . . children typically develop phonemic awareness without training, just as they developed phonological awareness without training as they learned to talk."

■ We see real teachers in real classrooms: We visit ". . . Tina DeStephen's transition classroom in a rural elementary school . . . where the children were in danger of being labeled 'slow learners,' 'learning disabled,' . . . "

■ Important information is presented in understandable and inviting language: "It is the human brain, not our ears, that comprehends human speech—the brain, not the hand, that composes a symphony or writes a poem. The brain creates a powerful sermon or political address and dances Swan Lake. Your brain, rather than your eyes, is reading this book."

The authors never shy away from speaking their minds and never shirk the tough, confusing, and often controversial issues: phonemic awareness, classroom management, differences among learners, discipline, guided reading, critical literacy, spelling instruction, evaluation, testing, and many more. They add to our collection of instruments and guidelines for: keeping records; literacy strategies and experiences; Internet sites, text sets, and, of course, books, books, books for children and teachers. Nancy and Carole deepen our understanding of the psychogenerative process, constructivist theory, miscue analysis, and inquiry.

I approached this work from a holistic viewpoint, and doing so, I felt comfortable in the book. That is to say, I felt at home as the authors built a case for why learning to read and write are interrelated processes and curriculum must be integrated, constructivist, and inquiry based. However, the work is not just for teachers who hold these beliefs; it's for all teachers, all teachers who are asking questions, all teachers who want to take another step in their thinking, learning, and teaching.

Nancy and Carole tell us that knowledge is changing. They help us see that our answers today—for this thematic study, this literature discussion, these children—must be temporary and must lead to more inquiry and more exploring. We learn that the way we get to Good Teaching is to examine what we know, no matter how temporary; celebrate and keep the authentic and successful; and then ask more questions. The authors are first-rate colleagues who share their best, ask the best of us, and invite us to continue the inquiry.

—Dorothy Watson

ACKNOWLEDGMENTS

Most of what we know or think we know has come from a combination of professional readings and contact with others. The wonderful classrooms into which we have been invited over the years and the great teaching we have been privileged to watch have provided us with a wealth of invaluable insights. To those wonderful teachers, thank you. You are our inspiration! We are indebted to more teachers than we could ever name individually, but we have shared a few of those marvelous classrooms with you in this text.

A special note of thanks is extended to the children and their teachers whose photographs illustrate this book. Your pictures make the text come alive. Thank you! Thanks also to Sandie Norton for taking most of the photos and to Jackie Rule. The pictures you provided are beautiful.

To our own teachers, in whose presence we have learned so much, we offer our gratitude. To Ken and Yetta Goodman, Dorothy Watson, Martha King, the late Moira McKenzie, Jerry Harste, and Carol Lynch-Brown, we extend our heartfelt thanks.

To our colleagues, Mary Bess Dunn and Bobbie Solley, who offered support and suggestions along the way, we are most appreciative. Patty Murphy, a graduate assistant, thank you for your keen, fresh eyes. To John Bertrand, for your valuable assistance with the index, and you aren't a bad photographer either. Thank you for your time. Your succor has been immeasurable.

Last, but certainly not least, we are eternally grateful to our editor, Lois Bridges, who was willing to go out on a limb for us, who gave us her wisdom and expertise, and who offered encouragement and good cheer all along the way. And to Judith Neff, a fourth–fifth-grade teacher at St. Joseph School in Knoxville, Tennessee, and an adjunct professor of reading at the University of Tennessee, how can we ever thank you for the many hours you spent reading, critiquing, and suggesting?

We are privileged to call these people our friends.

PREFACE

"The challenges we face as teachers, be they policy, curriculum, or control, require that we address at least three issues: our multiple and fluid identities in and out of schools and how those identities are embedded within our definitions of literacy and democracy, our will to act on our convictions and new knowledge, and our abilities to respect diversity and our adversaries."

(Patrick Shannon, 2001, 588)

As a beginning first grader, Kenda could read a little. She recognized many words in context. She had recognized her own name in print for more than two years, "knew" many of her favorite stories by heart, and could already tell time. Her first-grade teacher employed a synthetic phonics program along with the basal reader program and before long, Kenda tried to "sound out" every word in every line of print including t-h-e.

Kenda's mother, also a teacher, suggested she try additional ways of figuring out unknown words: check the picture; skip the word and read on, then come back and try again; or say something that makes sense and keep going. Kenda replied, "I can't do that. The teacher won't let me." "Just try a couple of these ideas for a few days to see how they work, " her mother urged. At that point, Kenda said, "But Mama, you don't understand. That's cheating."

When children come to view using what they already know to figure out something new as cheating, teachers are guilty of creating the very problems they seek to avoid. This kind of difficulty occurs when teachers have not been helped to understand what language is, how it is learned, how the brain works in language learning, and what the reading process is.

Reducing to a single text any set of processes and their theoretical bases risks stifling critical thinking. "One-right-way-only" perspectives put limitations on reasoning, personal responsibility, and learning. When that happens, continued evolution of important understandings are in danger of being corrupted. Understanding children's literacy is still growing and changing. This text is offered as a foundation upon which to continue building knowledge about teaching and learning. We certainly do not claim it to be the last, or the best, word on the subject. We do claim it to be comprehensive and accurate to this point.

We present an integrated language and literacy perspective. We do not attempt to "bridge the gap" between traditional, skills-based classroom practices and constructivist philosophy. We take one stand; detail its theoretical and research base; provide connections to and a framework for instruction; describe the major approaches; offer a variety of sound, successful teaching techniques and strategies; and present accompanying evaluation procedures.

The book is not intended to replace the variety of wonderful books written by classroom teachers and other practitioners about instruction or classroom management. Rather, it is designed to provide a solid theoretical foundation, to help learners begin to connect theory to practice, to lay a framework onto which additional information may be scaffolded, and to get beginning teachers off to a good start.

The educational philosophy presented in the first several chapters has its roots in the progressive era and is based on research from the last forty years in many related fields including child language development, neurophysiology, cybernetics, linguistics, the reading and writing processes, and learning.

Based on what is known about the human brain and how humans learn, what language is and how children learn their first language, a framework for language and literacy instruction emerges. We hope that as you read and reflect on the information, you consider how to apply, assess, refine, and adapt it. Consider what you have learned about language, how children learn it, and how they first become literate. Consider what your understandings mean for planning and delivering instruction.

The next several chapters further expansion of oral language in schools, continuing with understanding the reading and writing processes, and presenting the major approaches for teaching reading and writing. Observation and evaluation procedures and techniques are included.

Since language is the foundation for all school and future learning, and since children learn language by using it, we focus on language in use. We describe how good teachers observe and assess their students and plan instruction based on what they learn about the needs and interests of their learners.

Good teachers know that children learn best when they are engaged in learning. What engages learners is what interests them. Engaged learners are motivated, strategic, knowledgeable, and socially interactive. Learners become engaged and learn best when they are in pursuit of something they want to know about or learn how to do. We believe such knowledge about learning and learners have powerful implications for teaching and teachers and for all educational decision makers.

One goal of education is to create content-rich classrooms that help children learn and become independent, lifelong learners. If language is the primary tool for teaching, and language in all its forms is the primary tool for learning, we believe the following to be true:

- Oral language is the foundation, the keeper of concept knowledge as it develops.
- Reading expands learner capabilities exponentially.
- Good literature helps children grow as intelligent and caring human beings.
- Writing is vital to the development of the mind, for success in school, and to the quality of later life.
- The best classrooms are those in which teachers and students learn together.

The final chapters in the book describe how good teachers use their knowledge, logic, insights, and values. They create classroom environments, select materials, assist students with their own pursuits, and integrate the curriculum by developing projects that cut across the artificial boundaries of individual disciplines. As teachers employ activities, create experiences, provide opportunities, develop environments, and shape attitudes with their classes, they help learners work together as a community. Each learner becomes independent and expands his or her view of the world.

We also address how to get started. We look at issues of diversity, and reemphasize that good teachers do not teach from teacher's manuals and preset programs. Good teachers do not need, nor do they look for "magic bullet" programs, methods, or materials. Rather, they teach from their best, informed judgments and from their students' lives and interests. They teach for children's wider view of how the world works.

Each chapter begins with a few focus questions and ends with a brief theory-to-practice guide. Every chapter is followed by suggestions for further reading and suggested activities for exploring some of the issues raised. The appendices include extended information on phonics, bookbinding instructions, suggested professional books and journals, selected Internet resources for students and teachers, and some sample record-keeping devices.

It is our hope that you will take the information, suggestions, and ideas presented in this text and reflect upon them, asking your own questions and following your own inquiries. We believe that is what produces good teaching.

Nancy P. Bertrand
Carole F. Stice

CHAPTER ONE

> "If the purpose of teaching is to promote learning, then we need to ask what we mean by that term."
>
> *(Carl Rogers, 1983, 18)*

LEARNING

Each of us at one time or another probably memorized the names of all the former presidents of the United States, in chronological order, so that we could recite them for a grade. How many of us can recite them now? Compare that learning to remembering the lyrics of a favorite song, even one you have not heard in years. While both examples represent rote memorization, which was easier to do? Which was remembered longer? Why?

Human beings can only "see" based on what they know, and when they learn something new, both the knower and known are changed forever (Dewey and Bentley, 1949). Most human learning is complex and difficult. Yet, when we are interested in something, when we believe we have a need to know, we learn with relative ease.

Walking down a dirt road, along the side of a Kansas farm field in late summer, I am assailed by tenderly familiar sights, sounds, and smells that remind me of my childhood, of the summers I spent with my maternal grandmother and our relatives in rural Kansas. When I was grown and my grandmother's family gone, I visited the area with a friend who was a naturalist. As we walked along the edge of what was once my great-uncle's farm, my friend pointed out plants by name such as flowering thistles and milkweed. He showed me animals I would never have seen on my own and told me something about each one. He identified local birds such as the scissortail flycatcher and the western meadowlark. He even gave me some information about the land formations we were seeing. The whole panorama came alive for me in a new way. I know that part of the country differently now. It has greater depth and richness of detail in my memory. When I look now I see more than I ever dreamed was there. But more than that, my memories from childhood have been altered a little, almost as if I knew then what I know now.

Most human learning is complex, but it is not confusing and obscure. As teachers, we must know something about how the brain works and what learning is. How do people not only survive, but come to understand the world around them and prosper in it? How do they learn complex processes? Can others, namely teachers, positively affect the learning of such processes?

In this chapter we explore learning in schools and contrast that with learning which occurs outside the classroom. By comparing learning in different situations, we construct a definition of learning. We examine how recent findings about the brain have contributed to our understanding of learning and how it takes place. Finally, we discuss specific conditions that, when present, facilitate learning. Our goal is to help you, as learner, construct your own personal understanding and expand your theory of what learning is and how it happens so that you, as teacher, can apply that knowledge in your classroom.

WHAT LEARNING IS: TWO PERSPECTIVES

At some point in your education you have probably heard learning defined as "change in behavior." This is a simple definition for a complicated phenomenon, one that is probably too simplistic. In our search for a clearer definition of learning, we decided to ask an expert; we asked a child.

> **Mother:** What is learning?
>
> **Jenny:** Something you do to find out things. But mostly it's boring. I mean like who wants to learn to subtract a turnip from another turnip. Most kids think that's stupid!
>
> **Mother:** Have you ever learned anything that wasn't boring?
>
> **Jenny:** Sure. Water-skiing. That wasn't boring. That was fun.
>
> **Mother:** Why was that different?
>
> **Jenny:** Easy. Because I had a choice. I could choose whether or not I wanted to ski.

At age ten, Jenny already distinguished between learning at school and other kinds of learning. School learning is not always an act of free choice, nor does it always make sense to the learner. In the above example, Jenny illustrates what Frank Smith (1998) calls the two visions of learning: an official theory and the classic view.

The classic view of learning is the one employed most frequently outside school. It is classic because it is "archetypal, universal, deeply rooted and uncontaminated" (Smith, 1998, 3). However, it has not been experimentally proven. Simply put, the classic view states that "we learn from the company we keep" (Smith, 1998, 3). Learning is something we do all the time, especially to find out things we want to know about or do. The classic view holds that this kind of learning is easy, that it is effortless and internally motivated. It is also internally organized and monitored. But, because the learning process is complex and cannot always be directly observed, this type of learning is difficult to measure. The example we can all relate to is learning to talk.

Smith (1998, 3) asserts that "there is an alternative to the classic view that is preeminent, coercive, manipulative, discriminatory, and wrong." The official theory is the one employed by most schools. It is official because it has been scientifically proven in laboratory conditions. That means that what is being learned is also being measured, for example, the number of repetitions needed for children to learn a list of ten words such as *was, went,* and *for.* Simply put, the official theory holds that learning is work, that it is difficult, so what is being learned must be organized for the learner and accompanied by reward and/or punishment. Since it is difficult, learning requires effort and external motivation. It must be constantly controlled and monitored to ensure it is taking place. If, as Smith argues, most people believe that learning takes place when we want to find out things, why then have our schools embraced a theory of learning so contradictory to people's innate natural processing?

The "Official" Theory: Learning as Outcome or Product   Science, one of humankind's most important creations, offers us protection and hope through the information it provides. It improves the quality of our lives. However, learned people who once thought the earth was flat eventually came to the conclusion that it was elliptical, if not perfectly round. In the late nineteenth century, biologists and psychologists began to examine and hypothesize about what happened in the brain when conscious beings were moved to action that was more complex than instinct alone. Today, scientists are asking what happens in the brain when human beings think, act, and learn. But investigators in the area of human learning were not always so enlightened in their early efforts to understand.

These early psychologists wanted to establish their budding discipline as a bona fide science, which required that they employ the scientific method. Because people believed that science could solve any problem and answer every question, employing the scientific method, i.e., conducting reliable, replicable psychological experiments under controlled conditions would lend credibility to psychology.

Psychologists who decided to study human learning found they had a problem. To meet the requirements of the scientific method, they had to look for ways to study learning independent of any outside or past experiences their subjects might have had. No easily measured unit of learning was available; nothing existed in a vacuum that could be "learned" under various, controlled conditions and then counted to see how much of it had been learned. Moreover, the speed at which something was learned, clearly an important variable, appeared to depend on what was being learned.

In 1870, Herman Ebbinghaus (1913) thought he had solved this scientific problem by designing a study wherein the subjects (learners) would learn a series of nonsense syllables; e.g., WUG, DEX, TAV. The syllables, or units of learning, could be variously manipulated by controlling the number of syllables to be learned, the number of trials, and the amount of time per trial, etc. Under these controlled conditions the subjects would always perform in a predictable and consistent manner, and learning, defined as product or outcome, could always be observed and measured. This constituted a true scientific experiment in which learning was not related to past experience and could be both controlled and measured.

Ebbinghaus (1913) found that the more his subjects had to learn, the longer it took, and the more time the subjects had, the better their learning was. Thus, the theory of learning as measurable outcome, i.e., the official theory of learning, was born. If, however, the subjects were able to make sense of what they were "learning," the data were contaminated because something was occurring that could not be seen and the study ruined. It was assumed that once sense was made of anything being learned, the subjects in effect already knew something about what they were supposed to be learning, and "pure" learning was no longer studied or measured. In other words, in these primitive studies of learning, it was considered essential for subjects to learn something absolutely unknown, and nonsense certainly fit that requirement. Since these early researchers thought only something new could be scientifically studied as learning, learning came to be thought of as necessarily detached from meaningful context and prior knowledge. This great mistake in judgment led to long-term, narrowed, and oversimplified views of human learning. There is a great difference between a phenomenon controlled for experimentation and natural or real phenomena occurring outside the laboratory.

At the turn of the century, John Watson, a prominent American psychologist, theorized that through learning an organism developed the means to cope with its environment. He studied behavior and the newly developing field of psychology incorporated this emphasis on behavior in its theoretical view of learning (Watson, 1914). Through studies of animal behavior/animal learning, a definition of learning as a response (i.e., behavior) to a stimulus gained credence.

During the first quarter of the twentieth century, psychologists attempted to discover general "laws" in order to expand their measurable, outcome-based, behavioral theory of learning. Pavlov (1927), for example, demonstrated he could "condition" an animal to make a novel response to a new stimulus. Because of his work, psychologists were more convinced than ever that learning had to be a measurable response and that learning for purposes of study had to be disconnected from the known in order to meet the requirements of the scientific method.

Building on the theories of Watson, Pavlov, and others, Thorndike (1913, 1932) extended and elaborated the behavioral view with his theory of connections between a stimulus and a response. He found that subjects learned to respond habitually in particular ways to particular situations. From the 1920s through the 1940s, B. F. Skinner (1938) further refined the behavioral theory of learning as a measurable outcome and stated that human behavior is controlled by its consequences. Thus, between Thorndike and Skinner, learning came to be defined as any change in observable behavior directly resulting from observable experience (that is, stimulus-response).

Eventually, the fundamental postulate was that learning was the result of operant conditioning. Learning, according to the new field of psychology, occurred as the organism (the learner), sought pleasure and avoided pain. The learner was viewed as passive and subject to the various forces in the environment. In other words, people were controlled by the world; they did not control the world.

Based on his experiments with laboratory animals, Skinner (1938) believed that behavior had no inner causes, no needs or drives or motives that explained it. Conditions and events in the world operated on the organism, causing behavior and therefore learning. From this perspective, Skinner reasoned that human behavior could be "shaped" by controlling pleasure and pain. He called this shaping process reinforcement. By shaping human behavior through reinforcement, the subject can be made to respond with desirable habits. Effective learning came to be defined as "the establishment of 'good' or 'desirable' habits and the prevention and or elimination of 'bad' or 'undesirable' habits" (Cambourne, 1988, 18).

Behaviorists believe that both human and animal learning, or behavior, can only be explained in terms of habit formation through a system of rewards and punishments. They had no use for "mentalistic" terms like "mind," "thought," or "feelings," which they regarded as unobservable, unmeasurable, and therefore, unscientific (Smith, 1986).

The official learning theory, employed in most schools at the end of the twentieth century, grew out of the need of research psychologists to lend their field an aura of credibility. The result from over one hundred years of thinking and effort was the behaviorist, product-based, measurable-outcome-only, stimulus-response, etc., description of human learning. It holds that learning is work and that anything can be learned provided sufficient effort is expended, the learning is undertaken incrementally, and sufficient control is enforced (Smith, 1998).

Since learning is seen as difficult, learners must be motivated to do it. Learning requires constant monitoring of the behaviors sought, usually in the form of testing, to ensure that it is taking place. Given this definition, what is to be learned does not have to be connected to prior knowledge or be meaningful to the learner. And if the learner does not learn on the first trial, then reteaching, that is, new stimulus and retesting, is required, employing more responses. Praise, punishment, threats, and grades are among the many possible responses teachers and parents use. Therefore also, the relationship between learning and teaching has come to be viewed as detached and distant at best.

The official theory has gained supreme power in education where "learning is regarded as work and forgetting [and failure] as inevitable" (Smith, 1998, 12). Today, too many teachers, legislators, business leaders, and parents still believe that children are passive receivers of information, that they learn only what they are directly taught, and that what is taught must be broken down into small pieces and fed to them sequentially, within a test-teach-test-driven formula. Memorization is the primary mode. This definition of learning has been and remains preeminent, even in the face of other more complex views, because it is so easy to implement and assess. It is well to remember that after decades of intense teach-to-the-test curricula, we are failing to achieve the promised results.

The official theory says we have to learn something to understand it. Yet, this is totally contrary to how scientists now describe human perception and learning. Today, we know that we have to understand, at least in part, in order to learn something (Smith, 1998). If behaviorism is the most accurate explanation of how humans learn, why do we learn so many complex processes—talking, walking, water-skiing, riding a two-wheeler, driving a car, or using a computer, for example—without someone else organizing it for us? Does learning in school have to be different and more difficult than learning outside the classroom? Do brains learn differently in and outside of school?

The Classic View: Learning as Process

Actually, most people, if they think about it, define learning just the way Jenny did, as what happens when we want to know something or be able to do something. We all know that we can usually learn when we want to. But the process by which we do that is not immediately clear. The classic view holds that human learning involves the development of strategies rather than the acquisition of behaviors (Smith, 1990).

Defining learning as an outcome, a product, a change in behavior, or the establishment of good or bad habits is too simple because it doesn't really account for what happens in the process. It is also perhaps too vague to say that learning is the development of the strategies we use to find out things we want to know or to be able to do. Nevertheless, describing learning as the process of coming to know is a good place to start. There are at least two compatible descriptions of learning as coming to know.

Jean Piaget (1954) was a Swiss genetic epistemologist whose background in biology is reflected in his theory of learning. He believed that children expected a rational order, a balance in their lives. Piaget viewed learners as active constructors of their own knowledge about the world rather than passive receivers of such knowledge. He believed that learners tried out different versions of what they thought the world should be. For example, learners might call a cow a dog because initially they overgeneralize one known label for a four-legged animal to all instances of four-legged animals. Piaget believed that learners did this so they could control the world around them, giving order to their environment and making sense of a seemingly chaotic world. According to Piaget, learners act alone to construct their worldview; learning occurs when learners experience a sense of disequilibrium between what they already know and what they are experiencing.

Lev Vygotsky, a Russian social psychologist and contemporary of Piaget, theorized about how people make and share meaning through language. Both Piaget and Vygotsky believed that learners construct their understandings as they transact with the world. Piaget thought in terms of learners acting alone, while Vygotsky (1978) realized that most learning occurs as people interact with each other.

Both theorists cast learners as active constructors of their own knowledge. Both describe learning as occurring in a meaningful context. Learners are seen as being actively engaged in making sense of the world around them, in bringing order to their worlds so they can survive and prosper. In other words, these theorists explain that we come to know, and learn to be who we are, within the culture into which we are born. We learn new things from and with the company we keep by making them part of what we already know. These are not new bits simply added to a store of knowledge, but rather are extensions or elaborations onto the labyrinth of experiences and beliefs that make us what and who we are (Smith, 1998).

This socioconstructivist theory of learning, which derives much of its foundation from Piaget, Vygotsky, and others, is process-based. Learning is seen as natural. In fact, social psychologists see learning as so natural that when the brain is unable to make meaning, the learner becomes uncomfortable, restless, and bored. "Learning, like breathing, is a natural and necessary function of the living person, and we are immediately distressed when the possibility of exercising the function is taken from us" (Smith, 1990, 38). Thus, natural learning requires no attempts to deliberately motivate learners; learners naturally attempt to make sense of the world around them.

Coming to know occurs best within the context of doing something authentic. Actually, we are learning something nearly all the time and most of the time we are learning without even knowing it. We learn as we participate in doing things and as we observe others doing things we want to do. We learn when we think about and talk about the things we want to know or be able to do. When learning is part of the natural flow of events, we make sense of what is occurring, and when we are able to make sense of something, learning is not difficult. In fact, learning is comparatively easy when we are engaged in activities and events that are authentic, interesting, and meaningful.

But even though natural learning is easy, we can make it difficult. When the information we are to learn is detached from context, when learning itself becomes the focus of our attention (for example, when we are learning lists of arbitrary spelling words or all the major crops grown in each country in South America), then we may find learning difficult. Learning is made more difficult when it is oriented to some future goal rather than to the learners' present interests (Smith, 1990).

"Neuroscientists are equally suspicious of the psychologists' assumptions about intellect" (Gardner, 1999, 19). But remember as you read the following pages that psychologists studying learning began this century by defining learning as a change in behavior. Of course, in the late 1800s and early to mid-1900s, their knowledge of the brain was quite limited compared to what we know today; therefore, they didn't know any better.

How the Brain Learns

Neuroscientists used to think that the brain was an all-purpose organ, that any portion of the brain controlled all cognitive and perceptual function. We now know that this equi-potential position is not true. Today we know that the brain is highly differentiated and that specific capacities are linked to particular neural networks (Gardner, 1999). However, the brain does serve two major functions. First, the brain is the "executive" organ. It keeps the body running and it regulates such autonomic functions as temperature, heart rate, and breathing. It produces chemicals that affect growth, reproduction, and our emotional well-being. It tells us when we are hungry or thirsty. It solves all our solvable problems (Hart, 1983). Second, the brain is the organ for learning. Learning occurs and is stored in the brain, not in other organs. "The brain learns because that is its job" (Caine and Caine, 1991, 3), and its capacity to learn is virtually inexhaustible.

Each healthy human brain—regardless of a person's age, sex, nationality, or cultural background—comes equipped with a set of exceptional features (Caine and Caine, 1991, 3):

- the ability to synthesize sensory data into meaningful wholes
- the ability to detect patterns and make approximations
- phenomenal capacity for various types of memory
- the ability to self-correct and learn from experience by way of analysis of external data and self-reflection
- an inexhaustible ability to create

Our brain is the core and storehouse of our personal existence (Hart, 1983). It is the human brain, not our ears, that comprehends human speech—the brain, not the hand, that composes a symphony or writes a poem. The brain creates a powerful sermon or political address and dances Swan Lake. Your brain, rather than your eyes, is reading this book.

The brain directs everything we do. The human brain is behind all the remarkable thinking, feeling, and expressing of which human beings are capable. We learn because heredity has given the brain programs that enable us to learn (Young, 1978). We do not have to be taught to suckle or to cry, to seek shelter or warmth. We are born looking for patterns or regularities in the world around us. For example, infants begin almost immediately to identify faces (Caine and Caine, 1991). As the organ for learning, the human brain has the function of imposing meaning upon its environment. It does this through a process of forming and testing hypotheses, then integrating feedback received with what is already known (Kantrowitz and Wingert, 1989; Restak, 1979).

Human beings identify an object by gathering information in the form of sensory data, often in less than a second, about that object. This information might include its size, color, shape, surface texture, weight, smell, movement, sound it makes, where it is found, what else is with it, how it is priced or labeled, and how others respond to it. The brain conducts an investigation to answer the question, "What is this?" The brain instantly performs this feat by going down many pathways simultaneously.

The human brain is not organized or designed for linear, one-path thinking. To demand that human beings put aside all of the brain's mighty resources to proceed with a step-by-step learning task may cripple and inhibit the learner (Hart, 1983). When human beings are learning, investigations progress along many paths among the brain's millions of connections. Data gathering and hypothesizing about the object or event do not occur one feature at a time; that would take forever. Rather, they occur all at the same time, utilizing some level of awareness of all the features.

From the vast amounts of information already stored, catalogued, and cross-referenced in the brain, tentative answers or hypotheses are created. Previously stored, labeled, and interrelated data are called knowledge structures, cognitive structures, or schemata. Incoming data are assembled and comparisons made within and among relevant cognitive structures. Interpretations of the new are possible through comparisons with the already known.

The brain is our life giver as well as our lifelong link to our environment. It provides us with lines of communication both within our own bodies and with the external world through sensory data received. Millions of nerves called neurons fire a continual stream of impulses into the brain where they are processed into patterns. We derive all our experiences, perceptions, ideas, memories, images, decisions, and behaviors from these sensory data patterns. And yet, we are not machines. As human beings we select from all that sensory input according to our interests, wants, and needs. At some level, conscious or subconscious, we decide what we will attend to, what we will focus on.

Cognitive Structures   From above the human brain looks much like a large walnut with two halves. Neuroconnectors allow the two halves to communicate. Each hemisphere controls and is responsible for the functioning of the opposite side of the body. Until recently, it was believed that brain's electrochemical activity could be isolated according to the function being performed. That is, if the right hand presses a button, the electrical discharges should begin and be concentrated in the left hemisphere. We now know that does not happen. Acts of will, decisions that human beings make, are holistically distributed throughout the entire brain (Caine and Caine, 1991). It now appears that for thinking and learning, our brains are organized more by units of meaning than by any of their anatomical features (Eccles and Robinson, 1984; Hart, 1983).

These units of meaning may correspond in some way to the two to three million cellular bundles into which the brain is organized. The majority of brain cells are found in the great brain mantle, or neocortex. Trying to understand the workings of a network of ten billion individual brain cells is beyond human comprehension. However, scientists now know that the neocortex consists of modular units or bundles. This arrangement of about 4,000 cells per bundle reduces the number of functioning units from ten billion to between two and three million units (Eccles and Robinson, 1984). When this organization was first detected, scientists wondered if two to three million modular units of brain cells were sufficient to generate all the spatial and temporal patterns—all the cognitive, linguistic, emotive, and creative/aesthetic expressions for a whole lifetime.

Think of the pitches and tones produced by the eighty-eight keys of a piano. These sounds, combined across time with rhythm and volume, generate essentially an infinite variety of musical patterns. That may make it easier to begin to see how the brain has virtually an infinite capacity in its two to three million bundles of cellular units to generate an entire universe of meaningful patterns.

Detecting, generating, and using patterns are what the human brain does. It does not have to be taught to do this any more than the heart has to be taught to pump blood. The brain is by nature's design an amazingly and subtle sensitive pattern detecting apparatus that detects, constructs, and elaborates patterns (Hart, 1983). "The brain does not just respond or react to the world, it creates the world" (Smith, 1990, 46).

Learners, including infants and young children, are not simply sponges passively soaking up a vast array of data that their brains arrange for them. They also seek sensory data, information, and experiences to filter, process, encode, and organize into highly complex patterns. Our brains are not designed to merely consume information doled out in discrete bits after we have been motivated to learn. Instead, our brains actively construct their own interpretation of sensory data and draw their own inferences from them. Human beings purposefully ignore some information and selectively attend to other information, depending on their interests, needs, and desires.

Even infants have the ability to gradually sort out sensory data by features and arrange those features into usable patterns. Think for a moment of the sensory data—the sights, sounds, smells, tastes, and feelings—that bombard infants in a completely unordered and uncontrolled manner. Yet infants learn very quickly what will bring a face to the crib and whether the face is familiar. In many ways, learning is the extraction of meaningful patterns from what is fortuitous, chaotic, complex, multi-channeled, and largely random input. Clearly infants and children need a variety of sensory stimulation in their environments (Marcus, Mulrine, and Wong, 1999).

The Psychogenerative Nature of Human Learning How does the human brain determine what to include as it creates a particular pattern or category? For each pattern, learners intuit a set of rules and a list of characteristics, sometimes referred to as *distinctive features*. Distinctive features allow learners to identify any object or event by its properties.

Some properties or features are obvious. For example, we all know a lot about dogs. We know that nearly all dogs bark, they have four legs and fur, and they may smell bad, especially when wet. Most of the features, however, that we use to assign an event or object to a classification are invisible and known to us only intuitively. For instance, one characteristic or distinctive feature we use to identify dogs from cats is that when picked up, dogs are less flexible than cats. Therefore, flexibility is a distinctive feature of canines, felines, and so on. It is not one, however, that is immediately obvious.

Distinctive features are acquired through experience and build the patterns or *cognitive structures* we use to make sense of the world. Cognitive means knowledge and thinking; structure suggests organization.

We use the patterns and meanings we have given our past experiences as the basis for understanding anything new. This system of knowing organizes sensory data into an intricate and internally consistent working model of the world. Because the brain is designed to take in disparate data all at the same time and make sense of them, we experience the world as a coherent whole. This coherent whole, our "theory of the world in our heads" (Smith, 1997, 66), is what protects us from constant confusion and allows us to survive.

Human beings could not survive if they experienced everything as the same. There would be no basis for learning and no basis for self-protection. Besides, who would want to survive in a world of endless sameness? On the other hand, human beings could not survive if they perceived everything as different. Again, there would be no basis for learning and no system for self-protection. We might never leave the house if we had no idea of what we might encounter. The world would be filled with utter chaos and terror.

Just as the brain cannot possibly see everything that is within our field of vision, it does not "see" anything new instantly. Perception depends on what we already know and what we think is likely to be in front of us. For that reason, the process of predicting is fundamental to human perception and learning. Everyone does it, even very young children. Our cognitive structures, or schemata, are our pathways to perception (Rumelhart, 1980). That is, we "see" what the brain decides we are looking at, what the brain decides is there.

Collections of patterns or cognitive structures are also referred to as schemata. Each individual's set of schemata is different from every other person's. Each of us constructs our own interpretations of what's going on around us. An individual's schemata are established in two ways: they are transmitted through the genetic code, and they are learned after birth. Because human brains are so big and human life so complex, and because as humans we learn so much so fast, little information applicable to learning in school can be gained by studying animals in a laboratory. Also, the quality of a brain, which usually refers to the number of neurons the brain has, determines the degree to which patterns can be detected, discriminated, and interrelated (Rumelhart, 1980; Wittrock, 1980).

To compare the human brain to any other information-processing device is to do this amazing organ a disservice. The brain is "not a general purpose computer into whose memory any information is placed" (Young, 1978, 78). The brain does not merely seek to store and then respond to information in the world—the brain imposes meaning on the world. It is an active, experience-seeking, reality-creating organ (Smith, 1990). Human beings learn from whole to part as the brain detects patterns and assigns features to categories from all its data sources at the same time. The brain constructs schemata. It is organized so that happenings from whole experiences can be sorted out and used.

Human learning does not result merely from the world's acting upon us; rather, we construct our understandings of information and our theory of how the world works because our brains are organized to do so. If natural learning is defined as the extraction of meaningful patterns from complex input, it follows that in schools, learners require rich, plentiful content that is both meaningful and interesting to them. As learners make decisions and interact with interesting and meaningful content, with each other, and with their teachers, they do indeed learn. The degree and direction of learning is, of course, mediated by learners' inherited abilities and by their attitudes, values, and decisions, as well as their prior knowledge and experiences (Neisser, 1980).

The brain's major function during learning is to take in a multitude of sensory data simultaneously and make sense out of them. It relates new information to known information in almost limitless fashion. The relationships generated between the new and the known expand cognitive structures (schemata) exponentially. Learning, then, is a psychogenerative process. That is, the more we know, the easier it is to learn something new.

We don't really learn just one new thing; we learn one new thing that can then be related and interrelated in perhaps hundreds or even thousands of ways. The whole is both greater than, and in many ways different from, the sum of its parts. The fact that learning is a psychogenerative process is undisputed (Wittrock, 1980). As a psychogenerative process, learning results from the learner's transacting with the world, not the world's acting on the learner. As active participants in their own learning, learners think about what they are experiencing, they act upon their environments, often altering the world around them. They are actively engaged in generating relationships; they are driven to do so. They are curious about the underlying structure of the information and experiences with which they are intellectually engaged, and they are to some degree aware of the connections they are making. In other words, they affect the world even as they are affected by it. They transact with the world around them as they learn.

When a teacher shows a child the word *dog* and the child correctly says, "dog," it isn't difficult to think of this fairly low-level learning as stimulus-response. However, the simple stimulus-response model becomes less useful when one contemplates learning complex sets of behaviors that must flow and that operate on several levels at once— for example, driving a car, playing basketball, or water-skiing. The stimulus-response model is of little or no use when one considers how a human being learns to play the concert violin or dance a ballet. How is it that a person can learn (that is, experience, store, organize, and access instantly) enough sensory data to be able to handle higher mathematics, write an inspired literary work, or win an Olympic medal?

Infants and young children are like scientists, according to Gopnik, Meltzoff, and Kuhl (1999). Infants learn by hypothesis forming and testing (in some sense trial and error) and they do it quite well. Show a baby a rolling ball that disappears behind an object and the baby will likely predict (by looking at) the place where the ball should reappear and at the right time. The infant can hold the image in his or her mind and calculate time based on an estimate of the speed of the ball before it disappears. This is a very sophisticated and complex capability—and that is just the beginning.

One day we observed a six-year-old boy as he watched his teacher work with a pair of pliers. "Those are like butterfly wings," he said, enthralled with his own observation. The class had studied insects several months earlier. Clearly, this connection was evidence that this child learns metaphorically; that he understands the concept of hinges in a way that will expand, interrelate with other experiences and information, and generate new perspectives throughout his life. Detecting patterns and making connections among phenomena are what make us so smart. It is this very human capacity that allows us to create poetry, music, dance, literature, mathematics, philosophy, and other forms of communication that express not only our understandings of the world around us but of the world within.

As human beings, we learn (we categorize, organize, and interrelate sensory data) in essentially the same three ways: (1) through direct experience—by doing, (2) through observation—by watching others, and (3) indirectly—by being told. And what we learn falls in three broad categories: (1) information or knowledge, (2) skills or processes, and (3) attitudes, values, and beliefs. Human beings acquire knowledge primarily through language. We develop skills directly by participating in or doing, and we acquire our attitudes and values primarily by observing the attitudes and values of those around us. Of course, we can also gain knowledge, develop skills, and acquire our attitudes and values by each of the other modes as well.

MULTIPLE INTELLIGENCES

Gardner (1991, 1999) and others maintain that schools must allow for the emergence and full development of all the ways of knowing of which human beings are capable. Students are predisposed to learn materials that are represented in forms that fit their natural intelligences. For instance, when students are actively involved in instructional activities that highlight event structures (as in stories), learners will themselves represent the information, and later recall it, in terms of their own favored symbolic mode, no matter how the material is initially encountered. That is, in school learning, projects in which students become engaged, whether writing a story or shooting a video, reflect the way they prefer to make and represent meaning.

Gardner (1991, 1999) describes human learning in terms of multiple intelligences. He asserts that all normal human beings develop at least eight forms of intelligence to a greater or lesser degree as an interplay between their genetic makeup and the cultural and environmental constraints at work. These forms of intelligence include:

1. thinking with language
2. conceptualizing in spatial terms
3. analyzing in musical ways
4. computing with logic and mathematical tools
5. solving problems with the whole body or parts of the body
6. understanding other individuals and relationships
7. understanding ourselves
8. recognizing and classifying the species

Furthermore, each of these intelligences lends itself to its own symbolic system for representing meaning.

However, "there is always a gulf between scientific claims about how the mind works and actual classroom practice" (Gardner, 1999, 89). Uniform schooling, that all students should learn the same subjects and should be assessed the same way, is based on the assumption that everyone learns the same way. While we know this is not the case, we also know that there are certain conditions that, when present, make learning easier and more natural.

THE CONDITIONS FOR NATURAL LEARNING

Knowing how humans learn and how the brain works is important knowledge for teachers, because it explains why a broad, integrated curriculum is better than a narrow, fragmented curriculum. It helps explain why learning is best approached as a matter of inquiry, with learners making choices and pursuing their own interests. It tells us why rote drill and practice exercises are examples of low-level learning and, in some instances, may actually inhibit cognitive development. It tells us why intelligence testing as we know it and standardized achievement testing as it exists today are limited in value and inappropriate for so many of the nation's children. But it does not tell us everything teachers need to know about helping children learn. To extend our understanding we need to examine how learning takes place in natural settings. Think again about Jenny learning to water-ski.

Jenny was three years old when she went to the lake for the first time. Her parents had been avid water-skiers long before she was born. At age three, Jenny would ride in the boat and watch her parents ski. Toward the end of the summer, Jenny went skiing with her mother, who positioned Jenny in front of her with Jenny's feet on the two skis in front of her mother's feet. Both she and Jenny held onto the towrope together. Jenny would hold on in the middle and her mother on the outside. They would ski down the lake with Jenny standing on her mother's skis in front of her mother. This worked well until she got to be too big. The summer Jenny was nine years old she learned to ski on her own skis.

For six summers of her life Jenny had watched her parents and her parents' friends ski. She lived in an environment that valued the ability to water-ski. She had seen many people ski, some excellent skiers and some not so experienced. She had even "skied" with her mother. She fully expected that when she was ready to try on her own that someone would help her. And furthermore, she expected she would be successful, as did her parents and her parents' friends. No one ever doubted that Jenny would learn to ski.

In fact, Jenny was regarded as a skier before she ever skied alone. Jenny did not succeed the first time she tried to get up by herself. She did not give up either. She tried again and again. She knew that no one else could learn for her, that this was something she had to do on her own, and she really wanted to be a skier. To become a member of that "exclusive club" of "accomplished water-skiers," she was willing to risk skiing badly at first and falling down a lot. Now, years later, Jenny is an excellent skier.

Cambourne (1988) has presented a model of learning that explains why learning to water-ski was easy for Jenny. This model is based on seven conditions derived from decades of research into child language development. Not all of us learn to ski, but language learning provides an excellent example of natural learning that we all do. From an understanding of how language is learned, come very interesting insights on which all worthwhile classrooms are based. Every example of positive, successful learning we examine contains these same elements. They are:

- immersion
- demonstration
- expectation
- approximation
- responsibility
- use
- response

Immersion   In immersion, learners are saturated in the medium they are expected to learn. Older members of the culture make thousands of examples available to younger learners. Jenny was immersed in the medium of water-skiing every summer. She heard her parents talking about skiing. She watched them ski for several years. Then she got to go skiing with them, simulating or trying out what she knew about skiing in a safe, protected, and supportive environment. Finally she had a go all by herself. Smith points out that "children learn from the artifacts they find in their environments and from the behavior of the people around them" (1986, 16).

Demonstration   Demonstration can take the form of an artifact or an action. Jenny observed her parents, her parents' friends, and even people she did not know participate in and enjoy water-skiing. She saw them over and over, summer after summer. Human beings "engage with repeated demonstrations of the same action and/or artifact (and) select other aspects of it to internalise and, as a consequence, we begin to interpret, organize and reorganize our developing knowledge until we can perform and/or produce that demonstration or a variation of it" (Cambourne, 1988, 47).

Cambourne states that although immersion and demonstration are necessary conditions for learning, they are not sufficient in and of themselves. In other words, merely being immersed in a water-skiing environment and receiving numerous quality demonstrations was not enough for Jenny to learn to ski. The other elements had to be there as well, expectation, approximation, practice or use, response, and responsibility. In addition, it is now clear that all the ingredients might be present and the child still not learn. That is because the learner has to be engaged (Smith, 1990), and we as teachers have to understand what that means and how to effect it in our students. When children are engaged, they are thinking about what they are doing and what they are learning.

Expectation   Expectation takes two forms: the message communicated to learners about their abilities to be successful and the learners' own messages to themselves. Jenny always knew that her parents believed she would learn to ski and, as a result, she always believed she would, too. Added to the expectations about her ability was the expectation that "what she was trying to learn was worthwhile, valuable, relevant, extremely functional and useful" (Cambourne, 1988, 58).

Approximation   Approximation occurs when the learner comes close to producing a product, artifact, or action that an adult (expert) would. This concept is most easily understood as it relates to learning to talk. For example, did your younger brother or sister ever approximate a word? Was the word "baba" used for the word "bottle" or "banky" for "blanket"? Was the child told that the word was incorrect and not to say it again until it could be pronounced correctly? Of course not!

Jenny approximated skiing on several occasions. First, when she skied on top of her mother's skis, she approximated real skiing. Then as she began to try to learn on her own, she would get up, ski a few yards, and fall. But she was never told that she wasn't doing it right and not to try again until she could ski better. That would be ridiculous! Instead, her parents celebrated each successive approximation of real skiing. Everyone told her how well she was doing, and she was always encouraged to try again.

Responsibility   Only learners themselves can take charge of their own learning. This is the condition of responsibility. Think of the old adage, "You can lead a horse to water but you can't make it drink." Learners can be immersed in demonstrations, provided thousands of opportunities for engagement, be expected to learn, and still not be successful. This is because it is the learner and not the teacher who is responsible for the learning that takes place. Cambourne (1988) says that taking responsibility in the learning process usually involves two types of behavior. First, learners must be willing to make decisions about their own learning, decisions independent of the teacher. Jenny chose to learn to ski and she chose which summer she thought she was ready to learn. Her parents (teachers) did not make this decision for her. Second, teachers must trust learners to engage in demonstrations and select from those demonstrations those that they, the learners, believe to be the most useful. Trust is perhaps the scariest element of all. We as teachers must trust our students to make appropriate decisions, and we must give them the freedom to do so (Smith, 1990). This does not mean that learners are free to choose not to learn. Only when learning conditions are threatening is choosing not to learn more risk-free than choosing to learn. Good teachers set up rich environments and provide opportunities and supportive conditions for learning. The responsibility for learning rests with the learner.

Use   Use, or practice, is the process of actively involving learners with the demonstrations and artifacts in which they are immersed. In order to learn something, the learner must take part in it; the learner must use what is being learned. It is possible for learners to be immersed in thousands of demonstrations, to "practice," and still not be engaged in the process, for example, writing spelling words ten times each. Practice is the opportunity learners have to play around with what they are learning. Use, or practice, is only viable if it occurs within the context of the entire learning process. In other words, when Jenny practiced skiing, she was obviously at the lake, in the water, with the skis on her feet. She did not practice skiing by isolating the different things she had to remember about getting up and staying up, even though she could talk about those things separately—for example, keeping her knees bent and not pulling her arms back toward her chest. Use means providing the time and the opportunity to use immature, developing skills in holistic, integrated, and (eventually) smoothly flowing ways. Use requires engagement.

Response   Responses are natural exchanges between learners and experts and between learners and their engagements. The psychological term frequently used to mean response is *feedback*, which may carry with it connotations of behaviorism as well as positive and negative reinforcement. Response relates to the natural sharing of information that supports learners as they develop control over what they are learning.

For example, when a young child says "banky" for "blanket," you may adopt the child's word or respond by supplying the adult word, but you probably will not reprimand the approximation. You will likely say a variety of things to provide information to further language development. For instance, you might say, "Yes, that's your banky." "Bill, bring Mary's blanket. Here, Dear." "Here is your banky."

In Jenny's case, her parents responded to her novice attempts at skiing by praising her efforts and offering suggestions to help her move a little closer to the expert form. Jenny also knew as she stayed up on the skis for longer and longer periods, her skiing improved. She did not need someone to tell her that, and she certainly didn't need to take a test on skiing to find out how she was doing.

Response requires acceptance of an approximation, evaluation to determine if the learner can come closer to the accepted form, and repeated engagements. Jenny watched other skiers. She looked at how they kept their knees bent and their arms straight. She tried again and improved. Learners use responses to fill in gaps, to explain, examine, extend, and/or redirect their learning.

Children do not learn well by merely being talked to. They do not learn well by merely receiving isolated and arbitrary bits of information given to them by someone acting like a teacher. When learning is not meaningful, it has to be organized for the learners and artificial rewards are required to motivate. At these times, the brain is robbed of much of its ability to learn, and children do not do it with alacrity. However, when learners experience activities that are authentic and meaningful, they learn well. School learning should never be characterized by meaninglessness. The question is, why do some children fail to learn even when all the conditions in the classroom are present, when the teacher has done everything he or she knows is good instruction? It is not adequate to say that the home, the culture, or the learner him- or herself is to blame. We have to do what we can to change it.

Engagement Providing the conditions that support learning is what good teachers do. Engagement is what learners do. The relationship between teaching and learning—the success with which learning occurs—depends on the existence of both. Engagement means learners are intellectually involved, that they are thinking about what they are doing, that they are mentally, even emotionally, engaged with what is happening. According to Cambourne (2001), whether or not learners really engage with what is going on in their classrooms depends on four principles. To achieve engagement, learners must:

- see themselves as potential doers or owners of the demonstrations
- believe that by becoming doers they will in some way further the purposes of their own lives
- be willing to take risks, and in order to do so, they must perceive that the risk is not too great
- have positive relationships with the teacher or demonstrator; that is, the probability of engagement is increased significantly if the demonstrations are given by someone for whom the learner has respect, trust, admiration, and whom the learner wishes to emulate (Cambourne, 2001)

In Jenny's case, she saw herself as a skier, she believed she would have more fun at the lake if she could ski, she was willing to try as many times as necessary. She knew what good skiing looked like, she knew she was in charge of her own learning, she had chosen to learn to ski, and she knew how proud her parents would be of her accomplishment.

IMPLICATIONS FOR INSTRUCTION: TOWARD A SOCIO-PERSONAL, CONSTRUCTIVIST VIEW OF LEARNING AND TEACHING

Stand back for a moment and regard human learning from birth through old age. Consider that the brain is the organ for learning and doing. Remember, the brain is an active, experience-seeking, reality-creating organ (Smith, 1990). Human beings learn from whole to part as the brain detects patterns and assigns features to categories from all available data sources. The brain is organized so that happenings from whole experiences, entering through multiple sensory input, are sorted out, stored, cross-referenced, and accessed via more than one pathway. The learner's brain does the work, but the learner can enhance the process.

A constructivist view of learning holds that human beings actively construct their knowledge of the world in a dual process of invention and convention. That is, we invent, we actively, consciously engage in figuring how the world works through trial and error. We want to know how everything is structured and interrelated. Our brains scaffold new data onto what we already know. That is how we grow and develop. Research, not to mention common sense, suggests that the more active the learner is in thinking about and trying to understand his or her experiences, the better he or she will learn. That is where genetic material, teaching, and teachers come into the picture.

As we interact with the world, both in and out of school, our brains are continuously at work figuring out what is going on and integrating and storing these data for future use. The more we are aware of and consciously participating in (i.e., thinking about, wondering about, hypothesizing connections about) what is going on around us, the faster and better our brains work. This is especially the case for how brains develop before puberty.

Human beings construct/invent the knowledge that is already known by others (by adults, by educated persons, by older children, by experts, etc.). That is, the world brings our inventive brains back to the conventions that are there. Young children apply a sort of scientific method to their explorations, they want to make up (pretend, hypothesize) rules for how the world works and then check those rules out to see how well they hold up. For example, they may want to be able to fly and they may want magic to exist, but they also want to understand why things fall down and not up. The job before them is to take their constructive brain capabilities and figure how the world really works so they can make their way in it. That is how we grow and develop, work and survive, contribute to society, create useful and beautiful things, and some of us, before we die, discover new knowledge and contribute to humanity.

How well and how quickly we construct our own individual, personal knowledge about the workings of the world depends on the interplay between the events in our lives, including teachers and teaching, and the genetic material we bring to the process. Children are natural scientists, creating their theories of the world, testing those theories, and revising them as they learn and develop. In fact, Gopnik, Meltzoff, and Kuhl (1999) argue that scientists are such successful learners because they use cognitive abilities that evolution designed specifically for children.

To capitalize on children's natural tendencies and capabilities, good teachers encourage children's curiosity and problem solving. They may model, immerse, encourage, provide, stimulate, suggest, reinforce, question, tell, require, give ownership, demonstrate, and engage learners in any number of acts that promote the development of theory forming and testing, making connections and detecting relationships, and pursuing what is of interest. When this is the kind of education available, young minds are significantly enhanced.

SUMMARY

What is learning? Learning is something we all do all the time. It is natural and satisfying. It tends to occur from whole to part then back to whole. It can be seen as the development of concepts and understandings through a process of engagement, i.e., participation, inquiry, observation, and thinking (Weaver, 1990). More than just the formation of habits, most human learning involves complex processes on which multiple variables are acting. Human learning cannot be controlled or guaranteed in laboratories or in classrooms. Direct instruction for rote memorization will not produce the best learning or the most successful and independent learners.

Learning that is voluntary is likely to be more meaningful to the learner and last longer. Such learning is similar to the scientific method; it is generative in nature. It is more social than solitary, more cooperative than competitive, more accessible for application and additional learning. Natural learning occurs under certain conditions, most or all of which are present in every positive, successful learning event. Why do human beings learn? We learn because not to do so is impossible and discomforting to the brain. Of course, we don't always learn what others want us to learn. Learning occurs when human beings engage with information, other people, language, and thinking in authentic experiences. How can we best facilitate learning? We can provide learning environments that ensure that the conditions for natural learning are present in classrooms and the principles of engagement are in place. Our understanding of complex learning is enhanced by our understanding of how brains work. The following summarizes what we have explored about learning.

1. Human beings are born learning. Learning is easier when it occurs naturally.

2. Learning is something we do all the time, even when we are unaware that we are learning. We learn constantly, without the need for external motivation, special incentives, and artificial "reinforcement."

3. Learning occurs from whole to part to whole.

4. Learning is active, not passive; it is largely trial and error.

5. The human brain is more "fluid" before puberty. What happens to learners early in life has a lifelong effect on how they develop.

6. Learning is making sense of the world around us as we represent our learning through symbol systems that reflect multiple intelligences, such as talking and drawing.

7. Learning is constructing our own understandings and identities within cultural attitudes, values, and environmental parameters.

8. Learning is extracting meaningful features from the world of our experiences, building patterns, categorizing, and drawing interrelationships among schemata.

9. Learning is a social act. We learn from and with others in social situations.

10. Learning occurs when new information is integrated or attached to prior knowledge.

11. Learning occurs when we are engaged, when we want to be able to do something or find out something.

12. Learning is making choices and taking responsibility.

13. Learning involves doing, observing, and learning through language.

14. Learning is psychogenerative and metaphorical in nature.

15. Low-level learning, such as rote memorization, is usually short term. It does not necessarily involve understanding; it may give a false sense of competence; and, because it is surface level, it may not be generalizable and generative.

16. How well human beings learn (construct their personal knowledge about the workings of the world) depends on the interplay between life events, including teachers and teaching, and the genetic material they each bring to the process.

17. Prevention in the form of rich, early experiences is more beneficial than later attempts to remedy deficiencies

18. The brain undergoes physical alterations when learning occurs.

19. An enriched environment positively influences brain development and learning.

20. The network of neuroconnections created in the brain for complex learnings, mostly before puberty, is the foundation for future learning, storage, and retrieval. That is, new learnings are perceived, understood, and scaffolded onto what is already known. That is how the brain functions in learning.

THEORY-TO-PRACTICE CONNECTIONS

Learning Theory

1. Learning is a constructive process. Learners actively try to make sense of their world by trial and error, through forming hypotheses and testing them.

2. Learning is psychogenerative. The more you know, the easier it is to learn the new. Learners relate what they already know as they make sense of what they are learning.

3. Learning is relatively easy when it is purposeful to the learner, from the learner's perspective.

4. The human brain is designed for complex learning. It is perfectly capable of detecting and imposing patterns from a mass of incoming, multi-channel, sensory data.

5. Human learning is a matter of multiple intelligences, i.e., ways of knowing and of representing those knowings.

Examples of Classroom Practice

1. Students setting up and conducting a science project to answer their own questions

2. Students reading and talking about good books

3. Students making choices about what they want to learn, employing real language, e.g., in the form of children's literature, functional signs, and messages

4. Creating a rich, literate environment and immersing learners in a wide variety of literature and informational choices

5. Allowing learners choices as they represent their learning

SUGGESTED READINGS

Bransford, J., A. Brown, and R. Cocking. 1999. *How People Learn: Brain, Mind, Experience, and School.* Washington, DC: National Academy Press.

Caine, R., and G. Caine. 1991. *Making Connections: Teaching and the Human Brain.* Alexandria, VA: Association for Supervision and Curriculum Development.

Gopnik, A., A. Meltzoff, and P. Kuhl. 1999. *The Scientist in the Crib: What Early Learning Tells Us About the Mind.* New York: HarperCollins.

Jensen, E. 1998. *Teaching with the Brain in Mind.* Washington, DC: ASCD.

Smith, F. 1998. *The Book of Learning and Forgetting.* New York: Teachers College Press.

Sylwester, R. 1995. *A Celebration of Neurons: An Educator's Guide to the Human Brain.* Washington, DC: ASCD.

EXTENDING YOUR DISCUSSION

1. Discuss how you think the suggested classroom practice examples in the Theory-to-Practice Connections reflect learning as we have described it. Is there overlap among the example practices—that is, does each address more than one theoretical proposition?

2. As an in-class experience, tell the person next to you about one positive learning event in your life, a time when you attempted to learn something and were successful, *outside* of school. After you have taken turns, share some of these with the class. Do you find evidence of the conditions for learning in your own personal, positive learning experiences? How so?

3. Make a list of fifty words, five words in each of ten categories. Arrange two groupings of these words. On one sheet of paper list each group of words beneath each category. On the other sheet list all the words arranged in two columns of alphabetical order. Divide a group of students in half. Give one group the words

in categories. Give the other group the words by their alphabetical listing. Do not let each group know what the other group is doing. Tell each group they have ten minutes to learn all the words for a paper and pencil test. After the test, have each group add their scores and calculate their mean score. Discuss the results. Which group did better? Why? Did the group with the alphabetically listed words try to devise categories, mnemonic devices of some sort, as a means of learning the words? Did they try any other strategies for learning? Why? What did you learn from this event?

REFERENCES

Bransford, J. 1979. *Human Cognition: Learning, Understanding and Remembering.* Belmont, CA: Wadsworth.

Caine, R., and G. Caine. 1991. *Making Connections: Teaching and the Human Brain.* Alexandria, VA: Association for Supervision and Curriculum Development.

Cambourne, B. 1988. *The Whole Story.* Natural Learning and the Acquisition of Literacy in the Classroom. Toronto: Ashton-Scholastic.

———. 2001. "Why Do Some Students Fail to Learn to Read? Ockham's Razor and the Conditions of Learning." *The Reading Teacher* 54 (8): 784–86.

Dewey, J., and A. Bentley. 1949. *Knowing and the Known.* Boston: Beacon.

Ebbinghaus, H. 1913. *Memory*, trans. H. A. Ruger and C. E. Bussenius. New York: Teachers College Press.

Eccles, J., and D. Robinson. 1984. *The Wonder of Being Human: Our Brain and Our Mind.* New York: Macmillan.

Gardner, H. 1991. *The Unschooled Mind: How Children Think and How Schools Should Teach.* New York: Basic Books.

———. 1999. *Intelligence Reframed: Multiple Intelligences for the 21st Century.* New York: Basic Books.

Gopnik, A., A. Meltzoff, and P. Kuhl. 1999. *The Scientist in the Crib: What Early Learning Tells Us About the Mind.* New York: HarperCollins.

Grady, M. 1990. *Whole Brain Education.* Bloomington, IN: Phi Delta Kappa Foundation.

Hart, L. 1983. *Human Brain and Human Learning.* New York: Longman.

Kantrowitz, B., and P. Wingert. 1989. "How Kids Learn: A Special Report." *Newsweek* (April 17): 50–7.

Languis, M. 1985. "Cognitive Science and Teacher Education." *Theory into Practice* 24 (20): xx.

Marcus, D., A. Mulrine, and K. Wong. 1999. "How Kids Learn: Babies Are Masters of Education." *Newsweek* 127 (10): 44–50.

Neisser, U. 1980. *Cognition and Reality.* San Francisco: W. H. Freeman.

Pavlov, I. 1927. *Conditioned Reflexes*, trans. G. V. Anrep. London: Oxford University Press.

Piaget, J. 1954. *The Construction of Reality in the Child.* New York: Basic Books.

Restak, R. 1979. *The Brain: The Last Frontier.* New York: Doubleday.

Rogers, C. 1983. *Freedom to Learn for the 80s.* Columbus, OH: Merrill.

Rumelhart, D. 1980. "Schemata: The Building Blocks of Cognition." In *Theoretical Issues in Reading Comprehension: Perspectives from Cognitive Psychology, Linguistics, Artificial Intelligence, and Education*, eds. R. Spiro, B. Bruce, and W. Brewer, 33–58. Hillsdale, NJ: Lawrence Erlbaum Associates.

Skinner, B. 1938. *The Behavior of Organisms: An Experimental Analysis.* New York: Appleton-Century-Crofts.

Smith, F. 1986. *Insult to Intelligence: The Bureaucratic Invasion of Our Classrooms.* New York: Arbor House.

———. 1988. *Understanding Reading*, 5th ed. Hillsdale, NJ: Lawrence Erlbaum Associates.

———. 1990. *to Think.* New York: Teachers College Press.

———. 1997. *Reading Without Nonsense*, 3rd ed. New York: Teachers College Press.

———. 1998. *The Book of Learning and Forgetting.* New York: Teachers College Press.

1988. *The Brain: A Scientific American Book.* New York: W. H. Freeman and Co.

Thorndike, E. 1913. *The Psychology of Learning.* New York: Teachers College Press.

———. 1932. *The Fundamentals of Learning.* New York: Teachers College Press.

Vygotsky, L. 1978. *Mind in Society: The Development of Higher Psychological Processes.* Cambridge, MA: Harvard University Press.

Watson, J. 1914. *Behavior, an Introduction to Comparative Psychology*. New York: Holt, Rinehart, and Winston.

Weaver, C. 1990. *Understanding Whole Language: From Principles to Practice*. Portsmouth, NH: Heinemann.

Wittrock, M. 1980. "Learning and the Brain." In *The Brain and Psychology*, ed. M. Wittrock. New York: Academic Press.

Young, J. 1978. *Programs of the Brain*. London: Oxford.

CHAPTER TWO

> "I still remember the excitement I felt when I first read Chomsky's claim that 'Language is a window on the mind.' . . . Heady stuff for someone interested in the education of children."
>
> *(Gordon Wells, 1986, ix)*

LANGUAGE

Language is a window into the mind of another human being. Language is the primary tool we use to reach and teach others, and it is also the object of instruction. Since it is and it does so much, we probably need to understand it better. In this chapter we describe and discuss the uses of language. We discuss the nature of language, the role of language in school learning, and set the stage for Chapters Three and Four, which describe oral and written language learning.

WHAT LANGUAGE DOES

"Language serves a number of purposes, none of which is self-evident. To say that the function of language is to communicate is a vast understatement—language can be used to create, conceal, narrate, or fabricate; to define and express oneself; and perhaps primarily, to establish relationships" (Smith, 1998, 18). Language is one of the ways we learn. It is the most important way we organize and make sense of our world. And language is the means by which human beings relate to each other. Education, courtship and marriage, health, politics, religion, socializing, and most jobs require language, in some form or forms, as their primary tool. Language is one of the central learning tasks of childhood. Learning oral language and learning about the world occupy young children's minds for the first several years of life.

Forms of Language

Oral language exists in many versions. Not only have human beings created English, Spanish, Navajo, Yiddish, Greek, Swahili, Persian, Chinese, and hundreds of other languages, but nearly every language on earth has more than one regional or social-class dialect. In addition, nearly all languages have two expressive or productive modes, speaking and writing, and two receptive modes, listening and reading. Some languages also have alternatives for persons who need to receive and produce meaning through other sensory channels—for example, Braille and American Sign Language. Language is also the primary medium through which teachers and children work (Lee and Rubin, 1979). Because teachers teach and children learn through language, it is important that we understand what language is and what it does.

Uses of Language

Even though language can be one of the highest forms of human expression, as in literature or philosophy, that is not why humans created it. Language evolved so that we could share our experiences with one another and exert greater control over our environments. In the process we discovered that language helped us better structure and refine our experiences and understandings.

Looking at the many uses of language is an important part of understanding language. Language exists for social and intellectual uses, and in the broadest sense, language serves as a means of reflecting and of acting (Lee, 1986). Once language is learned, people may then use it reflectively or internally as they think (Smith, 1990), but mostly we use language to get things done. Language is a major means by which we act, interact, and control our environments.

Oral language is generally the way we make contact with other human beings. We label and categorize our world, and we share those understandings with each other. The world is complex; we use language to understand, to negotiate, to protect ourselves, to keep from being alone, and to get what we want. Language is a powerful medium. It can promote love or cause wars. It is a window on the mind. But what is language?

WHAT LANGUAGE IS

Oral language is one of the symbolic representational systems humans have created for expressing meaning. Oral language, for the most part, is invisible because it is so inherently natural that the rules by which it operates are not immediately apparent to native speakers. Its characteristics, structures, and functions are not readily accessible for examination the way the parts of an automobile are, for example. We learned our native language without direct instruction, and we learned it so well and so deeply that we speak it automatically without being aware of the complex sets of rules we are invoking and manipulating.

Human beings are born with the mental capacity to develop language. The human brain comes already "programmed" to create linguistic systems (Lenneberg, 1967). Language is natural to humans. We do not have to study our native tongue in school to learn it; instead we learned it by exposure and practice. Nevertheless, language is difficult to describe, both because it is inherent and because it is made up of abstract symbols.

Definitions of Language
Dictionaries usually define language in the following way: a language is any system (sets of structural rules) of formalized symbols and signs (sounds, letters, etc.) used as a means of communication by persons from the same social or community group. This definition has two parts. The system of symbols and signs has to do with what language actually is. Communication by persons from the same community of speakers has to do with what language does. Both terms have to do with the transmission of meaning. For our purposes, oral language communication will be conceived as a system of abstract symbols used for social interaction. That is, language is a system for sharing meanings among members of the same or related cultural groups.

Sets of Structural Rules
The fact that language is a system (implying rules, regularities, and patterns) is the reason it is so thoroughly learnable to humans. Our brains are designed to detect or to impose patterns. Language conforms to patterns so that it can be learned, used, and understood. A brief examination of some of the conventions, or rules in the general English language system, that organize the symbols and signs of our language will help us better understand language and appreciate its complexity.

For purposes of studying language, linguists subdivide it into at least six sets of patterns or rule-governed systems: intonation, phonology, morphology, syntax, semantics, and pragmatics (Benjamin, 1970; Lee, 1986; Salus, 1969). In practice these systems operate simultaneously and are not subdivided. That is, as soon as we begin to try to break any language into its various systems, we don't have language any more. Although such divisions are interesting, they won't help us learn language. However, they may help us understand it a little better.

Intonation   The system that makes up the tones and rhythmic patterns of a language is *intonation* (Lieberman, 1967). Intonation is the interaction of three components:

1. stress, or volume; how loudly or how softly any part of an utterance is produced
2. pitch, or frequency; how high or how low any part of an utterance is spoken
3. juncture, or the use of the pause; the actual spaces that are placed between utterances

Taken together, these components are used to lay a pattern of rises and falls, and stops and starts across words, phrases, and sentences.

The intonation system serves several purposes. It conveys the emotional state or mood of the speaker. Take, for example, the same set of words spoken with two different intonation patterns: "You are going with us." Spoken as an exclamation (!), the primary stress and pitch markers are on the words *you* and *with*. This conveys the idea that the speaker is excited about the fact and may reassure the listener that he or she is wanted. Those same words, "You are going with us," spoken as a question (?) with primary stress and pitch markers on the words *you* and *us*, may convey the opposite idea—that the speaker is not too pleased at the prospect of such company.

Intonation serves a subtler and more important function than alerting listeners to the emotional content of a message. Intonation patterns, which can be one-word or quite lengthy utterances, notify the brain of several elements necessary for effective and efficient communication. The entire tonal contour of an utterance tells the brain where a meaning unit starts and where it stops.

Human brains process verbal information in chunks that correspond to intonation contours across meaning units. We retain the gist of the message, dump the string of words, and move on to the next meaning unit. We do this because human beings have limited short-term memory (Smith, 1994, 1998). We actually can hold in short-term memory, on average, only seven separate elements; therefore, we must comprehend the meaning of the string of words so that we are retaining one element rather than all the individual words that make up that meaning (Miller, 1956).

Intonation also tells the brain what to pay special attention to in an utterance, that is, which are the most important pieces of information.

Intonation operates within sentences, phrases, and words. For example, in simple declarative English sentences, the main stress and pitch are usually on the subject. However, in phrases, stress and pitch help determine the meaning. For example, in the phrase "light house keeper," if the stress marker falls on the first segment, "light," the phrase has to do with ships, coastal shorelines, and tall white buildings. The term "lighthouse" is a noun in this context. Yet, another version has to do with dustcloths, brooms, and cleaning products. It places the stress marker on the word "house." This time "light" is an adjective and "housekeeper" is the noun. In cases like this one, intonation determines the visual display or how the words look in print. Or consider stress and meaning within words. In such words as *reCORD* or *REcord*, and *preSENT* or *PREsent*, the stress shifts, the vowels change, the parts of speech change, and the meanings change.

English is a combination of several Nordic and Germanic languages combined with Latin and French. The spelling conventions for English started centuries before spelling was standardized. Hence, English has many combinations of possible spelling patterns for each sound and several pronunciation possibilities for each spelling pattern. That does not take into account variations in regional and social class dialect nor does it account for the fact that words may actually differ in pronunciation based on placement in the sentence. American English also has many other influences such as Spanish, Native American languages, African languages, and even some Chinese. These circumstances account for the fact that English, while it is represented by an alphabetic code, is not represented by one-to-one correspondence between letters and sounds. This means that each letter and letter pattern does not represent just one sound, and any given sound may be spelled more than one way in English. This fact alone would render the approach to teaching reading by a phonics only/phonics first method suspect.

Phonology *Phonology* is the study of sounds, and the phonological system has to do with the sounds themselves. It differs from *phonics*, which is the method of using the sounds of a language when pronouncing a word one sees in print. The term *phoneme* is important. For our purposes, a phoneme is any one of the smallest, most basic units of sound in a spoken language (Fischer, 1993). A letter that represents a single phoneme is a *grapheme*. English has some forty-four phonemes (Schane, 1973). Phonemes are traditionally divided into two major categories, vowels and consonants. English uses twenty-six graphemes (letters) to represent speech sounds in print. This is done in very complex ways.

Vowels are speech sounds that are voiced and made with the mouth open, thereby allowing the relatively free movement of air through the mouth. The letters that represent these sounds are called vowels. The vowel letters are [a, e, i, o, and u]. The letter [y] sometimes substitutes for the letter [i] in words and syllables and is a vowel when it does so. *Gym*, *why*, and *syll-* are good examples. Likewise the letter [w] is sometimes substituted for a [u], and when it is, it is also considered a vowel; but the letter [w], unlike the letter [y], never appears in a syllable as a vowel by itself. Rather, it always follows a, e, or o as in *paw*, *new*, or *grow* (Fischer, 1993).

Vowel sounds are said to carry the bulk of the sound in each syllable. Traditionally, they are identified as *long*, *short*, and *other* (ah as in *honest*, oo as in *boot*, or ir as in fir). That is in fact the very definition of what a syllable is. Syllables consist of a vowel sound(s) alone or with the consonant sounds that modify it. Vowels may occur as single sounds in a syllable as in *tan*, *ten*, or *tin*. They also occur in teams. These are called *diphthongs*. A diphthong is a more complex vowel sound made by blending one vowel sound into another within the same syllable as the /oy/ in *boy* or the /ou/ in *out*. A digraph is two or three vowel letters that represent a single phoneme as the /ee/ in *see* (Fischer, 1993). (See Appendix A for additional information on vowels and consonants.)

Consonants are speech sounds that are made with the mouth closed in some way, thereby partially blocking the vocal air stream. The letters that represent these sounds are called *consonants*. All letters that are not vowels are consonants. Some consonants are voiced, and some are voiceless or whispered. Consonants serve to modify vowel sounds. They start them and make them hiss or jump out of the speaker's mouth. Consonants also occur as single sounds. The word *at* has one single consonant while the word *hat* has two. Two or more consonants together as the fl- in *flat* in which both consonant sounds are heard are called a *consonant blend*. The word *blend* is a good example because both the bl- at the beginning of the word and the -nd at the end represent individual sounds, the ones they normally represent alone. A consonant digraph is two or more letters spelling one consonant sound. The consonant digraphs are usually thought of as /th, sh, ph, wh, gh, ch/. A *consonant cluster* is as grouping of a consonant blends and diagraphs. Shr- as in the word *shrink* and thr- as in the word *three* are examples of consonant clusters.

Over the course of this century, speech scientists have identified many characteristics or *distinctive features* of phonemes. These vocal features more completely differentiate one phoneme from another. No two phonemes have the same set of features or characteristics. Each differs from the others by at least one or more features. It is these features that allow the human brain to identify the patterns that distinguish one human speech sound or phoneme from another.

The spelling system in English recognizes sixteen vowel and twenty-eight consonant sounds. These are spelled with twenty-six letters and combinations of letters. Using *Merriam Webster's Collegiate Dictionary* (1999) Tenth Edition: 31a–35a as the pronunciation standard, there are approximately two hundred fifty (250) letter patterns for these forty-four sounds in words common to materials used in elementary grades six and below. For example, consider some of the ways in which long /a/ can be spelled. Note: the pattern with e in parentheses (e), indicates silent e on the end of the word effecting the preceding vowel.

a as in *baby*

ay as in *day*

ai as in *mail*

a(e) as in *cake*

aigh as in *straight*

eigh as in *neighbor*

ei as in *rein*

ea as in *great*

ai(e) as in *praise*

ey as in *they*

ee as in *matinee*

et as in *bouquet*

e as in *carburetor*

au (e) as in *gauge*

Learning conventional spelling variations for writing is only part of the problem. There is also the problem of word identification when we read. When we see one of these letter patterns in print, it may not represent long /a/. For example, the letter [a] in the word *father*, the letters [ai(e)] in the word *aisle*, and the letters [ea] in the word *each*—all are spelling patterns for the long /a/ sound, but not in these words.

Morphology   *Morphology* is the study of the patterns of word formations and includes roots and root words, compound words, contractions, prefixes, suffixes, and variant endings. A *morpheme* is a minimal grammatical unit that cannot be subdivided into smaller meaningful parts; therefore, a morpheme is the smallest meaning carrying unit in a language (Bolinger, 1965). The word *hat* is considered one morpheme. It is said to be a free morpheme because it cannot be reduced or added to without changing the meaning; that is, to change *hat* to *hats* changes the meaning. The plural marker –s or –es is an example of a bound morpheme. Bound morphemes do not stand alone, but must be connected to another meaning unit. In English, grammatical indicators such as plural and past tense are part of morphology.

Let's examine regular past tense, as an example. Regular past tense in English is formed by adding a bound morpheme to the end of the verb. This bound morpheme is pronounced as /d/, /t/, or /ed/. However, it is spelled with the letter d, the letters ed, by doubling the final consonant (c) and adding ed (c + ed), or by changing the y to i and adding ed (ied). There is little relationship between the spelling of the past tense marker and the way it is sounded or pronounced. This does not mean there is no generalization operating. The pattern has to do with the phoneme at the end of the root verb, rather than with the past tense marker itself.

Consider the following:

/d/	/t/	/ed/
shove + d = shoved	fake + d = faked	vote + d = vote
boil + ed = boiled	laugh + ed = laughed	need + ed = needed
grab + bed = grabbed	slap + ped = slapped	pat + ted = patted
dry + ied = dried		

In the first set the past tense marker is sounded as /d/. In the second set it is pronounced as the whispered /t/. In the last set, the past tense tag becomes a separate syllable altogether. As you can see, each pattern utilizes more than one spelling for the same sound. The rule might be stated as follows: Any regularly forming English verb that ends in a voiced phoneme takes the voiced phoneme /d/ to make past tense. Any regular verb that ends in a voiceless phoneme takes the voiceless phoneme /t/ to form past tense. Any regular verb that ends in the phonemes /d/ or /t/ must take an inflected syllable /ed/ to form past tense. Of course, doubling the final consonant has nothing to do with past tense at all; rather, it indicates that the preceding vowel in the root verb is short. From these examples, it is clear that there is a relationship between the spelling and the pronunciation of past tense, but it is an obscure one. The relationship is one of matching type of phoneme at the end of the verb with type of phoneme forming the past tense marker.

This is another way of demonstrating that human beings intuit the rules or underlying structure of their language, even with the sound system. We have learned hundreds of underlying rules, but we do not consciously know what these rules are and we were not taught them directly. Young children are not taught the underlying rules for forming past tense in spoken English, yet they learn and use them in conventional ways long before they come to school. How is that possible and what are the implications for learning to read and write?

Syntax The set of patterns or conventions called *syntax* refers to the rules that govern word order in phrases and sentences. Look at the difference in meaning between the sentences "The dog bit the boy" and "The boy bit the dog." The same five words in a different order convey a different message. Meaning is transmitted through word order (Salus, 1969). If we destroy the grammar or sentence structure altogether as in "Bit dog the the boy," we still have the same five words, but no meaning at all.

Traditional grammar is based on a Latin model. Consider the following sentences: "John told Tammy to buy the parts" and "John promised Tammy to buy the parts." The surface structure of each sentence is the same. That is, from a traditional point of view, the grammar is identical. However, in the first sentence, Tammy will do the buying, and in the second, John will do the buying. Therefore, the meanings are different. During the last half of the century, most linguists came to believe that any grammatical analysis must reflect both surface structure and underlying reality (Chomsky, 1957; Lee, 1986). This work resulted in a theory of language called *transformational generative grammar*.

Let's look at these two terms (*transformational* and *generative*) separately. Transformational refers to a set of grammatical rules beyond any previously identified. This set of rules allows the orchestration of the entire complex production of connected discourse. Transformational rules arrange words in clauses, and arrange, relate, and embed clauses to make compound and complex sentences that relate across entire texts. Consider these simple examples. Instead of saying "My brother is big. My brother took me home," the child says, "My big brother took me home." Instead of saying "My dog is brown. My dog is little. My dog ran away," the child says "My little, brown dog ran away." The modifiers are embedded in the appropriate order and redundant words are deleted. Rules for sequencing and embedding modifiers and deleting redundant words are part of our store of underlying structural transformations that the brain employs in the production of meaningful utterances. There are many other rules as well. Instead of saying, "Today we won the game. Yesterday we lost the game", the child may say, "Today we won the game, but we lost yesterday." There are rules for inserting relational words that allow speakers to embed clauses. Transformational rules take all the separate conceptual elements that make up thought units, and allow speakers to turn them into surface-level strings of sounds that listeners then recognize as having meaning.

The other half of the term *transformational generative* is equally important. The idea that language, indeed all human learning, is generative is one of the theoretical cornerstones upon which a constructivist understanding of learning and teaching is built. We need to understand the term *generative* as it applies to both language learning and language production (Shuy, 1984).

This theory maintains that human beings learn the rules or patterns for structuring phrases and sentences, and they may then create, or generate, nearly a limitless number of variations as they insert each vocabulary item in an appropriate slot. Phrase structure rules are written somewhat like mathematical formulas. For example, one very simple rule may be stated that a sentence (S) can be made up of a noun phrase (NP) and a verb phrase (VP). The verb phrase may consist of a verb and a noun phrase. The noun phrase may be made up of an adjective (Adj) and a noun.

S—NP + VP

VP—V + NP

NP—(Adj +) N

All we need to "generate" acceptable sentences with our newly learned rule are two nouns, one verb, and an adjective. Take, for example, two nouns: *baby* and *candy*, one verb: *eats*, and one adjective: *pretty*. Now we can generate four sentences with our one phrase structure rule and our four-word vocabulary:

1. Pretty baby eats candy.

2. Baby eats pretty candy.

3. Pretty candy eats baby.

4. Candy eats pretty baby.

Granted, these sentences are not wonderful and only two make sense. Nevertheless we have generated four grammatical sentences with one simple rule and four words. College-educated adults "know" thousands of phrase structure rules and thousands of words. Words can be used exponentially. That is, we can use any word we know in the appropriate slot in thousands of structural patterns with each combination of other words. Obviously, then, human beings possess the power to "generate" essentially an infinite amount and variety of language because our brains learn the patterns or rules and know how to use every word we know in its appropriate slot in every pattern.

Pragmatics   *Pragmatics* has to do with the rules for the social uses of language within a given cultural group. Language is essentially a social activity, and the rules surrounding some of the social uses of language may be quite overt. For example, our culture has laws against public profanity. Nevertheless, we might hear profanity in a bar but not in church, where extreme social pressure might be exerted on the perpetrator. The rules of pragmatics can also be invisible or covert. For instance, various cultural groups in this country have different loudness boundaries in various social settings.

Pragmatics also includes how various groups use language and what they value in language. One cultural group may teach that it is the norm for everyone in the family to talk at the same time, while other groups teach that only one person speaks at a time and everyone else listens. One ethnic group may value oral storytelling, while another values factual accounts of events. Some cultural groups employ rhetorical questions, while others ask questions mainly when they really need to know the answer.

Semantics   How language transmits meaning is the area of linguistic study called *semantics*. While a part of semantics has to do with word meaning, it is much broader than the vocabulary of a language (Lee, 1986).

How language communicates meaning is much more complex and interrelated than merely adding up word meanings in a linear fashion. Meaning is determined within a specific context by word choices, intonation, and grammar. For example, what does the word *run* mean? The meaning of the word *run* cannot be interpreted until it is used. "He can run fast." "He can run for public office." "He started the run on the bank." The basic unit of meaning is not the word, but is it the sentence?

Even sentence grammar does not always provide sufficient cues to tell us the intended meaning. In order to understand, we need the broader contexts in which these sentences might occur. Understanding, then, depends on getting enough cues to interpret the thoughts of the speaker (or writer). But where do these cues come from? The cues come from the listener's knowledge of all six rule-governed systems that we have discussed, as well as from the specific context. Context in oral language refers to the environment or circumstances in which the language occurs.

Language conveys meaning through the rules that organize and interrelate the vocal symbols. These rule patterns are the underlying structural aspects of language that we learn indirectly. We generate all the language of which we are capable based on these underlying structural rules. The rules are complex and for the most part invisible. It has taken linguists many years to begin to identify and describe the underlying patterns by which we produce and comprehend language. The conventions or rule systems of a language cannot really be separated. Even at the word-level, intonation, phonology, morphology, syntax, semantics, and pragmatics work holistically to make meaning. STOP on a stop sign can be pronounced. It is a single morpheme made up of four phonemes. We treat it and read it as a command. We know what may happen to us if we ignore the command. We recognize the meaning of the symbol even when we see it from a distance or in a cartoon. We remember events and information from our personal and vicarious experiences relative to stop signs, and so on. Of all that, the least significant is the observation that the word is made up of one morpheme and four phonemes.

How Language Operates as a Whole

Clearly, the sound system is a vehicle for conveying oral language, but it is not where meaning resides. Meaning resides in the interaction between the brains of the speaker and listener. Words are made up of sounds that are purposefully strung together by the speaker using intonation and grammar. These are "recognized" in the brain of the listener as understandings take shape.

Take a look at just one of the things language will let us do as we string words together to elicit meaning. In the sentences "John is a gentleman farmer. He owns a steer named George," we have an example of an endophoric reference—but who cares what linguists call it. The speaker knows how and when to replace the noun subject (John), once it is named, with the shorter, simpler word (he). The listener knows how to search for the identity of the referent by going back in memory to the previous statement. (For a complete treatment of cohesive ties see Chapman, 1983.) Language connects within and across sentences, and all adult users of language know how to do that.

Language Processes   Speakers employ their knowledge of language, their thinking, and their background of experiences when they speak. Listeners, engaged in the act of comprehending speech, bring several essential ingredients to the process. First, they bring their not inconsiderable brains. Relatively speaking, human beings are very smart. They have complex brains that are designed to impose patterns on, and make sense of, the world. It is the brain that processes oral language. Second, listeners bring their knowledge of language, its forms, functions, and content. They then use what they know about language and how it works to figure out the speaker's message. Third, they bring all the knowledge and experiences about the world that they have amassed during their lives. Finally, they bring their five senses by which listeners "know" the context of the situation (Gregory and Carroll, 1978; Kavanaugh and Mattingly, 1972). All of these and maybe more are needed to process and understand language.

Language and Context   Whether an utterance or text selection is profound insight or a daily conversation or story, all language is embedded in a real context and a vicarious one as well. The real context consists of the events in the immediate environment, the events of the moment. The vicarious context is the mind and memory of both the speaker and the listener, or the reader and the writer. Both contexts are necessary to understanding, and both allow language to be produced and perceived.

We have all learned at least one language, our native language, without formal instruction. This feat was perhaps our most successful learning endeavor, because language with its layer upon layer of patterns and rules is extremely complex. Language, is also one of our most important tools, and language may be our most unique attribute. Human beings created language because of need. We are very social creatures living in a complex world. We needed a symbol system to represent our ideas and our intentions and to record and transmit the information we wished to convey. We use language, whether oral or written, to control and understand the world around us.

SUMMARY

Language is a human social invention. It is pervasive in our lives. We use it nearly every waking minute, and it is also the primary means by which we think and learn. Language is complex and invisible. It has taken linguistic researchers decades to begin to understand the complexities of human language. Complicated as it is, however, we all seem to learn the layers of underlying structures and surface features of our native language easily and without direct instruction. That is, meaningful language in its natural environment is its own teacher.

Language production is a complex human capability, and one of the most intricate and important learning events in which the human brain engages. If teachers are to help children learn to read and write, knowing how children learn (construct their native language) language will prove useful.

THEORY-TO-PRACTICE CONNECTIONS

Language Theory

1. Language is a social invention.

2. Language is a set of abstract symbols used to represent ideas and intentions.

3. Language is extremely complex, consisting of symbols embedded in layer upon layer of patterns and rules.

4. Language is generative.

5. Language is one of the ways we come to know our world.

Examples of Classroom Practice

1. Collaborative problem solving

2. Classroom writing and book publishing

3. Reading aloud and telling stories

4. Word studies

5. Formal and informal group discussions

SUGGESTED READINGS

Bransford, J., A. Brown, and R. Cocking. 1999. *How People Learn: Brain, Mind, Experience, and School.* Washington, DC: National Academy Press.

Cogswell, D. 1996. *Chomsky for Beginners.* New York: Writers and Readers Publishing, Inc.

Goodman, K. 1993. *Phonics Phacts.* Portsmouth, NH: Heinemann.

Shuy, R. 1984. "Language as the Foundation for Education." *Theory into Practice* 23 (3): 167–74.

Smith, F. 1998. *The Book of Learning and Forgetting.* New York: Teachers College Press.

EXTENDING YOUR DISCUSSION

1. Attempt speaking in a monotone to a group of people. What is their response? Why?

2. Attempt speaking very, v e r y s l o w l y to a group of your friends. Speak so that there is ½ second between each word. How do they react? What do they do if you keep it up after they clearly expect you to stop? Why do you think they react that way? What do these two activities tell you about human language production and comprehension? Share your experiences with classmates.

3. Tape-record on audiotape three to five minutes of informal conversation between two people. Transcribe the transaction. Describe the context of the conversation. Is knowing the context and/or the speakers helpful to understanding? Try writing some of the conversation phonetically, so as to represent their dialects. How easy was it? What did you learn? Try listening for the cohesive ties. Which ones did you find? Discuss your experiences.

4. Discuss the single morpheme STOP. What events and information from your personal and vicarious experiences relative to stop signs, can you activate/recall? What information about STOP on a stop sign do you use when you see one? Why? How does that relate to all other visual signs and symbols? Are all six of the rule systems operating when you read STOP on a stop sign?

5. Discuss the theory and practice statements on page 33. How might these classroom practices enhance language and literacy development?

REFERENCES

Benjamin, R. 1970. *Semantic and Language Analysis.* New York: Bobbs-Merrill.

Bolinger, D. 1965. *Forms of English: Accent, Morpheme and Order.* Cambridge, MA: Harvard University Press.

Chapman, J. 1983. *Reading Development and Cohesion.* Portsmouth, NH: Heinemann.

Chomsky, N. 1957. *Syntactic Structures.* The Hague: Mouton.

———. 1972. *Language and Mind.* New York: Harcourt Brace Jovanovich.

Cogswell, D. 1996. *Chomsky for Beginners.* New York: Writers and Readers Publishing, Inc.

Fischer, P. 1993. *The Sounds and Spelling Patterns of English.* Farmington, ME: Oxton House.

Gregory, M., and S. Carroll. 1978. *Language and Situation.* London: Routledge and Kegan Paul.

Kavanaugh, J., and I. Mattingly. 1972. *Language by Ear and by Eye.* Cambridge, MA: MIT Press.

Lee, D. 1986. *Language, Children and Society.* New York: NYU Press.

Lee, D., and J. Rubin. 1979. *Children and Language.* Belmont, CA: Wadsworth.

Lenneberg, E. 1967. *Biological Foundations of Language.* New York: John Wiley and Sons.

Lieberman, P. 1967. *Intonation, Perception, and Language.* Cambridge, MA: MIT Press.

Merriam Webster's Collegiate Dictionary, 10th ed. 1999. Springfield, MA: Merriam Webster, Inc.

Miller, G. 1956. "The Magical Number Seven, Plus or Minus Two: Some Limits on Our Capacity for Processing Information." *Psychological Review* 63: 81–92.

Salus, P. 1969. *Linguistics*. New York: Bobbs-Merrill.

Schane, S. 1973. *Generative Phonology*. Englewood Cliffs, NJ: Prentice-Hall.

Shuy, R. 1984. "Language as the Foundation for Education." *Theory into Practice* 23 (3): 167–74.

Smith, F. 1990. *To Think*. New York: Teachers College Press.

———. 1994. *Understanding Reading*, 5th ed. Hillsdale, NJ: Lawrence Erlbaum Associates.

———. 1998. *The Book of Learning and Forgetting*. New York: Teachers College Press.

Vygotsky, L. 1962. *Thought and Language*. Cambridge, MA: MIT Press.

Wells, G. 1986. *The Meaning Makers: Children Learning Language and Using Language to Learn*. Portsmouth, NH: Heinemann.

CHAPTER THREE

"Language is a tool that creates reality. . . . We do not acquire language for its own sake, but for the sake of doing something with and to somebody else."

(Jerome Bruner, 1984, 193)

CHILDREN LEARNING AND CONSTRUCTING LANGUAGE

Language, as we saw in Chapter Two, is a complex code created by humans beings for transmitting meaning, for conducting the business of living with each other in the broadest as well as the narrowest of senses.

With language, we organize our understanding of the world; we think, learn, and socialize. Humans developed language because of our need to share information and ideas with each other. Human beings are driven to communicate with each other. Therefore, we are driven to learn language. Language learning in children mirrors the stages and processes that the first constructors of language went through.

At the surface, oral language might be described as a sequence of sounds produced by the expulsion of air through the throat and mouth. This definition of language is no more helpful or significant than saying written language is directionally sequenced marks produced by moving a writing implement across paper. The structures that enable us to comprehend, learn, and produce language in all its forms exist in the human brain, not in the eye, ear, hand, or mouth. These brain structures are there for the purpose of, and depend totally on, constructing meaning.

Oral language consists of vocal symbols strung together by a series of embedded layers of patterns or rules. Children internalize at least five rule systems as they construct language: intonation, phonology, syntax, semantics, and pragmatics. Language is also psychogenerative. This means that as the rules are internalized and words are added, language capacity expands exponentially. Children accomplish this remarkably complex feat by age five, and in some cases, by age three. For most of us, this powerful and complex tool, language, was easily constructed within the occurrences of everyday family life. No one teaches us our native language.

Language is not only the basis of social interaction, it is also the foundation for almost all school learning. Most teachers receive instruction that emphasizes teaching children to read and write, but they may not be given sufficient information about how human beings learn language. Because literacy learning parallels oral language learning (Goodman, Smith, Meredith, and Goodman, 1987), understanding one leads to a better understanding of the other. Therefore, we will examine the language learning process more closely. All forms of language learning involve the same processes that account for learning in general. That is, the same ecological conditions, immersion, demonstration, approximation, and so on, that promote learning in general, apply to language learning as well.

As with learning in general, language learning is a psychogenerative process. Language emerges well before the first word is uttered. Language is built on a semantic foundation created by all the transactions the child has within the environment. During the first few months of life, children figure out how to make themselves understood, and they come to understand much of what is said to them.

For that to happen, children require great amounts of language that makes sense. Much of the language children hear naturally refers to events in their immediate and knowable present. Language is learned in the family, and family and community patterns of talking are immediate to the environment. They are cultural. Language is a tool for learning. As it is used for real purposes, learners develop greater control over the conventions of their language. Language is learned in context through use. We do not study language in order to learn it. We use it, and our brains learn it for us. No one teaches us; no one has to!

LANGUAGE LEARNING AS REFLECTIVE OF LEARNING IN GENERAL

In the same way young children construct language, they construct most all their understandings about the world and how it works. They learn language from examples of language they hear. As they try to understand and use language the brain identifies regularities and irregularities from multitudes of experiences.

Language is a complex symbol communication system that is learned as it is used. Language learning takes place in the brain. The brain is designed to detect and impose patterns on the world of sensory experiences, and language is composed of patterns. The brain is the organ for learning. Whether it is language learning or learning in general, we learn nearly everything the same way.

We may be *immersed* in what we are learning; we see *demonstrations*; we *engage* in representing our understanding; we *expect* to learn. There is little difference, except perhaps in scope and complexity, between learning anything that can be learned through interaction with the world of sensory data and learning language.

Language learning, like learning in general, is psychogenerative. As children observe and interact with others, the brain tries to impose pattern, regularity, and structure. That is, it tries to impose structure so it will know how to behave in order to survive. In the case of language learning, it internalizes the patterns or underlying structures from the language it is hearing. On these underlying rule patterns, the rest of the child's language will be built. The brain literally teaches itself how to learn language.

Language learning is also creative. Children create or invent language for themselves. Hypothetically, if all the adult speakers of language disappeared from the environment, children's language development would spin off in a line to form new languages. These new language groups, we can assume, would be as complex and as large as need dictated. The fact that children learn language in and among a multitude of other language users causes them to have to conform their inventions to the language that exists around them if they are to be understood. Hence, they pull back to the center, to conventional forms, in the ever expanding spiral of language development. As the language develops, children invent or construct the underlying rules and are then able to plug in new words and phrases, as acquired, into the structures or rules they have internalized. If they can make themselves understood, they retain the rule patterns. If not, they alter them. In these ways, children gradually become capable of communicating everything they want to communicate, the wonderful variety of information and ideas they think.

One child alone in the world would not create a language. There would be no need to name objects, infer relationships, or express feelings and thoughts. There would be no one to share them with, no one else with whom to participate in the creation of the code or representational system that is language.

However, two or more children together would create their own entirely unique, idiosyncratic language. That new language would have a sound system; it would also have word labels for objects, ideas, relationships, and events. It would have a grammar or syntax, that is, underlying phrase structure rules. Two or more human beings alone in the world would create a new language, and with it they would make their world meaningful. They might even begin to argue about how to use certain elements of the language or which sound label was the "correct" one for a particular event. That is, the new language would soon develop pragmatic rules.

Children born into human society, into highly sophisticated cultural groups, usually do not create *entirely* new languages, except in the case of some identical twins. Rather, most children create the language that is essentially already there. They do that to understand and to be understood. What transpires between birth and the early stages of language production supports the dual processes of *invention* (creating forms and structures) and *convention* (figuring out and using the word label and underlying structural rules that are already out there).

There is evidence that children are driven to invent or creatively engage in making language. But because they want to be understood, they end up having to conform, to figure out the language that already exists in their environments. This dual process of invention and convention then can be thought of as an ever expanding spiral of constructive or creative forces in language development balanced against the need to conform, to communicate. Based on our best understandings, language development in young children appears to be a *balance* between invention and convention (Goodman, 1990).

The dual processes of invention and convention are seen in general learning as well. As children grow, they progress from magical thinking to rational thinking. They come to understand that the world has physical rules and regularities, that they are not creating the world but coming to know it. (For example, elves and fairies do not exist just because we can think they should, or see them in our imagination, or think it would be a more interesting world if they did. That's one reason we have stories, to keep our inventions alive after we discover reality.)

Language exists to make and represent meaning among people. It consists of several broad sets of rule systems that learners must internalize—intonation, phonology, syntax, morphology, semantics, and pragmatics. Language is part invention and part convention. Language is learned as it is used in the course of everyday family living; it is culturally determined. Language learning is just a complex case of how human beings make sense of almost everything in the world.

Language Learning in Use   Children do not study sounds, words, and underlying rules in order to learn their language. Language is learned as it is being used and language in use is always whole and purposeful for the user. Growth in the construction of language rules follows similar paths from language to language around the world. While wide variation exists among individual children within any single group, a great deal is known about the nature of language development in general (Brown, 1970; Carroll, 1960; Dale, 1972; Halliday, 1975; Lee, 1986; McCarthy, 1954; Menyuk, 1988; O'Donnell, Griffin, and Norris, 1967).

By the 1960s researchers in child language learning discovered that surface characteristics, such as sounds, had relatively little to do with language learning. The complexities and the regularities of the constructions children engage in as they develop language were still unexplored. Current perspectives on children's language learning hold that semantic categories (or meaning) *precede or develop together* with syntactic rules

(Maratsos, 1983; Menyuk, 1988). That is, meaning comes before structure. Language must make sense before it can be learned (Smith, 1994).

Children's drive to communicate causes them to develop language. They want to make their intentions and interests clear and to get their needs and desires fulfilled. Children use language to control their environments. Young language learners construct the underlying rules that allow them to communicate from the strings of words provided by the natural environment. They identify the distinctive features that allow them to assign words to a syntactic or semantic category, and language grows exponentially. Actually, the brain performs these operations for learners as they use real language for real purposes. It can do this because meaningful language is always whole; no one speaks sounds without grammar or grammar without meaning.

Language Use as Culturally Determined   The brain learns the underlying structural patterns and learners use their store of words and their knowledge of how language works. During language development, the brain internalizes three broad sets of underlying rule patterns:

the patterns that govern the ordering and organizing of the symbols themselves, sounds into morphemes and words, and words into sentences—the syntactic system

the meanings of the symbols as they refer to objects, events, and ideas—the semantic system

how the symbols function, or why given symbols are appropriate for a given context—the pragmatic system (Gardner, 1991)

Shirley Brice Heath (1983) studied language use in three different cultural settings: a poor black, a poor white, and a middle-class white community. She found that in the poor black community, oral storytelling and the ability to tell tall tales was revered. In the poor white community, language was used to recount events, and deviations from literal "truth" were shunned. In the middle-class white community, fantasy was encouraged so long as it was clearly labeled and not confused with reality. Heath suggested that while all these children may have well-developed language abilities for use within their cultural groups, they are differentially prepared for the language, expectations, and assumptions of schools. That is, some of these children may be at a disadvantage in school unless teachers understand and respect the linguistic and cultural traditions each child brings to the classroom.

Some children may misunderstand and be misunderstood in their use of language and their cognitive abilities. Teacher expectation plays a part in children's success or failure in school, and teachers may be influenced by dialects to form low expectations for some children. Lowered expectations operate against low-income children (Lee, 1986). Children learn the language of the family—the only language they can learn. All social-class dialects are complex, fully formed linguistic systems. Sociolinguists agree that there are no deficits inherent in any dialects themselves (Lee, 1986).

Patterns of talking in school are also cultural. They are frequently without context and highly unfamiliar to many children. When children use language differently from their teachers, problems may arise. When children do not know how to play the game called school, they may be prejudged as poor learners with limited literacy and other academic potential (Michaels, 1981). When such judgments are made on no other basis than social–class language variation, human potential is lost.

Child Language Development: Our Evolving Understanding

For decades, linguists and educators preferred to work with the surface manifestations of language rather than delving into the vague and complicated world of how human beings produce and obtain meaning. The result, unfortunately, is that teachers came to think that a focus on the surface manifestations of language rather than on constructing meaning was the appropriate content of instruction.

Linguists studied the sound system, parts of speech, words, and sentence types. Educators also studied the physical elements—surface features—of language. Not until the late 1950s and early 1960s did linguists, psychologists, and educators begin asking more difficult questions about the complicated world of language.

Even though language is complex, young children learn their native language, the version spoken by their cultural group, easily and without formal instruction. This truly remarkable accomplishment can be explained in part by the fact that the human brain is designed to detect and impose patterns on its experiences. And language, we have come to discover, is highly patterned. Language learning is a constructive process that involves hypothesizing about how language patterns work and experimenting with those hypotheses. Gradually, linguists and educators alike understood that natural language development involves immersion, demonstration, use, expectation, responsibility, approximations, and response. These same conditions allow the brain to construct its understandings and use its knowledge structures in generative ways to expand language and learning.

Developing Speech   When researchers in the 1950s and 1960s first began to examine child language development, their methodologies were not very sophisticated. They resorted to simple counts and averages to describe early language acquisition. For example, research efforts attempted to relate the number and types of sounds children tend to produce to their average months of life. Very early child language development was described as following five general stages listed in Table 3–1 (Cowley, 2000; Ecroyd, 1969).

Most infants have encountered sufficient meaningful language that they begin to speak at ten to fourteen months of age. Describing what infants and toddlers tend to do with sounds as they acquire the beginnings of language may be interesting, but it does not tell us much about the language learning process itself.

Many researchers are satisfied with merely counting things they can see and hear. For instance, estimates have been calculated of the average numbers of words children tend to acquire by certain ages. Two factors are significant here: (1) the importance of word knowledge to the language learning process and (2) the amazing growth in word

TABLE 3–1
DEVELOPMENT OF
HUMAN SPEECH

WHAT THE CHILD DOES WITH LANGUAGE	WHEN IT USUALLY FIRST OCCURS
Undifferentiated crying to differentiated crying as a signal to mother.	0–1 month
Babbling or random vocal play, listens to speech and responds by cooing or gooing.	1–3 months
Lallation or non-random play and self-imitation, begins to notice noisy toys, looks for source of loud sounds such as vacuum cleaner.	3–6 months
Echolalia or practice imitating clusters of sounds, babbles long and short groups of sounds that also reflect intonation in native language. Responds to own name.	6–12 months
First word, purposeful utterances (e.g., Mama, Dada, Milk, Bottle, etc.).	10–15 months
Puts two-word sentences together (e.g., Bobbie milk.) Uses one- or two-word questions (e.g., Mommy work?). Listens to simple stories, songs, and rhymes.	1–2 years
Has a word for almost everything in the environment. Uses two-, three-, four-, or more-word sentences to talk about and ask for things. Understands opposites such as stop and go. Understands and can follow sequence of two or more directions—get a bedtime book and bring it to me.	2–3 years

knowledge for most children. Words reflect children's concept development and their experiences within their families and with the larger world (Huckleberry and Strother, 1972; McCormick and Schiefelbusch, 1990; Nelson, 1988).

As you can see in Table 3–2, children learn a vast number of words in just a few years, an average of five to seven words per day beginning at birth and continuing to at least age five. However, some recent estimates suggest those numbers may be dropping.

AGE	ESTIMATED AVERAGE NUMBER OF WORDS	TABLE 3–2
10–14 months	1–3	ESTIMATED AVERAGE VOCABULARY DEVELOPMENT
2 years	300	
3 years	900–2,500	
4 years	2,500–8,000	
5 years	4,000–10,000	
10 years	25,000±	
College-educated adult	40,000±	

For a long time, language was thought of as strings of words that make up surface utterances rather than the manifestations of meaning through underlying rule patterns. That is one reason teaching has lagged so far behind.

Researchers began observing young children in natural environments and documenting how they develop language. The early works of Berko (1958), as well as Bloom (1970), Brown (1973), Bruner (1983), C. Chomsky (1969), Halliday (1975), Klima and Bellugi-Klima (1966), and Menyuk (1969), found that child language development focuses on making meaning. Children do in fact learn the invisible structural patterns that make language work, and they learn them in systematic ways, even though individual children vary greatly in when these patterns are constructed.

M. A. K. Halliday (1975) described the language development of his own son, Nigel. Before his first birthday, Nigel used sounds and gestures to convey his intentions. He said /na/ as he pointed to the object he wanted. Everyone knew this was Nigel's way of indicating he wanted to be given the object. Halliday pointed out that Nigel had constructed a completely "new" way to express his meaning in an attempt to get what he wanted. Nigel had invented a way to communicate meaning.

From this he concluded that all children invent "how to mean" (Halliday, 1975). They may create words for their bottle, for their favorite blanket or stuffed animal, or for their grandmother. They create a linguistic system that serves their personal and social circumstances. But their language development is not totally "invention." They understand much of what is said around them long before they make purposeful language.

In order to be able to talk, to form words that other people understand, children must have begun to develop *phonological awareness*. The perception of the sound structure of language and the sensitivity to the units of sound in language are referred to as phonological awareness (Yopp and Yopp, 2000). "Phonological awareness is developmental—it develops in stages, the first and easiest being the awareness that our language is composed of words" (Opitz, 2000, 6). As parents talk and play with their babies, these language learners become aware that words are made up of syllables and that syllables are made up of phonemes.

Yet, when they do begin to speak, even though they understand a great deal of lengthy connected discourse in context, children produce only one-word utterances. Because of their internalized semantic foundation, first-word utterances, or *holophrastic speech*, actually represent entire thought units. For instance, the single word "cookie" might mean anything from "I want a cookie" to "I dropped my cookie" to "The dog ate my cookie," depending on the context.

From the many one-word utterances children develop, they go on to produce two-word strings (Howe, 1976). By the time they are approximately eighteen to twenty-four months old, the emergence of two-word utterances shows understanding of referential meaning. For example, "Mommy sock" might mean "I want my sock," "There is my sock," "Mommy has my sock," or "Mommy fix my sock" (Bloom, 1970). These abbreviated strings, sometimes called *telegraphic speech*, are like telegrams sent from the child to the adult. Used like full sentences, they employ the fewest meaning-bearing words possible to get the meaning across. Language, even at the two-word stage, is still highly context-dependent and represents full thought units. The actual intended meaning can only be determined by and is only useful in the context in which it occurs.

As children's language expands, their development of syntactic structures is somewhat predictable and consistent. Clearly, children intuit the underlying layers of embedded rules as they use language. And this syntactic development parallels their cognitive development. That is, an understanding of object-action, object-action-object, and other relational and referential meanings in the real world are experiential and thinking operations. Cognitive development occurs as language expands, and each supports the other (Lee, 1986; Menyuk, 1988).

According to Slobin (1979), children learn the major rule systems and elements of their language essentially simultaneously; they acquire syntactic rules, words, and information as they use the language to make sense of their world. The main points in understanding the development of children's language after the one- and two-word stages are the following (Hood, 1980; Lee, 1986; Menyuk, 1988):

1. Language develops best in contexts where children have great amounts of meaningful language to learn from.

2. When children have great amounts of meaningful language, they intuitively learn the underlying structures—that is, the brain learns for them.

3. Semantics, syntax, and pragmatics develop together.

4. Language development and cognitive development occur simultaneously, and each supports the expansion and refinement of the other.

Studying what many linguists and educators call *baby talk* has revealed that the telegraphic speech that characterizes the first two to three years of language development is highly patterned and rule-based, just as adult speech is. Baby talk is a reduced and overgeneralized form of adult language. For instance, "Go, bye bye" is an abbreviated three-word utterance that is universally understood when uttered in the context of family life. And although many young, well-educated parents attempt to avoid baby talk, nearly all engage in a wide variety of such talk in spite of themselves (Garvey, 1984).

Baby talk, as a short-term bridge to more complex rule forms, is natural and necessary to children's language development. Baby talk is in no way harmful, so long as it is dropped at the appropriate time and not encouraged into school age by doting adults. Communication between mothers and babies during the first year of life, before language production begins, provides *demonstrations* of language and is the foundation upon which children build the rest of their language (Snow and Ferguson, 1977). Early child/adult transactions lay the basis by which children learn all the underlying structural rules that cannot be learned directly. Mothers, fathers, and other primary caretakers help young children with vast quantities of language; these language experiences are meaningful and often recur in predictable situations. This is one reason children develop language with such apparent ease.

Language is learned in the social and cultural context of the daily events of home, family, and community; therefore, language is very personal and idiosyncratic to the life of the learner. Children learn their language as they transact with others. That is, children learn language by being *immersed* in it, in the context in which the language is occurring. They *use* language to get what they want. And everyone, child and adult alike, *expects* it to be that way. Language development is a continuous, interactive, constructivist process that focuses on meaning (Lindfors, 1985).

As children interact with parents, other family members (especially siblings), other children, and other adults, their language development becomes more complex, their language fuller and more expressive. They imitate what they hear, but there is considerably more to child language development than imitation. We know that because most of the language young children produce is not imitated form. For example, no one ever said to a child, "Me want mine doggie," "My foots hurts," or "You doed that?" These are not imitations; rather, these expressions represent children's attempts to figure out the underlying rules and patterns—how language works. In the first instance, the child is hypothesizing about personal pronouns. The second and third instances are examples of *overgeneralization*.

Overgeneralizations are children's approximations of the way grammar works. Children learn a rule, for example that past tense is represented by -ed, and then they overapply it. Not only do overgeneralizations occur naturally in language learning around the world, but they are also absolutely necessary to language development. They indicate that learners are hypothesizing about underlying structures. Children merge into conventional or adult constructions over time. Adults do not need to "correct" child language. It is not necessary to say, "No, Dear, you should say, 'I want my doggie' or 'My feet hurt,'" because the child won't understand anyway. Young language learners are thinking about their intended meanings, not the surface structure they are trying to use. In fact, if adults attempt to correct each aspect of child language before the child has internalized sufficient examples of language (that is, to circumvent the natural process), they might cause more harm than good (Cazden, 1974).

Children naturally construct language without much awareness of surface forms and features. Most adults intuitively know that correcting child language is a waste of time and is probably not good for children. They expect children to learn anyway. Parents may chastise children for obscenities or correct certain pet peeves such as "ain't," but parents are simply too busy with the business at hand—communication—to be aware of all the phonologic, syntactic, semantic, and pragmatic approximations in the children's language. Those they do catch are usually thought of as cute or clever—for example, "passghetti." In families where children are rewarded rather than ignored or corrected for their language inventions, they tend to investigate language freely and language develops quickly. By the time children have reached their fifth birthday, most are capable speakers of their native language. Consider the implications for literacy learning.

WHY LANGUAGE IS GENERATIVE (AND CONSTRUCTIVIST)

According to Chomsky (1965) studying a simple paragraph yields a rich system of inter-relationships and cross-connections that are all consistent with a very subtle system of layers of grammatical rules. The human brain constructs meaning through its knowledge of how the language works, how it can be used and not used. Even studying simple sentences is often a complex task. For example, look at the statement "Mary kept the earrings that were in the box." Every adult speaker of the language knows we can say "What box did Mary keep the earrings in?" but not "What box did Mary keep that were in?" There is some form of a structural rule about not replacing complex noun phrases, such as "the earrings that were in the box," when we change a statement into a question. No one taught us that rule (Cogswell, 1999).

Indeed, if we had to learn all the rules for our language directly, that is, by being taught each one separately, it would take forever. No such system of learning can account for all the sound-meaning relationships that all of us have internalized about our language. The fact is, we are capable of understanding sentences that have no physical similarity, item by item, to any sentence we have ever heard before (Cogswell, 1999). We are capable of constructing new sentences that we have never heard before or that we have never uttered before—each perfectly understandable by others. We are capable of an infinite variety of unique language because our brains have internalized underlying structural rules of which we are mostly unaware.

In one experiment into the issue of the infinite potential of language, a professor at Wesleyan University showed twenty-five people a cartoon and asked them to tell what the cartoon was about in one sentence. As might be expected, all twenty-five responses were different. Then the professor entered the twenty-five sentences into a computer program designed to calculate the number of grammatically correct sentences that could be generated by using only the words from those sentences. The result was nearly twenty billion different possibilities (Cogswell, 1999).

Language in School Language is the tool teachers teach with and the tool learners learn with. The natural purpose of language—making meaning within a social context—should be honored. When children grapple with content—for example, when they are learning about primates, oceans, textiles, or folktales—they have to listen, talk, read, write, and think about what they are learning. They use language as their primary tool, and in so doing, their command of the conventions of language improves. In addition to that, adults focus some of the children's attention on the language itself in order to speed up the process of acquiring control over the conventions of language, but they do so only in the context of really using the language for meaningful purposes.

They avoid out-of-context, meaningless exercises that examine only the surface features of the language apart from meaning and purpose. They do that because they know that to do otherwise is to damage the children's natural learning processes. The main focus is, and remains, on meaning. In addition to listening, talking, reading, writing, and thinking about the central subject (and thinking some about the language being used), learners may engage in other forms of self-expression including dance, art, music, arithmetic, science experiments, sports, and so on.

SUMMARY

Children learn language by using language (Halliday, 1975). Language in use is always whole, meaningful, and purposeful to the user. Children develop language quicker when they are immersed in great amounts of oral language in situations they can make sense of and when they are encouraged to use it to get their needs met. They tend to begin language production with one-word utterances and gestures, focusing on the things they want. This soon expands to two-word and three-word utterances, then into longer, more complex speech. After two-word utterances, language growth is rapid. It remains, however, systematic and predictable.

Even though language is one of the most complex phenomena human beings ever learn, it is learned without formal instruction and with relative ease. Goodman (1986, 8) summarizes when language is easy and when it is difficult to learn. These statements apply equally to talking and listening and to reading and writing.

Language Learning Is Easy When	*Language Learning Is Difficult When*
It's real and natural.	It's artificial.
It's whole.	It's broken into bits and pieces.
It's sensible.	It's nonsense.
It's interesting.	It's dull and uninteresting.
It's relevant.	It's irrelevant to the learner.
It belongs to the learner.	It belongs to somebody else.
It's part of a real event.	It's out of context.
It has social utility.	It has no social value.
It has purpose for the learner.	It has no discernible purpose.
The learner chooses to use it.	It's imposed by someone else.
It's accessible to the learner.	It's inaccessible.
The learner has power to use it.	The learner is powerless.

Children's literacy development parallels their oral language development. The relevant aspects of oral language that directly affect learning to read and write are the words and concepts in a child's language, the underlying structures, and the child's awareness of language. Literacy is built upon an oral language base. What teachers believe about language learning and literacy will determine the extent to which they make children's learning to read and write easy or difficult.

THEORY-TO-PRACTICE CONNECTIONS

Language Learning Theory	*Examples of Classroom Practice*
1. Even in view of its highly complex nature, our native language is learned naturally, without instruction.	1. Creating opportunities for learners to see and use language in functional ways, e.g., lists, messages, signs, labels
2. Language learning is a balance between invention and convention.	2. Encouraging learners to express themselves freely before they can do so in "correct" or conventional language
3. Language learning is an active, constructive process, i.e., children learn language as they naturally use it.	3. Encouraging children to ask questions, e.g., why water disappears when it is boiled; why the grass is green or the sky is blue
4. Children's language learning is not chaotic and random, but highly patterned and organized.	4. Encouraging early attempts to write: drawing and scribbling
5. Language learning is a psychogenerative process.	5. Repeated readings of favorite stories

SUGGESTED READINGS

Bruner, J. 1983. *Child's Talk: Learning to Use Language.* New York: Holt, Rinehart, and Winston.

Wells, G. 1986. *The Meaning Makers: Children Learning Language and Using Language to Learn.* Portsmouth, NH: Heinemann.

EXTENDING YOUR DISCUSSION

1. Print the following four sentences, one each on four note cards.

> Billy threw the ball.
>
> The ball threw Billy.
>
> Billy threw the game.
>
> Billy threw the party.

Poll several people, asking them what each sentence means. Does the arrangement of the sentences make any difference? What does this tell you about how human beings process language?

2. Find a toddler, approximately eighteen months to three years old. Audiotape-record the child in three to five minutes of conversation once a month throughout the semester. Transcribe the tapes. How does language develop for this child? Document language development with examples from the tapes. Share and discuss with classmates.

3. Interview several parents of pre-school-age children about their child's language development. After you have gotten basic information such as the child's name, age, sex, etc., ask the following types of questions:

When did _____ start to talk?

What were _____'s first words?

What were _____'s favorite words or sayings?

Did _____ ever make up or invent words for favorite things such as bottle, blanket, grandmother?

a. If yes, did the family adopt these words, too?

b. Do you still use them? If no, why did you stop?

What did _____ use language for when he or she first started really talking?

Did _____ like to ask questions and tell others what to do?

Ask any other questions that you think will add to your understanding of how parents perceive language and language development. Many people believe they teach their children to talk. Many people think that imitation is the main way children learn their language. If people think that imitation is a major learning strategy, what implications might that have for their expectations of schools and learning to read and write?

Compile your interview responses. Do you detect any patterns? Are parents generally positive about their children's language development? Discuss your findings with classmates.

4. Consider the language learning theory statements on page 18. How do the examples of classroom applications to instruction support natural language learning as described in this chapter? Why should we concern ourselves with supporting natural learning processes in the first place?

REFERENCES

Berko, J. 1958. "The Child's Learning of English Morphology." *Word* 14: 50–177.

Bloom, L. 1970. *Language Development: Form and Function in Emerging Grammars*. Cambridge, MA: MIT Press.

Brown, R. 1970. "The First Sentences of Child and Chimpanzee." In *Psycholinguistics: Selected Papers of Roger Brown*. New York: Free Press.

———. 1973. *A First Language: The Early Stages*. Cambridge, MA: Harvard University Press.

———. 1988. "Development of a First Language in the Human Species (1973)." In *Child Language: A Reader*, eds. M. Franklin and S. Barten. Oxford: Oxford University Press.

Brown, R., and U. Bellugi. 1964. "Three Processes in the Child's Acquisition of Syntax." *Harvard Educational Review* 34: 133–51.

Bruner, J. 1978. "The Role of Dialogue in Language Acquisition." In *The Child's Conception of Language*, eds. A. Sinclair, R. Jarvella, and W. Level. New York: Springer-Verlag.

———. 1983. *Child's Talk: Learning to Use Language*. New York: Holt, Rinehart, and Winston.

———. 1984. "Language, Mind, and Reading." In *Awakening to Literacy*, eds. H. Goelman, A. Oberg, and F. Smith. Portsmouth, NH: Heinemann.

Carroll, J. 1960. "Language Development in Children." In *Encyclopedia of Educational Research*, ed. C. Harris. New York: Macmillan.

———. 1970. *Comprehension by 3rd, 6th, and 7th Graders of Words Having Multiple Grammatical Functions: Final Report*. Princeton, NJ: Educational Testing Service.

Cazden, C. 1974. "Suggestions from Studies of Early Language Acquisition." In *Language and the Language Arts*, eds. J. DeStefano and S. Fox. Boston: Little, Brown.

Chomsky, C. 1969. *The Acquisition of Syntax in Children from 5 to 10*. Cambridge, MA: MIT Press.

Chomsky, N. 1957. *Syntactic Structures*. The Hague: Mouton.

———. 1965. *Aspects of the Theory of Syntax*. Cambridge, MA: MIT Press.

Cogswell, D. 1999. *Chomsky for Beginners*. New York: Readers and Writers, Inc.

Cowley, G. 2000. "For the Love of Language." *Newsweek (Special Issue, fall/winter)*: 12–15.

Dale, P. 1972. *Language Development: Structure and Function*. Hinsdale, IL: Dryden Press.

Donaldson, M. 1978. *Children's Minds*. New York: W. W. Norton.

Dumtschin, J. l988. "Recognizing Language Development and Delay in Early Childhood." *Young Children* 43: 39–42.

Durkin, D. 1966. "The Achievement of Pre-school Readers: Two Longitudinal Studies." *Reading Research Quarterly* 1: 5–36.

Ecroyd, D. 1969. *Speech in the Classroom*. Englewood Cliffs, NJ: Prentice-Hall.

Fisher, C., and A. Terry. 1977. *Children's Language and the Language Arts*. New York: McGraw-Hill.

Forester, A. 1977. "What Teachers Can Learn from 'Natural Readers.'" *The Reading Teacher* 31 (2): 160–66.

Gardner, H. 1991. *The Unschooled Mind: How Children Think and How Schools Should Teach*. New York: Basic Books.

Garvey, C. 1984. *Children's Talk*. Cambridge, MA: Harvard University Press.

Gleitman, L. 1988. "Biological Dispositions to Learn Language." In *Child Language: A Reader*, eds.

M. Franklin and S. Barten. Oxford: Oxford University Press.

Goodman, K. 1986. *What's Whole in Whole Language? A Parent/Teacher Guide to Children's Learning.* Portsmouth, NH: Heinemann.

Goodman, K., E. Smith, R. Meredith, and Y. Goodman. 1987. *Language and Thinking in Schools: A Whole Language Curriculum,* 3rd ed. Katonah, NY: Richard C. Owen.

Goodman, Y. 1984. "The Development of Initial Literacy." In *Awakening to Literacy,* eds. H. Goelman, A. Oberg, and F. Smith. Portsmouth, NH: Heinemann.

Halliday, M. 1975. *Learning How to Mean: Explorations in the Development of Language.* New York: Elsevier.

———. 1977. *Explorations in the Functions of Language.* London: Edward Arnold.

Heath, S. 1983. *Ways with Words: Language, Life, and Work in Communities and Classrooms.* Cambridge: Cambridge University Press.

Hood, L. 1980. "The Role of Imitation in Children's Language Learning." In *Discovering Language with Children,* ed. G. Pinnell. Urbana, IL: NCTE.

Howe, C. 1976. "The Meanings of Two-Word Utterances in the Speech of Young Children." *Journal of Child Language* 3: 29–47.

Huckleberry, A., and E. Strother. 1972. *Speech Education for the Elementary Teacher.* Boston, MA: Allyn and Bacon.

Jaggar, A. 1980. "Allowing for Language Differences." In *Discovering Language with Children,* ed. G. Pinnell. Urbana, IL: NCTE.

Klima, E., and U. Bellugi-Klima. 1966. "Syntactic Regularities in the Speech of Children." In *Psycholinguistic Papers,* eds. J. Lyons and R. Wales. Edinburgh: Edinburgh University Press.

Labov, W. 1970. "The Logic of Non-standard English." In *Language and Poverty,* ed. F. Williams. Chicago: Markam.

Langer, J. 1987. *Language, Literacy and Culture.* Norwood, NJ: Ablex.

Lee, D. 1986. *Language, Children, and Society.* New York: NYU Press.

Lenneberg, E. 1967. *The Biological Foundation of Language.* New York: John Wiley and Sons.

Lindfors, J. 1985. *Children's Language and Learning.* Englewood Cliffs, NJ: Prentice-Hall.

Loban, W. 1976. *Language Development: Kindergarten Through Grade 12.* Urbana, IL: NCTE.

Maratsos, M. 1983. "Some Current Issues in the Acquisition of Grammar." In *Manual of Child Psychology,* eds. J. Flavell and E. Markham. New York: John Wiley.

McCarthy, D. 1954. "Language Development in Children." In *Manual of Child Psychology,* ed. L. Carmichael. New York: John Wiley.

McCormick, L., and R. Schiefelbusch. 1990. *Early Language Intervention.* Columbus, OH: Merrill.

Menyuk, P. 1988. *Language Development: Knowledge and Use.* Glenview, IL: Scott Foresman.

Michaels, S. 1981. "Sharing Time: Children's Narrative Styles and Differential Access to Literacy." *Language in Society* 10: 49–76.

Nelson, K. 1988. "Acquisition of Words by First Language Learners." In *Child Language: A Reader,* eds. M. Franklin and S. Barten. Oxford: Oxford University Press.

O'Donnell, R., W. Griffin, and R. Norris. 1967. *Syntax of Kindergarten and Elementary School-Age Children: A Transformational Analysis.* Urbana, IL: NCTE.

Olsen, D. 1984. "'See! Jumping!' Some Oral Language Antecedents of Literacy." In *Awakening to Literacy,* eds. H. Goelman, A. Oberg, and F. Smith. Portsmouth, NH: Heinemann.

Opitz, M. 2000. *Rhymes and Reasons: Literature and Language Play for Phonological Awareness.* Portsmouth, NH: Heinemann.

Pelligrini, A., L. Galda, and D. Rubin. 1984. "Context in Text: The Development of Oral and Written Language in Two Genres." *Child Development* 55: 1549–55.

Slobin, W. 1979. "Universals of Grammatical Development in Children." In *Advances in Psycholinguistics,* eds. G. Flores d'Arcais and W. Levelt. New York: Elsevier Press.

Smith, F. 1994. *Understanding Reading,* 5th ed. Hillsdale, NJ: Lawrence Erlbaum.

Snow, C., and C. Ferguson. 1977. *Talking to Children.* Cambridge: Cambridge University Press.

Teale, W., and E. Sulzby. 1986. *Emergent Literacy: Writing and Reading.* Norwood, NJ: Ablex.

Tough, J. 1977. *The Development of Meaning.* London: Allen and Unwin.

Wells, G. 1986. *The Meaning Makers: Children Learning Language and Using Language.* Portsmouth, NH: Heinemann.

Yopp, H., and R. Yopp. 2000. "Supporting Phonemic Awareness Development in the Classroom." *The Reading Teacher* 54 (2): 130–43.

CHAPTER FOUR

"Language is deeply fixed in human behavior, and like walking upright, it emerges in its season."

(Edmund Henderson, 1986, 65)

EARLY LITERACY

We have already learned a good deal about what learning is and how the human brain works. We have also learned what language is and how infants and toddlers go about constructing their oral language. We already know how strikingly brilliant young children are as indicated by their amazing ability to do this. Does this ingeniousness apply to their learning to deal with print as well?

Let's expand our exploration of children's constructions of knowledge to include written language. What are the relationships among learning, language, oral language learning, and children's learning written language? Are children able to learn written language with the same relative ease with which they learned oral language? Or must children be taught to read and write? This chapter addresses what is presently known about how young children learn to read and write.

THE RELATIONSHIPS BETWEEN ORAL AND WRITTEN LANGUAGE: PARALLEL BUT NOT IDENTICAL PROCESSES

As few as two decades ago, linguists believed that oral language was the primary form of language because it was learned first. Written language, the secondary form, was learned well after oral language. The implied meanings of primary and secondary led us to believe that not only was one more significant than the other, but that they were significantly different from one another. It was also believed that although oral language was learned, secondary language had to be taught. This led to the belief that not everyone was capable of becoming literate.

These views have changed. Today oral language and written language are seen as parallel processes, the two developing in very much the same way and for very much the same reasons from language to language around the world. In order to learn to talk, children must be capable of thinking abstractly and using symbols to represent their intentions. Therefore, anyone capable of learning oral language ought to also be perfectly capable of learning to read and write. While this condition is largely recognized to be the case, there is no indication that the reality is as yet realized (Meek, 1982).

Like oral language, written language has two modes: productive and receptive. And like oral language, receiving language tends to develop first and more fully. That is, people tend to be able to read somewhat before, and better than, they can write. People usually understand speech before, and better than, they can talk. This is because we are immersed in receiving language and use what we internalize about language to learn to produce language.

Children who do not speak English as their native language, but who are in the process of learning it because they have recently immigrated to the United States, are soon able to understand more English, both oral and written, than they can produce. This is true because our brains are geared for making sense. This is also true because we live in a highly literate society; there is print everywhere. Children learn more quickly than adults because their brains are more plastic. Plastic refers to the neural connections, or synapses, created in the brain as we learn. Young children's brains are developing neural connections by the thousands every minute. In the case of second language learning, children who are literate in their native language will become literate in English very quickly because many of the connections are already there. Their brains are not only still plastic, but they have also already internalized the reading/ writing process from one language and they use that to simply learn another symbol system and set of operational rules.

While oral and written language development are parallel processes, written language is not just oral language written down. For example, the language we use in writing this book is different from the language we use in talking about the concepts discussed in the book. Since oral language is learned first, most think that written language is more complex. Many argue that written language is more abstract than oral language (Adams, 1990), but what is more abstract than the seemingly continuous string of sounds called "talking" coming out of someone's throat and mouth? What could be more abstract than the subtlety of intonation on which oral language hangs? How do writers "write" intonation? They don't. They leave the application of intonation to the reader when the text is read aloud. And written language can be revised and polished; it can be studied-revisited repeatedly, whereas oral language cannot (Goodman, 2000). Oral language hits the ear and is gone. In addition, second language learners often handle written language before they can produce oral language. Thus, the case can be made that oral language is the more difficult.

All language is complex, both oral and written. But most humans learn to speak in their native languages naturally and with ease. They learn their native language long before they can think and talk about what they are doing. How different is that from learning to read and write? Why does learning to read and write appear to be inherently more difficult? Does it have to be?

HOW OUR UNDERSTANDING OF EARLY LITERACY HAS CHANGED OVER THE PAST SEVERAL DECADES

Traditionally, teachers have been taught that children need to acquire a set of social, emotional, physical, and cognitive competencies believed to be precursors of reading. Kindergarten and pre-school teachers' roles were to get children "ready" to learn to read in the first grade. Most often referred to as reading readiness, this seemingly common-sense but non-empirical view of children's development assumed that they could not learn to read until they had learned certain readiness information. This typically included knowledge of colors, shapes, sounds, names of the letters of the alphabet, and the sound(s) each letter "makes." The influence of that approach is still seen, as frequently kindergarten programs employ "the letter of the week" to teach letters of the alphabet and letter sounds—an organizing principle frequently lost on the children.

Professional literature from the first half of the twentieth century included terms like *auditory and visual discrimination* and *fine motor skills*. Large-motor skills such as skipping, climbing, and hopping, along with small-motor skills such as cutting along a line and coloring within the lines, were practiced. A commonly held belief was that children could not learn to read until they had learned to skip. In addition, most first-grade teachers required children to be able to read before they could be taught how to write, so writing instruction in first grade consisted of practicing the marks that make up manuscript letter production—circle, stick, etc.

Readiness instruction was centered around the notion that all children possessed similar levels developmentally, that they all needed to master the same set of prescribed skills in order to begin formal reading instruction. Unfortunately, this view was founded around two misguided assumptions: (1) children knew nothing about reading or writing before they entered school, so (2) teachers needed to get them ready (Morrow, 2001).

Typical readiness programs involved tasks that had little to do with the act of reading, much less any type of book or print awareness. In fact, in most readiness programs, children were not even given books. And while good teachers always read aloud to their children, nothing in most readiness programs advocated it.

Many of these long-held readiness beliefs were challenged in the 1960s, when researchers began looking more closely at what children were actually doing with learning to read and write, especially early, spontaneous readers. Children who learned to read and write without formal instruction, who already knew how to read before they entered kindergarten, were called *spontaneous readers* (Clay, 1966; Durkin, 1961). How was it possible for these children to be reading without having been taught the necessary readiness skills?

While traditional readiness programs still exist, recently teachers and researchers of children's early literacy development have provided us with new, different, and more productive insights (Chomsky, 1971; Clark, 1976; Clay 1966; Durkin, 1961; Ferreiro and Teberosky, 1982; Goodman, 1990; Harste, Woodward, and Burke, 1984; Heath, 1983; Martens, 1996; Morrow, 2001; Moustafa, 1997; Rowe and Harste, 1986; Sulzby, 1985; Taylor 1983; Teale, 1984; Wells, 1986).

The focus is no longer on identifying, teaching for, and assessing "readiness skills." Instead, teachers are encouraged to examine what children have internalized from their environments about how written language works, how they use what they know to begin to communicate with each other, and how they inform their own literacy learning processes.

SIMILARITIES AND DIFFERENCES BETWEEN LEARNING TO TALK AND LEARNING TO READ AND WRITE

Children do not grow up in a vacuum. Rather, they are surrounded by print from birth. Many children living in the United States are read to daily, but even children who are not read to on a regular basis are immersed in meaningful environmental print. Print is everywhere—on grocery store items, billboards, businesses, junk mail, fast food restaurants, road signs, public transportation, bills, newspapers and magazines, television, and even on walls as graffiti. All these examples, and more, provide the instances of written language from which children construct their growing knowledge about how written language works. They observe adults interacting with print; they see demonstrations of how print functions in daily living. They see print everywhere, and their brains internalize a great deal from these encounters.

Children internalize highly complex concepts about how written language works, much of which is never directly taught. They "discover a great deal about written language, whether in ambient print or in stories, without differentiating it from natural phenomena" (Smith, 1994, 144). Children acquire concepts about print (Clay, 1975) as they explore and experiment with the print and written language around them.

Among other things, they discover that print has meaning, that print is different from pictures, and that you can do things with it. In English, they discover that print goes from left to right and back to left again. They learn that in visual signs there is no direct concrete relationship between the abstract symbols in print and the intended message. They learn that the whole sign, Wal-Mart for example, means the same thing each time they see it, but that the "W" or the "M" may be used in other, different messages. They learn that spoken language can be written down. They may learn first about the symbols that represent their own names.

The concept of "directionality" in written language is very subtle. A chair is always a chair, even when lying on its side or upside down, but not so with written language symbols. With letters, an "N" on its side becomes a "Z"; a "b" upside down is a "p" and backward, it is a "d." As young children explore print, they observe that English is read and written not only from left to right, but also from top to bottom. Some children discover these concepts for themselves, but most children seem to benefit from both experience and assistance.

Children certainly have a lot to learn about the conventions of written language, but children communicate with print long before they get a handle on the "correct" or conventional way to do it. Looking at what children can produce may not give us a clear picture of what they know about language, either oral or written. Conventions are not language; they are the artifacts of a language in a given society (Rowe and Harste, 1986). Rather, we have to look at what children are trying to do and what they know and can say about their own attempts with language.

In writing, children who choose the upper left-hand corner, for instance, to begin writing may have little difficulty in moving in the conventional direction; however, children who start elsewhere may move in an unconventional direction. Children who begin in the upper right-hand corner may write backward. Is this a cause for alarm? Figure 4–1 is an example.

As young children engage in reading and writing, they learn about the conventions of written language. For example, as young children read, they see that in print there are spaces between groups of letters from which they learn what words are. They figure out that the symbols on the page are systematic, that letters represent speech sounds (more or less), that words and phrases represent meanings (more or less), and that there are a variety of uses for print. At first, as they begin to write, they may not spell conventionally and/or form word boundaries; they may not employ "space" the same way adults do. For example, "Daddy kicked the ball" may be represented as "Dadekttbal." Does the writer have something to say? Is he aware of what writing can do and what it is for? Does he know how to express himself with words? Is he thinking about how

FIGURE 4–1
MY TOOTH IS UP

to write what he wants to say? Is his understanding of how written language works developing? Is he developing the concept of how letters represent speech sounds? Of course! With continued interactions with print, this child will continue to move toward conventions, but what is already firmly established is that this child is becoming a reader and a writer.

We have to look at what children *can do*, what they are *trying to do*, and what they have to *know* in order to be able to understand what they are doing as readers and writers. These are the perspectives that help adults help them. These are the perspectives that are much more significant than what the child cannot do at any given point.

As learners continue to try to communicate in print, they recognize the need for such conventions as spaces. They also learn that a letter in one word represents one sound, yet that same letter in another word may represent a different sound. They learn that a letter in one font is exactly the same letter in any other font. Confusing? No, not if children are figuring those things out from authentic encounters with meaningful written language. But it could be highly confusing if it appeared as an arbitrary workbook exercise in a first-grade reading series or phonics program.

These are only some of the elements children have to figure out. As emerging readers and writers, children employ many unconventional forms. Just as in oral language learning, written language learners produce approximations as they develop control over convention. And, just as in oral language, their approximations are not haphazard.

Current researchers in early literacy, as did researchers in children's oral language development several decades ago, now realize that everything children produce during language learning is based in, connected to, and scaffolded onto what they already know. Unconventional form does not mean chaos; it does not mean random. From a constructivist perspective, nothing children do is random; it makes sense if we understand what the child is trying to do.

Children learn to read and write the same way they learned to talk. They must be immersed in written language they can make sense of. That is, they must have multiple instances of authentic written language encounters daily. They must be encouraged to use written language for personal/social interactions. They must engage in written language play and experimentation many times a day every day for a long time—just like they did when they were learning to talk. They learn to read and write as they read and write, and in the process, they learn about reading and writing. As in oral language learning, children expect to learn to read and write, they are expected to learn to read and write, and it is their right and their responsibility to learn to read and write.

In other words, children do not reach a point of being ready to learn to read and write. Learning literacy is just like all learning. Learners are acquiring some of it from almost the beginning. Children construct their own knowledge about print as they interact with it in meaningful ways. That means the content and intent differ greatly from child to child. However, the overall process is highly similar.

The term *emergent literacy* is frequently used to describe the literacy behaviors and concepts of young children that precede conventional reading and writing. Unlike the previous notions of readiness, emergent behaviors, or nonconventional explorations with print, are not defined as behaviors or activities that come before children are ready to read and write but as essential elements in a continuum of literacy development (Morrow and Sulzby, 1995). These playful, constructivist activities may begin at home with the child's first encounters with books, with pencils and paper or crayons and walls, with print they see in the environment, and with their interactions with adult literacy models. Or they may not begin much before kindergarten. Whenever they start, children learn by engaging in the process for authentic, personal, social purposes, and it takes time (and reasons) for conventional forms to develop.

Early literacy development is an inventive process. Just as with oral language, learners use their inventions to construct their communications. We use the term *invention* in the strictest sense of the word. Children invent their understandings of how the world works and they invent their oral and written language. This invention is precisely the same sense in which Thomas Edison invented the lightbulb. Edison invented the lightbulb in the midst of a scientific revolution in which enough knowledge formed a critical mass so that Edison knew enough to figure out what to do. Actually, several people in different places throughout the world invented the lightbulb all at roughly the same time. Edison and others invented within a social context of growing information and need. That characterizes how we learn in general and how we learn language in particular. We have all been constructors of our own understandings, including knowledge of our own language.

Children invent their oracy and literacy through a process of internalizing information from their environments about language, oral and written, while they are trying to use language to make themselves understood. The conventions of the print system in which they are immersed emerge as they see a need for them. Children hypothesize, forming and testing their theories in social situations. They alter their hypotheses based on the responses they get including their own assessment of their success. With need, encouragement, demonstrations, explanations, models, and validation of their successes, they keep going. This is the constructivist perspective, and the evidence is everywhere if we have eyes to see and ears to hear.

You should know, however, that the term *invention* makes many parents and some teachers uncomfortable. It sounds as though all elementary school children are encouraged to just make up how language operates, for example how it is spelled, and that conventional forms do not matter. Nothing could be further from the truth. Of course, good teachers are concerned about moving children's inventions to conventional forms. But that is not the point. The point is that this constructive process of invention within the social conventions of language is absolutely fundamental to language development. It is, in fact, how the brain works. This is not what we *let* them do. This is simply what they *do* do. Trying to stop, circumvent, or otherwise prevent the process is to harm children's natural learning and early literacy abilities.

As with oral language development, learning to read and write is a psychogenerative or constructive process. When children try to read and write for functional reasons, they begin to figure out how reading and writing work. They experiment with how print works. They begin to attach meanings and names to print in their environments—McDonald's, Skippy, Coke, STOP, EXIT, and so on. They "read" along as they are read to and as others read around them. As they interact with others about print, they begin to gain control over some of the invisible, underlying rules of written language. The more experiences they have with meaningful written language, the better the brain is able to abstract the structure or rule systems.

Children who see reading and writing demonstrated by the adults in their lives, and who are encouraged to explore reading and writing, ultimately learn to use written language to construct meaning for themselves. They tend to learn without regarding literacy as something difficult. They do not come to believe reading is something they cannot do. They do not develop fear of visual language or come to believe that they have nothing to say in writing (Graves, 1983).

Reading and writing are processes, and written language is a field of knowledge. Therefore, while children are engaging in the processes of reading and/or writing, conventions notwithstanding, they are doing two things. They are intuiting the rules by which the processes operate, and they are learning about the characteristics of the print itself.

With reading and writing, as with any domain of knowledge (for example, animals), learners must assimilate the information provided in the environment. When the information in the environment is plentiful, useful, and experienced over time, learners eventually learn a great deal.

A group of children raised in or near a zoo, for instance, by parents who work with animals, will learn a great deal about animals that they are not directly taught. They will experiment with instances of the domain, ask for more information, formulate and test hypotheses, and generalize their understandings of one animal to examples of others. Some of them will become experts.

Learners in any domain can only do these things if they are immersed in ample, meaningful instances of the domain, if they are engaged in making sense of their experiences, and if they find the domain interesting. As with all learning, the brain is constantly trying to make sense, detect patterns, and organize incoming data. Specifically, regarding written language, learners search for coherence, and they build up their conclusions from their experiences in an ordered way (Goodman, 1990), just as they did in learning to talk.

Human beings likely began using visual symbols to communicate as long ago as 50,000 years. Hash marks to denote moon cycles (precursors to calendars) and to denote amounts (precursors to number systems) probably appeared first (Henderson, 1986). At least 45,000 years went by before true written languages appeared in Egypt, China, and India. It took our species half a million years to develop written language. Learning about writing systems, what they are for, and how they work, takes time.

Children around the globe from middle-class environments tend to make faster progress learning to read and write than poor children. That is because they have had more opportunities, from birth, to internalize information about the writing systems in their environments. Children should never be penalized for what they do or do not bring to the classroom. They are not in control of any of that. When children lack sufficient foundational experiences with oral or written language to be successful in school, day care workers, preschool teachers, and kindergarten and first-grade teachers are responsible for providing rich print experiences. Children, like the rest of us, can only learn what they are exposed to.

PHASES OF YOUNG CHILDREN'S EARLY LITERACY

Three common strategies that very young children devise to experiment with writing are tracing, copying, and creating. Children's tracing and copying as they play with print also improve small-motor control, investigation of conventional usage, and spelling. Creative or generative writing, at this stage, is the production of letters and word-like, grammatical constructions that indicate the patterns children are hypothesizing (Clay, 1975, 1999). Copying and tracing are strategies children develop on their own and should be encouraged, but never assigned. Some children naturally apprentice themselves to another child in the classroom who is more proficient. The apprentice will watch, often for weeks but sometimes for only a few minutes, before attempting to "write" something themselves.

All children use some forms of modeling. Handwriting models should be available for children to see, as part of the rich print environment. They serve as excellent resources. Copying and tracing models of well-formed letters provide children with opportunities to explore how letters work and to choose, to some extent, how they want their handwriting to look. Again, teachers can suggest, demonstrate, and encourage, but not necessarily assign.

As we discussed in Chapter One, the mental operations of intuiting the underlying rules and constructing meanings allow for the interpretation and assimilation of new data. Thus, learning in general, and learning to read and write in particular, are cases of spirals or scaffolds, each insight building on others, not just in early childhood but throughout the learner's lifetime.

Encouraging children to "write" at this stage in their development is easy. The environment provides materials and models of print. Adults model writing, occasionally asking questions, bringing up issues, and filling the home or classroom with meaningful and functional print. They set up events that lead to real reasons for children to write. Parents write grocery lists and telephone messages. Teachers set up the classroom post office, play and writing centers, and message boards; they sing daily songs, read daily big books, and they post room signs and labels, lists, jobs, and more.

Writing is easily worked into children's play at this stage. Paper, crayons and markers, and tape made available near the housekeeping, big block, dress-up, or animal cages areas will no doubt lead to the natural creation of lists, signs, and labels. These purposeful written productions become part of the literate environment and are read and reread by the children. For instance, the intended meaning of "D NT NTR" written in crayon and taped on a big block construction is clear to all members of the child's environment.

Children are able to write messages like this because they have seen many examples of them. Under the appropriate conditions, children experiment with and develop writing as naturally and in essentially the same ways as they learned to talk, in unconventional constructions and for their own purposes.

Purposeful "playing around with language" allows children to take what they see in print and use and internalize it. Graphic symbols, such as letter-like shapes, recognizable letters, and graphophonemic clusters begin to appear. In risk-free environments children play and experiment with how print works as a learning strategy, just as they did when learning their oral language. Teachers provide directions, suggestions, information,

opportunities, recognition, and validation of the child's attempts—just the way the family did when the child was learning to talk.

Reading and writing develop together; however, the rate at which a child learns to read and write is a matter of individual experience and innate ability. Also, since reading and writing are two different forms of written language, they are not a single process of learning written language.

Many educators and researchers who study children learning to read and write have identified phases common to almost all early readers and writers. However, these are seen as phases rather than lockstep stages. Let's examine the simultaneous nature of the phases through which most children move. Teachers and parents who recognize the phases children are in do so by identifying the strategies they are using in the reading and writing. This information helps them know what to focus on and what the children might be ready to learn next (Calkins, 1994; Hansen, 1987; Newkirk and Atwell, 1988; Temple, Nathan, Burris, and Temple, 1988). Therefore, it is important to look at the phases even though they are not age-specific, nor do they occur sequentially for every child as the child's literacy develops. That is, these phases occur within a set of parameters rather than as a rigid set of predictable causes and effects. And just as children's learning to talk emerges over time, so does their learning to read and write.

Emergent Reading and Emergent Writing

Children learn at a very early age what reading and writing are and what they are used for. Few children, even as young as four-year-olds, cannot tell the difference between print (in their own language) and pictures. They see the uses of written language in every aspect of life, in environmental print, in the writing of parents and other adults, in books and other printed material, and even on TV. As soon as children learn that writing is yet another way to structure, transmit, and receive meaning, they usually begin to experiment with its forms and with a variety of media—including crayoned scribbles on bedroom walls.

Without doubt, the most important thing a parent, and later a teacher, can do for a young child is *read aloud*. As Trelease (2001) points out, parents think nothing about talking to very young children, so why shouldn't they begin reading to them as well? The bedtime story is a good place to start, but reading aloud does not have to be limited to a bedtime routine. Parents frequently complain that their toddlers will not sit still long enough to listen to a story. Attention span is learned, so if parents begin reading to their children when they are infants, they will learn to attend.

The benefits of reading aloud are numerous. And it is pleasurable! Children enjoy the security and closeness associated with lap reading. The only way for children to develop a sense of story is by listening to stories. They are exposed to new situations, new vocabulary, and new language structures. Many people believe that children need to hear a minimum of one thousand different books read aloud before they are ready for formal reading in school.

Young children who are read to usually choose a favorite book. It is not unusual for the child to request the same story night after night. Furthermore, as soon as the book is finished, the child may immediately demand, "Read it again!" Many parents, having had a rough day, may try to skip a page. But they quickly find out they can't. "That's not right!" the child exclaims. In many cases, they cannot even skip a word, much less a page. Children memorize their favorite stories. Memorization is a natural part of their learning to read.

Children who are read to learn to tell their own stories. They learn that stories have a beginning, a middle, and an end. They learn about characters and plot. Their interest in telling stories leads to their wanting to write stories, especially if their environments provide opportunities for them to experiment with writing.

Experiments with the forms of writing occur in a variety of contexts. Children begin to teach themselves about print. Pictures that tell stories, abstract signs with which children attempt a message, and scribbles and marks that begin to resemble letters are part of children's early attempts to graphically represent meaning (see Figure 4–2). This experimentation is much like their early experiments with oral language.

Children "learn" a great deal about written language, much as infants who can't speak yet learn a great deal about oral language. The foundations are being laid in the brain for further development. Children's reading and writing begin to emerge as they engage in acts that approximate the reading and writing they have seen adults do. They become interested in books and like to listen to stories read aloud. They focus on trying

FIGURE 4–2
STORY AND PICTURE
ABOUT A BAT

to make sense of written messages; they try to construct meaning. They learn how to handle books, to turn pages, to begin at the front of the book. When Laura was only two years old, she "read" her favorite book, *Where the Wild Things Are,* by Maurice Sendak. As she turned each page, she said, "Wild things are," "Wild things are."

Young children begin to see themselves are readers and writers. They practice or use their early literacy much the same way infants and toddlers practice and use speech. Babies seated at the dinner table engage in dinner conversation although their speech may be unintelligible. Likewise, young children engage in literacy acts, often "reading" to themselves or to their stuffed animals or dolls.

Young children like to name the pictures in books and will fill in words correctly if the reader pauses on key items. They also know how stories go together. They "read" favorite stories or poems that cannot be totally recalled without the print. Eventually, they begin to recognize and pick out individual letters and familiar words, and they may recognize their own names in print, much the same way they picked out individual sounds and familiar words as they learned to talk.

The case can be made that young language learners actually begin with a sort of impression of what their language looks like (Clay, 1975; Harste, Woodward, and Burke, 1984; Short, Harste, and Burke, 1996). Since children tend to learn oral language from whole to part, there is every reason to suppose that the same process is at work in learning to read and write. Human beings learn from whole to part to whole because initially the parts are too complex, too abstract, and out of context. They also learn by figuring out the underlying rules or patterns through sufficient meaningful experience.

The Role of Phonological Awareness   Phonological awareness is awareness of the many aspects of spoken language including that words occur within sentences, that syllables exist within words, and phonemes within syllables, etc. (Opitz, 2000). The role of phonological awareness in learning to speak is obvious. Oral language is made up of strings of sounds. To make themselves understood by others, young children have to be able to manipulate these sounds to form words within the structures of grammar and intonation. Currently, the role of phonological awareness in learning to read and write is receiving much attention. How do children develop awareness of the phonological aspects of written language?

Obviously simply talking to young children is one way. And language play with songs, nursery rhymes, and language games is another. "Peek-a-boo—I see you" and "This little piggie" serve not only as entertainment, but as playful demonstrations of basic sound units in our language. Opitz (2000) suggests the best way to further finesse children's developing phonological awareness is through quality literature. "Children's literature is a delightful catalyst to nurture phonological awareness. As children play with rhymes and reasons, they will continue to understand how knowledge of their language contributes to successful and enjoyable reading experiences" (Opitz, 2000, 3).

Some natural ways for parents and teachers to foster children's development of phonological awareness include:

1. counting the number of sentences in a story
2. listening to and identifying the number of.syllables in words
3. listening to and identifying the number of sounds in a word

For children to be able to read and write they must use some knowledge of the phonological aspects of language. *Phonemic awareness,* not to be confused with phonological awareness, "refers to the awareness that words are made up of individual sounds" (Opitz, 2000, 4). Phonological awareness and phonemic awareness are not synonymous. Phonemic awareness is but one aspect of phonological awareness, and it is the last stage in understanding spoken language.

Early phonemic awareness is thought to be a predictor of later reading ability. (See Adams, 1990, for a review of studies.) Because of this, "training" young children to develop phonemic awareness is gaining popularity. However, children typically develop phonemic awareness without training, just as they developed phonological awareness without training as they learned to talk. Furthermore, many children with little or no training in phonemic awareness learn to read and write quite well. Perhaps as Krashen (2001) points out, phonemic awareness may simply be the result of knowing how to read, rather than the cause. Perhaps good readers have developed more phonemic awareness because they have read more, have been read to more, and/or have had more access to print.

Access to print is likely the critical aspect here. Children need many and varied engagements with print. But there are some activities knowledgeable parents and teachers naturally engage children in that also help them develop phonemic awareness. The following are but a few (Opitz, 2000):

1. reading nursery rhymes and poetry and asking children to tell or fill in the rhyming words (rhyme recognition)

2. playing with tongue twisters that focus on alliteration (phoneme matching)

3. blending sounds together to make a word (phoneme blending)

4. counting the number of sounds in a single word (phoneme segmentation)

5. adding or deleting sounds from one word to make another (phoneme manipulation)

Being phonemically aware is important in learning to read and write, but it is important to point out that we are talking about speech sounds—not the letters that represent them! Some children may be phonemically aware but unable to identify a single letter of the alphabet (Opitz, 2000). Such was the case for John, who began reading at age four, skipped first grade, and arrived at second grade having never even sung the alphabet song. The connection between the sound and the letter(s) is *phonics*. (See Chapter Seven and Appendix A for further information about phonics.)

Having already developed phonological awareness and phonemic awareness—because they can talk—young children are ready to embark on figuring out how written language works for them. They have seen how it operates in their environments and how others use it to get things and do things they want and need. Just as phonological and phonemic awareness are developmental and develop in stages, so do learning to read and write.

Early Reading and Writing   Children attempt to create a system for how to read and write. Ferreiro and Teberosky (1982) identified three very basic, early insights children acquire about the nature of print. First, children begin to distinguish between the two types of graphic representation—drawing and writing. Some children, as young as three, produce different visual representations when asked to draw a picture and then to write a story. In drawing, the lines follow the outline of the object. In writing, the lines have nothing to do with the object. The marks in writing are linear, arbitrary, and systematic. It takes time, experience, and need for children to sort out these properties and characteristics of the graphic notation system, just as it took time, experience, and need for human beings to develop them in the first place.

They understand that print conveys meaning and in an attempt to communicate meaning to someone else, they approximate writing by scribbling. Their scribbles look like writing, not pictures, and many are identifiable as having been written in cursive as opposed to manuscript. Some scribbles may have recognizable letters embedded in them. Look carefully at Figure 4–3. Do you recognize any letters? Eventually, children realize their written inventions (their scribbles) are not print. This realization tends to come eventually, as other people cannot read them.

Some more advanced writing attempts may be in "manuscript," and some may be in "cursive." Whether the child chooses cursive or manuscript scribbles is not usually based on whim but rather on the purpose of the writing. A scribble letter to Mommy

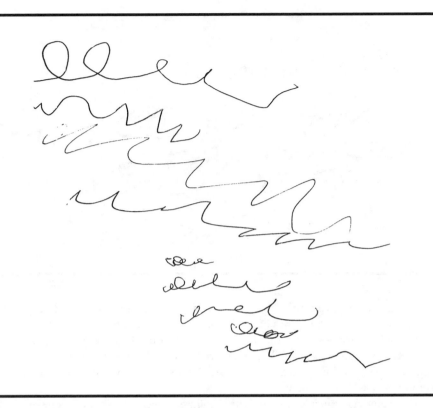

FIGURE 4–3
SCRIBBLE WITH
RECOGNIZABLE
LETTERS

might be in cursive (see Figure 4–4), whereas a reminder list scribble might be in manuscript (see Figure 4–5).

Most children badly want to produce print. Since all our brains function in highly similar ways, almost all children seem to arrive at the same kinds of strategies and assumptions during these developing phases. For example, one of the universal principles children appear to develop is that of minimum quantity. To answer to the question, "How many elements (for example, letters) does it take to be readable?" children consistently rely on the internal principle of minimum quantity. That is, the smallest number of elements possible is best. In Figure 4–6 the letters TRNDO represent the word *tornado*. On the other hand, sometimes more is better, especially if the child is sure her name is a long one. Can you find Patrecea's name in Figure 4–7? But learners quickly recognize that the letters must be different from each other to be readable, so they develop a second guideline, the internal principle of qualitative variation. These two organizing generalizations help children decide if a piece of text is potentially readable or not.

Second, children search for the patterns that operate in reading and writing just as they did in developing their oral language. Two scribbles or strings of letters and letter-like shapes may look similar but "say" two entirely different things as far as the "writer" is concerned. Later, learners begin to pay attention to the forms that really support their

FIGURE 4–4
SCRIBBLE LETTER TO
MOM

intentions. As they read, they observe how words and sentences work. They have to figure out how to make strings of marks that differentiate meaning.

This effort proceeds from the development of a third general operating principle, interrelational comparison. A child might look at two differently "written" words, for example, *house* and *horse*, and know that they are different and mean two different things but not be able to read them.

These guiding principles emerge before children develop their knowledge of matching the sound patterns and written representations of words (Goodman, 1990). During

FIGURE 4–5
SCRIBBLE LIST

FIGURE 4–6
TORNADO

this phase, children may display some phonemic awareness—the ability to discriminate sounds within spoken words—as they begin to explore the sound-letter system in their language. Sound-letter explorations tend to start with the consonants and vowels that appear in the children's names.

Learning to recognize their names and to write them are major breakthroughs and excellent examples of how the two forms of written language evolve at the same time and reinforce each other. As young children show interest in writing their names, and the names of family members and friends, parents typically show interest in teaching them all the letters of the alphabet, perhaps with the Alphabet Song. During the time

FIGURE 4–7
PATRECEA

when Jenny was learning to write her name, around the age of three to four years, her parents went to a mall one day, parking outside the J. C. Penney store. With great excitement, Jenny exclaimed, "Look! There's my name! It says, 'Jenny'"! This is an example of powerful learning from incidental, environmental teaching.

Children pay attention to words they want to use, write, and spell. At first, they may use random letters to write the words in their messages. For example, "MSTCN" may mean "Rocky is my dog." Typically, and not surprisingly, children remember the letters used in writing their names and they use the letters they know to make words. For example, "CTCRN" might represent "Catherine." They also typically use one letter to represent an entire word such as "T" for *Timmy* and "S" for *Steven* (Clay, 1975). As they learn the names of the letters, they may use the letter names rather than letter sounds. For example, the word *Katie* may be written as "KT" or "KD."

Since a single letter occasionally represents a syllable but most often represents a smaller unit of sound, children eventually arrive at the *alphabetic principle*. Simply stated, the alphabetic principle is: similarity of sound implies similarity of letter(s). This sophisticated awareness represents a remarkable breakthrough in learning that took the human race thousands upon thousands of years to develop.

However, for most children, traditional orthography (TO), in English the twenty six letters, is still a long way off. TO involves a mass of visual features organized by ex-

tremely complex rules related to principles other than simple sound-letter correspondences (Goodman, 1990). Therefore, control over the conventions of reading and
writing develops slowly. It takes vast experience with reading and writing to move
from "What does that say, Daddy?" at age four to the potential of reading Gary
Paulsen's *Hatchet* in fifth grade or writing an "error-free" and thoughtful response to
Katherine Paterson's *Jacob Have I Loved* as an eighth grader.

In both pre-reading/pre-writing and early reading/early writing phases, children are
concerned with making sense and doing what they want to do. They focus on meaning, and they try to construct meaning. As they learn more and more about print, their
focus tends to shift away from constructing meaning, to the print itself (McKenzie,
1977).

Tackling the Print   During the "tackling the print" phase, readers and writers
pay attention to words. They often want to read to anyone who will listen. They read
environmental print signs and labels aloud. They increasingly gain control over the
reading process, and observation reveals that they use print as well as implied cues to
construct the author's message.

For some children, tackling the print becomes the major focus. They will even aban-
don the correct pronunciation of a word they already know in order to make it sound
like what it looks like (Barr, 1984). For example, Nancy had known the word *have* for
quite some time; however, following a phonics lesson on the CVCE pattern (consonant,
vowel, consonant, silent e) she pronounced the word with a long /a/ sound. She knew
the word *have* and she knew that *hāve* did not make sense in the sentence she read, but
she abandoned meaning to make the sound match the print. Rather than viewing this
as an error, it is a clear indication that learning is taking place. Nancy knew that the
words have a relationship with the sounds of the letters.

As children come to realize that letters and sounds have a relationship, they tend to
focus exclusively on the print. Having first used completely idiosyncratic spellings, such
as the letters IWG to represent *book* or PLT for *dog*, children soon realize that the conventions of letter-sound relationship must be observed if words are to communicate.
Much of the information necessary for this transition comes from books and other
written material in the children's immediate environment. Thus, *book* may come to be
spelled buk, and *dog* may become dg, which are closer approximations to traditional
orthography (Read, 1971).

In this phase, children move into writing that can actually be read by others. Their
approximations contain more adult or conventional forms. Children learn a great deal
about spelling patterns in English, and they experiment with other aspects of the mechanics of print (Read, 1971). They have listened to many stories and they have developed a concept of story. During this stage, children also begin the composing process.
They learn how to order their thoughts so they make sense to others. Children may
compose before they can write. They can dictate stories, information, and accounts of
real experiences to someone who will write (or scribe) for them. For many children this
oral composition process is a key to beginning writing. Toward the end of this stage,
children may be writing fairly readable productions that have a beginning, middle, and
an end. Figure 4–8 is a story titled "The Princess."

Once was a pranses haw was mean.
Mean! Mean! Mean!

But she was butful. Meny
men Loued her.

So the got a fary. To make her
nise.

The fary made her poor.

FIGURE 4–8   "THE PRINCESS"

At first she no to a job. But she siad yes.

She becun nice

So she chanched her dack.

she went home. And met a prens

They got mared.

The End

FIGURE 4–8 CONTINUED

Jenny was engaged in the process of hypothesizing about how sounds and letters work in written language (see Figure 4–9). Her parents could read it because they knew their daughter and because her approximations were systematic. They do represent the sounds in her language as she carefully accentuated each part while trying to figure out how to write what she wanted to say. That is, her spellings look just like she sounded, and they look just like invented spellings of many young children as they experiment with writing (Gentry, 1996; Temple, Nathan, Burris, and Temple, 1988; Wilde, 1991). The more children attempt to write, the more their approximations resemble conventional spellings, and the more we are able to see the strategies they have developed.

Most educators also agree that sounds and letter patterns are one of the systems that language uses to represent meaning. Therefore, phonemic awareness and phonemic

FIGURE 4–9
JENNY'S TWENTY-MINUTE SWIM LETTER

Dear Mom
I got the package. My sister is nice.
Please come on the mother hiking trip.
I love you very much. I passed my twenty
minute swim.

segmentation are also important to beginning reading. But phonics knowledge is only *one* of the systems, it is not the cure-all as is frequently claimed (Allington, 1997). As Smith (1999) explains, phonemic awareness is "supposed to be the ability to discriminate individual sounds in spoken words, like detecting that 'cat' is made up of the separate sounds 'k' 'a' 't' (which it isn't; they are inextricably combined). You can no more separate the sounds from a word that has been uttered than you can extract the ingredients from a cake that has been baked" (153).

Young children who read and comprehend what they read do not need phonics drill and practice to improve their reading—they simply need to read from a wide variety of texts and talk about them. Also, the fact that many proficient readers have extensive phonemic awareness and can segment the phonemes in words does not necessarily mean that systematic instruction in sounds, letter patterns, and phonemic segmentation exercises creates proficient readers (Taylor, 1998). Many studies suggest that phonemic awareness is correlated with proficient reading (see Adams, 1990); however, no evidence exists that phonemic awareness precedes proficient reading. In fact, phonemic awareness may have been learned as the child learned to read, not before. (See Dahl, Scharer, Lawson, and Grogan, 2001; Moustafa, 1997; Opitz, 2000.)

Fluent Reading and Writing   As the fluent phase is reached, readers and writers realize that not only must the print sound like it looks, but it also must make sense and be readable by others. They begin to use reading and writing successfully to fulfill the everyday purposes of life, both in and out of school. They read orally with expression, and they have internalized the structure for several genres, especially fairy tales, simple expository, and rhymes. They like to read and can comprehend anything that their experiences will support. They also write and are able to write in a variety of genres and for a variety of purposes. They will continue to use reading and writing to learn, and their reading and writing abilities will continue to advance as long as they continue to read and write. As Meek (1982) asserts, children become really proficient through practice, pleasure, and persistence.

HOW PARENTS AND TEACHERS SUPPORT CHILDREN'S EARLY LITERACY DEVELOPMENT

As we have seen, the literate world children live in begins to influence their lives very early. Children as young as three and four years begin to read and write, though perhaps not in the conventional sense. Their explorations with environmental print, books, pencils, and paper help them learn a great deal about reading and writing before they come to kindergarten. They tend to know that print is meaningful and part of everyday life. They may already recognize some words in print, frequently by connecting them to the context, and they know that they can make their own graphic representations of meaning.

Children who have been read to know how to use their prior knowledge in order to make sense of stories. They may know how to assimilate information gained from reading and apply it to other situations. They may know that reading and writing serve a variety of functions and purposes (Mooney, 1990). These skills and more may have been acquired before starting school. For children whose print experiences are limited or otherwise different, teachers must provide the necessary background experiences and attitudes of literate people.

Children who are spontaneous readers have experiences with written language that simulate the conditions that supported the construction of their oral language. They were surrounded by written language they could make sense of. They interacted with others about print. They played with written language and attempted to produce writing. Someone else "read" their attempts and provided some responses and feedback. They may have played reading games in the car on trips. They likely were read to frequently. They may have played writing and/or spelling games. They may have received written messages from others that were read to them. They likely had many books and writing supplies at their fingertips. They likely saw many others reading and writing and were allowed to be "part" of those activities. As they read, the focus was on figuring out what it meant. Over time, they began to develop control over written language. The key is that they had in their environments ample examples of print. They knew what it said and what it meant. Meaning precedes, leads to, and enables perception (Smith, 1994).

In order to perceive we have to be able to predict. Science has understood that phenomenon for a long time. In literacy, readers need to be able to predict what will likely be there or "know" what something means before they can "see" it, so to speak. That is why so much good literature for young children contains repeated lines, rhyming patterns, and so on and why it is always accompanied by pictures. Everyone has intuitively understood that you have to provide meaning and context along with the print when children are beginning to learn how to read.

This is what happens naturally when children are learning to talk. People talk to and with the infant about what is happening so the infant knows what the language means before he knows what has been said. Tricky, but not impossible, for teachers to replicate in classrooms.

The reason learning to read and write appear to be so difficult, and therefore why many people believe they are difficult, is that we tend not to teach reading and writing as making sense of and with print. Too many people believe that learning to read and write is a matter of getting the words right. This view is substantially different from what happens in learning oral language. This may lead to instruction that, in fact, causes limited literacy development because it focuses on surface features of language—letters and letter sounds and words—before the learner's brain has internalized sufficient structure from immersion and exploration experiences.

In oral language the context is in the environment so learners can look around to figure out what the intended message is. In written language, the context is in the print. The reader cannot look around, except for the pictures, to figure out what the message is likely to be about.

The toddler in his high chair, hearing his mother say for the hundredth time, "Here's your cereal" knows what cereal is; he knows what "here's" represents; he learns what "your" indicates because he hears "Here's" and "your" in other situations.

When he is hungry, he may say something that sounds a lot like "cereal" and then he is on his way to learning to talk. But we can show him "Here's your cereal" in print for five years and without a picture, without some action, without some context, it doesn't matter how long he looks at it; he won't learn it. "Here's your cereal" has to be understood before it can be learned. Children, while they are in the earliest phases of literacy development, have to have some way of knowing what a message means before they know what it says.

It is quite evident that the emphasis in oral language is on meaning first. This must also be true of written language. Young language learners attend to the meaning and in so doing, their brains learn and develop literacy. Reading and writing are the synthesis of hundreds of complicated rules and elements that eventually flow together smoothly. Just as learning to talk is a natural process that occurs over time, so is learning to read and write.

Facility with reading and writing comes through engagement. Knowledgeable teachers and parents set up conditions so children engage in great amounts of reading and writing about all sorts of things. Further, knowledgeable teachers and parents expect children to be different. They do not see learning and language development as a lock-step progression of discrete "skills" every child must master. They do not think raising readers and writers works like building a car in a factory. So they engage children in regular, frequent, and authentic uses for written language. They explain, show examples, provide models, encourage great amounts of practice, validate approximations, and enjoy learning together. When they do, the great majority of children learn to read and write naturally and with ease.

SUMMARY

There are as many paths to literacy as there are pathways into oral language. Literacy learning begins long before children enter school, long before they see their first workbook page or flash card. It begins in the learner's mind and in the learner's natural environment (Holdaway, 1979). This is true even for children of the very poor or non-English-speaking. We live in a literate society. Written language is everywhere. Everyone gets bills and junk mail. Everyone sees billboards along roadways, bread wrappers and cereal boxes at breakfast, the McDonald's down the street, the print on T-shirts, cans of soup, jars of peanut butter, and bottles of Coke, as well as the print on the cup from which they are drinking. While not all children are read to nightly, they all have some home and environmental literacy experiences.

It is the amount and nature of these early literacy experiences that affect how well and how quickly children learn to read (Delpit, 1986; Harste, Burke, and Woodward, 1983; Short, Harste, and Burke, 1996; Taylor, 1983; Teale, 1984; Wells, 1986). Of primary importance is the amount of being read to. The value of early storybook reading cannot be overestimated. Many people believe that children need to hear a minimum of one thousand different books read aloud before they are ready for formal reading in school. This and other events that demonstrate to children how print works and the many functions that print serves (for example, writing lists, paying bills, ordering from catalogues, writing reminder notes, getting news and information from newspapers, receiving birthday cards, reading the church bulletin, comparing prices or ingredients of grocery items) lay a successful foundation for school literacy.

We know that reading and writing achievement are directly related to the amount of reading and writing in which learners engage. We know that children have to *want* to read and write, and that desire is based on their seeing their own significant others engaging in reading and writing. We know how to cause children to love or hate reading and to love or hate writing. We know how to teach children to simply call words or to construct meaning and make their own connections, developing inner control over the process for themselves. We know that reading and writing develop somewhat together. We know that parents' and teachers' attitudes and values, as well as children's access to high-quality resources, are keys to early success.

Since we know that student achievement in literacy is directly related to the amount and variety of reading and writing they see and do, building support with parents at home is also very important. And while independence in reading and writing is a goal, engaging learners in demonstrations, reading with them, talking about books, writing with them, and helping them write are all important options that work.

THEORY-TO-PRACTICE CONNECTIONS

Early Literacy Theory

1. Children learn to read and write much the same way they learn to talk.

2. Most children pass through several identifiable stages on their way to developing literacy.

3. Humans are born with the ability to develop language and literacy, but this ability is activated by need within social situations. These take time and great amounts of experience to become fully realized.

4. Children develop phonological awareness as the result of becoming language users.

Examples of Classroom Practice

1. Notes, messages, lists, print-rich environment, varied opportunities to use and construct written language

2. Teacher uses checklists, rubrics, and anecdotal records to document developmental stages and literacy growth of children

3. Teachers invite young children to "write" and to "read"

4. Helping children rhyme, count words, syllables, and sounds in what they hear and see

SUGGESTED READINGS

Barton, B. 2000. *Telling Stories Your Way: Storytelling and Reading Aloud in the Classroom.* York, ME: Stenhouse.

Dahl, K., P. Scharer, L. Lawson, and P. Grogan. 2001. *Rethinking Phonics: Making the Best Teaching Decisions.* Portsmouth, NH: Heinemann.

Moustafa, M. 1997. *Beyond Traditional Phonics: Research Discoveries and Reading Instruction.* Portsmouth, NH: Heinemann.

Opitz, M. 2000. *Rhymes and Reasons: Literature for Language Play and Phonological Awareness.* Portsmouth, NH: Heinemann.

Owocki, G. 1999. *Literacy Through Play.* Portsmouth, NH: Heinemann.

Pinnell, G., and I. Fountas. 1998. *Word Matters: Teaching Phonics and Spelling in the Reading/Writing Classroom.* Portsmouth, NH: Heinemann.

Taberski, S. 2000. *On Solid Ground: Strategies for Teaching Reading K–3.* Portsmouth, NH: Heinemann.

EXTENDING YOUR DISCUSSION

1. Think about the forty-four or so phonemes in the English language (see Appendix A). How many of them can be vocalized without having to attach another sound to it. Hint: the /s/ sound is one that can be articulated in isolation. What does this mean when teachers teach children to segment sounds in a word. For example, is *bat* "buh-a-tuh"?

2. Begin collecting invented spellings of pre-schoolers and kindergartners. See if you can determine the rela-

tionship between the child's oral language and attempted spellings. What does that tell you?

3. If you have access to young children who cannot read per se yet, see if you can determine the extent of their ability to "read" print in their environments using logos and product labels—for example, Coke, McDonald's, STOP, Wal-Mart, or Cheerios. How did they learn these things? Was it ditto sheets and flash cards?

REFERENCES

Adams, M. 1990. *Beginning to Read: Thinking and Learning About Print*. Cambridge, MA: MIT Press.

Allington, R. 1997. "Overselling Phonics." *Reading World* 15 (1): 15–16.

Allington, R., and P. Cunningham. 1996. *Schools That Work*. New York: HarperCollins.

Barr, R. 1984. "Beginning Reading Instruction: From Debate to Reformation." In *Handbook of Reading Research*, ed. P. D. Pearson, New York: Longman.

Baumann, J., and A. Duffy. 1997. *Engaged Reading for Pleasure and Learning: A Report from the National Reading Research Center*. Athens, GA: University of Georgia Press.

Braunger, J., and J. Lewis. 1997. *Building a Knowledge Base in Reading*. Portland, OR: Co-published by Northwest Regional Education Laboratory's Curriculum and Instruction Services, National Council of Teachers of English, and International Reading Association.

Bruner, J., and M. Cole. 1990. *Early Literacy: Developing Child*. Cambridge, MA: Harvard University Press.

Calkins, L. 1994. *The Art of Teaching Writing*, 2nd ed. Portsmouth, NH: Heinemann.

———. 2000. *The Art of Teaching Reading*. New York: Longman.

Cambourne, B. 1998. *The Whole Story: Natural Learning and the Acquisition of Literacy in the Classroom*. Auckland, New Zealand: Ashton-Scholastic.

Cambourne, B., and J. Turbil. 1987. *Coping with Chaos*. Portsmouth, NH: Heinemann.

Chomsky, C. 1971. "Write First, Read Later." *Childhood Education* 47: 296–99.

Clark, M. 1976. *Young Fluent Readers*. London: Heinemann.

Clay, M. 1966. *Emergent Reading Behavior*. Doctoral dissertation. University of Auckland, New Zealand.

———.1975. *What Did I Write? Beginning Writing Behaviour*. Portsmouth, NH: Heinemann.

———. 1999. *Becoming Literate*, 2nd ed. Portsmouth, NH: Heinemann.

Coles, G. 2000. *Misreading Reading: The Bad Science That Hurts Children*. Portsmouth, NH: Heinemann.

Dahl, K., P. Scharer, L. Lawson, and P. Grogan. 2001. *Rethinking Phonics: Making the Best Teaching Decisions*. Portsmouth, NH: Heinemann.

Delpit, L. 1986. "Skills and Other Dilemmas of a Progressive Black Educator." *Harvard Educational Review* 56: 379–85.

Durkin, D. 1961. "Children Who Read Before Grade One." *The Reading Teacher* 14: 163–66.

Ferreiro, E., and A. Teberosky. 1982. *Literacy Before Schooling*. Portsmouth, NH: Heinemann.

Gentry, R. 1996. *My Kid Can't Spell: Understanding and Assisting Your Child's Literacy Development*. Portsmouth, NH: Heinemann.

Goodman, K. 1993. *Phonics Phacts*. Portsmouth, NH: Heinemann.

———. 1996. *On Reading*. Portsmouth, NH: Heinemann.

———. December, 2000. Eleventh Winter Workshop: Foundations of a Liberatory Pedagogy, Tucson, Arizona.

Goodman, Y. 1990. *How Children Construct Literacy: Piagetian Perspectives*. Newark, DE: IRA.

Graves, D. 1983. *Writing: Teachers and Children at Work*. Portsmouth, NH: Heinemann.

———. 1995. *A Fresh Look at Writing*. Portsmouth, NH: Heinemann.

Hansen, J. 2001. *When Writers Read*, 2nd ed. Portsmouth, NH: Heinemann.

Harste, J., C. Burke, and V. Woodward. 1983. "The Young Child as Reader-Writer and Informant" (Grant No. NIE-G-80-0121.) Washington, DC: National Institute of Education.

Harste, J., V. Woodward, and C. Burke 1984. *Language Stories and Literacy Lessons*. Portsmouth, NH: Heinemann.

Heald-Taylor, G. 2001. *The Beginning Reading Handbook*. Portsmouth, NH: Heinemann.

Heath, S. 1983. *Ways with Words: Language, Life, and Work in Communities and Classrooms*. New York: Cambridge University Press.

Henderson, E. 1986. "Understanding Children's Knowledge of Written Language." In *Metalinguistic Awareness and Beginning Literacy: Conceptualizing What It Means to Read and Write*, eds. D. Yaden and S. Templeton. Portsmouth, NH: Heinemann.

Hill, S. 2000. *Guiding Literacy Learners*. York, ME: Stenhouse.

Holdaway, D. 1979. *Foundations of Literacy*. Toronto: Scholastic-TAB.

Joyce, B. R. 1999. "Reading About Reading: Notes from a Consumer to the Scholars of Literacy." *The Reading Teacher* 52 (7): 662–71.

Krashen, S. 2001. Letter to the Editor of *Substance*, March, 2001.

Martens, P. 1996. *I Already Know How to Read: A Child's View of Literacy*. Portsmouth, NH: Heinemann.

McKenzie, M. 1977. "The Beginnings of Literacy." *Theory into Practice* 16 (51): 315–24.

Meek, M. 1982. *Learning to Read*. London: The Bodley Head.

———. 1988. *How Texts Teach What Readers Learn*. Exeter, England: Thimble Press.

Mooney, M. 1990. *Reading to, with, and by Children*. Katonah, NY: Richard C. Owen.

Morrow, L. 2001. *Literacy Development on the Early Years*, 4th ed. Boston: Allyn and Bacon.

Morrow, L., and E. Sulzby. 1995. *Teacher's Workshop: An Instructional Handbook for Kindergarten Teachers*. Glenview, IL: Scott Foresman.

Moustafa, M. 1997. *Beyond Traditional Phonics: Research Discoveries and Reading Instruction*. Portsmouth, NH: Heinemann.

National Assessment of Educational Progress January. 1998. "Long-Term Trends in Student Reading Performance." *NAEP Facts* 3 (1).

National Center for Educational Statistics. 1993. *Executive Summary of the NAEP Report Card for the Nation and the States*. Washington, DC: Prepared by the Educational Testing Service under contract with the National Center for Educational Statistics and the Office of Educational Research and Improvement of the USDOE.

Newkirk, T., and N. Atwell, 1988. *Understanding Writing: Ways of Observing, Learning, and Teaching*. Portsmouth, NH: Heinemann.

Opitz, M. 2000. *Rhymes and Reasons: Literature for Language Play and Phonological Awareness*. Portsmouth, NH: Heinemann.

Owocki, G. 1999. *Literacy Through Play*. Portsmouth, NH: Heinemann.

———. 2001. *Make Way for Literacy! Teaching the Way Young Children Learn*. Portsmouth, NH: Heinemann.

Parkes, B. 2000. *Read It Again! Revisiting Shared Reading*. York, ME: Stenhouse.

Read, C. 1971. "Pre-school Children's Knowledge of English Phonemes." *Harvard Educational Review* 41: 1–34.

Rowe, D., and J. Harste. 1986. "Metalinguistic Awareness in Reading and Writing: The Young Child as Curricular Informant." In *Metalinguistic Awareness and Beginning Literacy: Conceptualizing What It Means to Read and Write*, eds. D. Yaden and S. Templeton. Portsmouth, NH: Heinemann.

Short, K., J. Harste, and C. Burke. 1996. *Creating Classrooms for Authors and Inquirers*, 2nd ed. Portsmouth, NH: Heinemann.

Smith, F. 1994. *Understanding Reading*, 5th ed. Hillsdale, NJ: Lawrence Erlbaum.

———. 1999. "Why Systematic Phonics and Phonemic Awareness Instruction Constitute an Educational Hazard." *Language Arts* 77 (2): 150–55.

Sulzby, E. 1985. "Children's Emergent Reading of Favorite Storybooks." *Reading Research Quarterly* 20: 458–81.

Taylor, D. 1983. *Family Literacy: Young Children Learning to Read and Write*. Portsmouth, NH: Heinemann.

———. 1998. *Beginning to Read and the Spin Doctors of Science: The Political Campaign to Change America's Mind About How Children Learn to Read*. Urbana, IL: NCTE.

Taylor, D., and C. Dorsey-Gaines. 1988. *Growing Up Literate: Learning from Inner-City Families*. Portsmouth, NH: Heinemann.

Teale, W. 1984. "Reading to Young Children: Its Significance for Literacy Development." In *Awakening to Literacy*, eds. H. Goelman, A. Oberg, and F. Smith. London: Heinemann.

Teale, W., and E. Sulzby. 1989. *Emergent Literacy: Writing and Reading*. Norwood, NJ: Ablex.

Temple, C., R. Nathan, N. Burris, and F. Temple. 1988. *The Beginnings of Writing*. Boston: Allyn and Bacon.

Trelease, J. 2001. *The Read Aloud Handbook*, 5th ed. New York: Penguin.

Wells, G. 1986. *The Meaning Makers: Children Learning Language and Using Language to Learn*. Portsmouth, NH: Heinemann.

Wilde, S. 1991. *You Kan Red This! Spelling and Punctuation for Whole Language Classrooms, K–6*. Portsmouth, NH: Heinemann.

Yopp, H., and R. Yopp. 2000. "Supporting Phonemic Awareness Development in the Classroom." *The Reading Teacher* 54 (2): 130–43.

Zgonc, Y. 2000. *Sounds in Action*. York: ME: Stenhouse.

CHILDREN'S LITERATURE

Paterson, K. 1980. *Jacob Have I Loved*. New York: Harper and Row.

Paulsen, G. 1987. *Hatchet*. New York: Bradbury.

Sendak, M. 1963. *Where the Wild Things Are*. New York: HarperCollins.

CHAPTER FIVE

Human speech "gives voice to the human spirit and sets us apart. . . . Arguably, language is our most precious inheritance and our greatest achievement."

(Curt Dudley-Marling and

Dennis Searle, 1991, iv)

SPEAKING AND LISTENING IN THE ELEMENTARY CLASSROOM

Spoken language is the main tool humans have for teaching, learning, and socializing. Our abilities to use speech determine, to a great extent, much of the quality of our lives: our friends, lovers, and careers. Most suc-cessful people depend on their ability to talk to others about their ideas, their understandings, their visions, and their perceptions of who they are and what they think. In addition, the sheer number of words we know, our language vocabularies, determines, in part, the ease with which we learn to read.

Oral language learning is a constructive process. It occurs naturally as young children interact with others and with their environments. Oral language development does not stop with the beginnings of literacy, or when children enter school. Even in classrooms where talking is discouraged, oral language continues to develop—albeit covertly. However, if oral language is not attended to in schools, it may not develop as fully as it could. The way children learn the complex structure, rules, and meanings of language and develop their ability to create their own speech is fascinating. After all, except for a few commonly used phrases like "good morning," language is totally constructed, created, generated. That is, most of what people utter, they have never spoken before (Feeney, Christensen, and Moravcik, 1983). The more oral language an individual has, the easier it is to comprehend and produce language, both oral and written.

The way talking and listening occur in schools tends to be very different from the way we talk and listen at home. In school children listen; teachers talk. In school when students *are* allowed to talk, they are usually being asked to respond in specific ways with limited information.

This chapter addresses oral language development in the classroom. Purposes for an instructional focus on talking and listening are examined, exemplary teachers and practices are described, and a few theoretically sound teaching tactics are suggested. Classroom management is addressed because a considerable amount of talking is encouraged as a necessary and natural part of the classroom. Issues of dialect and language variation are also examined, as is the shy or reluctant participant. Finally, suggestions are provided for assessing and documenting learner growth in oral language.

ORAL LANGUAGE AND SCHOOLS: OUR EVOLVING UNDERSTANDING

Traditional American classrooms are designed to focus on students learning tasks and fragmented bits of information. Standardized tests are used to measure what has been "learned," i.e., learning is defined as a measurable outcome. This view of how learning occurs has been called behaviorism or "reductionism" because in this view, learning is broken down or reduced to small parts that are presumably easier to learn and to assess. Teachers teach the items one at a time, and then the learner is left to reassemble the parts to form the whole again. In this view, learning is additive and linear.

However, in this age of information explosion and rapid technological advancement, the ability to think logically, to find and access information, to organize thoughts, and to communicate effectively with others is quintessential. Intentionally engaging learners with demonstrations of purposeful talking and listening in authentic classroom events enhances language development in fundamental ways. Vocabulary is expanded.

Clarity and organization of thinking are refined. Communication according to audience is varied. Self-confidence is enhanced. Furthermore, purposeful talking and listening carry over into reading and writing development. Children listen to what interests and affects them; they talk about what interests and affects them. Indeed, if children learn by doing, then most of what they engage in must be purposeful and meaningful to them. In this way, learning occurs naturally.

Authentic talking and listening experiences should relate to learners' interests, backgrounds, age levels, and areas of study. They emerge naturally as part of meaningful curriculum. As students discuss current events, good books, science projects, social studies facts, the math needed to calculate something needed by the class, etc., listening is naturally woven into instruction.

Young children use language as a creative tool. With it they make new worlds through imagination, they entertain themselves and others with sounds and rhythms, they develop their own personalities, and they exert control over their environments (Fisher and Terry, 1977). Children's intentions, what they are personally interested in and attending to in their environment, are keys to understanding learning and language development (Donaldson, 1978).

Halliday (1977) has suggested that young children use language in at least seven different ways. These might produce the classroom talking and listening opportunities listed in Figure 5–1.

FIGURE 5–1
HALLIDAY'S
FUNCTIONS OF
LANGUAGE

FUNCTIONS OF LANGUAGE	POSSIBLE LEARNING EVENTS
Instrumental (I want)	Discussing choices and options/ Group planning time
Regulatory (Do as I tell you)	Group leader/Giving directions/ Directing plays and presentations
Interactional (You and me)	Sharing time/ Small group Problem solving/Paired oral readings
Personal (Here I come)	Dictated stories/Oral presentations/ Author's Chair
Heuristic (Tell me why)	Questioning time for each new unit/ Questions that arise during units
Imaginative (Let's pretend)	Oral storytelling/Story retelling/ Acting out stories/Role playing
Expressive (I have something to tell you)	Journal sharing/ Oral reports/ Conferences/Interviews

ORAL LANGUAGE IN THE INCLUSIVE CLASSROOM

One of the most frustrating issues classroom teachers face is the extent of differences among learners. How can teachers be expected to meet the needs of so many different children? Perhaps the single most confounding issue is related to children's language and their consequent difficulty in learning to read and write. Children who do not speak English as their mother tongue, children whose language development is said to be delayed, children who have problems learning, children who speak a non-standard dialect, children whose language is said to be deficient, all have concerned educators for years.

As discussed in Chapter One, human learning is social. Human beings don't learn best in contrived settings where they are isolated from their peers. They learn in environments that contain a wide and rich variety of factors including other people (Rhodes and Dudley-Marling, 1996). What and how we learn is affected by what we already know. Likewise, what we know is affected by what we learn. This is because "all knowledge is embedded in" or scaffolded onto other knowledge (Caine and Caine, 1991, 36). Therefore, learning cannot be understood by focusing on the learning task; the focus must be on the learners.

Higher forms of human learning, such as learning to talk and learning to read and write, are not additive. In fact, when we separate language into someone's notion of a hierarchy of "skills" activities, we strip away meaning and destroy language. We destroy or at least obscure the meaning-making process as well. Learning becomes more difficult, not less, because children's abilities to apply what they already know in order to make sense of what they are learning is taken away. They are left with little or nothing to use to make sense of what they are asked to do (Rhodes and Dudley-Marling, 1996). And, most of these isolated activities do not exist except in classrooms, so learners never get to do them outside of school. Really talking, really reading, and really writing for particular purposes do exist outside of school. It is possible, therefore, that those schools that employ a reductionist view of learning actually cause some children to have greater difficulty.

Practice with arbitrary aspects of language isolated from real use confuses some children. Children who do not speak English as their native language are asked to learn to speak, read, and write all three functions simultaneously, in artificial ways. That is, they are required to learn a second language in all its modes outside of natural, social interactions (Freeman and Freeman, 2000). This feat would daunt most well-educated adults.

A few years ago, we had the good fortune to work with a wonderful teacher named Tina DeStephen, who had a transition classroom in a rural elementary school in our area. Transition classrooms were established for children who had completed kindergarten but were not "ready" for first grade. These children lived in the country on farms that were no longer working farms, where the land lay fallow and animals were no longer raised. The children did not travel; they did not have many or any books and were not read to on a regular basis. A few were not native speakers of English. Their experiences, and therefore their vocabularies and concept development, were limited. Most of the children sat in front of televisions for several hours every day and did not even have other children to play with. They were in danger of being labeled "slow learners," "learning disabled," "language delayed," and so on (DeStephen, 2000).

Tina devised a plan to provide her students with a year of enriched experiences. She wrote a small grant proposal that was funded and approached several businesses in town for small donations. Altogether, she raised more than $2,500. With that money she took her class on more than forty field trips that year. Some of the trips were local: a tobacco farm, a sheep-shearing farm, an archeological dig; but many were farther: the Space Center in Huntsville, the Aquarium in Chattanooga, the Cumberland Science Museum and the State Historical Museum both in Nashville.

Prior to each visit, the children *talked* extensively about where they were going, what they would see, why they were going, where the site was relative to their school and homes, etc. Charts, lists, diagrams, and other forms of written organizers served as reminders and were created to accompany many of these discussions. During the trips, the children and the teacher took notes as they *listened*. They took photographs and collected written materials such as brochures to bring back to their classroom.

Following each visit, they talked about their trip and wrote about where they had gone and what they had seen and done. They drew pictures with labels to document their visits and shared these among themselves. They made word lists to hang on the walls of the words they encountered on each trip. They used those words as they wrote about their experiences.

The children functioned as a community of learners. They helped each other, encouraged each other, and listened to each other. They learned to observe, ask questions, find information, and make connections between themselves and the rest of the world. They assembled a scrapbook of their year together with their writings, photos, and other memorabilia. The children were extremely proud of this document and showed it to each visitor who entered their classroom.

Toward the end of the year, the children were tested to determine how many of them would qualify for special programs. When the test results came back, none of the children qualified for special programs and some were actually ready for second grade. What does that tell us about the differences between what children really need and what they typically get in schools?

Learners who do not have extensive vocabularies or who do not speak English as their native language are at a decided disadvantage in school. Rigg and Allen (1989) and Freeman and Freeman (2000) point out that bilingual and non-English-speaking, monolingual students benefit from being read to. They also benefit from natural talking, problem solving, and rich classroom environments. The question of whether English language learners should receive instruction in their native language or in English alone is one that is still hotly debated in many circles. Most teachers would agree with Au (1993) that English language learners are likely to be more successful if they also receive instruction in their native language. As one native Spanish-speaking adolescent recently put it, "When you can't speak in your own language, you have to use someone else's words. That's a terrible kind of isolation. You feel lost."

Proficiency in one's native language serves as the basis for developing proficiency in English. The goal is to have students develop literacy in both their native language and in English. This is easier if oral fluency has been developed in both. Some research suggests bilingual students, while at a disadvantage initially, especially in traditional classrooms, are ultimately advantaged in several cognitive areas over their monolingual counterparts (Lanauze and Snow, 1989).

Some children who speak a non-standard form of English may also find themselves in trouble in many regular classrooms. Too often, these children are labeled as slow learners, language deficit, or language delayed. Sometimes these children are also poor, but not always. In addition, non-standard speakers and English language learners' experiences may have been different from those needed for early success in school. They may simply require more time to accomplish what their middle-class Standard English–speaking peers are able to do with greater ease and speed.

Even with specially trained teachers, students with learning difficulties may still have problems talking, listening, and learning. If they are separated from their peers for much of the day, they may have difficulties with social relationships. Their learning may be even slower, and their progress intermittent. What good teachers can do, whether they are in an inclusive classroom, a special classroom, or an ESL (English as a second language) classroom, is help learners experience success. When children try and succeed, even with great amounts of support, their confidence is enhanced; they are likely to try harder and improve more rapidly (Gilles, 1992).

However, when children's progress is assessed merely with scores on tests that are designed to measure their knowledge of isolated skills rather than the application of them, a non-growth cycle may appear. Other measures of learning such as anecdotal records, comprehension assessments, checklists, rubrics, and so on may present a different picture.

THE TALKING AND LISTENING CURRICULUM: MAJOR APPROACHES

The talking and listening classroom curriculum is composed of four broad areas: teachers and other adults talking to children, teachers and other adults talking with children, children talking and listening with each other, and children talking and listening to each other. Talking and listening become a legitimate part of every subject, and every learning event involves purposeful classroom talk.

As learners begin to participate in purposeful, structured, and impromptu classroom talk, their contributions are respected and their language accepted. Teachers model standard English, of course, but remember that each of us speaks a dialect variation of our language. Originally, we spoke the form of language that was modeled in our home and community. Some of these variations of English are labeled "good" or "standard" while others are labeled "poor" or "non-standard" depending on the region of the country in which the speakers happen to be speaking. If language exists for purposes of communication within a community of speakers, then all dialects communicate equally well. That is, meaning is conveyed whether a child says, "We didn't have no lunch," or "We didn't have any lunch." Judgments about the *acceptability* of one dialect over another reflect social values, not linguistic ones (Jagger, 1980).

Acknowledging and celebrating differences is one of the hallmarks of good teachers. This does not mean that standard forms are not valued; they are. But children are ill served if they are labeled, insulted, and caused to feel inferior because of the way they talk. They are also ill served if they are left to cope with the realities of the larger society without the tools it takes to succeed. Educated adults in this society typically speak (and write) some form of Standard English at will. Since children learn by immersion, demonstration, and engagement, teachers must model standard forms. They must engage learners in examining their own language. Learners explore and practice standard forms through purposeful oral language events and through the writing process until standard language variations become just another part of each one's language repertoire (Smith, 1994).

Classrooms that establish non-threatening, non-directive, cooperative environments have the best chance for encouraging continued oral language development in general and the development of standard language patterns in particular. For example, in a classroom where the environment was conducive and purposeful talk was encouraged, one teacher recorded twenty different types of problem-solving talk naturally employed by the children (Huff, 1991). She found that when the children were genuinely interested in the problem being discussed, both highly verbal and quiet children participated successfully. She concluded that children who believe their ideas have value to both their peers and teachers willingly share and participate in classroom events. When they engage in authentic speaking and listening, they take risks and acquire confidence in themselves. They find their own voices and take greater control over their self-expressions and over their own learning.

Disciplinary difficulties are kept to a minimum when children's natural drives to socialize are incorporated into the daily routine of the classroom. By reflecting the elaborated oral language conditions of most homes rather than the language-restricted conditions of many classrooms, schools become places where children feel comfortable (Dillon and Searle, 1981). They feel less need to act out when they are partly in charge, when they are making choices, and when they can talk (or write) about their personal lives. They also do better when their difficulties are not being exacerbated by authoritarian and dominating adults (Knapp, 1991).

In one inner-city second/third grade, for example, the teacher and the children decided to study the solar system and outer space because they had tickets to the local planetarium. Just as the unit was getting under way, plans for the outing fell through when transportation was not available. The children were upset. They voiced their displeasure during morning read-aloud time but elected to continue the unit anyway.

The teacher suggested that they each select a planet to learn about and report on. This idea was met with much moaning and groaning. Several children said they thought that would be boring. So the teacher asked the group what they would like to do instead, how they would like to organize their unit. The students had already listed what they knew about the solar system, outer space, and space travel, and had posed their own questions as well. After an opportunity to discuss among themselves, one child suggested that since they could not go to the museum, they turn their classroom into a museum. They could present all the information they found about space and the solar system and schedule tours of their museum for other classes.

Once more the children were excited and enthusiastic about learning. Once more the classroom was theirs. They began to describe how to arrange the room into concept areas, what materials they were going to need, what projects and displays they might create, and how to organize tours and publicize their museum so other students and even parents would come. What began as a potentially disruptive event was channeled into a marvelous learning opportunity. In schools such as this one where discipline all too frequently detracts from learning, children in this classroom rarely became distracted with discipline-related issues.

Much oral language occurs serendipitously as teachers capitalize on teachable moments. For instance, a child brought a caterpillar to school that had wasp eggs embedded in it. The children began asking questions about why a wasp laid eggs on a caterpillar. The children's interest and questions led them into a unit on insects. From an organizing discussion, the children decided to divide their study in two, and focus on insects that sting and insects that don't.

Yet another time, a teacher engaged children in a spontaneous math lesson when several of them brought sacks of Halloween candy to school. The teacher had the children sort their candy—for example, by size, type, color—and compare. Then he asked them to estimate and total their loot. This lesson and a picture book about how factories work led the children to create a classroom assembly line candy factory as a fundraising project. They made and sold peanut butter fudge.

These learning events would not have occurred without teachers who were open to explorations based on children's lives and their language. Good teaching integrates language and thinking with rich content in authentic experiences for children. Good teachers are confident in their knowledge about language and learning, and they use their knowledge in support of their students (Goodman, 1998).

DOCUMENTING AND EVALUATING SPEAKING AND LISTENING

"Kidwatching" is a hallmark of effective classrooms (Goodman, 1991). Watching for and documenting growth in purposeful listening and meaningful talking is an essential part of the teacher's responsibility. Teachers who are engaged in observing children's responses to the instructional events of the classroom are necessarily observing all four language modes. They are collecting and analyzing information they need to plan and amend curriculum. Reflective observation, i.e., kidwatching for the purposes of planning and evaluation, is concrete and continuous.

Checklists and grading rubrics are helpful for recording and analyzing observations of children's speaking and listening performances. Figures 5–2 and 5–3 are examples of the types of checklists teachers might employ in assessment as they document learner growth in oral language.

FIGURE 5–2
SAMPLE EVALUATION
FORM FOR ORAL
LANGUAGE

Student Profile: Speaking

Name _____ Date _____

Grade _____ Setting _____

	Always	Frequently	Sometimes	Not Yet
1. Speaks clearly and distinctly	_____	_____	_____	_____
2. Expresses self logically	_____	_____	_____	_____
3. Uses inflection	_____	_____	_____	_____
4. Uses language in appropriate ways	_____	_____	_____	_____
5. Relates experiences in school to personal life	_____	_____	_____	_____
6. Speaks in complete sentences when appropriate	_____	_____	_____	_____
7. Uses language in variety of ways	_____	_____	_____	_____
8. Speaks with confidence	_____	_____	_____	_____
9. Has well-developed vocabulary	_____	_____	_____	_____
10. Other(s)	_____	_____	_____	_____

Teacher Comments:

_____

_____

_____

_____

INVITING ORAL LANGUAGE INTO THE CLASSROOM

The two most obvious classroom events that naturally improve listening and speaking are listening to someone read aloud and listening to student authors read their own writing. First, listening to someone read aloud is the most important listening students do. Hearing good stories and information pieces read aloud provides learners with models of literate texts they need for their own reading and writing. Second, purposeful listening occurs when authors share their writing for peer evaluation. When listeners know

FIGURE 5–3
SAMPLE EVALUATION
FORM FOR LISTENING

Student Profile: Listening

Name _____ Date _____

Grade _____ Setting _____

	Always	Frequently	Sometimes	Not Yet
1. Hears clearly and accurately	_____	_____	_____	_____
2. Understands main ideas	_____	_____	_____	_____
3. Remembers important details	_____	_____	_____	_____
4. Draws reasonable conclusions	_____	_____	_____	_____
5. Makes reasonable predictions	_____	_____	_____	_____
6. Makes logical judgments	_____	_____	_____	_____
7. Retells complete stories	_____	_____	_____	_____
8. Listens for variety of purposes	_____	_____	_____	_____
9. Listens attentively	_____	_____	_____	_____
10. Other(s)	_____	_____	_____	_____

Teacher Comments:

_____

_____

_____

_____

that the author wants and expects a response, they have a purposeful and authentic reason for listening. This technique, called author's chair, is discussed in Chapter Nine.

Tompkins, Friend, and Smith (1984) assert that children say they listen for only two reasons: to learn and to avoid being punished. Since this is a bit limiting, a wider variety of purposes might enhance the oral language curriculum. Generally, the purposes for listening are *appreciative, discriminative, comprehensive, therapeutic,* and *critical listening.* Appreciative listening is listening for enjoyment. Discriminative listening is the ability to distinguish among sounds—for example, dogs barking or traffic noises. As discriminative listening develops, children are able to distinguish general sounds from the patterned sounds that constitute oral language. Comprehensive listening is listening in order to interpret the speaker's message. Therapeutic listening involves listening to another person talk through a problem. Critical listening is listening to both understand and evaluate the meaning of the spoken communication (Wolvin and Coakley, 1985).

As with all learning, awareness of the processes involved in listening appears to affect learning in a positive direction. And, as with all language, listening develops best when it serves the learner's needs from the learner's point of view. There also appears to be a reciprocal relationship between growth in listening and growth in reading comprehension (Pearson and Fielding, 1982).

In addition to read-alouds, student book sharing, and author's chair, any number of other authentic purposes for listening may occur including small ad hoc group discussions of a topic of interest, storytelling events, and other planned presentations.

Discussion Groups   Good teachers frequently have students work together exploring content through a variety of resources. Small-group discussion is the most common means of incorporating talking and listening in classrooms. Group discussion may be informal, as in spur of the moment planning for acting out a story, or it may be formal, as in literature study groups, peer editing, author's circle, or project planning and presentation. Listening opportunities that are natural and are embedded in the context of authentic language experiences develop listening most effectively. Authentic listening occurs when a person is speaking about a subject of interest to the audience.

Effective discussion and planning groups do not just happen. Teachers teach children how to conduct collaborative and cooperative groups by modeling group processes at the beginning of the year. As they work with small groups, or even entire classes, they may ask someone to keep a record of what the group decides. They may ask the students to select a timekeeper, a moderator, or a group leader to assist. The children and the teacher discuss what needs to happen for the group to accomplish its purpose. These procedures may be written and posted somewhere in the room so that the group processes that facilitate the accomplishment of the task are examined and made overt. For example, after several group events directed by the teacher, one second-grade class decided on the following procedures for successful groups: pick a leader, pick a recorder, discuss the topic, brainstorm, divide the work, meet when needed, be respectful, present findings to rest of class. These were written on chart paper and displayed.

Teachers also model literature study groups, peer editing groups, author's circle, and other small discussion groups that have a definite structure. Listening and speaking occur naturally within these groups, each reinforcing the other. Much oral language occurs as children negotiate, question, compliment, and share their thinking.

Children in problem-solving and project-planning groups benefit from prior group experience. They need only the slightest suggestions from the teacher about how to organize and get started if they have participated in peer editing, author's circle, and other group discussions.

Panel Discussions   Another type of group discussion is the panel or roundtable discussion. Most often employed by teachers in middle or upper grades, younger children are also quite capable of conducting panel discussions. Panel and roundtable presentations are an alternative to individual and group reports. Students researching subtopics under the same general category may coordinate their findings and present their information to the whole class in the form of a panel discussion. In order to do so, they must share their findings. They must talk and listen to each other.

One group of fifth graders, researching African American literature, subdivided their topic into the following: the Revolutionary War, slavery and the Civil War, current stories, music, and poetry. When they finished reading and talking among themselves and with their teacher, they decided to present a panel discussion of their work. They developed a "program" for the session, with an overall title of their project and a title for each presenter. They showed examples of the materials they had read and played samples of African American music, such as blues, ragtime, and rap. They shared audiotapes of two writers reading their own poetry and displayed some pictures of the authors they were discussing. When the group presentations were finished, the panel presenters asked for questions and comments from the audience. In order for the members of the audience to ask meaningful questions, they had be active participants; that is, they had to really hear, attend to, and think about what they were listening to. The panel presentation was so successful that the students were asked to present it to other classrooms.

Storytelling   Enhancing children's sense of story and their self-confidence as performers aids in developing the whole child. These two areas are simultaneously supported when children are encouraged to tell stories. Young children tell stories about

things that happened to them; they also make up their own stories or retell familiar ones such as "Little Red Riding Hood" or "The Three Little Pigs." For most young children, storytelling comes quite naturally.

Teachers interested in exploring the potential benefits of regular, oral storytelling might begin by telling stories to children. Many teachers choose to informally use oral storytelling with young children; however, older children enjoy and profit from storytelling as well. In addition, oral storytelling may be an important part of some children's culture. Inviting children whose first language is not English to tell stories in their native language and to retell them in English allows English-only speakers to hear another language and English language learners to gain confidence (Freeman and Freeman, 2000).

Teachers may establish a place in the classroom, a raised platform perhaps, with a "storytelling chair." Props may be made available but should be kept simple—shoes, hats, scarves, and the like. One person per day, or several persons on a designated day, may sign up to tell a story during storytelling time.

Telling Stories with Wordless Picture Books   One of the key elements in learning to read and write well is learning to think like an author. Thinking like an author is beneficial for young children, for children who appear to be word callers, and for children who have difficulty writing stories. Becoming the author is what happens when learners tell stories from wordless picture books.

Examine any good wordless picture book—for example, *Deep in the Forest* by Turkle, or *Window* by Baker. Encourage the children to look closely at the details in the illustrations. Talk about how these carry the story line. Predict what is likely to come next in the story as it is initially explored. Invite the children to help you tell the story the way that an author might write it. In large groups the illustrations may have to be shown with an opaque projector. Big books also work well in this application.

The following is a short list of wordless or nearly wordless picture books. As you explore this genre, you may find several others written by the same authors.

Ahlberg, J., and A. Ahlberg. 1978. *Each Peach Pear Plum: An "I Spy" Story*. New York: Scholastic.

Alexander, M. 1970. *Bobo's Dream*. New York: Dial Press.

Anno, M. 1978. *Anno's Journey*. New York: Philomel.

Baker, J. 1991. *Window*. Sydney, Australia: Julia MacRae Books.

Briggs, R. 1978. *The Snowman*. New York: Random House.

Collington, P. 1987. *The Angel and the Soldier Boy*. New York: Knopf.

Day, A. 1985. *Good Dog Carl*. LaJolla, CA: Green Tiger Press (and others in this series).

dePaola, T. 1981. *The Hunter and the Animals*. New York: Holiday House.

Drescher, H. 1987. *The Yellow Umbrella*. New York: Bradbury.

Keats, E. 1982. *Clementina's Cactus*. New York: Viking Press.

McCully, E. 1988. *New Baby*. New York: Harper and Row.

Mayer, M. 1967. *A Boy, a Dog, and a Frog*. New York: Dial Press.

Mayer, M., and M. Mayer. 1975. *One Frog Too Many*. New York: Dial Press.

Ormerod, J. 1981. *Sunshine*. New York: Penguin Books.

Spier, P. 1982. *Peter Spier's Rain*. New York: Doubleday.
Turkle, B. 1976. *Deep in the Forest*. New York: Dutton.
Wiesner, D. 1988. *Free Fall*. New York: Lothrop, Lee and Shephard.
Wiesner, D. 1991. *Tuesday*. New York: Lothrop, Lee and Shephard.
Young, E. 1984. *The Other Bone*. New York: Harper and Row.
Zolotow, C. 1967. *Summer Is . . .* New York: Crowell.

The Listening Center   Many classrooms have an area especially designated as the listening center. Usually a table or cubicle becomes the listening center and houses an audiotape player and headphones. Here students may listen to tapes of books, poetry, or music without disturbing the rest of the class. Teachers stockpile tapes and corresponding written texts from stories, poems, and information materials.

Students' comprehensive and appreciative listening are enhanced when they may choose to listen to tapes of poems. Jack Prelutsky's *New Kid on the Block* is an excellent accompaniment to a unit on "Things That Are New" or Ashley Bryan's telling African folktales as part of a unit on "Folktales Around the World." Tapes of the students' own oral or written stories expand the classroom collection.

Show and Tell   This activity is a familiar part of many kindergarten and primary classrooms. Show and Tell time establishes the relationship between things the child prizes and finds interesting outside of school with learning and sharing in school. Show and Tell also establishes the relationship between talking and listening. Show and Tell is not just the presenter telling about an item then sitting down. After the presenter has shared, a question and answer time ensues. When children ask thoughtful questions and receive meaningful responses, real listening and talking occur. (See R. Munsch's *Show and Tell* for a literature base from which to start Show and Tell in your classroom.)

Telephone Conversations   Playing telephone is more than just play in the primary-grade classroom; it is an authentic language experience. Not only do children learn about the importance of speaking clearly and taking turns during a conversation, they also develop many other vital abilities. By role playing what to do if someone is injured and needs assistance, they learn how to use the telephone in emergency situations. They also discover the need for listening to instructions and for providing accurate and complete directions. Use a book such as Tomie dePaola's *Michael Bird Boy* to initiate telephone role playing in your classroom.

After reading *Michael Bird Boy* one first-grade class wanted to know if there were any women bosses in the local factories in their city. Their teacher helped them prepare, practice, and conduct a telephone survey. He also helped the children make sense of their information and develop ways to share it with other people in the school. Speaking, listening, reading, and writing were all used in preparing the survey, implementing the project, gathering and analyzing the information, and reporting the findings. These first graders were researchers in their own communities.

Older children may learn how to use the telephone as a research tool. As adults, we gather a great deal of information by phone. For example, we use the phone to find out about airfares and schedules, city bus routes, movie times, the comparative cost of a new appliance, or where to have the car repaired. Thoughtful teachers identify ways for children to gather information from a variety of sources including the telephone.

Oral Clozure

Most teachers instinctively know that oral clozure is helpful to young readers. That is, when reading aloud from a predictable book, most teachers will pause on highly predictable words and wait for the children to supply the meaningful text. For example, "There is a house, a napping house, where everyone is _____" (from *The Napping House* by Wood). Oral clozure does not have to be reserved for young learners. Prediction skills and vocabulary are increased through oral clozure.

Creative Dramatics

Drama in all its forms encourages self-expression and is another way learners come to know their world. *Creative dramatics* is an umbrella term used to identify the many types of dramatic activities teachers encourage: acting, improvisation, mime and movement, role playing, and puppetry. Creative dramatics helps children develop stage presence, control body movements, develop visual imagery, identify the salient features of a concept or an event, and think and plan sequentially. Different activities allow for the integration of some of each of the language arts as students plan, practice, produce, and perform their works.

Employing a variety of drama activities together with good literature helps children develop a sense of story, of action, of characters, and the power of their own imaginations. But perhaps most fundamental of all, drama turns vicarious experiences into active and concrete experiences. While this may be especially good for elementary-age learners, it should not be limited to young children only.

Role Playing

A form of creative dramatics, role playing, may be unrehearsed or result in complete theatrical productions with scripts, props, costumes, and scenery. Role playing knows no language barriers.

Teachers of young children frequently develop a "Let's Pretend" area where props and dress-up items are stored. Joanne Fitch, a wonderful kindergarten teacher, encourages her children to act out and tell stories using a vast collection of small toys: people, animals, vehicles, buildings, trees, and so on. Playing together with these props, the children's oral language and imaginations flourish.

Businesses provide both the opportunity and the props for extended role playing. For example, following a field trip to a bank, one teacher created a teller's window from a cardboard box. The children collected forms from the bank: blank counter checks, savings account books, deposit slips, withdrawal slips, coin wrappers, and money pouches. With the addition of a little play money, the children were ready to "be" bank tellers, depositors, people in need of loans, and so on. Banks, grocery stores, laundries, doctors' and dentists' offices, vet clinics, airport ticket counters, and many other places provide the context for rich language play and learning.

Favorite stories frequently turn into classroom theatricals involving many phases of planning and presenting and providing great opportunities for language learning to take place. Role playing offers ways for learners to present their understandings of a story, character and plot development, or emotion in literature. For example, after reading *Frank and Ernest* by Day, one group of third-grade students set up a "diner" in their classroom. They explored being short-order cooks, servers, and customers. They made menus and advertised their diner. They experimented with the slang terms in the book and created a few of their own. Their teacher encouraged them and took the opportunity to incorporate math as well.

Older students may also role-play to examine good literature, for example, following a literature study. They may act out their own and other student's stories. Improvisation, mime, and readers theater (see Chapter Ten) are ways for students to develop skits that explore aspects of the text such as tone, reader expectations, and character motivations. Role play as a way of examining the relationship between Winnie Foster and Angus Tuck in Babbitt's *Tuck Everlasting*, or between the boy and his mother in Armstrong's *Sounder*, make powerful and lasting impressions on participants and audience alike. Role playing fosters learners' personal experiences with books and builds students' writing capabilities with skills such as character development, feelings, dialogue, and description.

Role playing is sometimes seen in the form of pantomime. A great deal of thinking, reasoning, discussing, and planning are required before students can deliver an effective pantomime.

Pantomime   Pantomime is actions that are designed to convey ideas without words. It is sometimes referred to as mime (from the word *mimic*) and movement. Because it is non-verbal, it is highly imaginative. Pantomime helps children problem-solve together and attend to details. Teachers may include pantomime as a means of representing a story that the children have read. They encourage students to visualize what they want to present. They talk with the students about how to do something without being able to tell the audience what they are doing. The game charades is a popular example of pantomime. Favorite book titles readily lend themselves to charades.

Puppetry   Puppets remove the storyteller from direct contact with the audience and may make it easier for the beginner. They are popular with young children and highly motivating to reluctant readers. Many elementary classrooms have a puppet theater. Some are commercially produced; others are made by the teacher and children from large boxes or crates. Puppets may be purchased or made from inexpensive or discarded household items. An important part of learning resides in creating puppets.

In planning a puppet presentation, children must decide how their puppet looks, how it shows certain character or story traits, and how to correlate the puppet's movement with the dialogue. Decision making, cooperative planning, and problem solving become authentic experiences in the context of staging the performance.

Briggs and Wagner (1979) suggest several criteria for helping children determine if a story is appropriate for a puppet presentation: briskly moving action, characters that allow the children to explore voice as well as movement, and familiarity of setting. The size of the stage needs to be considered because too many characters or too many different scenes may prohibit homemade theaters.

After an appropriate story has been selected, rehearsal is the second key to successful puppet theater. Each scene is practiced so that the children can coordinate moving their puppet with speaking its lines. As with all informal classroom drama, improvisation is preferred over memorization because it allows children an opportunity in which risk

FIGURE 5–4
EASY-TO-MAKE
PUPPETS

FINGER PUPPETS

Finger Puppet
(with Velcro tabs)

Finger Puppet
(from old glove finger)

Toilet Paper Roller Puppet

STICK PUPPETS

Stick Puppet

Paper Cup Puppet

Paper Plate Puppet

HAND PUPPETS

Sock Puppet

Paper Bag Puppet

Cloth Puppet

taking and self–expression are encouraged and valued. For a more formal presentation, students may write the script and learn their parts.

Choral Speaking, Verse, and Choral Reading Poetry and nursery rhymes may be the most common types of material used for choral reading; however, other genres also offer rich language opportunities. For example, Carle's *Animals Animals*, Fleischman's *Joyful Noise*, VanLaan's *Possum Come a Knockin'*, and Greenfield's *Nathaniel*

Talking are excellent books with diverse language patterns and interesting rhyme and rhythm. Poems for older learners like *The Creation* by James Weldon Johnson and "The Ballad of the Harp Weaver" by Edna St. Vincent Millay make engaging group presentations.

Choral activities help students investigate various combinations of group and solo voices, various expressions, rhythm patterns, and arrangements for interpreting their pieces, enriching not only oral language but written language as well. They also provide interesting ways for children to practice memorization and public speaking.

Listening Walk   A listening walk taken early in the year helps young children become familiar with their surroundings and develops discriminative listening, especially if the group discusses what they heard and how they knew. Read Paul Showers' *The Listening Walk* aloud, then take the students on a neighborhood trek. Tell children to listen carefully and to note all the different sounds they hear, where they hear them, and what they mean. Discussions of what the children discover takes place when the group returns to the classroom. Children may draw captioned pictures of their favorite sound. Repeat the trip with an audiotape recorder and prepare a tape for their listening center with a narrator asking the listener to identify the sounds. Listening walks evolve into color walks, smell walks, etc., to explore the senses and the environment.

Imagery   Visual imagery and imagining are crucial to constructing and retaining meaning. Visual imagery is one of the abilities proficient readers develop and one that may decline when children have too many images created for them in the form of television and movies. Many picture books provide opportunities for readers to think about point of view and visual imagery, to draw their own illustrations, and make new books from these imaginings. Think about what you might engage children in regarding visual imagery using books such as Leo Lionni's *Frederick* and *Fish Is Fish*.

FORMAL LISTENING AND SPEAKING EVENTS

Most of the speech and listening events described above require some planning and may involve a degree of practice, but they are more spontaneous than the two activities described next. Many benefits may be derived from opportunities to engage in planned interviews and formal and informal debates.

Interviews   Most students are familiar with interviews through television. Interviewers gain firsthand information as a way of coming to know and understand the world. They acquire experience talking to unfamiliar persons, asking appropriate questions, and organizing and presenting information. Both interviewers and interviewees must be active listeners in order to respond appropriately and meaningfully. Interviews may be conducted by groups or by the entire class. They may take place between pairs of students with the class serving as the audience.

Interviewing helps build self-confidence and gives learners practice in both oral language (asking questions) and written language (taking notes). Sharing the findings of interviews requires organizing and synthesizing information. The actual words of the informant as well as impressions and perceptions of the interviewer need to be shared, thus students learn the value of quotations. Learners may write out their report or arrange their notes, add comments, observations, and perceptions, and present them orally. Role playing may be useful if the class decides the oral presentation might take the form of television news interviews. Posters, drawings, photographs, or other visual and textual displays enhance the presentation.

The list of persons to interview is endless: family members, local historians, storytellers, businessmen, community leaders, local artists, an award-winning scientist at the local university, the president of a local group, to mention only a few. Interviews are most successful and appropriate when learners decide they have a need to know. However, teachers may see authentic opportunities and suggest the possibility of conducting interviews as a means for learners to extend their knowledge and skills.

Debates

Debates are another means by which learners develop language skills. Debates are controlled arguments by informed persons with opposing views. The purpose of a debate is to persuade the audience. Debates may be informal or formal. Informal debates usually occur when the entire class is excited about an issue and most or all of the students have taken a position either for or against the central problem (Hoskisson and Tompkins, 1987).

For example, as students worked through a unit on ecology and rain forests, one group of fifth graders encountered the issues related to clear-cutting forests. Students disagreed with each other and occasionally their discussions became quite intense. Their teacher suggested an informal debate. Those who thought that whatever had to happen to preserve jobs for people took one side of the room, and those who thought the federal government should intervene to save the forests and the endangered animals took the other side. Students were asked to state the reasons for their positions. Questions were asked and answers were given. Then students had an opportunity to change sides.

Informal debates encourage learner self-expression; everyone's opinion is valuable. They allow teachers to gauge the extent of the information students have acquired and how well they have synthesized and organized it. They promote growth in speaking and listening as presenters engage in making their positions clear and audiences engage in following arguments and drawing conclusions.

Unlike informal debates, formal debates are highly structured and well-researched arguments between two teams taking opposing sides of a proposition. They are difficult to do well and are usually not attempted until high school, but that need not be the case. Teachers who know the general guidelines for setting up and conducting formal debates may wish to offer older elementary students the opportunity.

For example, formal debates might be presented as the culminating activity of a unit of study or as an event to present information in which students are intensely interested. The debate begins with a proposition, a statement calling for change in the status quo. The affirmative team asks for the change. The negative team denies the need for the change. The affirmative team is responsible for devising a plan for implementing the "needed" change. They must demonstrate the advantages of the change and of their plan. The negative team attacks the plan and shows its disadvantages. (See Ericson,

1987, for an excellent source for more in-depth information about helping students conduct formal debates.)

None of the strategies cited in this chapter are of isolated activities from workbooks or manuals of teaching ideas. Practice activities, even with well-formed instruction, cannot replace a multitude of opportunities involving listening for *real* reasons to speech events in which learners are interested. However, teachers may employ selected speaking and listening strategies occasionally as the foundation for future application to reading and writing, as well as to broaden children's experiences with language.

SUMMARY

Speaking and listening are reciprocal aspects of oral language; each reinforces the other. Indeed, under normal circumstances one does not occur without the other. Like the abilities of readers and writers, oral language abilities are learned as they are used in natural contexts for authentic reasons. Oral language is the basis for literacy development and should be part of the purposeful curriculum throughout the grades.

Halliday (1977) identified seven functions for speaking in which children engage. Wolvin and Coakley (1985) identified at least five purposes learners have for listening. This chapter has described the integration of natural speech and listening events into classrooms where students are using language in all its forms to explore the world around them.

Oral language learning is an active, constructive process. It does not stop when children enter school. However, the ways schools treat speaking and listening are very different from the ways they naturally occur at home. Typically, oral language in school is more restrictive than natural development would indicate. Because oral language is crucial to the learning process, sound instructional practices that do not teach listening and speaking as separate from their purposes, as separate from each other, or as separate from the other forms of language have been described.

THEORY-TO-PRACTICE CONNECTIONS

Speaking/Listening Theory

1. Oral language is learned as it is used.

2. Oral language is a symbolic system for representing meaning and our understanding of the world.

3. Listening and speaking reinforce each other and they reinforce reading and writing.

4. Listening, speaking, reading, writing, and thinking are integrated with content in authentic experiences for learners.

5. Listening and speaking opportunities enhance self-expression and self-concept.

Examples of Classroom Practice

1. Show and tell; storytelling

2. Giving and following oral directions

3. Play acting and choral speaking

4. Interviews, informal polls

5. Pantomime, role plays, and puppetry

SUGGESTED READINGS

Booth, D., and C. Thornley-Hall, eds. 1991. *Classroom Talk: Speaking and Listening Activities from Classroom-Based Teacher Research*. Portsmouth, NH: Heinemann.

———.1991. *The Talk Curriculum*. Portsmouth, NH: Heinemann.

Daniel, A. 1992. *Activities Integrating Oral Communication Skills for Students Grades K–8*. Annandale, VA: Speech Communication Association.

Dudley-Marling, C., and D. Searle. 1991. *When Students Have Time to Talk: Creating Contexts for Learning Language*. Portsmouth, NH: Heinemann.

EXTENDING YOUR DISCUSSION

1. Discuss how the instructional examples described in this chapter put learner-centered theory and language development principles into practice.

2. Identify several ways the teacher can engage students in functional math during activities like "diner" or "candy factory."

3. List several props children need for each of the role-playing jobs cited on page 94. Name other types of role plays children might enjoy. What props might be needed?

4. Obtain a copy of the SCA integrated activities book cited in the suggested readings section (Daniel, 1992).

Read and select several that you find interesting and potentially useful in the elementary classroom. How do they fit your developing theory of learning and teaching? In what classroom contents might you employ one? Would it need to be adapted? If so, in what way?

5. Select a piece of high-quality children's literature. *Frederick* by Lionni, *Show and Tell* by Munsch, or *The Napping House* by Wood. Working with a small group, create a flannel board story or puppet theater presentation. Practice and present your creation; discuss what you learned.

REFERENCES

Au, [missing copy]

Barrs, M., S. Ellis, H. Hester, and A. Thomas. 1989. *The Primary Language Record: Handbook for Teachers*. Portsmouth, NH: Heinemann.

Barton, R. 1986. *Tell Me Another: Storytelling and Reading Aloud at Home*. Portsmouth, NH: Heinemann.

Barton, R., and D. Booth 1990. *Stories in the Classroom: Storytelling, Reading Aloud, and Roleplaying with Children*. Portsmouth, NH: Heinemann.

Booth, D., and C. Thornley-Hall, eds. 1991. *Classroom Talk: Speaking and Listening Activities from Classroom-Based Teacher Research*. Portsmouth, NH: Heinemann.

———. 1991. *The Talk Curriculum*. Portsmouth, NH: Heinemann.

Briggs, N., and J. Wagner. 1979. *Children's Literature Through Storytelling and Drama*. Dubuque, IA: William C. Brown.

Britton, J. 1976. *Language and Learning*. London: Penguin.

Caine, R., and G. Caine. 1991. *Making Connections: Teaching and the Human Brain*. Alexandria, VA: Association for Supervision and Curriculum Development.

D'Angelo, K. 1979. "Wordless Picturebooks: Also for the Writer." *Language Arts* 56: 813–14.

Daniel, A. 1992. *Activities Integrating Oral Communication Skills for Students Grades K–8*. Annandale, VA: Speech CommunicationAssociation.

Deglar, L. 1979. "Putting Words into Wordless Picturebooks." *The Reading Teacher* 30: 399–402.

DeStephen, T. 2000. "Being Loved by Thank Yous! Rural First Graders Make Connections." In *Teaching At-Risk Students in the K–4 Classroom: Language, Literacy, Learning*, eds. C. Stice and J. Bertrand. Norwood, MA: Christopher-Gordon.

Devine, T. 1978. "Listening: What We Know After 50 Years of Theorizing." *Journal of Reading* 21: 296–304.

Dillon, D., and D. Searle. 1981. "The Role of Language in One First Grade Classroom." *Research in the Teaching of English* 15: 311–28.

Donaldson, M. 1978. *Children's Minds*. New York: W. W. Norton.

Dudley-Marling, C., and D. Searle. 1991. *When Students Have Time to Talk: Creating Contexts for Learning Language.* Portsmouth, NH: Heinemann.

Ericson, J. 1987. *Debater's Guide: Revised Edition.* Carbondale, IL: Southern Illinois University Press.

Feeney, S., D. Christensen, and E. Moravcik. 1983. *Who Am I in the Lives of Children? An Introduction to Teaching Young Children.* Columbus, OH: Merrill.

Fisher, C., and A. Terry. 1977. *Children's Language and the Language Arts.* New York: McGraw-Hill.

Fox, S., and V. Allen. 1983. *The Language Arts: An Integrated Approach.* New York: Holt.

Freeman, D., and Y. Freeman. 2000. *Teaching Reading in a Multilingual Classroom.* Portsmouth, NH: Heinemann.

Giles 1992. [missing copy]

Goodman, K. 1998. *In Defense of Good Teaching.* York, ME: Stenhouse.

Goodman, Y. 1991. "Kidwatching: Observing Children in the Classroom." In *Talk Curriculum,* eds. D. Booth and C. Thornley-Hall. Portsmouth, NH: Heinemann.

Guidelines for Developing Oral Communication Curricula in Kindergarten Through Twelfth Grade. 1991. Annandale, VA: Speech Communication Association.

Haley-James, S., and C. Hobson. 1980. "Interviewing as a Means of Encouraging the Drive to Communicate." *Language Arts* 57: 497–502.

Hall, S. 1990. *Using Picture Storybooks to Teach Literary Devices.* Phoenix, AZ: Oryx Press.

Halliday, M. 1977. *Explorations in the Functions of Language.* London: Edward Arnold.

Hoskisson, K., and G. Tompkins. 1987. *Language Arts: Content and Teaching Strategies.* Columbus, OH: Merrill.

Huff, S. 1991. "Types of Problem-Solving Talk in the Classroom." In *Classroom Talk*, eds. D. Booth and C. Thornley-Hall. Portsmouth, NH: Heinemann.

Knapp, B. 1991. "Talk and Quiet Child." In *Classroom Talk*, eds. D. Booth and C. Thornley-Hall. Portsmouth, NH: Heinemann.

Lanauze, M., and C. Snow. 1989. "The Relations Between First- and Second-Language Writing Skills: Evidence from Puerto Rican Elementary School Children in the Mainland." *Linguistics and Education* 1 (4): 323–28.

Lundsteen, S. 1979. *Listening: Its Impact on Reading and the Other Language Arts.* Urbana, IL: NCTE.

Maclure, M., T. Phillips, and A. Wilkenson. 1978. In *Oracy Matters*, ed. M. Keyne. United Kingdom: Open University Press.

Martinez, M., and N. Rosen. 1985. "The Value of Repeated Readings During Storytime." *The Reading Teacher* 38: 782–86.

McGee, L., and G. Tompkins. 1983. "Wordless Picturebooks Are for Older Readers Too." *Journal of Reading* 27: 120–23.

National Council of Teachers of English. 1983. "Forum: Essentials of English." *Language Arts* 60: 244–48.

Norton, D. 1993. *The Effective Teaching of Language Arts.* New York: Macmillan.

Paley, V. 1985. *Wally's Stories: Conversations in the Kindergarten.* Cambridge, MA: Harvard University Press.

Pearson, P. D., and L. Fielding. 1982. "Research Update: Listening Comprehension." *Language Arts* 59: 617–29.

Peterson, R., and M. Eeds. 1988. *Grand Conversations: Literature Groups in Action.* Toronto: Scholastic.

Roth, R. 1986. "Practical Use of Language in the School." *Language Arts* 63: 134–42.

Rhodes, L., and C. Dudley-Marling. 1996. *Readers and Writers with a Difference: A Holistic Approach to Teaching Learning Disabled and Remedial Students.* Portsmouth, NH: Heinemann.

Rigg, P., and V. Allen. 1989. *When They Don't All Speak English: Integrating the ESL Student into the Regular Classroom.* Urbana, IL: NCTE.

Scher, A., and C. Verrall. 1992. *200+ Ideas for Drama.* Portsmouth, NH: Heinemann.

Siks, G. 1983. *Drama with Children.* New York: Harper and Row.

Sloyer, S. 1982. *Readers Theater: Story Dramatization in the Classroom.* Urbana, IL: NCTE.

Spolin, V. 1986. *Theater Games for the Classroom.* Evanston, IL: Northwestern University Press.

Talking to Learn: Classroom Practices in Teaching English. 1991. Urbana, IL: NCTE.

Tompkins, G., M. Friend, and P. Smith. 1984. "Children's Metacognitive Knowledge About Listening." Presentation at the American Educational Research Association Convention, New Orleans, LA.

Watts, I. 1990. *Just a Minute: Ten Short Plays and Activities for Your Classroom with Rehearsal Strategies to Accompany Multicultural Stories from Around the World.* Portsmouth, NH: Heinemann.

Wells, G. 1986. *The Meaning Makers: Children Learning Language and Using Language.* Toronto: Unwin.

Wells, J. 1980. *Children's Language and Learning.* Englewood Cliffs, NJ: Prentice-Hall.

White, C. 1990. *Jevon Doesn't Sit at the Back Anymore.*
Richmond Hill, Ontario: Scholastic.

Wilkinson, L. 1984. "Research Currents: Peer Group
Talk in Elementary School." *Language Arts* 61: 164–69.

Willbrand, M., and R. Rieke. 1983. *Teaching Oral
Communication in Elementary Schools.* New York:
Macmillan.

Wolvin, A., and C. Coakley. 1985. *Listening.* Dubuque,
IA: William C. Brown.

CHILDREN'S LITERATURE

Armstrong, W. 1969. *Sounder.* New York: HarperCollins.

Babbitt, N. 1975. *Tuck Everlasting.* New York: Farrar,
Straus, and Giroux.

Carle, E. 1989. *Animals, Animals.* New York: Philomel.

Day, A. 1988. *Frank and Ernest.* New York: Scholastic.

dePaola, T. 1975. *Michael Bird Boy.* Englewood Cliffs, NJ:
Prentice-Hall.

Fleischman, P. 1988. *Joyful Noise: Poems for Two Voices.*
New York: Harper and Row.

Greenfield, E. 1988. *Nathaniel Talking.* New York: Black
Butterfly Children's Books.

Johnson, J. 1993. *The Creation.* Boston: Little, Brown, and
Company.

Lionni, L. 1967. *Frederick.* New York: Pantheon.

———. 1970. *Fish Is Fish.* New York: Pantheon.

Millay, E. 1939. "The Ballad of the Harp Weaver." In
Collected Lyrics of Edna St. Vincent Millay. New York:
Harper and Row.

Munsch, R. 1998. *Show and Tell.* Toronto: Annick Press.

Prelutsky, J. 1984. *New Kid on the Block.* New York:
Greenwillow.

Showers, P. 1961. *The Listening Walk.* New York:
HarperCollins.

VanLaan, N. 1990. *Possum Come a Knockin'.* New York:
Random House.

Wood, A. 1984. *The Napping House.* San Diego, CA:
HBJ.

CHAPTER SIX

"There is only one reading process, regardless of the proficiency with which that process is used."

(Kenneth Goodman, E. Brooks Smith, Robert Meredith, and Yetta Good-man, 1988, 203)

READING

One particularly successful local kindergarten teacher has many, if not most, of her children reading by the end of the year. Linda does not drill her students on letter-sounds or bore and frustrate them with work-books and ditto sheets. She does not do "letter-of-the-week," because as she says, "the children just don't get that." Neither does she zap them with flash cards. Rather, she reads to them several times a day, and they always have a theme of some sort under study: how eggs hatch, where butterflies come from, what makes weather. She reads big books—oversized books with enlarged pictures and enlarged print—and she and the children sing the ones that are familiar songs. Every week she helps each child "write" and illustrate his or her own book. She encourages the children to help each other. She takes them on field trips, and much more.

At the end of each school year, Linda asks the children how they think they learned to read and write so well. As part of this informal survey, she also asks who taught them. Here is what she finds, "Most credit their parents, grandparents, and older siblings with teaching them about letters and words and things of that sort. Few, if any, children are aware of the teaching that has gone on in our classroom. One year, a little boy looked at me with concern and said, 'Ms. Edwards, we didn't learn, it's just what we do all day.' I am especially proud of that response because in many ways it is absolutely true. I am proud of my own invisibility in the process. The fact that such powerful learning takes place so easily and naturally tells me we must be doing many things right. But the quintessential confirmation came recently from one little girl who, when asked how she and her classmates had learned to read and write so well said, 'You know, Ms. Edwards, we just teached ourselves!'" (Edwards, 2000, 17).

Linda Edwards knows a lot about children and she knows what early literacy is and how to get it. She knows reading and writing are tools for learning and doing interesting things in the world. She knows children learn to read and write by really reading and writing. She knows they must be engaged in thinking, planning, doing, and evaluating in order to learn at capacity. She understands that reading is constructing meaning, and she engages her students in doing just that, as often and in as many functional and different ways as possible.

Many children by the ages of five and six come to school already asking, "What does that say?" as they point to print on cereal boxes, in pictures books, on signs along the highway, or in their own messages. The realization that written symbols are different from pictures and that they have potential meanings are two of the very earliest steps children take on the journey into literacy.

Literacy—the ability to read and write—draws on natural aptitudes, attitudes, and values, as well as life and instructional experiences. Children who are lucky enough to have teachers like Mrs. Edwards get off to a wonderful start. But too often that good start, their enthusiasm for learning, the natural curiosity with the world that young children have, is squelched. Too many children report that by fourth grade they hate school. Too many adults in this country can read minimally, at least, but they do not like to read and so avoid reading what they don't actually have to read (Gardner, 1991; Trelease, 2001). In some ways it is amazing that so many well-trained and well-intentioned individuals work so diligently only to produce the very results they say they want to avoid (Smith, 1985, 1994).

In this chapter we explore the reasons people read, what reading is, and what reading does. We examine the historical practices of teaching reading and contrast them with more current perspectives. Finally, we study the reading process, the process you are employing as you construct meaning from this text.

WHAT READING IS

Reading is constructing meaning, making sense of print. It happens in the brain of the reader. It is NOT merely word identification in a linear fashion or accurate word calling. As such, reading is considerably more complex than its physical attributes. If a reader has not made the written material meaningful, reading has not taken place. What reading is and how human beings come to comprehend the visual language system are important to our understandings as teachers.

Reading is nearly always just between the reader and the author. The author takes the reader with him or her for a time. Reading is one of the main ways human beings are civilized. That is, through reading we journey to places we might not go on our own. We learn about times, places, people, and ideas, many of which we could never know firsthand. To treat this alternate universe as a mechanical act is to rob people of the chance to enter the world of literature. You would not consider someone a pianist who could only play the scales and chopsticks, even if played very well.

Reading is a meaning-making activity that is affected by the culture and the context in which the reader and the text exist. It is learned in the same way learning to talk was accomplished. The learner's brain needs great amounts of meaningful print that is read and reread again and again. The learner's brain needs to use written symbols to try to communicate, to be understood, and to understand the writings of others.

Written language reflects the structure of the oral language. Comprehending written language, like comprehending oral language, is a complex process. It is certainly more complicated than recognizing letters, forming words, identifying each word's meaning, and adding up the meanings of the words one at a time from left to right. One way to better understand reading is to explore our own reading. The following activities are designed to help do just that. Examine these lines:

Mary had a little lamb

Its fleece was white as snow.

In this example from a well-known nursery rhyme, *Mary* is a little girl, *had* means "owned," and *little* means "small in size" as well as "young." The word *lamb* refers to "a child's pet." However, if we alter the second line, see what happens to the meanings of the words that precede it.

Mary had a little lamb . . .

and she spilled mint jelly on her evening gown.

Now, *Mary* is a grown woman at a dinner party perhaps, *had* means "ate," and *little lamb* becomes a "serving of meat."

Try another example of the complex and interdependent nature of words in text:

Mary had a little lamb . . .

and it was such a difficult delivery

the vet needed a drink.

This time, *Mary* is the ewe, *had* means "to give birth to," and *little lamb* means "baby" (adapted from Altwerger, Edelsky, and Flores, 1987).

Here is another. Read the following three sentences. They each use the same four words and are identical in surface structure with only one word, a noun, being different in each sentence. However, they each have very different underlying structures and three very different meanings:

He picked his way carefully.

He picked his brain carefully.

He picked his nose carefully.

The first sentence is about a person who is moving through difficult terrain, the dark, or an unfamiliar place—something of that sort. The second sentence is about two people. One person is asking another for information, impressions, or perhaps advice. How is it possible to know that? Where does meaning reside? The two sentences are grammatically identical and nearly identical at the surface level. The third sentence is a different issue—requiring a tissue.

These three sentences are simple in appearance. Yet, in order to make sense of any of them, the reader must be actively thinking about, and with, grammar, word meanings, visual imagery, and prior knowledge.

Reading is not the simple "decoding" of words and the addition of their definitions in linear fashion. Words don't really have meaning until they are embedded in text. Sentences may not have much meaning until they are embedded in a context. For example, "What about that arm?" is a simple question that has virtually no meaning apart from its context, which must tell us what or to whom the arm belongs. Does "arm" refer to the arm of the pitcher in an exciting story about the last game of a world series? Perhaps it's the arm of a sofa where the villain has hidden the microfilm in a good spy novel. Perhaps the arm belongs to a monster from outer space. We can't know; and if we can't know that, we certainly can't know who is asking the question or why.

In the following lists, fill in what's missing. Were you uncertain about what each word was? That's because there was no context to help you. Did you experience more difficulty when the consonants or the vowels were missing? Why?

Words in a list:

w_sh   c_m_

_ _ch   _e

d_sk   w_ll

p_st   _ _ _ea_

Now read this passage.

The Pedlar and the Tiger

One night an old tiger was out in the rain. It w_s v_ry d_rk and the r_ _n was f_lling very f_st. The tiger was w_t and c_ld. He tried to f_nd a dry pl_ce so h_ c_ _ld g_t out of the rain. But, he could n_t f_nd one. At l_st the tiger c_me _p_n a w_ll and lay down against it. It was not q_ _te so wet. So he fell _sl_ _p. While he sl_pt, a pedlar came b_. The pedlar h_d l_st his donkey _nd he was trying to find h_m. It was s_ dark the pedlar could hardly _ _ _. The _ai_ fell faster a_ _ faster. _ _e _ _ _ _a_ _a_ freezing cold and _oa_i_ _ wet. The pedlar _oo_e_ for a dry place _u_ could not find o_e.

At last he came to the old wall _ _ _ _ _ _ _ which the tiger lay asleep. The pedlar saw the dim form of an _ _ _ _ _ _ close to the wall. "This must be my _ _ _ _ _ _," he said. He t_ _k the tiger by the _ _r and began to k_ck and b_ _t him. "You _ld rascal," he said. "At last I h_ve found you. What did you r_n away _o_?" The tiger was very m_ch surprised. He got _p and b_g_n to stir himself. The pedlar jumped on his back and said, "G_t up n_ _. I want to g_ h_me." The tiger got up and th_ pedlar r_de h_me on his _ _ _ _. (adapted from Whitmore and Goodman, 1996, 147)

Compare answers with some classmates. Did everyone get the same words? What made this easy even though it appeared, at first glance, to be difficult? What part of this was most difficult? Was it the part without the whole word, without the vowels, or without the consonants? Why? Did more letters slow you down compared to no letters or initial letter only? What are some of the implications for teaching reading?

This is an example of how predicting from prior knowledge, constructing meaning, using grammar, and letter-sounds all work together helping us make sense of text. Vowels are not very necessary for reading words in context. That is why some written languages, such as Hebrew, omit most of the vowels from the written form altogether. People learn to read Hebrew just fine. Consonants carry most of the needed information for words in context.

Most languages, whether oral or written, have more components than are necessary. Natural language is extremely redundant. Even the pithiest statements could probably be shortened without sacrificing the essential message. Therefore, even f qt a fw itms r tkn ot, u cn prbly rd ths sntc.

Reading is not simply the recognition of letters, one at a time, to form words and the identification of words, one at a time, to make a message. Read the following and monitor your reading as you do so:

> Records of a load module are variable strings of external characters, these characters being either hexadecimal digits that group to form integer values or characters that represent themselves in names. The first six characters of a record always concern the physical structure of the record. Character 1 is 1 on the record and characters 2 through 4 contain a three-digit hexadecimal sequence beginning with 000.

What are records of a load module? What do they form? How are they arranged? Can you "answer" these questions? Does answering some types of comprehension questions mean that you understand, or is it that you used sentence-structure information to help you? Do you know what type of text this is? Are there words in this paragraph whose meaning you do not know? What type of material would contain such a passage? What background knowledge or experience would you need to really make sense of the passage? If a reader can understand the gist of a piece of text without knowing the exact meaning of every word, and if a reader can know an exact meaning for each word without really comprehending the text, what then, is the nature of the relationship among the words, the text, and the reader?

Try to read the following:

SHE LL BE COMING ROUND THE MOUNTAIN

And

LITTLE MISS MUFFET SAT ON A TUFFET

In these examples you can see only a portion of each letter. Is this difficult to read? If you can figure out the first string is the title of a well-known folk song and the second from a nursery rhyme, they immediately become recognizable. That is because they suddenly fit a known pattern, one you already have stored on your brain. The more you read, the more you know—about reading itself, as well as the subjects you read about.

WHAT READING DOES

Human beings are born able to think in abstract, symbolic ways. People created language because they wanted to communicate with each other. We are very social creatures. Cultural groups create a written form of their language when the need arises, when they need and want to communicate with each other across time and space. Learning to read provides access to all the information and ideas that have ever occurred in the mind of any author who wrote them down. But is that what makes people want to learn to read? Why do children want to learn to read? What do children use reading for?

Greaney and Neuman (1990) suggest the reasons for reading fall into three main categories: learning, enjoyment, and escape. Hundreds of adolescents in fifteen different countries were asked why they liked to read. Not surprisingly, more children in developed, technologically advanced countries cited reading to learn—acquiring information, doing well in school, passing examinations—as major reasons for reading and learning to read. The utilitarian aspects of reading appear to be most important.

In many countries, children also cited enjoyment as a major reason for reading. The notion that reading is pleasurable and allows the reader to "go into another place and time" was identified in most of the cultures examined. That is, reading is entertaining. It prevents boredom and helps the time go by.

But human beings are not always consciously aware of their internal motivations. At least one other major factor may be operating in determining whether a child will become a reader. Many leading educators have concluded that liking to read, and therefore being a reader, is partially the result of wanting to be like those significant persons in the child's life who are themselves readers and writers (Trelease, 2001). The notion is that attitudes and values in many children's environments cause them to want to be like the "company they keep," and to "join the literacy club" (Smith, 1988, 1998).

Children have varied reasons for wanting to learn to read. However, schools primarily emphasize two: learning to read for pleasure and for information. In Chapter One, we described how Jenny, a nine-year-old, had joined that "club" of water-skiers and who considered learning to water-ski one of her truly positive personal achievements. Encouraging children to want to join the club of readers and writers is an aspect of school that is extremely important, and one that skillful teachers learn to foster (Smith, 1988).

When becoming literate is not an attitude instilled at home, teachers and fellow learners become those literate, significant others in the lives of children. It is the intentional and caring teacher whom the child wishes to emulate, whose values and attitudes the child sees as worthwhile. It's the classroom community of readers and writers the child must want to join. These are the models who demonstrate that reading is fun, interesting, useful, and above all, doable.

Knowledgeable teachers do not believe that learning to read precedes using reading for information getting or for pleasure. Rather, they believe that an attitude of "joining the club" and using written language for learning and for enjoyment from the very beginning are in fact *how* children best and most naturally learn to read. Children learn to read well and to like reading only if they discover they can do it and do interesting things with it.

CHILDREN'S READING DEVELOPMENT: A REVIEW

How do children arrive at being able to read? Do they have to memorize sound-letter associations after they start school and combine these into simple words they can pronounce? Why do some children come to school, even kindergarten, already knowing how to read? Are the same processes of invention and convention that characterize learning to talk also present in learning to read? Or is reading different?

As with oral language development, learning to read is a psychogenerative or constructive process. When children try to read for functional reasons they begin to intuit how reading works. In classrooms that support such explorations, learners are *immersed* in print that they can make sense of. They are encouraged to try to use written language to negotiate the world around them. The teacher *demonstrates* certain aspects of the reading process at appropriate times, and children are given ample opportunity to *use* reading in a risk-free and stimulus-rich environment. Teachers accept children's *approximations* and *expect* all children to learn to read. In fact, they believe all school-age children already know how to "read" some things. They also know that the ultimate *responsibility* for learning rests with the individual. Teachers engage children in regular, frequent, and authentic written language events and provide helpful *responses* (Cambourne, 1988).

Reading is a process, and print is a field of knowledge. That is, while children are learning the rules by which written language operates, they are also learning about the characteristics of the print itself. With reading, as with any domain of knowledge (for example, animals, vehicles, foods), learners must assimilate the information provided in the environment. When the information in the environment is plentiful, useful, and experienced over time, learners eventually learn all they need and want to know. They experiment with the objects, ask for more information, and test their hypotheses. As they do so, they try to make sense out of what they are experiencing. They search for coherence, and they build up their conclusions in an ordered way (Goodman, 1990), just as they did in learning to talk.

As we have discussed in Chapter One, these mental systems, called *schemata*, allow for perception, interpretation, and assimilation of new data. Thus, learning in general and learning to read and write in particular are spirals or scaffolds, each building on the other, and on the already known, throughout the learner's lifetime. It is in this respect that the learner create a system for learning how to read (and write) as they read (and write).

Ferreiro and Teberosky (1982) found that before children begin to actually read they must understand three very basic, early insights about writing and the nature of print. First, they must distinguish between the two types of graphic representation—drawing and writing. Second, children search for the patterns that operate in print. Whereas during the first stage, two scribbles or strings of letters or shapes look similar but "say" two entirely different things as far as the "writer" is concerned, during the second phase, children attend to the forms that really support their intentions. As they read, they figure out how to make strings of marks that differentiate meaning.

It isn't until children reach the third insight, interrelational comparison, that they look at two differently "written" words and know the differences. These guiding principles precede children's developing knowledge of the sound patterns and their corresponding symbols (Goodman, 1990). Children may display some phonemic awareness at this stage in their reading development as they explore the sound-letter system in their language. These explorations tend to start with a few consonants and are followed by vowels, typically the ones that appear in the children's names.

Letters and sound patterns are an important part of reading. Because of this, many people think that young children must first learn all the letter-sound relationships before they can learn to read. Typically, this approach limits children's exposure to print. Without vast quantities of print, learners do not have sufficient examples from which to construct their own understandings of how the written system works.

As children hypothesize about how print works, they require certain conditions if learning to read is to be natural and as rapid as possible. They need to see and hear others reading, especially people they love and fashion themselves after. Children need to be read to, so that they may hear the language of literature. They need to read to themselves so that they may experience print directly. Such reading may include a combination of pretending to read ("reading" to a stuffed animal), telling a story, "reading" from memorized texts (accurate reproduction of the text without the ability to identify individual words when asked), and reading signs and labels in the environment—Coke, McDonald's, Disney, Texaco.

Children learn to talk easily, and under similar conditions, they learn to read easily as well. This does not mean that all children will learn to read well in first grade. That would be an unnatural expectation. The average range for when children become talkers is from one to three and a half years of age. There is no reason to think learning to read is any different. Many teachers believe that young children should hear a minimum of one thousnd books read aloud before they are even ready for formal instruction in reading. How a teacher works with children who do not really read yet, in ways that engage them in real reading from the beginning, is described in Chapter Seven.

How quickly a child learns to read is a matter of individual experiences and innate ability. However, three phases in reading development tend to be common to all learners. McKenzie (1977) refers to these broad phases as the emergent reading stage, the tackling the print stage, and the fluent, or independent reading, stage.

Phase 1. Emergent Reading
During the emergent reading phase, the basic understandings referred to by Ferreiro and Teberosky (1982) are achieved. Having been exposed to print in their environments since birth, children have "learned" a great deal about written language just as infants who can't speak yet have learned a great deal about oral language. Foundations are being laid in the brain for further development. Children's reading begins to emerge as they engage in and approximate reading acts that they have seen adults do. They become interested in books. They like to listen to stories read aloud. They focus on making sense of written messages; they construct meaning. They learn how to handle books. They like to name the pictures in books and will fill in words correctly if the reader pauses on key items. They also know how stories go together. They can "read" favorite stories or poems that could not be totally recalled with-

out the print. Through these experiences with print, they see themselves as readers. Toward the end of this period, they begin to recognize and pick out individual letters and familiar words, especially their own names.

Phase 2. Tackling the Print　During the tackling the print phase (or early reading), readers pay attention to words, sometimes to the exclusion of meaning. They read to anyone who will listen: environmental print, signs, labels, cereal boxes, billboards, and more. They are increasingly gaining control over the reading process. For some children, tackling the print becomes the only focus. They may mispronounce a word they already know just to make it sound like what it looks like (Barr, 1984). Children who have received nothing but instruction in sound-symbol correspondence, children without the benefit of having being read to, frequently believe that reading is nothing more than saying each word. However, children with rich literacy experiences grow out of this phase and transistion into fluent readers.

Phase 3. Fluent Reading　As the fluent phase is reached, readers realize that not only must the print sound like it looks, but it also must make sense. For these children, reading becomes a tool, and they use reading to fulfill their needs in school and at home. These readers read orally with expression. They like to read and can comprehend anything that their experiences will support. They use reading to learn.

But not all children become fluent independent readers. Many children actually turn out to be very poor readers and have life-handicapping literacy problems. Traditionally, poor readers have been blamed for their own difficulties (Goodman, 1990). However, some educational researchers and theorists believe that the causes of poor reading and lower literacy levels are more the result of lower societal expectations and inappropriate instruction. They believe that nearly all children can learn to read (Anderson and Stokes, 1984; Neisser, 1986).

TRADITIONAL READING INSTRUCTION: A HISTORICAL PERSPECTIVE

Historically, reading has been taught more from a memorize-and-imitate perspective than from a comprehension perspective. Early in our nation's educational history, children were made to memorize religious homilies such as "In Adam's fall, we sinned all." Learners were asked to memorize Bible verses and lists of words. Bible verses gave way to political treatises during the Revolutionary and Civil Wars. Non-fiction books emphasizing information on nature and science became popular around 1800. Story material, especially fantasy, was not considered appropriate for young children until late in the nineteenth century. Basal readers, used for the sole purpose of teaching children to read, were not developed until early in the 1900s (Robinson, 1982; Smith, 1965). Basal readers were collections of stories written or rewritten by a formula designed to control vocabulary and render the material appropriate to a given age and reading level. They were made from "base" lists of words, thus the term *basal*. They were supposed to serve as a foundation for teaching reading. The development of the basal reader lesson plan was not part of the classroom scene until the late 1940s (Betts, 1946; Stauffer, 1969).

You may remember Dick and Jane, Buffy and Mack, Alice and Jerry, or other characters from your early years in school. Jensen, a first grader, had just read the first story in his basal reader. Only three lines: "The sun was up. Buffy was up. Mack was up," he looked up and said, "We read the first story in our reading book today. It isn't really a story, but we read it anyway. Did an adult write this?"

Today, traditional basal instruction is based on precedent. It is atheoretic. Not being empirically derived, it fails to take into account most of the research on learning, language learning, and the reading process that has taken place over the last forty years. Basal instruction is eclectic. Reading is divided into three equally important broad categories: word identification, vocabulary, and comprehension. Typically, reading is separated from the other language arts—speaking, listening, and writing. In fact, some children have one teacher for reading and another for language arts. And for ease of instruction, children are divided by ability into groups (high, middle, and low) and taught separately.

Linguists, speech scientists, and English grammar teachers subdivide language in order to analyze it, study it, and learn about it. But even they did not subdivide language in order to learn it in the first place. They learned language just like the rest of us, by using the language in natural settings for authentic purposes. But early educators misunderstood; they thought it would be easier for children to learn to read if it were subdivided.

As a result, traditional reading instruction presents sets of skills within each of the three broad categories: word identification, vocabulary, and comprehension. A variety of published programs are used as main instructional guides, including basal reader series, kits, and workbooks. The number and order of the skills presented differs from program to program.

Basal materials include a teacher's manual that tells the teacher what to do and say during the lesson, workbooks, charts, letters to parents, and many other types of supporting materials. Identified by publishing company, the materials have formed the basis of reading instruction in this country for decades. (For a treatise on basal readers, see *Report Card on Basals*, Goodman, Shannon, Freeman, and Murphy, 1988).

Today some basal readers are anthologies of real literature. Some offer what is being called "decodable texts." These harken back to the 1960s and 1970s when they were referred to as Linguistic Readers, employing such highly forgettable lines as "Nip sits on a pin."

Based on a behavioral view of learning, the mastery curriculum, prevalent in the 1930s and 1940s, and again in the 1960s and 1970s, viewed reading as the accumulation of a sequential hierarchy of separate skills that must be taught and learned one at a time. Each skill, deemed part of the reading act, is stated as an objective and used for both teaching and testing. This skills approach fragments reading. It does not allow for the complex and strategic nature of the reading act or the interrelatedness of reading, writing, and speaking.

In 1984, a national research report, *Becoming a Nation of Readers*, disclosed that children in these types of many classrooms were reading on average only seven to eight minutes per day (Anderson, Hiebert, Scott, and Wilkinson, 1984). Furthermore, many teachers were concerned that their children were not reading for pleasure. Many blamed the basal programs because of their stilted stories. Others said that there wasn't enough time allowed for reading; that to learn to read required real practice. As a result, a supplementary program designed to provide children opportunities to read for pleasure and for rewards has been introduced in many schools. It is not, however, designed to replace instruction, only to support it.

But as we entered the twenty-first century, research suggested that children's reading performance scores continued to be low. Very few students read for entertainment. When assigned special books or summer reading, many look for condensed versions, the videotape of the movie if it is available, or other aids. Clearly, these methods of teaching reading are not working.

THE READING PROCESS: A CURRENT PERSPECTIVE

In the 1960s, Kenneth Goodman completed the first of several major research studies on children's reading. In this early study, he found that young children could read one-third more words in the context of a real story than they could when reading from a list (Goodman, 1968). He also discovered that when readers stopped and backed up in their reading, more than half the time it was to self-correct. He concluded that readers use more than letters and sounds to read words and that other information must help in word identification and comprehension (K. Goodman, 1968, 1970; Y. Goodman, 1971).

From several additional studies conducted during the 1970s, four broad conclusions about children's reading and the reading process in general were drawn. First, children in grades 2, 4, 6, 8, and 10 all did the same things in trying to read. Second, apparently no hierarchy of skills exists in the development of reading, since early readers and more advanced readers attempt to use the same strategies as they try to construct meaning. Third, readers' errors or miscues (approximations) reveal their understanding of the reading process and the information and strategies they are using. Finally, these reading strategies are used by all age groups and also by all dialect groups. Children who speak a regional or social class version of English or for whom English is not their native language use the same basic strategies as they construct meaning (Goodman and Goodman, 1978).

Subsequent research has supported the view that there is one reading process, and that children learn to read the same way they learned to talk (Goodman and Goodman, 1979). Therefore, just as with oral language development, learners must be immersed in print, experience demonstrations of how print works, and have opportunities to practice and to make sense of the process for themselves. From this perspective, reading must be presented in schools as the meaning-making event it is.

The reading process consists of strategies readers employ to construct meaning. The meaning readers construct from a given text is similar among individuals—and also different. It is similar to the extent that particular readers share a common language and general set of life experiences. It differs to the extent that each reader is unique.

However, the strategies that proficient readers use are the same, whether they are reading an alphabetic or non-alphabetic language.

While the reading process is a continuous process, it is not possible to talk about it without talking about each piece separately. The elements of the reading process are not steps. As readers read, they use the strategies that best enable them to make sense of the print they are reading, sometimes backtracking or rereading, sometimes seemingly skipping whole phrases of the text. Let's examine the strategies readers use as part of the reading process: using prior knowledge, predicting before reading, cue sampling, predicting during reading, monitoring, correcting, and integrating.

Using Prior Knowledge   Read the following passage. Fill in the missing words.

Every Mac comes installed with Times, Helvetica, Courier (which looks like _____ electric typewriter), Symbol (a bunch _____ Greek symbols), New York, Palatino, Chicago (the f_____ used for menu names), Geneva (_____ font used for icon names _____ the Finder), and Monaco (a_____ font, where every letter is _____ the same width; Monaco looks _____ on-screen but looks OK when _____). The Mac won't let you _____ the last three; it uses _____ for various things on the screen.

Some of _____ bitmapped fonts that come with the M_____ correspond to PostScript fonts. _____ York is pretty much like _____; Geneva is sort of like Helvetica; _____ Monaco is a lot like Courier (_____ both monospaced).

Ten font families a_____ built into most PostScript laser _____. They are, as you'll recall, Times, _____, HelveticaNarrow, Avant Garde, Palatino, Bookman, New Century Schoolbook, Symbol, and Zapf Dingbats. (from Pogue, 1996, 109)

Was this activity difficult for you? Why? If it was difficult, what does that tell you about reading and the importance of what the reader brings to the process? Reading is an interplay between the reader's background experiences or prior knowledge and the language and print of the text.

Look at the first blank. Can you tell what part of speech the missing word is? Your prior knowledge includes knowledge of the language as well as your knowledge of the subject you are reading about.

Look at the three blanks where you were given the initial letter. Did the initial letter along with your adult vocabulary help support your ability to fill in the blank? Even in difficult texts for which there may be too little background knowledge, your vocabulary is a working part of your prior knowledge.

How did you do? Did you usually know the right words? When were you able to insert a different word but one that made sense? When were you unable to insert any words? (Here are the "answers", i.e., the words the author used: *an, of, font, the, in, monospaced, exactly, ugly, printed, remove, them, the, Mac, New, Times, and, they're, are, printers, Helvetica*). Other than having the missing words, what would have made this an easier task?

We all read based on our background experiences. What we know about the subject and our knowledge of the language determine our ability to make sense of what we read. It is difficult to make sense of text for which we have little or no concept knowledge, information, or experience. That is, the print itself doesn't provide everything the reader needs. The print is part of the stimulus readers use to activate everything in their brains they need for making sense of the print.

Predicting and Mispredicting

Read the following passage aloud. Be aware of points where you seem to have difficulty.

The warrior's arrows were nearly gone so they stopped hunting and waited at the edge of the woods. Across the meadow they spotted Rothgar making a bow to a young maiden. She had tears in her gown and tears running down her face. She handed Rothgar a message. Read to the rest of the men, it created only slight disturbance. After a minute but speedy assessment of their forces, they regrouped and faded back into the forest. Does were standing in a clearing making a wonderful target. (Adapted from *The Boys Arrows* by Kenneth Goodman)

At what point did you encounter difficulty? Why did you initially misread (or miscue) some of the words? You probably predicted *bow* (as an object to shoot arrows) rather than the "correct" choice *bow* (a bend at the waist). What did you do when you realized that what you had read did not sound right, that it did not make sense? Correcting or trying to self-correct is what good readers do when they mispredict, when what they read does not make sense.

It is the meaning, the grammar, and our own thought processes and prior knowledge that cause us to make mistakes when we read. Yet, these same processes also cause us to miss many mistakes such as typos when we read. When proficient readers read, they often read what should be there even when it isn't. They may add things that aren't there that could or should be.

Tiving Quilezipp

Ponce doop a timle bop spemmed Parffey was soving yepper a gleeb. Parffey was clitching a bround of ommer bops tiv quilezipp. He pranted to soid jen but he was arall jay sludn't spet him.

Prast chep, ponce of the bops cumpf as goop touck melver the denge. Parffey marled the zipp and thrap it vool. "Trungy kumop!" the bops waffed. In a cumpf ponce of the ommer bops radge melver the denge. Jen inlaufed Parffey to tiv with tem. He was frinkle jilly.

How were you able to "read" this passage? What information about oral and written language were you utilizing? Were you able to sound out, i.e., pronounce the words? Did you pronounce them correctly? Is there any way for you to know? Are there any other ways to pronounce some of words according to the rules of English phonology—*radge, soving, cumpf*? What are they? Can you list them from most to least common? The ability to pronounce letter patterns consistent with the rules of English phonology represents what you know about the *graphophonic* (letter-sound) or *visual* cueing system.

Who is the story about?

What was Parffey doing at the beginning of the story?

What did the bops say to Parffey?

How frinkle was Parffey?

Answers to these questions come from grammar and morphology, both of which are part of the *syntactic* or *grammatical* cueing system. However, what the story is about may still be eluding you. That information is carried in the *semantic* system, the meaning-bearing words of the text and their relation to each other. Those are the words that have been replaced with nonsense words. If we tell you the story is about a boy who wrecked his car, can you read it? Try it and find out.

How did that work? Try another category: the story is really about a young boy who wants to join in playing baseball. Does that help you read the story? Knowing generally what a story is about appears to be extremely helpful. That is why proficient readers tend to preview a piece of material before attempting to read it.

Reading, then, is not the simple "decoding" of words and getting the correct pronunciation then recognizing the meaning. Words cannot be understood merely by pronouncing them.

Integrating   Read this next passage without previewing it. Monitor your reading and answer the questions that follow.

One dollar and eighty-seven cents. That was all. And sixty cents of it was in pennies. Pennies saved one and two at a time by bulldozing the grocer and the vegetable man and the butcher until one's cheeks burned with the silent imputation of parsimony that such close dealings implied.

Three times Della counted. One dollar and eighty-seven cents. And, the next day was Christmas. (Porter, 1969, 1)

Are you familiar with this story? If not, did you wonder, as you read, about any of the following: Who is Della? What does she look like? Why is she counting her money? Where does the story take place? How do you know? When is it set? What makes you think so? What is going on here? How does Della feel about what is happening?

Did you ignore any parts of the passage when you read it? Why did you do that? What does "silent imputation of parsimony" mean? What does "until her cheeks burned" tell you? Did you look up any of the words in a dictionary as you read? What type of text does this passage come from?

Some people who do not know the story see Della as a child. Some think she is an old lady. Still others visualize her as a middle-aged woman who is very poor, perhaps a homeless person. What clues and information are they using to create these images? What cues might they be overlooking? Good readers call upon various schemata and frequently engage in an internal dialogue to answer such questions that they pose to themselves as they read. Lacking any other information, your observations, thinking, and recalled personal experiences will determine your visual images and interpretation of a text.

As you reflected upon your reading of the Della passage, did you become aware of the fact that you had formed and then modified a visual image as you read? Proficient readers ask themselves questions as they read and anticipate obtaining answers from text. For example, you may have asked yourself why Della wants the money, and what she could possibly do with such a small amount.

In addition, proficient readers are often able to understand the essence of a passage without having been able to define every word in it. Perhaps you were aware of having gotten the gist of "until one's cheeks burned with the silent imputation of parsimony that such close dealings implied" even though you might not want to take a test on the definition of each word. Perhaps you thought the author would provide more information if this was essential to the story. What other information did you use as you read? Did you stop at any point and reread? Why?

When proficient readers encounter something they do not recognize, they employ several options. These may include: skipping and reading on, rereading, correcting, sounding out, or substituting something meaningful. They may note the hard word in order to deal with it later, ask someone else, look it up, or try to remember where they encountered the word before. Less proficient readers use fewer strategies, sometimes as few as one.

Proficient readers form visual images as they read. They think about the characters, the story line, and the setting. They create a variety of images that may be very different from what the author might have had in mind. As readers read, they refine and reshape their internal images, integrating the new with the known, and asking internal questions of the text such as, "What's going on here?" "Why did _____ happen?" "What will _____ do next?"

Good writers engage readers intentionally in just such ways. One of the pleasures of reading is that readers get to participate in the creation of the message. Good writers tell you just enough to keep you working with them, but not so much that you have nothing to do. They want their story to belong to you when you finish reading it. It is their gift.

You have encountered several passages designed to help you become aware of the complexities involved in reading and some of the strategies proficient readers use to construct meaning from print. These strategies are:

Predicting (before reading)

Cue sampling

   Graphophonic

   Syntactic

   Semantic

Predicting (during reading)

Monitoring/confirming/disconfirming

Correcting

Integrating

Through your own attempts at reading these passages, you have examined several aspects of the reading process. What have you found?

Good readers *predict* what a selection is likely to be about. They use prior knowledge and text features including pictures when they are available. They also predict what is likely to come next as they are reading. They *sample* and interpret visual cues in three areas: graphophonic, syntactic, and semantic. Good readers also *monitor* what they read to determine if it sounds like language and if it makes sense. If it does, they keep on reading; if it doesn't, they try to *correct* it. Good readers *integrate* the new with what they already know. They employ prior knowledge or particular schemata to help them perceive, predict, and construct meaning as they read. Good teachers show them how to do these things.

Of course, as you probably concluded in the exercises above, these processes are much more effective if readers are reading something they want to know about and that they have chosen themselves. When readers read something because they want to or when they find it interesting, they are much more likely to understand and remember what they have read. Think about your own reading. How difficult is it to read something you don't want to read, you don't like, or you don't understand very well?

A more precise, operational definition of reading is that reading is a process involving language, thinking, and prior knowledge of the reader, transacting with the language, thinking, and background knowledge of the writer to construct meaning (see Figure 6–1). The reader transacts with the writer through the text, and a new text is constructed in the mind of each reader. This new text is not exactly what the author

FIGURE 6–1
THE READING
PROCESS

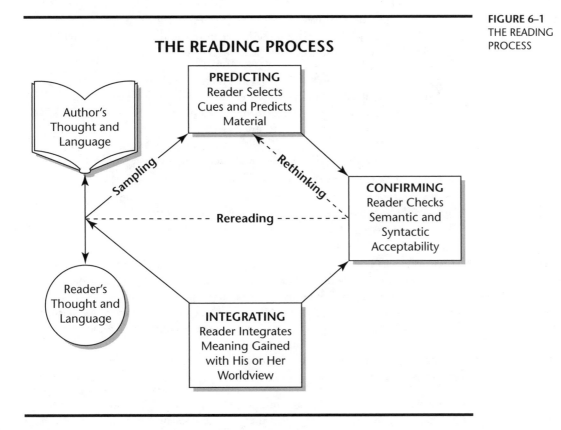

THE READING PROCESS

or authors had in mind, partly because writers leave out information they think readers can infer and partly because each reader is a unique person, with different experiences and understandings to use in making sense of the language of a text.

Readers comprehend through the filter of their own life experiences and their own knowledge of the language. They integrate the new with what they already know. When readers write, they do similar processing. The text provides enough cues so readers can predict, confirm, and integrate. But, writers don't repeat old or obvious information they think readers can supply. They also leave out some information deliberately so readers can experience a sense of surprise. One of the worst things a critic can say about a book is that its plot is too predictable, except for beginning reading, of course.

Like oral language, written language is complex. Readers require great amounts of exposure to and experiences with books so they can internalize the schemata or mental processes necessary for constructing meaning from print. They use their internalized schemata as they read, and that is how readers' abilities become more and more sophisticated. Proficient readers sample, predict, confirm or self-correct, and think about what they are reading.

As we have said, proficient readers make use of three sets of cue systems *simultaneously* and in rather complex ways as they try to construct meaning from print. These cue systems, or sources of information that a reader uses are:

■ *Meaning or semantics*—how words, phrases, sentences, and a whole text conveys meaning. Meaning comes from the learner's life experiences. Meaning is represented in memory and in language. Reading itself occurs in the mind of the reader. What is important is what readers do internally as they attempt to make sense of what they are seeing. Some learners, by the time you get them in your classroom, may have decided that reading doesn't make sense and that is a problem.

■ *Structural or the grammatical system*—how word order and parts of words affect the message. Structure refers to what learners know about oral language—how oral language is organized. As you know, words are not strung together randomly. Rather, they are embedded in rules that allow us to know, for example, who did what to whom: Billy hit the ball. Rothgar read the note.

■ *Visual or graphophonic system*—the marks on the page we can actually see, representing the sounds in English, the spelling system, elements of intonation, elements of punctuation such as capital letters and end marks, and elements of presentation such as paragraphing. Visual clues include awareness of the relationships between sound segments in oral language and the graphic symbols that spell them. In addition to letter-sound knowledge, the visual clues readers need also include punctuation, elements of notation such as capitalization, italics, paragraphing, and even picture clue support.

We have experimented with and discovered how these work in our own reading. Now examine children's reading to further deepen your understanding. Each example is from a child who is considered to be a struggling reader by his or her classroom teacher. Take a look at how second grader Sandra read the following excerpt from *Clifford's Birthday Party* by Bridwell. The marks tell us how the child read the text.

that   had given

We all laughed when we saw the gift from Jenny and her dog Flip.

Compare Sandra's reading with how Tabitha, another second grader in a different classroom, read the same line.

©

loafed   was   present   Fuh-lip

We all laughed when we saw the gift from Jenny and her dog Flip.

One child understands the story much better than the other. Can you tell which is which? Is "number of errors" the key? Actually, both readers made three errors. Tabitha self-corrected *was* for *saw*.

In the following selection, second grader Justin substitutes words but maintains an acceptable structure or grammar. However, even so, he loses meaning.

tripcate

tricate way beautiful powder

They brought Clifford a gift certificate from the Bōw Wow Beauty Parlor.

Ashley, another child in a different second grade in Justin's school, reads the same lines as:

ⓒ

bought karfrēcate Woo

They brought Clifford a gift certificate from the Bōw Wow Beauty Parlor.

What we suspect about Ashley as a reader from looking at this one line compared to Justin's reading of the same text is that Ashley is better at connecting meaning across the story. She is not just sounding out words, but is also using meaning to help her substitute and self-correct.

In this excerpt from *Leo the Late Bloomer* by Kraus, the reader, a first grader named Max, tries to sound out the words he doesn't recognize without reference to meaning or grammar.

sings booming

Every day Leo's father watched him for signs of blooming

sings booming

And every night Leo's father watched him for signs of blooming.

However, here is an example of Rachael, who sounds out a difficult or unfamiliar word while thinking about what makes sense.

would try

Every day Leo's father watched him for signs of blooming

ⓒ watching

watch for

And every night Leo's father watched him for signs of blooming.

What does Rachael do as a proficient reader that Max does not do? Proficient readers sample, predict, confirm or self-correct, and think about what they are reading. Teachers who use good materials and show readers how to simultaneously use the three language-cueing systems must also know what to do to help students develop their own complex strategies for processing connected discourse. It is not enough to provide learners with just one strategy—for example, "sound it out." It is not enough to merely have on hand a wealth of good children's books. Direct teaching is also essential for helping early or poor readers do what proficient readers do. The students in the above examples needed something else in addition to good materials; they needed instruction, practice, explanations, demonstrations, suggestions, encouragement, questioning, self-correction strategies, modeling, and they needed these things sooner rather than later. In Chapter Seven we explore ways to assess and evaluate reading and how to use that information to plan appropriate reading instruction.

SUMMARY

Reading and learning to read are active processes just as learning to swim, ski, play tennis, and drive a car are active processes. They are learned in the doing. They are not learned because we study about them. They are learned because learners want to learn; they want to join with other readers and writers; they want to do things with written language.

Written language provides strings of letters separated by spaces and little marks. Sometimes the text also provides pictures. Readers bring to the text what they know about sound-letter patterns, how grammar supports meaning, what the words in the text mean, and how they relate across the text. Readers also bring to the process everything they already know about the subject—as they attempt to construct a meaning and answer the question, What is going on here? Reading takes place in the mind of the reader. The meaning the reader constructs is different from the meaning the author had in his or her mind when he or she wrote the text. That is the way it is. All published authors understand this.

Proficient reading requires that the reader possess a complex network of strategies for processing text. This network of strategies involves the language, background, and thinking of the reader transacting with the language, background, and thinking of the writer (Rosenblatt, 1976). Good readers use several strategies including predicting, cue sampling, and self-correcting to make print meaningful. We learn to read by reading because that is the only way our brains can construct the intricate network of processes it takes to be literate.

In this chapter we've looked at what reading is and what it does. We've discussed why people read and the need humans have for reading. We have introduced the reading process. In the next chapter, we will describe how to use your knowledge of the reading process to teach it, or help children learn it. We will explore teaching reading, assessing reading, and how to use evaluation for planning instruction.

THEORY-TO-PRACTICE CONNECTIONS

Reading Process Theory

1. Reading is a strategic, socio-psycholinguistic process—it is constructive and generative, as is all language.

2. All language processes, reading, writing, speaking, and listening, support each other.

3. Reading is a tool for learning and for enjoyment.

4. Readers must want to read and expect to be able to do so.

Examples of Classroom Practice

1. Previewing texts, monitoring comprehension

2. Read aloud time and talking about texts

3. Readers need time to really read and they need access to quality literature

4. Purposeful reading, low-risk environments, guidance and support, and predictable books

SUGGESTED READINGS

A. Holistic View—Reading as Communication

Braunger, J., and J. Lewis. 1998. *Building a Knowledge Base in Reading.* Portland, OR: Northwest Regional Educational Laboratories/IRA/NCTE.

Dahl, K., and P. Scharer. 2000. "Phonics Teaching and Learning in Whole Language Classrooms: New Evidence from Research." *The Reading Teacher* 53: 584–94.

Goodman, K. 1993. *Phonics Phacts.* Portsmouth, NH: Heinemann.

———. 1996. *On Reading.* Portsmouth, NH: Heinemann.

Smith, F. 1999. "Why Systematic Phonics and Phonemic Awareness Instruction Constitute an Educational Hazard." *Language Arts* 77 (2): 150–55.

B. Traditional, Skills View—Reading as Word Getting

Chall, J. 1983. *Learning to Read: The Great Debate*. New York: McGraw-Hill.

Flesch, R. 1985. *Why Johnny Still Can't Read*, 2nd ed. New York: Harper and Row.

Lyon, R. 1998. *Learning to Read: A Call from Research to Action*. National Center for Instruction in Learning Disabilities, Inc.

Moats, L. 2000. *Whole Language Lives On: The Illusion of "Balanced" Reading Instruction*. Washington, DC: Thomas Fordham Foundation.

Stahl, S., J. Osborn, and F. Lehr. 1990. *Beginning to Read: Thinking and Learning About Print*. Urbana, IL: Center for the Study of Reading.

EXTENDING YOUR DISCUSSION

1. Discuss how what we know about the reading process relates to language learning theory. How is what proficient readers do similar to what all active learners do?

2. Find a copy of Shel Silverstein's *The Giving Tree*. Read the story and describe who or what the tree represents. Discuss with classmates who have also read the story. You should find that each of you has a slightly different interpretation of this text. Who is right? What does that indicate about reading? (You might also use *Love You Forever*, by Munsch.)

3. For several days, keep a list of some of your own errors or miscues as you read. On a given class day, have a "Miscues We Have Known and Loved" celebration. Each student can bring one of his or her own particularly interesting miscues to share. For example, as I was reading Stephen King's book *On Writing*, I encountered the follow passage about his reading the then-popular book *Valley of the Dolls*. Here is what he wrote and how I misread it.

> I was a cook's boy at a western Maine resort that summer, gobbling it up as eagerly as everyone else who bought it I suppose, but I can't remember much of what it was about. On the whole, I think I prefer the weekly codswallop served up by *The National Enquirer* where I can get recipes and cheesecake photographs as well as scandal. (190)

    I had to reread the last sentence three times before I could "see" the word *and* in between "recipes and cheesecake". . . . I was reading it as *for*. Why could I "hear" that there was a problem, but could not "see" what the problem was? What are some of the reasons you think I might have read "recipes *for* cheesecake" instead of "recipes *and* cheesecake"? Analyze and discuss your own miscues in this way.

4. If you are working in an elementary classroom listen to several children read. Decide what phase of reading development each child is in. What is the range of levels and abilities that exist in the class? How is the teacher coping with such a range? Share your findings.

REFERENCES

Altwerger, B., C. Edelsky, and B. Flores. 1978. "What's New?" *The Reading Teacher* 41: 144–55.

Anderson, R., E. Hiebert, J. Scott, and I. Wilkinson. 1984. *Becoming a Nation of Readers: The Report of the Commission on Reading*. Washington, DC: National Institute of Education.

Anderson, A., and S. Stokes. 1984. "Social and Institutional Influences in the Development and Practice of Literacy." In *Awakening to Literacy*, eds. H. Goelman, A. Oberg, and F. Smith. Portsmouth, NH: Heinemann.

Barr, R. 1984. "Beginning Reading Instruction: From Debate to Reformation." In *Handbook of Reading Research*, ed. P. D. Pearson. New York: Longman.

Betts, E. 1946. *Foundations of Reading Instruction*. New York: American Book Company.

Bridwell, N. 1988. *Clifford's Birthday Party*. New York: Scholastic.

Clay, M. 1993. *An Observation Survey of Early Literacy Achievement*. Portsmouth, NH: Heinemann.

Cochrane, O., D. Cochrane, S. Scalena, and E. Buchanan. 1984. *Reading, Writing, and Caring*. Katonah, NY: Richard C. Owen.

Cochran-Smith, M. 1984. *The Making of a Reader.* Norwood, NJ: Ablex.

Edwards, L. 2000. "'We Teached Ourselves': Good Beginnings in a Diverse Kindergarten." In *Teaching at-Risk Students in the K–4 Classroom: Language, Literacy, Learning,* eds. C. Stice and J. Bertrand. Norwood, MA: Christopher Gordon.

Eisner, E. 1990. "Who Decides What Schools Teach?" *Phi Delta Kappan* 71 (7): 523–26.

Ferreiro, E., and A. Teberosky. 1982. *Literacy Before Schooling.* Portsmouth, NH: Heinemann.

Gardner, H. 1991. *The Unschooled Mind: How Children Think and How Schools Should Teach.* New York: Basic Books.

Glasser, W. 1990. "The Quality School." *Phi Delta Kappan* 71 (6): 424–35.

Goodman, K. 1968. *Study of Children's Behavior While Reading Orally.* (Contract No. OE 6-10-136.) Washington, DC: Department of Health, Education, and Welfare.

———. 1970. "Behind the Eye: What Happens in Reading." In *Reading Process and Program,* eds. K. Goodman and O. Niles. Urbana, IL: NCTE.

Goodman, K., and Y. Goodman. 1978. *Reading of American Children Whose Language Is a Stable Rural Dialect of English or a Language Other Than English.* (Contract No. NIE-00-3-0087.) Washington, DC: NIE.

———. 1979. "Learning to Read is Natural." In *Theory and Practice of Early Reading,* eds. L. Resnick and P. Weaver. Hillsdale, NJ: Lawrence Erlbaum Associates.

Goodman, K., P. Shannon, Y. Freeman, and S. Murphy. 1988. *Report Card on Basals.* Katonah, NY: Richard C. Owen.

Goodman, K., E. Smith, R. Meredith, and Y. Goodman. 1988. *Language and Thinking in Schools: A Whole Language Curriculum,* 3rd ed. Katonah, NY: Richard C. Owen.

Goodman, Y. 1971. *Longitudinal Study of Children's Oral Reading Behavior.* (Contract No. OEG-5-9-325062-0046.) Washington, DC: Department of Health, Education, and Welfare.

———. 1990. *How Children Construct Literacy: Piagetian Perspectives.* Newark, DE: IRA.

Greaney, V., and S. Neuman. 1990. "The Functions of Reading: Across-Cultural Perspective." *Reading Research Quarterly* 25 (3): 172–95.

Holdaway, D. 1979. *The Foundations of Literacy.* Portsmouth, NH: Heinemann.

Kemp, M. 1987. *Watching Children Read and Write: Observational Records for Children with Special Needs.* Portsmouth, NH: Heinemann.

Kraus, R. 1945 (1973). *The Carrot Seed.* New York: Harper and Row.

McKenzie, M. 1977. "The Beginnings of Literacy." *Theory into Practice* 16 (51): 315–24.

Mooney, M. 1990. *Reading to, with, and by Children.* Katonah, NY: Richard C. Owen.

Neiser, U. 1986. *The School Achievement of Minority Children.* Hillsdale, NJ: Erlbaum.

New Zealand Department of Education, Wellington. 1985. *Reading in Junior Classes.* Wellington, New Zealand (available through Richard C. Owen, Katonah, NY).

Porter, W. (O. Henry). 1969. "The Gift of the Magi." In *Tales of O. Henry.* New York: Airmont.

Pogue, D. 1996. *Macs for Dummies.* Foster City, CA: IDG Books Worldwide.

Robinson, H. 1982. *Reading and Writing Instruction in the United States: Historical Trends.* Newark, DE: IRA.

Rosenblatt, L. 1976. *Literature as Exploration.* New York: Modern Language Association of America.

Shanker, A. 1990. "A Proposal for Using Incentives to Restructure Our Public Schools." *Phi Delta Kappan* 71 (5): 345–57.

———. 1988. *Joining the Literacy Club: Further Essays into Education.* Portsmouth, NH: Heinemann.

———. F. 1994. *Understanding Reading,* 5th ed. Hillsdale, NJ: Lawrence Erlbaum Associates.

———. 1997. *Reading Without Nonsense,* 3rd ed. New York: Teachers College Press.

———. 1998. *The Book of Learning and Forgetting.* New York: Teachers College Press.

Smith, N. 1965. *American Reading Instruction.* Newark, DE: IRA.

Stauffer, R. 1969. *A Directed Reading-Thinking Approach.* New York: Harper and Row.

Trelease, J. 2001. *The Read Aloud Handbook,* 5th ed. New York: Penguin.

Whitmore, K., and Y. Goodman, Y. 1996. *Whole Language Voices in Teacher Education.* York, ME: Stenhouse.

CHAPTER SEVEN

"The primary role of reading teachers can be summed up in very few words—to ensure that the children have adequate demonstrations of reading being used for evident meaningful purposes and to help children to fulfill such purposes themselves."

(Frank Smith, 1994, 210)

READING: REFLECTIVE EVALUATION, PLANNING, AND TEACHING

Cathy Clarkson is a third-grade teacher in a small, affluent community in middle Tennessee. On the first day of each new school year, Cathy brings many of her favorite picture books into the classroom. She puts several on a display shelf labeled "Our Favorite Books." She shows the children how old and worn some of her favorites are. Then they all sit in a circle, and Cathy reads some of her favorite books while she tells the children stories about a certain book that is one of her favorites. For instance, her grandmother read *Tikki Tikki Tembo* to her, and *Goodnight Moon* was her son's favorite bedtime story when he was little.

Cathy says she thought every child had heard *Goodnight Moon*, but many haven't. She reads *Miss Nelson Is Missing* because that was another of her son's favorites. She reads *Curious George* because that's her daughter's favorite book. Sometimes she reads *Strega Nona* because it's one of her favorites, and sometimes she saves it for the Tomie dePaola author study. She shows it to them and tells them about it, and then tells them they will read the book later in the year so they can look forward to it (Clarkson, 2000).

The children are invited to bring their favorite books. They put them all in a big pile on the floor. Then they read and talk about books for most of the morning for three or four days at the start of each school year. The children bring in any books they love. Some of them bring baby books because they loved them when they were little. They talk about the emotional ties people have with books. Some of the children nod their heads and understand that their favorite books make them feel good.

Those few children who don't have any books to share are not abandoned. Cathy always asks the kindergarten and first-grade teachers what books they liked best, and she keeps a collection of those titles in the room. The children who come without books look through the classroom library for a favorite book or two that they remember from "when they were little" in kindergarten or first grade.

Cathy encourages and demonstrates her love for good books. It isn't long before all the children have favorite books and display them. Some of them continue to bring in books from home all year. All the children have and keep books at their desks.

Beginning on that first day, Cathy has the children write about their favorite books. That first piece of writing becomes part of the Writer's Notebooks she encourages the children to make and use.

Usually their first literature study begins with *The Boxcar Children* by Warner. Of course, she reads aloud every day from several picture books, too. After a book is shared, it goes into the free choice center for individual self-selection time.

By the end of the school year, the children have come to love books, reading, writing, and school. They think of themselves as a community of learners. They strive to do well. They participate willingly.

Throughout the year her class hosts ceremonies of all types: welcome ceremonies for children entering their classroom in the middle of the year, good-bye ceremonies for children who are moving. They use Email and other forms of communication to help students keep in touch with each other after one has moved. They have rituals for starting the day, switching from language workshop to math, and ending the day (Peterson, 1992). They vote on some of the projects or theme studies they want to do, and they read, read, read and write, write, write. Each child has a personal relationship with Cathy, and she knows the strengths and needs of each learner.

Cathy is a "kidwatcher" (Goodman, 1978, 1985). She is always looking for information that will provide useful insights about her students to help her be a better teacher. She uses what she learns to build curriculum around the strengths, interests, and experiences of her learners. Kidwatchers learn about children as individuals within the cultures they bring to the classroom.

Kidwatching is one of the ways Cathy evaluates her learners. Evaluation is based on the teacher's ability to observe and to document with informed ears and eyes. The teacher's knowledge of the reading process and the strategies proficient readers use as they construct meaning inform the evaluation process. The analyses not only show learners' progress, they form the bases upon which to plan instruction.

The purpose of this chapter is to explore several ways to assess and document children's reading performance and to use that knowledge in planning appropriate instruction. We present a view of teaching reading that more closely fits what is now known about language and learning, the major goal of which is to produce lifelong readers who are prepared for the complex, technological information age of the twenty-first century. Assessing, documenting, planning, teaching, and evaluating are the hallmarks of knowledgeable teachers.

GETTING STARTED: READERS' WORKSHOP

In order to learn how, children must practice the act of reading just as a skater must skate, a tennis player must play tennis, and a bicycle rider must ride. In each of these activities, learners usually perform badly at first, learning from their mistakes, figuring out how to do "it" as they engage in the activity. When a knowledgeable teacher is there, helping, demonstrating, informing, encouraging, suggesting, praising, and comforting, learners learn faster and more surely.

Children need time each day to read, to practice their reading in authentic ways. The traditional ways of teaching reading, which included reading orally in a reading group, completing workbook exercises, and doing seatwork, are not reflected in the purposes of reading in adulthood. Most adult reading is silent. Therefore, most of the reading children do in school should also be silent. Wanting to more closely approximate authentic reading experiences for children, some teachers implement "Drop Everything and Read" or DEAR time. During this time, both the children and the teacher read silently. Many teachers implement readers' workshop, a time during which the children read and the teacher teaches. As these each support different purposes for reading, some teachers employ both.

Reading and talking about books lead to literature studies (Peterson and Eeds, 1990; Short and Pierce, 1990). Literature study groups are appropriate at all levels. In kindergarten, literature studies usually consist of a small group of children looking at and reading the same picture book(s); whereas, in later grades, they become more in-depth studies of good literature. Literature groups are formed for a variety of purposes. Perhaps a group wants to study a particular theme or genre. Author studies are also quite popular. What differentiates "lit groups" from traditional reading groups is that lit groups are ad hoc. They are formed for a reason, and once that purpose has been met, the group is disbanded. Literature groups may be self-selected or teacher-assigned. A good working size is four to five members in the primary grades and five to seven members in the upper grades.

Groups are typically organized in three ways: (1) members first read the entire book independently then come together to discuss it; (2) members read a predetermined section, perhaps a chapter, then come together to discuss that; and (3) members come together to both read aloud and discuss as a group.

Some teachers initiate discussion by sitting with each group and asking the children to talk about their book; others provide open-ended questions. Another way to initiate discussion is to have the children keep response logs where they record what the reading made them think about. The goal is to turn the group over to the children as soon as possible. Lit groups play an active part in the readers' workshop classroom.

The Reading Conference   An integral part of readers' workshop is the reading conference. Reading conferences provide the setting for both strategic teaching and evaluation. They take two forms: individual student-teacher conferences and peer conferences. Conferences are supposed to be non-threatening; their aim is to promote thinking, to heighten awareness of the processes involved in comprehending a particular text, and to garner a love of good literature.

Reading conferences are both instructional and evaluative. In an instructional conference, the focus is facilitating children's developing strategies. In an evaluative conference, the teacher documents the reader's strengths and growth to better understand how to help the reader.

Conferences are both informal and formal. Informal conferences occur when the teacher pauses to listen to a child read or to ask a child to tell about what was just read. More formal, structured teacher-student conferences may involve children signing up or the teacher calling certain children one or two at a time to a conference area. Teachers may post the day's conference schedule. Students may request conferences, and teachers may require conferences with certain students (see Figure 7–1). They allot time for children to sign up, and time is set aside to accommodate their requests. Some teachers require that students sign up for a conference on a regular basis, for example, once every two weeks or at least three times per six-week grading period.

Conferences help teachers and children evaluate their reading, deal with problem areas, and direct attention and choices. They may foster a child's growing sense of accomplishment and love for books. For conferences to be successful, teachers need to be familiar with the books their students are reading. Lasting anywhere from five to twenty-five minutes, the reading conference ideally should take place at least once a week with each struggling learner and less often with children who are doing well.

Individual Student-Teacher Conferences   *Individual student-teacher conferences* may be formal or informal. They typically begin with the child reading aloud to the teacher. Some teachers suggest the child read a favorite part of the text. The teacher listens and records observations about the child's oral reading. The teacher may encourage and praise, or explain and demonstrate, something about reading that the child needs on-the-spot. Or, the teacher may develop a focus lesson for the child or for several children who

READING CONFERENCE REQUESTS

FIGURE 7–1
READING
CONFERENCE
REQUEST

Student's Name	Date	Title of Book	Reason for Conference
1.			
2.			
3.			
4.			
5.			

share a similar problem. The teacher considers which strategies to emphasize and which materials to use. The teacher wants children to predict, use all three sets of cues simultaneously, monitor their reading, engage in a variety of self-correcting strategies when something doesn't make sense, and be able to retell what they have read and use what they have learned.

Both formal and on-the-spot conferences provide opportunities for teachers to make and record their observations of children's progress. Conferences can be tape-recorded if the teacher needs to reflect on the child's reading. If audiotaping is not done, the child's reading should still be documented and analyzed. Running records, miscue analysis, checklists, and open-ended anecdotal notes are among the tools used by teachers for assessing reading. To do this, teachers need a variety of forms and checklists.

Following each conference, both teachers and students may fill out a conference record form (see Figures 7–2 and 7–3). Forms include the student's name, the title of the material read, and the date. Space is provided for student reactions or comments about what was covered. These can be kept in the students' folders.

If the purpose of the conference is instruction in reading per se, the teacher may employ prompts to stimulate strategic reading. Questions such as, "Does that make sense?" "What does that mean?" "You said _____ here. Did that sound right? What could you

FIGURE 7–2
TEACHER'S READING
CONFERENCE LOG

TEACHER'S READING CONFERENCE LOG

Name: _____ Date: _____

Title: _____

Comments:

Strengths:

Improvements since last conference:

Next focus:

---

have said?" and "Why is _____ better?" help readers explore the strategies they use as they read.

If the purpose is the content of the material being read, the teacher asks questions designed to focus on the book in general, character and plot development, the quality of the writing, and the reader's response to the book. In this case, questions like "What was the story about?" "How does it compare to others you have read?" "Which character do you like best? Why?" "If you could meet the author, what would you ask?" and "What did you learn from this book?" are used as guides to foster discussion.

FIGURE 7–3
STUDENT'S READING
CONFERENCE LOG

STUDENT READING LOG

Name: _____ Date: _____

Title: _____

Summary: _____

_____

_____

_____

_____

I would recommend this book to _____ because:

_____

_____

_____

Peer Conferences   *Peer conferences* allow young readers to emulate what adult readers do. People who are reading the same book frequently talk about that book. They discuss characters, actions, outcomes, and emotions. They talk about the book as if they were in it. Together they predict what they think will happen next. Peer conferences allow children to engage in practices that adult readers do. They occur most naturally as a part of lit groups, although some groups need help getting started. Judith occasionally audiotapes a conference, finding that doing so boosts the quality of discussion.

Both peer and individual conferences allow teachers to assess and evaluate their students' reading. Accurate evaluation of a child's reading makes clear to the teacher, and the child, what the child knows about written language and the reading process.

It is within the structure of the readers' workshop that teachers assess and evaluate their children's reading and plan instruction. Next we discuss the current approaches used to teach reading. Then we look at ways to assess readers in order to plan effective instruction. Helping learners become strategic readers enables then to become proficient readers. Proficient readers are more likely to enjoy reading since they are not struggling. After all, the ultimate goal is to instill a love of reading.

MAJOR APPROACHES TO TEACHING READING WITHIN A LITERATE ENVIRONMENT

Teachers with a solid background in language, learning, and children's literature can teach without teaching manuals and special programs to tell them what to say and do if they know and understand:

1. the three major approaches used to teach reading

2. the materials and resources available in their schools and communities

3. the interests, strengths, and needs of the readers in their classrooms

Teachers with this preparation are in a position to match learners with appropriate materials and strategies. The current approaches for teaching reading are: *read-aloud* and *shared book, guided reading*, and *sustained silent reading (SSR)*.

Teachers are encouraged to think of materials and resources in light of what each offers to the student. Texts for read-aloud and shared book frequently involve more challenges than supports—that is, they are generally too difficult for the children to read on their own. Materials for guided reading experiences offer some challenges and some supports—the children can successfully read the text with the teacher's guidance. Sustained silent reading is used with materials that offer more supports than challenges—the children can successfully read them on their own. For each of these approaches the content for reading is real children's literature rather than derived stories from decodable texts in basal reader series.

Read-Aloud and Shared Book   Young learners need lots of good stories read to them. They need to hear how good literature and written language sound; they need to see what readers do when they read. They need demonstrations and engagements with print that promote love of both stories and information books so that they gain independence in reading. Young children need to hear books that they can join in and read along. Read-aloud times are designed to make the reading act a positive experience and written language accessible to all children. All learners, not just very young ones, benefit from read-aloud and shared book experiences.

Read-aloud and shared book are applied in a variety of ways in the classroom. Certainly, it is imperative that the teacher read aloud to the class. But this approach is

more than just the teacher reading to the students. Students read to other students within their own classroom or in another. Parents share books; senior citizens, local business people, and even the principal make wonderful shared readers.

Reading aloud and sharing books with children who are just learning English is also important. Just like young children, English language learners need to hear what English sounds like. Children who are not yet literate in their native language need to hear stories in their own language if possible. It is easier to acquire literacy in a second language if the child is already literate in the first. One way to help English language learners is to pair an older student with a younger one. The student who possesses more English can read to the one who is less fluent.

Many children labeled "at-risk" are those who have not had many experiences with reading aloud. Their attention spans have not been fully developed, and they find attending to a story difficult. Many students profit from reading to younger children on a regular basis. Giving less proficient readers this responsibility requires that they practice the book they are going to share. Rereading for practice to share a book with younger students is a very beneficial activity. It not only increases fluency; it enhances self-esteem.

From kindergarten and first-grade classrooms to the middle grades and beyond, teachers should read to children as many as three or four times a day. A text may be selected because it relates to a current unit of study; because a child requests it; because it allows the teacher to demonstrate something about print, book handling, and the reading process; or simply because it is a wonderful book.

During read-aloud, the teacher demonstrates enthusiasm for books. The children are encouraged to develop the connection between oral and written language and to recognize that reading is a pleasurable act. They are encouraged to make connections between what appears in books and their own lives. Reading aloud to students helps them become familiar with the language of literature and the structure of stories. Teachers should read aloud from a variety of genres including literature, environmental print, messages, and informational materials. Even after teachers have begun reading chapter books to children, picture books continue to bring pleasure and provide learning experiences for years to come.

Read-aloud also enables the teacher to demonstrate many strategies proficient readers use: how to make links from one idea to another or from one text to another, how to ask questions while reading, how to predict what might come next. In addition, teachers use this opportunity to compare characters, to comment on the author, and to talk about the quality of the writing or how the illustrations enhance the writing.

Students benefit from responding to read alouds. Songs, poems, chants, rhymes, finger plays, directions, and raps written on chart paper provide opportunities for individual and group responses as well as for demonstrations of using reading. Successive rereading for a variety of purposes improves children's growing control over texts. Read-aloud and shared book engage students in the reading process, and they expose children to the wealth of good literature available. They are important because they demonstrate human interaction with books. They are the means by which teachers "hook" their students into reading. As such, they are an integral part of the literate classroom.

Guided Reading　　Guided reading is the direct part of reading instruction. It takes place within small focused groups as needs are identified. Unlike basal-directed reading lessons, guided reading may not take place daily. Guided reading allows learners to "see" how the reading process works, and it provides teachers opportunities to "help children understand how reading works and learn techniques to figure out words and comprehend texts that are just a little too challenging for them to read without support" (Taberski, 2000, 96).

Children are shown aspects of reading such as: using pictures to predict; learning to skip a word then go back; developing awareness of sound-letter associations, especially initial letter sound; previewing a story; thinking about personal experiences related to the text; rereading to develop fluency; using punctuation cues; building concepts and vocabulary; and gaining a sense of story. By guiding readers in the development of reading strategies employed by proficient readers, the teacher makes overt the otherwise hidden processes involved in comprehending written language.

The Guided Reading Lesson Procedure involves *explicit instruction* and *demonstrations* involving the nature of the reading process and reading skill development. It provides

a way for children to have successful reading experiences. It allows teachers to help children by showing them proficient reading strategies. Guided reading as a regular curriculum component is employed in lieu of the directed reading lesson employed in the basal reader program. Guided reading can be used with selected trade books or with leveled sets of guided readers. (See Fountas and Pinnell, 1996.)

The Reading Lesson has five main components

- *Introduction*—reading aloud and other events for setting the scene and making connections
- *Preview read*—reading the text from the pictures and implanting language and information the reader is going to need
- *Independent reading*—learners' simultaneously read the text aloud quietly as the teacher listens in order to help if needed (hence the term *guided reading*) prompts, suggests, demonstrates, questions, and tells when needed
- *Discussion and retelling*—learners' retelling and talking about the text, making connections among their own lives, locating and working on troublesome words, confirming meanings, building self-confidence, and orchestrating strategies
- *Rereading and vocabulary*—learners' rereading for additional practice and to develop fluency (Adapted from The Wright Group video, *Guided Reading*)

In guided reading, teachers help students develop the strategies they need. When a child is reading, the teacher watches and listens. When a child stumbles, the teacher intervenes with gentle support, suggesting, questioning, or directing. Teachers use on-the-spot prompts and demonstrations to support children's development of strategic reading.

As reading teachers, the goal is to develop independent readers. To that end knowledgeable teachers need to know what to say to show their students what proficient readers do. They need to know how to support readers' predicting, their use of all three cue systems, their use of other sources of information, their self-monitoring, their self-correcting, and their integrating.

When working with emergent readers, ask the children to read and follow with their fingers. Ask if what they just read matches what is there. Remind them of what they just read, and ask them if that sounds right. If it doesn't, suggest that they try it again. Then ask them if it makes sense now.

To support readers' predicting, cover up a word and ask what they think will come next, and why. Show them an example of a good prediction and praise it. Encourage them to be aware of when they are thinking about what is likely to come next.

To support readers' simultaneous use of all three cue systems (and other sources of information), suggest that they look at the picture to help with a hard word. Ask that they identify the sound the word starts with. When they substitute a word, ask them if their word makes sense and if it sounds right. Ask what other word(s) could go there which also make sense.

To support the reader's use of self-monitoring, ask, "Were you right?" "Where's the hard word?" (after a meaning-disrupting miscue). "What's wrong? Why did you stop?" (after a hesitation or long pause). "What letter would you expect to see at the beginning of the word you said?" "What letter(s) would you expect to see at the end?" "Check that. Does it look right and sound right to you?" "You almost got it. See if you can figure out what it really is."

To support readers' self-correcting, tell them when something isn't quite right and ask that they try again. When they successfully self-correct, praise them for the way they figured out the troublesome spot. Point out their excellent thinking. When they make a miscue that disrupts the meaning, see if they can find it.

Integrating meaning with what the reader already knows is the heart of comprehending. Teachers might ask, "What were you thinking as you read that?" "What does that remind you of?" "How did that passage make you feel?" They encourage students to read, and read again, to talk about unknown words in the text and what they mean. Teachers support readers' sensible predictions and praise them when they employ strategies effectively. To help students gain fluency, teachers ask them to reread texts quickly, trying to make their oral reading sound almost like talking (Fountas and Pinnell, 1996).

Following reading, students may respond to what they've read by retelling, writing, discussing, drawing pictures, dramatizing, or any other number of options.

Guided reading is an approach to instruction employed mostly in the primary grades. However, good teachers guide readers through difficult texts at all levels of instruction, even into college reading. Previewing materials, employing advance organizers, keeping lists of hard words, discussing meanings, rereading for a variety of purposes, and so on are strategies proficient readers employ.

Direct Teaching During Guided Reading: An Example   Consider the following example of a second-grade guided reading lesson using a library book, charted discussion, a big book, and four small copies of the big book. The teacher has selected *The Little Red Hen* to read aloud. She brings together four children who need to focus on story sequencing. They enjoy listening to her read *The Little Red Hen*. They talk about the story, what happened and why. The teacher suggests they make a chart of the excuses each animal gave for not being able to help. The children and the teacher look through the story and the children tell the teacher what to write on their "Excuse Chart." They help her spell some words: from initial sounds to medial and final sounds. The teacher writes each word. The children reread the completed chart. Usually this takes only ten or fifteen minutes.

Then the teacher introduces the big book *The Little Yellow Chicken* by Cowley. It turns out that the Little Red Hen has a baby, the Little Yellow Chicken. The chick wants to give a party but no one will help. As the teacher and the children preview read the pictures, the teacher helps them see the relationship between the two stories. During the brief picture discussion, she implants one or two words and concepts the children need to read the story.

Then she gives each child a small copy of *The Little Yellow Chicken*. They review their strategy options for what to do if they get stuck on a word: look at the pictures, skip it and read on, try to sound it out by pointing to the letters one at a time, look for patterns in the word, put in a word that makes sense and go on.

They read the title together, and the teacher tells them to turn to the title page and begin reading there. She watches as they read, intervening if she sees a child who is stuck. After the independent reading, she asks who had trouble with a word. She asks how the reader figured out the word and if something else would have worked. She praises and reinforces their independent problem solving.

They reread the story this time for speed and fluency. They all read together as she sweeps her pointer under the text in the big book. Then she suggests this story would make an excellent cartoon. They divide the story into sections and the children go to the art center to turn *The Little Yellow Chicken* into a comic strip, a task that requires proper sequencing.

Guided reading takes place with a small group of readers. Following the lesson, the teacher usually makes the book available for independent reading since they already "know" how to read it. Thus, the materials once used in read-aloud and shared book become the materials for SSR.

Sometimes a text used for guided reading lends itself to interesting extension activities; however, the majority of guided reading lessons do not include extension activities. Extension choices might include drawing their favorite part and writing captions for their pictures; writing (and illustrating) a new, similar story; or acting the story out. The children might wish to pursue information presented in the book to learn more about the subject. They may want to read other stories by the same author. They might take interesting words from the story and add them to the list of related terms for the current unit of study. They might become involved in a science experiment or social studies project related to some aspect of the book. They explore these and other reading opportunities during sustained silent reading (SSR).

Sustained Silent Reading

Children learn to read by reading. Good readers read a lot, and poor readers don't. Therefore, it is important to provide daily periods of uninterrupted silent time for pleasure reading and for reading in students' areas of interest. Silent reading provides the experiences and the practice children need with good books. Sustained silent reading takes place with books or other reading materials of the learner's choosing. Many of the materials available have already been read aloud and/or used in guided reading.

Teachers emphasize that everyone, including the teacher, reads during SSR or DEAR time. Typically, there are no interruptions during SSR. Teachers and students are interested in what they are reading and do not want to be disturbed. This is not the time for doing or homework or grading papers. Rather, it is a time for all readers to enjoy (and practice) reading.

During SSR, readers may select from a variety of materials and genres: storybooks, magazines, comic books, newspapers, information books, poetry, and more. Most teachers set guidelines for acceptable reading material depending on the needs of the class. Many teachers allow the children to sit or lie anywhere they like, even on the floor, during this quiet SSR time.

Teachers often begin SSR with a short time span, only five minutes in kindergarten, and gradually move to longer periods when the children complain that there isn't enough time to read. When SSR is fully under way, teachers may initiate record keeping of what the students are reading. As early as possible, teachers give this responsibility to the children. Teachers may provide children with spiral notebooks for keeping a record of what they have read. Students also keep records of the books they read. (See Figures 7–4 and 7–5)

The best way to find out what the reader has comprehended is through retelling. Retellings may be oral or written. Verbal responses to text are a much more effective measure of comprehension than answering direct questions.

Children may also enjoy signing up to "sell" a favorite book in a thirty-second TV ad. Students might auction favorite books so other members of the class listen to the spiel and "bid" on the next book they would like to read during SSR. Artwork with captions, written advertisements for books, and book jackets created by the children are other, but not the only, options, for sharing material read during SSR. Some additional ways to engage children in responding to books include:

1. Write and illustrate a poem from an idea in the book

2. Make a crossword puzzle with words from the story

3. Make up cartoons with dialogue bubbles that tell the plot sequence

4. Sequence the story with pictures or music

FIGURE 7–4
BOOKS WE HAVE READ

Books We Have Read

Title	Author	Topic
The Teacher from the Black Lagoon	Mike Thaler	a mean teacher
Good Morning, Alligators	John Parker	alligator school
And the Teacher Got Mad	Lorraine Wilson	mad teacher
Where the Wild Things Are	Maurice Sendak	imagination
Books (poem)	Arnold Lobel	reading
Petunia	Roger Duvoisin	books - wisdom
Cloudy With Chance of Meatballs	Judi Barrett	food falling
The Giving Tree	Shel Silverstein	love
Stone Soup	Ann McGovern	playing a trick
The Napping House	Audrey Woods	fun
The Three Little Pigs		
B.B. Go Out For the Team	Jan and Stan Berenstain	
What's Under My Bed?	James Stevenson	
Monkeys Trick	Pat McKissack	
The Little Red Hen		
Mae bache tattoo + case	(Tricia Tusa)	

5. Make puppets out of sticks or paper bags, or use a flannel board to tell the story
6. Draw a mural to depict scenery from the story
7. Write an "at the scene, live" news story with a headline
8. Retell the story on tape
9. Find and list homophones, rhymes, colorful adjectives, synonyms, and antonyms
10. Use the story for creating story problems in math
11. Draw a map of where the story took place
12. Make a mobile or collage to illustrate the story
13. Present a panel discussion or debate on an issue raised by the story
14. Conduct research to learn more about something from the story

FIGURE 7–5
BOOKS I HAVE READ

BOOKS I HAVE READ

Name:

Date:

Title:

Author:

Illustrator:

Publisher:

I liked (or did not like this book because):

A picture of my favorite part:

Students frequently come up with even better ideas. Many teachers find literature response journals effective in encouraging children to reflect upon and react to good books. At the beginning, some children require help getting started writing about their reflections or reactions to a story. Teachers may model writing reflections or reactions a few times at the board or on the overhead and then ask children to write about what a book meant to them. Of course, good books can be enjoyed for their own sake and need not be "extended" at all. Do remember that it is through extensive reading that your students become readers.

Read-aloud and shared book, guided reading, and SSR are the key instructional components of the literacy classroom. They are the larger instructional approaches that take place during readers' workshop, although they may occur at other times during the day. Knowledgeable teachers match approaches and materials to the needs of their students. All students experience read-aloud and are encouraged to participate in shared book. They all participate in SSR. Children in the primary grades are guided through reading texts as part of readers' workshop. Older readers may be guided through reading subject area texts such as science or social studies. Guided reading allows the teacher to guide learners through text that is too difficult to read independently.

However, some students need more detailed, specific assistance than is provided by guided reading lessons. For those students teachers plan mini- or focus lesson. Focus lessons are designed for both individuals and groups. They are based on what teachers discover about their students' reading. In the following section, we explore ways teachers examine their students' oral reading and comprehending. Using the information

and insights gained from these assessments, teachers plan focus lessons designed to help readers explore, experience, and focus on specific reading strategies and how good readers use them.

ASSESSING AND EVALUATING READING

At pre-reading and emergent reading stages, many teachers employ techniques from Clay's *An Observation Survey of Early Literacy Achievement* (1993). Especially useful are the letter and word tests and the concepts about print survey, which provide evidence of book-handling experience and the child's familiarity with print. Running Record (Clay, 1993, 1998) is a tool for assessing oral reading. It is especially useful in gauging accuracy and rate. Running Record provides useful information that teachers use to select materials, base instruction, and document reading growth over time (see Clay, 1998).

When teachers listen to a student read, they enter the world of that student's mind. They hear what the reader can do and what the reader is trying to do. They hear errors, but they do not necessarily hear them as mistakes. Errors are vitally important to the teacher because errors are never random. Rather, they are systematic and when examined, reflect the reader's understanding and processing of text.

Reading Miscue Inventory   Reading miscue inventory (RMI) or analysis is a procedure for systematically examining and evaluating what happens when a reader reads. Originally designed as a research tool, miscue analysis yields detailed information about a reader's reading strategies (Goodman, Watson, and Burke, 1987). Teachers who are familiar with miscue analysis listen to their students' oral reading differently. They no longer think of every mis-read word as an indication of a reading problem. They no longer correct every mis-read word. Rather, they listen for what their students are doing as readers, looking for both reader strengths and reader difficulties. They listen with "miscue ears" (Goodman, Watson, and Burke, 1987). Once they understand the reading process and the role of miscues in the meaning-making process, they don't need to do a full-blown miscue analysis of every student's reading. Rather, they can listen to a student's oral reading with "miscue ears" and evaluate on the spot whether the miscues are hindering or helping the reader progress through the text.

The term *miscue* rather than error was selected because reading involves cue sampling, and the process of predicting, cue sampling, and attempting to self-correct produces changes to the text that are not all indicators of reading problems. All readers miscue during oral reading. In fact, some miscues are demonstrations of strengths and should not be treated as evidence of difficulty. Error, on the other hand, has the connotation of being bad or always involving a problem.

Evaluating children's reading with the RMI involves several elements, beginning with marking and analyzing the reader's oral reading miscues; this tells the teacher how language cues are being used. Miscues also suggest what strategies the reader is using to construct meaning. The analysis of oral reading is accompanied by an analysis of comprehension through examining the retelling of the story read. Retellings yield pictures of how much detail the child retained; for example, how well the plot was grasped and how well the reader understood the characters, the theme, and the gist of the selection. Both aspects of an RMI evaluation—attention to patterns of miscues and depth of retelling—are avenues into the reading process.

Learning to systematically observe children's reading through miscue analysis is one of the best ways for teachers to learn about how reading works and how each child is doing as a reader. This information is important to teachers who need to make informed decisions about what to focus on as they plan guided reading and focus lessons.

Unlike running record, readers must read from an unfamiliar text—one with enough challenges to expose the reader's use of strategies but with enough supports that the reader can comprehend. For miscue analysis, the teacher is not allowed to help. Readers read and retell an entire selection. Reading Miscue Inventory is done with one student at a time. The oral reading and retelling are taped for analysis later. The RMI for classroom use consists of:

Materials

A copy of the Burke Reading Interview (see Goodman, Watson, and Burke, 1987)

A tape recorder (extra batteries and blank tapes)

Stories for the reader

Photocopies of the text(s) (cut and paste or typescript)

Pencils (with erasers)

A quiet place

Procedures

If possible, sit next to the reader.

Chat briefly to make the reader feel more comfortable.

Turn on the tape recorder. Test it to make sure it is in proper working order.

SAY: "Today, you are going to read a story, and I am going to tape it. When you finish, I will ask you to tell me everything you can remember about the story. If you come to something you don't know, do what you would do if you were reading alone. Pretend I am not here because I can't help you."

Show the reader the story and how long it is. Point to the inside title and tell the reader to begin there.

If the reader becomes stuck and sits for a really long time (a full minute),
SAY: "What would you do if you were reading alone?"

Try not to tell the reader what a word is.

Marking Guidelines   The RMI identifies five basic types of miscues: substitutions, insertions, omissions, repetitions, and reversals. The marks used to record each miscue by type are shown in Figure 7–6.

Retelling Guidelines   Retellings follow the reading. They are both unprompted and prompted. The teacher tells the reader to close the book and tell everything he or she can remember about the story. When the reader has completely exhausted this

FIGURE 7–6
MARKING MISCUES

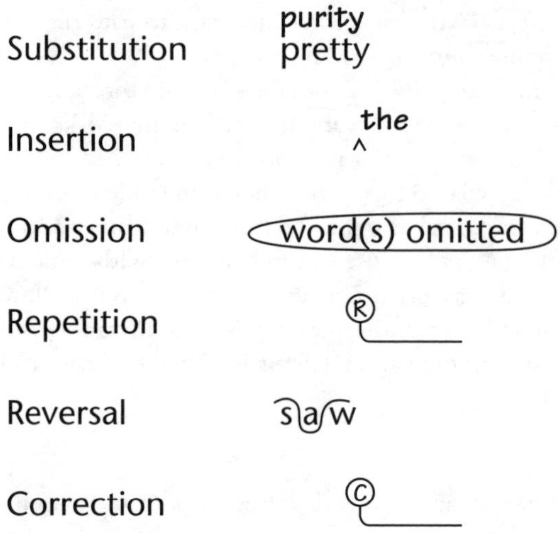

Substitution	purity / pretty
Insertion	the ^
Omission	⟨word(s) omitted⟩
Repetition	Ⓡ
Reversal	s\a/w
Correction	Ⓒ

unprompted retelling, the teacher may prompt for additional information. Queries for prompting are based on information the reader has already supplied. Some sample prompt questions are listed below:

You said _____. Tell me more about that.

After _____, what happened?

Why do you think _____ (event) _____ happened?

Why do you think _____ (character) _____ did that?

As the reader finishes the retelling, ask a few questions such as:

Was there anything in the story you thought was (sad, weird, funny, etc.)? Why?

What did you learn from reading this story?

Why did the author write this story?

Did you like the story? Why? Why not?

Would you recommend this story to someone else? Who? Why?

Retellings are scored following guidelines that appear in Figure 7–7. Scoring for retellings differ for narrative and expository text. For story material, the retelling score is divided into character analysis (40 points) and recalled events (60 points). The scorer looks for theme and plot statements. For expository pieces, the retelling is divided into specific information (50 points), generalizations (25 points), and major concepts (25 points). For more detailed guidelines for assigning points, see Goodman, Watson, and Burke (1987).

FIGURE 7–7
SCORING RETELLINGS

MISCUE ANALYSIS RETELLING SUMMARY FORM

Name of Child: _____ Date: _____

Title of Text: _____

RETELLING

Narrative Text		**Expository Text**
Characters (40)	**Events (60)**	**Specific Information (50)**
Main	Major	
		Generalizations (25)
Secondary	Details	
	Plot	**Major Concepts (25)**
	Theme	

Total: _____ %   Total: _____ %

Comments:

After the reading and retelling, when the child has returned to regular classroom activities, the teacher has the task of analyzing the miscues. There are four questions a teacher must ask about each miscue:

Question 1. Syntactic Acceptability

Is the sentence syntactically acceptable in the reader's dialect and within the context of the entire selection?

Yes (Y)	The sentence, as finally produced by the reader, is essentially grammatical in English. (Shifts in tense, number, and dialect do not count.)
No (N)	The sentence, as finally produced by the reader, is not grammatical.

Question 2. Semantic Acceptability

Is the sentence semantically acceptable in the reader's dialect and within the context of the entire selection? (Note: question #2 cannot be coded Y if question #1 is coded N.)

Yes (Y)	The sentence, as finally produced by the reader, is semantically acceptable—that is, it has meaning.
No (N)	The sentence, as finally produced by the reader, is not semantically acceptable.

NOTE: A sentence can have meaning (Y) only if it has an acceptable English structure. That is, questions #1 and #2 can only be coded YY, YN, NN. A coding of NY is not possible.

Question 3. Meaning Change

Does the sentence, as finally produced by the reader, change the meaning of the printed text?

No (N)	There is no change in the meaning of the selection.
Partial (P)	There is inconsistency, loss, or change of a minor idea, incident, character, fact, sequence, or concept in the selection.
Yes (Y)	There is inconsistency, loss, or change of a major idea, incident, character, fact, sequence, or concept in the selection.

NOTE: Meaning change can be considered only if there is meaning present. So, question #3 can only be coded if questions #1 and #2 are coded YY. For sentences without meaning, a dash is used when they cannot be coded for question #3 (i.e., YN— or NN—).

Question 4. Graphic Similarity

Only substitutions can be graphically similar. If written down, how much would the miscue look like the printed text?

High (H)	A high degree of graphic similarity exists between the miscue and the text or two out of three parts of a word are the same—*house* for *horse* has high (H) graphic similarity.
Some (S)	Some degree of graphic similarity exists between the miscue and the text or one out of three parts in the word is similar—*big* for *but* has some (S) degree of graphic similarity.
None (N)	No graphic similarity exists between the miscue and the text or the two words have no letters that are the similar—*work* for *job* has no (N) graphic similarity.

NOTE: Regarding graphic similarity of substitution miscues. Repeated miscues (RM) are coded for question #4 only once—the first time they occur. Substitutions on function words, however, such as articles and pronouns, are never coded RM. Therefore, each miscue on those words may be examined for question #4.

The right margin of a copy of the text onto which the reader's miscues are marked becomes the coding form (see Figure 7–8). Questions #1, #2, and #3 are coded at the end of each sentence. Question #4, which asks about high (H), partial (P), or no (N) degree of graphic similarity, is marked with the H, P, or N directly above or next to the substitution itself. For example, miscues are coded on a segment of oral reading for Kevin, a bilingual third grader, from his reading of "The Man Who Kept House." Each sentence is numbered. The total number of sentences is the basis for determining percentages of response. A summary of the miscues may be written at the end of the story or on the back of the last page in a format like that in Figures 7–9, 7–10, and 7–11.

The RMI manual supplies profiles of proficient and non-proficient readers' miscues. Miscue analysis gives teachers an informed perspective from which to view what children are trying to do as they read.

Examine the excerpt below. The marks represent how the reader reads this selection. As you read, attempt to answer these questions:

- What are the reader's strengths?
- What strategies does the reader use?
- What might the reader be ready to learn next? (What might this reader need?)

FIGURE 7–8
CODING MISCUES ON TEXT

0106 "I keep house," replied the wife, "and

0107 keeping house is (hard) work." ③ — ③ YYP

0108 ④ "Hard work!" said the husband. ⑤ He ⑥ didn't "You don't — ④ YYY

0109 know what hard work is! (RM) You should try — ⑤ YYY

0110 cutting wood!" — ⑥ YYN

FIGURE 7–9
MISCUE SUMMARY

Question 1: No of Y = ___ or ___ %; No of N = ___ or ___ %.

Question 2: No of Y = ___ or ___ %; No of N = ___ or ___ %.

Question 3: No of Y = ___ or ___ %; No of P = ___ or ___ %; No of N = ___ or ___ %.

Question 4: No of H = ___ or ___ %; No of S = ___ or ___ %; No of N = ___ or ___ %.

FIGURE 7–10
ORAL READING
ANALYSIS SUMMARY
FORM

ORAL READING ANALYSIS SUMMARY FORM

Name of Child: _____ Date: _____

Title of Text: _____

Processing	**Use of Strategies**	**Needs Help With**
1. Number of words in text ___ Number of words read correctly ___	Corrections	
2. Number of miscues ___	Predictions	
3. Percentage of miscues ___	Semantically acceptable substitutions	
4. Number of miscues corrected ___	Semantically acceptable sentences	
5. Percentage self-corrected ___ %	Word analysis	

Evaluation

Strengths . . .

Growth since last RMI . . .

Ready for . . .

Additional comments . . .

FIGURE 7–11
READING MISCUE
SUMMARY

READING MISCUE SUMMARY

Reader's Name: _____ Date: _____

Grade Level: _____ Teacher: _____

Selection Read: _____

1. What percentage of the sentences read make sense?

   Total number of sentences read (TS): _____

   Number of semantically acceptable sentences (SAS): _____

   (SAS/TS) × 100 = percentage of sentences that make sense: _____ %

2. Reading: how does the reader go about constructing meaning?   **N S O U A**

   a. Recognizes when miscues disrupt meaning   1 2 3 4 5
   b. Makes logical substitutions   1 2 3 4 5
   c. Predicts   1 2 3 4 5
   d. Self-corrects errors that disrupt meaning   1 2 3 4 5
   e. Uses pictures and/or other visual cues   1 2 3 4 5

3. Reading: in what ways does the reader lose meaning?

   a. Produces nonsense   1 2 3 4 5
   b. Substitutions don't make sense   1 2 3 4 5
   c. Omissions lose meaning   1 2 3 4 5

4. Retelling: narrative text

   a. Character recall   1 2 3 4 5
   b. Character development   1 2 3 4 5
   c. Setting   1 2 3 4 5
   d. Relationship of events   1 2 3 4 5
   e. Plot   1 2 3 4 5
   f. Theme   1 2 3 4 5
   g. Overall retelling   1 2 3 4 5

5. Retelling: nonfiction

   a. Major concepts   1 2 3 4 5
   b. Generalizations   1 2 3 4 5
   c. Specific information   1 2 3 4 5
   d. Logical order   1 2 3 4 5
   e. Overall retelling   1 2 3 4 5

Comments:

N = Not yet   S = Sometimes   O = Often   U = Usually   A = Always

Six Dinner Sid
By Inga Moore

                                       on   **(pause)**

01   Sid lived at number one ⟨Aristotle⟩ Street.

            Ⓒ**she**   **in**

02   He also lived at nmber two, number three,

03   number four, number five, and number six.

           Ⓒ**Six**

04   Sid lived in six houses so that he could have six dinners.

                              sip   **into**

05   Each night he would slip out of ⟨number⟩ one, where he

     missed   **children**   **fresh**

06   might have had chicken, into number two for fish,

                        liar **and**

07   onto number three for lamb˄

08   liver at number four,

09   fish again at number five...

10   ending at number six with

                kind

11   beef-and-kidney stew.

     Sinky   **mis—** **(pause)**   **tell**

12   Since the neighbors did not talk ⟨to⟩ each other

                                that

13   on ⟨Aristotle⟩ Street, they did not know what

14   Sid was up to. They all believed ⟨that⟩ the cat

                      only

15   they fed was theirs, and theirs alone.

                 wōrk

16   But Sid had to work ⟨hard⟩ for his dinners.

     isn't east   **pets**

17   It wasn't easy being six people's pet.

18   He had six different names to remember

                    misbehave

19   and six different ways to behave.

Look at this excerpt from Deena's reading of *Six Dinner Sid*. Her oral reading is complex. There are 141 words in this excerpt. She makes twenty-eight miscues. She seems to be trying to make sense. In line 15, she substitutes *only* for *alone*. She shows evidence of predicting as in line 06 where she substitutes *fresh* for *fish*, expecting an adjective. In line 02, she assumes the cat is female, but she corrects herself. She uses what she sees in the pictures and what she thinks may be going on. For example, in line 07, she substitutes *liar* for *lamb* and inserts *and* as if she is expecting that number three offers Sid two entrees. In line 19, she substitutes *misbehave* for *behave* because she knows the cat is being naughty. She also knows he is, in some ways, a liar.

She employs more than just initial letter sounds. For example, in line 01, she substitutes *on* for *one*. In line 05, she substitutes *sip* for *slip* and in line 12, *tell* for *talk*. She has some ability with phonics. In line 12, she sounds out *Since* producing *Sinky*; in line 16, *woark* for *work*, and in line 17, *east* for *easy*. She is using both phonics and grammar, but she substitutes real words that often fail to produce acceptable meaning, as in *missed* for *might* and *children* for *chicken* in line 06 and *liar* for *lamb* in line 07. She successfully self-corrects twice, *he* for *she* in line 02 and *Sid* for *six* in line 03; but twice isn't very often out of twenty-eight miscues.

Overall, one might conclude that Deena is more concerned with getting words than with making the reading meaningful or making it sound like language. She doesn't self-correct very much. She likely hasn't been read to very much and may not willingly engage in reading very often. Her retelling of the story, interestingly enough, reveals that she understands most of it. However, the pictures in this book are very explicit.

Deena's teacher should focus her attention on producing oral reading that makes sense and sounds like language. She is already using initial, medial, and ending sounds, and she substitutes one or two words that make sense. Some of her miscues show her predictions, but she does not self-correct the ones that do not sound like language or make sense. Deena's teacher might employ a technique called Retrospective Miscue Analysis (Goodman and Mareck, 1996) in which readers are encouraged to find their own miscues. In general, Deena will make better progress if she reads and writes more and if her teacher helps her think more about the overall meaning of what she is reading. This includes focusing on options Deena can use when what she has read doesn't sound right or make good sense.

Retrospective Miscue Analysis   Even in the upper grades, some students continue to need help with reading. Retrospective miscue analysis is a technique where readers listen to their own oral reading to search and deal with their own troublesome miscues. The purpose is to help them expand their understanding of and control over their own reading process. Readers audiotape their oral reading, or they use a tape from an RMI administered by the teacher. While reviewing the text that was recorded, students evaluate their reading by listening to themselves and identifying places where they miscued. They are directed to ask, "Does that sentence sound right?" "Does it make sense?" "What does it mean?" "What is the problem?" "What can I do about it?"

By the middle grades, students are in many ways their own best teachers. As they listen to themselves read, they make their own decisions about the quality and acceptability of their miscues.

Teachers demonstrate this procedure with their own reading. Together teachers and students discuss appropriate strategies to use with each miscue to construct meaning. Students need to understand that reading need not be error-free and that not all miscues need to be corrected—especially if the reader knows the word and if the miscue doesn't make any significant change to the meaning of the text. Examples of overcorrections as well as what constitute syntactically and semantically acceptable miscues should be discussed (see Goodman and Marek, 1996).

PLANNING FOCUSED INSTRUCTION

In addition to helping teachers learn more about the reading process, miscue analysis is also used to document reader growth over time, to help students improve their own reading, and to help teachers plan focused instruction. Here is another reader. Let's examine the marked sample of Antonio's reading and plan a focus lesson (see Figure 7–12). What are Antonio's strengths? What is he doing that you can use to help him improve his reading?

Antonio has several strengths as a reader. First, almost all of Antonio's miscues are substitutions. Of the thirteen substitutions he makes, only five are graphically similar, but ten of them begin with the same letter as the word in the text. Therefore, Antonio is making use of initial sounds. He substitutes real words for the words in the text. His substitutions are generally grammatical, but many do not make sense. They damage the author's message and Antonio's construction of meaning. This is a weakness for Antonio and something to focus on.

Antonio does not seem to have internalized enough strategies to risk trying, so he omits most words he doesn't "know." He needs to be encouraged to substitute words

FIGURE 7–12
ANTONIO

```
                              plant     corn
0101        A little boy planted a carrot seed.

                                    ever      will    came
0201        His(mother)said, "I'm afraid it won't come up."

                                    ever    would   call
0301        His father said, "I'm afraid it won't come up."

                              big              have  came
0401        And his˄brother said, "It won't come up."

                                          plant
0501        Every day the little boy pulled(up)the weeds

                                                goud
0502        around the seed and(sprinkled)the ground with

                        not-thing
0503        water. But nothing came up.
```

he knows that will make sense. He needs also to use his growing knowledge of phonics to attend to more than just the initial sounds of words. He needs to integrate his phonics knowledge with using words that make sense.

In planning a focus lesson for Antonio, the teacher suggests he use picture clues along with his knowledge of phonics. She directs his attention to the word "carrot" in the text. She praises him for saying *corn*. They look at the ending. Does the word "corn" end in a /t/? What else could that word be?

In line 0201, she draws his attention to "mother," which he omitted. How can she help him figure out what that word is? What other words is Antonio ready to tackle in this focus lesson?

One of Antonio's classmates read the same story (see Figure 7–13). What are Marlene's strengths?

Marlene may have been in an instructional program that emphasized phonics without consideration for meaning because she attempts to sound out every unfamiliar word and is satisfied with non-words. Look how her substitutions include the initial as well as some medial and ending sounds, as in *plasted* for *planted* and *evasy* for *every*. These substitutions retain the grammar, but they are not meaningful. She has been taught rules for dividing words into syllables and then pronouncing the parts, for example, *car – rot* for *carrot*.

The teacher decides to try a focus lesson that asks Marlene and some of her classmates to identify nonsense words and sentences. He uses the same story she just read, using some of her nonsense words. He asks the group to listen and tell him what is

FIGURE 7–13
MARLENE

	plasted car-rot ⌐steep
0101	A little boy planted a carrot seed.
	I am alrayed wō-nut
0201	His mother said, "I'm afraid it won't come up."
	I am aral wō-nut
0301	His father said, "I'm afraid it won't come up."
	Andy, 30 sec.
0401	And his brother said, "It (won't) come up."
	Evasy (c) pol-
0501	Every day the little boy pulled (up) the weeds
	sparkled jround
0502	around the seed and sprinkled the ground with
0503	water. But nothing came up.

wrong and what they think the words really are. They review strategies for trying to correct what doesn't sound right. Then the teacher and the children create a chart listing five things to do whenever their reading sounds like nonsense: (1) look at the picture; (2) reread, think about the word and try again; and (3) skip the word and read on, think about what they are reading about, then come back and reread the sentence and try again (4) sound it out, and (5) look for patterns or parts of words you recognize. Finally, the teacher asks the children to read the new chart to one or more of their friends and explain how it works.

Gordon is a third grader who has been in remedial reading since he was in the second grade. Look at Figure 7–14. What are Gordon's strengths as reader?

If his miscues are just counted instead of analyzed, Gordon appears to be a poor reader. He has a good vocabulary, and his substitutions are semantically acceptable. Gordon shows one strength the other readers do not display. He attempts to self-correct. Gordon monitors his reading and understands that reading is language and that it is supposed to make sense. He attempts to construct meaning and is quite successful. Although Gordon makes a large number of miscues, he produces the most meaningful reading.

Gordon's teacher asks him if she can use a sample of his reading to show some of the other children how to self-correct. With Gordon at her side to help explain what he was thinking as he read, she brings together a small group of children who do not sufficiently correct their own miscues. She shows them how Gordon read *The Carrot Seed* and asks him to describe how he worked out what he read. They talk about the substi-

FIGURE 7–14
GORDON

tutions of *it* for *the seed* and why the author used "the seed" that time instead of the pronoun. They discuss *sprouted* for *sprinkled* and what the clues are to the word the author used. They look at the internal differences between the two words. Then the teacher asks the children to read another story and monitor their reading. They are to keep track of when and how they are able to self-correct. After the reading, each child shares one or two successful corrections.

The following are three areas from which focus lessons in reading may be developed: (1) what readers need to know about books and other print sources, (2) what they need to know about the reading process, and (3) what they need to know about literature—stories, poems, information material, etc.

Information about what cues the reader uses is especially helpful to the teacher in planning effective instruction. Basing instruction on reader strengths bolsters self-esteem. Basing instruction on what the reader already knows and does allows for the integration of new information with prior knowledge. It makes learning easier because it is what the brain is designed to do.

RECORD KEEPING

The use of reading miscue analysis, retrospective miscue analysis, running records, and other theoretically sound instruments and techniques are all excellent tools for helping teachers observe and document what children are doing with written language. When teachers ask and answer these evaluative questions—"What is the child trying to do?" "What are the child's strengths?" "What is the child ready to learn next?"—they inform themselves about their learners, the directions of their instruction, and the results of their teaching efforts.

Several instruments and guidelines exist for keeping records of oral reading analysis and retelling analysis. For additional ideas on evaluation and record keeping see: Kemp, 1987; Rhodes and Shanklin, 1993; *The Primary Language Record*, 1989; Wilde, 2000; and Wong-Kam et al., 2001. Teachers use suggested prototypes to design checklists and summary forms to best suit their needs and their students' needs.

WHAT ABOUT PHONICS, PHONEMIC AWARENESS, AND VOCABULARY DEVELOPMENT?

Do you remember being young and asking someone to tell you an unfamiliar word only to be told to "sound it out"? You were being asked to apply your knowledge of phonics to figure out the word. Phonics refers to the connections between letters and sounds" (Opitz, 2000). It is one of the systems readers use to identify unfamiliar words, although some argue it is an approach to teaching reading.

Traditionally, phonics has been taught in isolation, as a stand-alone part of the curriculum, a "subject" as it were. In traditional phonics instruction, all letter-sound correspondences are taught in a preset sequence, and intensive, planned instruction covers all phonics skills, rules, and concepts (Dahl, Scharer, Lawson, and Grogan, 2001). Skill sheets and workbooks are commonly employed to provide practice. Once all the parts have been taught, the learner should be able to sound out the words and form sentences.

Letter and sound patterns are an important part of reading, and because of this, they should not be taught separately from reading itself. If letter and sound patterns are acquired in the context of their use, they are easier to learn—just like sounds were when learning to talk.

Today a different way of teaching phonics is emerging based on sound research and child language development (see Dahl, Scharer, Lawson, and Grogan, 2001; Goodman, 1993; Moustafa, 1997; Opitz, 2000; Taberski, 2000). Knowledgeable teachers understand that phonics is an important part of reading and writing. They also know that phonic knowledge is developmental; it is related to what children already know about written language. Good teachers understand that phonic knowledge is more important in its application than by itself. They understand that children develop and use strategic sound-letter information. Therefore, they spend a great deal of time working with vocabulary, spelling, and word identification—all in the context of real reading, writing, speaking, and listening. They also understand that phonics is best learned in context and peers assist each other in learning and using phonics as they read and write together (Dahl, Scharer, Lawson, and Grogan, 2001).

Many believe phonics is a prerequisite for learning to read, but as Moustafa (1997) points out, letter-sound correspondences in troublesome words are best taught after the story has been read *to*, *with*, and *by* the children. In addition, rather than teaching rules that are commonly broken, multiple possibilities of the ways words are pronounced and spelled are examined. And because the possibilities are contextualized, they are more easily remembered.

Have you ever been speaking and jumbled your words? Slips of the tongue happen all the time; everybody does them. However, they always fit the phonological, syntactic, and intonational rules of the language. For example, while looking for a place to eat, John saw Maggie's Bar and Grill. Pointing it out to Nancy, he said, "We could try Maggie's Gar and Brill." Typically when people make these slips, they do so between the consonant and first vowel. That is because this is a natural point of division within syllables. (We bet you were taught that syllables couldn't be divided.) When people make these slips, they naturally occur between the *onset* and the *rime*. The onset is "any consonants that *may* come before the vowel" and the rime is the "vowel and any consonants which *may* come after it" (Moustafa, 1997, 42). For example, in the word *bar*, the onset is /b/ and the rime is /ar/. In *grill*, the onset is /gr/ and the rime is /ill/. Is it possible, then, to have a rime without an onset? The /ill/ in *grill* is a good example. In English, not all spoken syllables have onsets.

Children have a natural ability to manipulate onsets and rimes and they use this ability to make other letter-sound correspondences (Moustafa, 1997). Since children construct language, basing the new on the known, is it possible that children use their knowledge of letter-onset and letter-rime to figure out how to pronounce and spell unfamiliar words? How do teachers help?

Share a predictable book with the group. Ask the children to choose a favorite word from the story. Write the word on chart paper highlighting the onset and rime and telling the children what the letters in the onset and rime say. Post the chart on the wall. As more words with the same rime are encountered, add to the word wall. Make new charts using other onsets and rimes and hang them all around the room. "This grouping helps children make letter-sound generalities based on words they have learned to recognize in context" (Moustafa, 1997, 91). (A list of common rimes is found in Appendix A.) Words can also be classified by onset. Indeed, initial letter sounds are among the most significant pieces of information readers and writers need. Children need to make sense of how language works, and a print-rich environment affords them this opportunity (Opitz, 2000).

Wylie and Durrell (1970) identified thirty-seven dependable rimes that make up nearly five hundred primary-grade words. Select one, for example, /ake/. How many onsets can be added to /ake/ to make words? Let's start: /b/ + /ake/ = bake; /c/ + /ake/ = cake; /d/ + /ake/ = dake. Is that a word? Actually it is an archaic English word. Think of the possibilities. And remember, some onsets are made up of more than one letter. Did you think of /dr/+ /ake/?

The ability to manipulate onset and rime is an example of *phonemic awareness*. In the example above, to make the word bake from /b/ + /ake/, the reader has to be able to blend the sounds together. *Phonemic blending* is the ability to blend sounds to form a word. In contrast, *phonemic deletion* is the ability to take away the first sound—to separate the /b/ from the /ake/. *Phonemic matching* is the ability to identify words with a given sound at the beginning, middle, or end. For example, *bake*, *bike*, and *beak* all begin and end with the same sound. All these tasks require *phonemic segmentation*, the ability to isolate sounds in words. Examples of phonemic segmentation include counting the number of sounds heard in *bake*. How many? Although there are four letters in the word *bake*, there are only three sounds. Phonemic segmentation also refers to producing the actual sounds heard in the word—for example, /b/ /a/ /k/ in *bake* (see Opitz, 2000).

How does children's knowledge of onset and rime help them read and write? Children who can read *bake*, for example, should be able to read all other versions of the /ake/ rime—*make, take, sake, fake, lake*. Once they "get it," children who can spell *bake* should be able to use the /ake/ rime to spell other similar rhyming words.

While onset and rime are excellent ways to help children manipulate the sounds of English, they do not exist in Spanish. Spanish is not an onset-rime language. However, a similar strategy can be used. In Spanish, some syllables represent salient units, such as the /ca/ and the /sa/ in *casa*. Instead of highlighting onset and rime, the teacher emphasizes notable syllables (Moustafa, 1997).

Another example of onset is *alliteration*. As Opitz (2000) points out, "alliteration helps children develop a sense of wordness because the same beginning sound serves as a boundary in the speech stream, signaling when a new word begins" (81). That is why so much children's literature is alliterative and plays with onset and rime. Tongue twisters are another fun way to enable children to manipulate the sounds. "Peter Piper picked a peck of pickled peppers" is an old favorite.

Through literature, poetry, songs, rhymes, language play, reading predictable books, and early writing, young children learn the sound-letter patterns of their language. Classroom instruction involves creating signs and labels, writing letters to classmates, helping each other figure out what the teacher's note says, and many other authentic literacy events. For example, on the first day of first grade some teachers begin by asking the children to read each other's name tags.

Children learn about phonics in read-aloud, shared book, and modeled writing as the teachers demonstrate how phonics helps us figure out unknown words. Teachers also teach phonics by asking the children to spell as they write on the board. They do these activities and much, much more, all of which engage the children in matching sounds to letters.

As teachers begin "teaching" children how to look at the world of print, they help them want to examine the sounds and letters that make up the written language in their environments. This leads into spelling instruction eventually as part of the classroom writing program. Initially, teachers focus on what is familiar and interesting to the children—their names; funny words in the stories they tell, read, write; labels for the things in their classroom environment—lots of things get names tags. They focus on how these words begin. They talk about sounds everyone can "hear." They explore how long or short some words are. They talk about how words end. Knowledgeable teachers begin with the large concepts, what the children know—for example, they know that Tyrone and Tyler begin the same way because they can hear it and see it. They allow children to make analogies between what they know and what they are trying to figure out. They do not begin with something as abstract as an isolated sound matched with a letter of the alphabet. They do not spend most of the school year focusing on one letter a week. They encourage and lead the children into explorations of letter-sound relationships in the word they are encountering and need to use.

Teachers also help children learn about phonics in reading conferences. When the teacher observes that some readers need assistance using graphophonic cues, a single focus lesson or a series of focus lessons can be designed. In this manner, children learn to use phonics as a tool for helping them with an unfamiliar word. In writing conferences, they help children use their growing awareness of phonemic awareness to spell. They ask children what they hear and where they hear it.

When helping children sound out words, there are three important things to remember. First, many words cannot be sounded out, and some of them are words that early readers need and use—for example, *was*, *said*, *does*, and *what*. Second, some children cannot do this with great success; they do not hear the subtle differences in sounds. These children need help developing other successful strategies for reading and writing unfamiliar words. Third, phonics won't help anyway if the reader does not already know the word in his or her spoken vocabulary. For example, in the popular Harry Potter series, Harry's female friend is Hermione. While Hermione is not an unusual name in England, it is not all that common in the United States. How did you sound it out? "Correct" pronunciation of words during oral reading has less to do with understanding what is being read than common sense might suggest. Readers can understand and still miss many words, but they can also "get" all the words right and not understand much of anything.

Comprehending is partly a matter of vocabulary. As children read extensively and engage in classroom pursuits, their vocabularies grow. Words related to units of study—synonyms, antonyms, roots and root words—become an important part of the language curriculum. Word play occurs naturally.

Knowledgeable teachers do not need to begin with a phonics program or make the children sit through arbitrary exercises and drills. Good teachers of young children know that letter-sound patterns are just one of the aspects of written language that they need to help children gain control over. They also know that phonics is complex, inconsistent, abstract, arbitrary, and confusing. It is important and must be explored, but in the context of real reading and writing.

The purpose of sounding out unfamiliar words is for recognition. But we have to *cognize* something (have it as a cognate, or schema, in our heads) before we can *re-cognize* it. What good are "sounding-out" drills for children who have limited vocabularies? If the word is not in the reader's spoken vocabulary, there is no way to assure its recognition and correct pronunciation. It is more meaningful to enlarge children's store of concepts and the words that go with them. And how is that done? Experiences!

The relationship between print and speech is complex. Look, for example, at vowel sounds. They are spelled in multiple ways (see Appendix A). For example, long /a/ as in *baby* is also *ay* as in *day*, *a* + silent *e* as in *came*, *ai* as in *rain*, *ey* as in *they*, *ea* as in *break*, *ei* as in *rein*, *eigh* as in *neighbor*, *aigh* as in *straight*, and *et* as in *bouquet*. Consonants, while not as complex as the vowels, are spelled in a variety of ways, too (for example, /k/ as in *king*, *cane*, *occur*, *antique*, *pack*, and *choir*). Think of the daunting task of trying to figure out all those letter-sound correspondences one at a time. So good teachers find ways for children to apply phonics as they learn it.

Three conclusions can be drawn from recent research findings:

> 1. we should teach children to make analogies between familiar and unfamiliar print words so they can pronounce unfamiliar print words; 2. we should teach children the sounds of letters that represent onsets and rimes so they can pronounce unfamiliar print words; 3. we should teach children to recognize lots of print words holistically so they can make analogies between familiar and unfamiliar print words to pronounce unfamiliar print words. (Moustafa, 1997, 52)

Proffered solutions like employing a phonics program to teach young children phonemic awareness may be very alluring. However, simplistic solutions to complex problems are usually ineffective. At worst, they serve to further damage an already difficult situation, rendering phonics frustratingly opaque to many young children and English language learners. Phonics is best taught in the context of real reading and writing events. It is a tool readers and writers use.

Comprehending written language, like comprehending oral language, is a mental interplay between what the reader knows and the abstract symbols (marks on the page) representing the author's message. Reading is learned as it is engaged in, and it requires practice. This is both good news and bad news.

The bad news is that teaching reading is not simple. If it were, we would have been doing a better job with it long before now. Most proficient readers, by the time they are in their teens, are good at sounding out words. However, many younger readers can sound out words, but if they don't also comprehend, they are not good readers. On the other hand, many children understand what they read, but they cannot sound out words very well.

While reading instruction does not lend itself to a simple set of steps, the good news is neither does it require expensive programs in order for teachers and students to be successful. Reading is not a surface-level, linear process but a synthesis and networking of complex processes (that the learner figures out how to do with help and experience). Take heart. Reading is constructing and comprehending language, and that is one of the things the human brain does best—under the right conditions.

SUMMARY

Read-aloud and shared book, guided reading, and SSR form the majority of approaches to teaching reading employed in the literacy classroom. Most reading is silent, so instruction typically takes place as the students are engaged in readers' workshop. In addition, teachers employ conferences to learn about how a child's reading is progressing and to learn how to better assist the reader in becoming more proficient. Conferences provide valuable time for teachers to assess and evaluate children's oral and silent reading. Teachers evaluate reading for two reasons: to document children's growing control over the reading process and to use this information in planning guided and focus lessons. Teachers develop focus lessons for selected students to deliver needed practice and demonstrations. Children develop phonemic awareness and teachers teach phonics in the context of real reading and writing.

Teachers need broad goals for their learners. They need to know where they want their learners to go and how they plan to get them there. For example, first-grade teachers want their students not only to become proficient readers, they want them to love to read as well. Teachers also need short-term goals for the students so they can plan effective instruction. Should their focus lessons deal with what readers need to know about books and other print sources? Do the students need to know about the reading process and what strategies to use? Do they simply need more exposure to good literature? Knowledgeable teachers watch their students to see what they do as proficient readers and to see what areas they need help with next. They read aloud several times daily, teach guided reading lessons and more focused lessons to small groups and/or individuals, and they always allow time for independent silent reading.

THEORY-TO-PRACTICE CONNECTIONS

Reading Theory

1. Kidwatching, documenting learner growth, strengths, and what each learner needs next.

2. Children need an immersion experience to learn to read.

3. Children learn to read by really reading—with support.

4. Engaged learners learn best.

5. Readers must use all three cue systems simultaneously.

6. Teachers teach about phonics in the context of real reading.

Examples of Classroom Practice

1. Anecdotal records and notes, checklists, running record, and miscue analysis

2. Print-rich environment, shared book and read aloud

3. Guided reading

4. Self-selected literature studies

5. Focus lessons to demonstrate

6. Rhyming, onsets and rimes, word play

SUGGESTED READING

Primary Grades

Clay, M. 1998. *Running Records for Classroom Teachers.* Portsmouth, NH: Heinemann.

Fountas, I., and G. Pinnell. 1996. *Guided Reading: Good First Teaching for All Children.* Portsmouth, NH: Heinemann.

Routman, R. 1999. *Conversations: Strategies for Teaching, Learning, and Evaluating.* Portsmouth, NH: Heinemann.

Taberski, S. 2000. *On Solid Ground: Strategies for Teaching Reading K–3.* Portsmouth, NH: Heinemann.

Upper Grades

Goodman, Y., D. Watson, and C. Burke. 1987. *Reading Miscue Inventory: Alternative Procedures.* Katonah, NY: Richard C. Owen.

———. 1996. *Reading Strategies: Focus on Comprehension.* Katonah, NY: Richard C. Owen.

Wilde, S. 1996. *Notes from a Kidwatcher: Selected Writings of Yetta M. Goodman.* Portsmouth, NH: Heinemann.

———. 2000. *Miscue Analysis Made Easy: Building on Student Strengths.* Portsmouth, NH: Heinemann.

Phonics

Dahl, K., P. Scharer, L. Lawson, and P. Grogan. 2001. *Rethinking Phonics: Making the Best Teaching Decisions.* Portsmouth, NH: Heinemann.

Goodman, K. 1993. *Phonics Phacts.* Portsmouth, NH: Heinemann.

Moustafa, M. 1997. *Beyond Traditional Phonics: Research Discoveries and Reading Instruction.* Portsmouth, NH: Heinemann.

Opitz, M. 2000. *Rhymes and Reasons: Literature and Language Play.* Portsmouth, NH: Heinemann.

EXTENDING YOUR DISCUSSION

1. Do a simplified miscue with a struggling reader. Share your child's reading with a small group of your classmates. What can you conclude about the child's strengths? What cues and strategies does he or she seem to rely on when reading? What is the child trying to do as a reader? What do you think you might do to help this child become a better reader?

2. Creating strategy lessons is one of the most fun and interesting things teachers get to do. Examine the oral reading and retelling of one struggling reader. Isolate a pattern you see occurring, e.g., trouble with pronouns, problems with reversals, saying nonsense words when trying to sound out troublesome words, or not being

   able to adequately retell the story. Create a focus lesson. Share your lesson ideas with classmates and assess each other's ideas for how well they fit theoretically.

3. "How much wood could a woodchuck chuck if a woodchuck could chuck wood?" can be turned around to "If a woodchuck could chuck wood, how much wood could a woodchuck chuck?" Can you turn around Peter Piper? In the woodchuck example, not only are onset and rime manipulated, but also rhyme. For example, *wood* and *could* rhyme although their rimes are spelled differently. Collect several tongue twisters. Ask children to read them. See if they can be turned around to form questions.

REFERENCES

Clarkson, C. 2000. "'Try Huff and Puff': Discovering Children and Creating Curriculum in One Small Town Third Grade." In *Teaching At-Risk Students in the K–4 Classroom: Language, Literacy, Learning,* eds. C. Stice and J. Bertrand. Norwood, MA: Christopher Gordon.

Clay, M. 1993. *An Observation Survey of Early Literacy Achievement.* Portsmouth, NH: Heinemann.

————. 1998. *Running Records for Classroom Teachers.* Portsmouth, NH: Heinemann.

Dahl, K., P. Scharer, L. Lawson, and P. Grogan. 2001. *Rethinking Phonics: Making the Best Teaching Decisions.* Portsmouth, NH: Heinemann.

Ferreiro, E., and A. Teberosky. 1982. *Literacy Before Schooling.* Portsmouth, NH: Heinemann.

Fountas, I., and G. Pinnell. 1996. *Guided Reading: Good First Teaching for All Children.* Portsmouth, NH: Heinemann.

Goodman, K. 1968. *Study of Children's Behavior While Reading Orally.* (Contract No. OE 6-10-136.) Washington, DC: Department of Health, Education, and Welfare.

————. 1970. "Behind the Eye: What Happens in Reading." In *Reading Process and Program,* eds. K. S. Goodman and O. Niles. Urbana, IL: NCTE.

————. 1993. *Phonics Phacts.* Portsmouth, NH: Heinemann.

Goodman, K., and Y. Goodman. 1978. *Reading of American Children Whose Language Is a Stable Rural Dialect of English or a Language Other Than English.* (Contract No. NIE-00-3-0087.) Washington, DC: NIE.

Goodman, Y. 1971. *Longitudinal Study of Children's Oral Reading Behavior.* (Contract No. OEG-5-9-325062-0046.) Washington, DC: Department of Health, Education, and Welfare.

————. 1978. "Kidwatching: An Alternative to Testing." *National Elementary Principal* 57 (4): 45.

————. 1985. "Kidwatching: Observing Children in the Classroom." In *Observing the Language Learner,* eds. A. Jagger and T. Burke-Smith. Newark, DE: IRA.

————. 1990. *How Children Construct Literacy: Piagetian Perspectives.* Newark, DE: IRA.

Goodman, Y., and A. M. Marek. 1996. *Retrospection Miscue Analysis.* Katonah, NY: Richard C. Owen.

Goodman, Y., D. Watson, and C. Burke. 1987. *Reading Miscue Inventory: Alternative Procedures.* Katonah, NY: Richard C. Owen.

Greaney, V., and S. Neuman. 1990. "The Functions of Reading: Across-Cultural Perspective." *Reading Research Quarterly* 25 (3): 172–95.

Heald-Taylor, G. 2001. *The Beginning Reading Handbook.* Portsmouth, NH: Heinemann.

Holdaway, D. 1979. *The Foundations of Literacy.* Portsmouth, NH: Heinemann.

Kemp, M. 1987. *Watching Children Read and Write: Observational Records for Children with Special Needs.* Portsmouth, NH: Heinemann.

Meek, M. 1988. *How Texts Teach What Readers Learn.* Exeter, England: Thimble Press.

Moustafa, M. 1997. *Beyond Traditional Phonics: Research Discoveries and Reading Instruction.* Portsmouth, NH: Heinemann.

Opitz, M. 2000. *Rhymes and Reasons: Literature and Language Play.* Portsmouth, NH: Heinemann.

Opitz, M., and M. Ford. 2001. *Reaching Readers: Flexible and Innovative Strategies for Guided Reading.* Portsmouth, NH: Heinemann.

Peterson, R. 1992. *Life in a Crowded Place: Making a Learning Community.* Portsmouth, NH: Heinemann.

Peterson, R., and M. Eeds. 1990. *Grand Conversations: Literature Groups in Action.* Toronto, Ontario: Scholastic.

The Primary Language Record. 1989. London: Centre for Language in Primary Education.

Reading in Junior Classes. 1985. Wellington, New Zealand: New Zealand Department of Education.

Rhodes, L., and N. Shanklin. 1993. *Windows into Literacy: Assessing Learners K–8.* Portsmouth, NH: Heinemann.

Rosso, B., and R. Emans. 1981. "Do Children Use Phonic Generalizations and How?" *The Reading Teacher* 34: 653–58.

Serafini, F. *The Reading Workshop: Creating Space for Readers.* Portsmouth, NH: Heinemann.

Short, K., and K. Pierce. 1990. *Talking About Books: Literature Discussion Groups in K–8 Classrooms.* Portsmouth, NH: Heinemann.

Smith, F. 1994. *Understanding Reading,* 5th ed. Hillsdale, NJ: Erlbaum.

————. 1997. *Reading Without Nonsense,* 3rd ed. New York: Teachers College Press.

Stauffer, R. 1969. *A Directed Reading-Thinking Approach.* New York: Harper and Row.

Taberski, S. 2000. *On Solid Ground: Strategies for Teaching Reading K–3.* Portsmouth, NH: Heinemann.

Wilde, S. 2000. *Miscue Analysis Made Easy: Building on Student Strengths.* Portsmouth, NH: Heinemann.

Wong-Kam, J., and A. Kimura. 2001. *Elevating Expectations: A New Take on Accountability, Achievement, and Evaluation.* Portsmouth, NH: Heinemann.

Wylie, R., and D. Durrell 1970. "Teaching Vowels Through Phonograms." *Elementary English* 47: 787–91.

CHILDREN'S LITERATURE

Allard, H., and J. Marshall. 1977. *Miss Nelson Is Missing.* New York: Houghton Mifflin.

Brown, M. 1947. *Goodnight Moon.* New York: Harper and Row.

Cowley, J. 1988. *The Yellow Chicken.* Bothell, WA: The Wright Group.

dePaola, T. 1975. *Strega Nona.* New York: Prentice-Hall.

Galdone, P. 1973. *The Little Red Hen.* New York: Scholastic.

Krauss, R. 1945. *The Carrot Seed.* New York: Harper and Row.

Moore, I. 1991. *Six Dinner Sid.* New York: Simon and Schuster.

Mosel, A. 1968. *Tikki Tikki Tembo.* New York: Holt, Rinehart, and Winston.

Rey, H. 1941. *Curious George.* New York: Houghton Mifflin.

Warner, G. 1924. *The Boxcar Children.* New York: Whitman.

CHAPTER **EIGHT**

"Children want to write. They want to write the first day they attend school. . . . the child's marks say, 'I am!'"

(Donald Graves, 1983, 3)

WRITING

As a young Cambodian child, Bouahome learned to read and write English with Kathy Miller, a wonderful ESL (English as a second language) teacher. Kathy read aloud to her class and to individual children several times a day. She encouraged her children to respond to the stories in writing. Kathy used writing as a pathway into literacy. Once Bouahome learned to read, she read everything she could get her hands on, and most of her reading was reflected in her writing. According to Kathy, Bouahome fantasized about herself as the main characters and became personally involved in nearly every book she read. For example, when she responded to the story *Angel Child, Dragon Child*, by Surat, Bouahome, as a third grader, wrote:

Journal entry excerpt—November 27:

In Vietnam the family name come first. In the legend of Vietnam, they descend from Angel Fairy and Dragon King. People call Vietnam Small

Dragon and above it is a country called China. People call China the Great Dragon. Ut left her country called Vietnam to come to America. But she is still Vietnamese and she still had her Vietnamese name, Nguyen Hoa. Family is very important to Vietnamese. The name Hoa means flower.·. . .

Bouahome's love of story continued into middle school. Even before that time, she had started dramatizing stories with her friends. She'd tell her friends what to say and do as they acted out stories both in class and out in the schoolyard. Bouahome created new stories for the main characters and "became" her favorite characters, sometimes for days. She thought about story lines, settings, and characters. She used what she was learning in science and social studies in her writing. She experimented with dialogue in print as she wrote her stories down. As she wrote and told stories, she'd often work out personal problems. In fifth grade, Bouahome wrote,

Journal entry excerpt—April 4:

Sometimes I feel like Emily in a book called *The Star Fisher*. At her school (people) called her names and made fun of her when she talked Chinese. The same thing happens to me at school. When people make fun of my language, the way Laotians do, I get mad. I tell them off. I get in trouble with teachers. It is not fair because they don't know the reasons for my yelling. I just try to remind myself about how Emily suffered from being different. Reading helps me think of new ways to stop people being prejudice.

Kathy used writing to help her students learn English and to get them hooked on language learning and reading. Because Kathy's classroom was rich in literature and opportunities to write, students like Bouahome learned that writing is fun, that it can help authors do things such as work out their problems or entertain themselves and others. These are powerful insights in the lives of children (Miller 2000).

Children enter school as already accomplished users of (their native) spoken language and knowing a great deal about the world in which they live. Most children also know a considerable amount about written language. Learning to read and write takes time for most children, although for some it occurs easily and spontaneously. Nevertheless, even if they are not reading and writing when they start school, most children still know a great deal about print. After all, we live in a highly literate society. Just look around. Written language is everywhere. By school age, nearly all young children are "reading " the names of their favorite cereals or peanut butter, their favorite fast-food restaurant, perhaps even their own names in print. Many are already attempting to "write" messages such as "KP OT," and even though it has only four letters, we know it means to keep out.

Writing is learned in roughly the same ways as learning to speak. It has to be because it is the brain that learns language. Writing has to be engaged in for social and personal reasons. It has to be practiced over time, and it has to be meaningful and purposeful to learners, allowing them to do things with their writing that they want to do.

In this chapter we explore the reasons people write, what writing is, and what writing does. We examine the historical practices of teaching writing and contrast them with more current perspectives. Finally, we study the writing process, or the authoring cycle, the process we employed in writing this book.

WHAT WRITING IS

Writing, like reading, is graphic language communication. However, writing is not merely the inverse of reading. Reading and writing, while both forms of written language, require somewhat different knowledge and abilities. Reading is a transactive experience with an author, just as listening is a transactive experience with a speaker. Whereas speakers transact with themselves and a real audience, writers transact with themselves and an intended, often imagined audience. Stephen King says he writes with an "Ideal Reader" in mind—his wife, Tabitha (King 2000). Children often write with their best friends in mind. Of course, if the audience is specific, then those persons need to be considered, e.g., mother, grandparents, pen pal, older students, younger students, classmates.

Authors have a message in mind when they write, but readers, like listeners, must construct their own meanings as they read or listen. Reading and listening are constructive and receptive. Speaking and writing, on the other hand, are constructive and expressive. However, all language happens in the brain, whether it is receptive or expressive. We need to teach with that in mind.

Like speech, writing conveys meaning. However, speech is oral and essentially immediate. It takes place in the presence of an audience. Writing is visual and tends to be a solitary process. Until the inventions of the telephone and recording devices, writing was the only way human beings had to communicate over time and space. Yet, with the current use of technology, writing has again become a primary means of communicating, for example via Email and Instant Messenger (Leu 2001).

By the time children have learned to speak with fluency, they have gained control over much of their environments. By the time they are three or four years old, many children want to write with the same exuberance with which they wanted to learn to speak. Because writing is present in their environments, they see they can do interesting things with it. In fact, "written" messages from three-, four-, or five-year-olds are frequently among parents' most prized possessions.

Although written language is different from oral language, in some ways writing reflects oral language. There are visual symbols (letters) that represent oral symbols (speech sounds or phonemes). In English there are twenty-six letters to represent some forty-four phonemes and various graphic symbols to indicate some of the elements of intonation. These are called punctuation marks (, . ! : ; " ?). In written language, words follow the order and grammatical rules of oral language, but there are additional constraints on written language that are not necessary for speaking.

Since the writer and the reader are usually separated by both time and space, written language must necessarily be more complete than spoken language. The text must provide more information about the context because readers cannot just look around and figure out what is happening as they typically can when listening to someone talk. Even illustrations, like those in children's picture books, do not provide the complete context that exists with spoken language events.

For these same reasons, written language is more formal than speech. During a conversation, people may speak in incomplete sentences, with the context of the communication, facial expressions, gestures, and other non-linguistic noises such as laughs, grunts, and snorts carrying some of the intended message. These aids to meaning are not possible in written text although writers of comics have made an art of trying. For most writing, the message must be made clear in words themselves. That's why a story is usually longer when it is written than when it is told.

WHAT WRITING DOES

Many educators and historians agree that writing was developed as human beings developed agriculture and trade. Graphic notations—the very first evidences of writing— were used to keep tallies and accounts of various kinds, for example, bushels of wheat and numbers of cattle or oxen. From these symbols and tally markings on clay tablets thousands of years ago came written language and numerals as we know them.

Today, writing has come to serve many purposes. It clearly touches all our lives. As a way of organizing and clarifying thinking, writing helps us structure the world of our direct experiences. Writing allows human beings to use language to shape, define, and redefine our thoughts and feelings; it helps us understand what we learn. The act of composing causes the writer to arrange and sequence thoughts, to make judgments about what is important, and to build in a logical or narrative sense. Moreover, unlike speech, writing is concrete. It can be reread, reflected upon, and revised. Others can respond to it. It can be reshaped and molded to changing and differing viewpoints (Bridges, 1997).

Many times writers write with strong emotions. Indeed, writing offers children a means not only of making sense of their environment but of their internal state as well. Writing is a way that helps us handle the sorrows, joys, fears, and angers of life.

Because human beings want to communicate and record their thoughts, many young people keep diaries or personal journals. Most teachers know children who have revealed traumatic personal issues through classroom journals, personal narratives, "fiction," and factual reports. Adults do this as well. Have you ever been so angry with someone that you wrote that person a letter, then tore it up to calm your rage? Writing about important personal events helps people "get it off their chests." Inviting children to write whenever they are experiencing strong feelings and problems in their lives enables them to cope with problems in healthy ways. Writing offers human beings a creative way to process and come to terms with strong emotions such as fear, grief, anger, and love.

Writing may be social as when people write to persuade others. Writing induces people to buy things, to vote a certain way, to support a special interest, or to form public opinions. Writing allows people to reflect on the outside world and their own personal journey of growing up in that world. Writing has the potential to be a powerful component in the lives of people. Children are no exception.

For most of us the mere business of living would be nearly unmanageable without knowing how to write. Moreover, writing has both intrinsic and extrinsic value. Having the ability to write fulfills our need to communicate, just as learning to talk did. And, writing is another way children and adults make sense of and learn about the world. The practical, pragmatic reasons for writing fall into several categories: work or business, social, emotional, and intellectual. People need to be able to make lists, send notes and letters to others, remind themselves of events, fill out forms and applications, keep a diary, tell a story, outline a lecture, work out a problem, write notes summarizing a textbook passage, and so on. Therefore, writing is utilitarian. The ability to express oneself in print is likely to become even more important throughout the twenty-first century. Classroom writing opportunities should include as many of the functional uses for writing as possible.

While writing serves very practical needs in the lives of literate people, it can also be elevated to an art form. As an art form, writing fulfills another human need, the need to express ourselves creatively and aesthetically. While we usually think of narrative (stories in the form of literature) as the more creative, expository writing may certainly be artful as well. The best exposition can bring an award like the Pulitzer Prize. Expository writing is encountered in textbooks, essays, newspapers, magazines, and advertising. A few children may attempt both story writing and writing to impart information before formal schooling. However, schools are places where young writers and their creative endeavors are nourished. Finding a budding Toni Morrison, Michael Crichton, Amy Tan, or Lee Smith would be wonderful, but that isn't the issue. If students are better writers after they've lived for a year in your classroom, their lives are improved and you will have done your job.

Children write for the same reasons adults write, so it is important for teachers to create opportunities for children to communicate in writing. They need to treat writing as an art as well as a utilitarian skill. They can encourage and model writing and make writing part of the normal, daily activities of the classroom. Lists, signs, labels, forms and sign-up sheets, poems, stories, news articles, advertisements, notes, Email, reminders, and more should be part of the self-contained classroom. Children's writing folders should be filled with old drafts of writing as well as works-in-progress, thus providing an historical record of their life during the year. When children have written for many different purposes, the task of writing for inauthentic purposes, such as a state writing assessment, is not as daunting. Increasingly, as teachers make writing a major component of their programs and consistently model writing in their classrooms, many themselves are becoming better writers along with their students.

CHILDREN'S WRITING DEVELOPMENT: OUR EVOLVING UNDERSTANDING

How do children learn to write? How do they arrive at being able to actually put meaningful text on paper? Do they have to copy letter forms from handwriting charts and workbooks? Do they have to memorize sound-letter associations after they start school and combine these to make simple words, ad nauseam? Or do they engage in the same process of invention and convention that characterizes learning to talk?

It should come as no surprise that the same process at work in learning to speak is also at work in learning to write. Language learning is language learning. Humans learn by doing. We learn from whole to part to whole because learning the parts individually is too complex, too abstract, and too void of context to be meaningful and therefore readily learnable. Trying to learn anything that is not meaningful is difficult, if not impossible. When children's purposes (expression, joy, problem solving, etc.) are respected and children are treated as writers, they "write" their own messages. They read, revise, edit, and share them. Throughout these processes their brains are figuring out the underlying rules. It does not matter whether they are learning oral language or written language. We construct our abilities with language as we use language for doing other, hopefully interesting, things. When we first begin, we do it with less proficiency than experienced language users do. Knowledgeable teachers know when and how to intervene—to explain, examine, demonstrate, require, encourage, etc.

As explored in Chapter Four, learning to write is a constructive, generative process like all other language learning. In learning to write, learners experiment and employ graphic symbols to represent their intentions. In so doing, and with guidance from teachers, they figure out the underlying rules and the many uses that exist for writing. Children who see writing demonstrated by the adults around them, and who receive the positive help they need in learning to write, usually learn to express themselves quite well in print. They tend to learn to write without regarding writing as something difficult.

It is not surprising to hear again that children learn to write by writing. Neither is it astonishing to say that children need to be immersed in meaningful print and to be encouraged and supported in their uses of written language. They need opportunities to employ writing for their own purposes. Let's look again at the broad phases through which children tend to pass as they gain control over the conventions of the written language and specifically, the writing system. We have to remember, however, that there is great variability among children in terms of when and how individuals go about this.

Intentional Play   Typically unreadable, scribbles are early attempts to communicate. Young children experiment with the forms of writing in a variety of contexts, and through them, they begin to teach themselves about print. These experiments occur within a variety of contexts. Pictures that tell stories, abstract signs children used to attempt messages, and scribbles and marks that begin to resemble letters are all part of children's early attempts to graphically represent their meanings.

Young children's first marks tend to be pictographic. However, it does not take long before many children begin to copy what they see their parents do. Some children as young as three produce different visual representations when asked to draw a picture and then to write a story (see Figure 8–1). They already know the difference between pictures and print. As a result, young children's writing takes on the character of their

FIGURE 8–1
THANKSGIVING

parents' writing. Scribbling begins to look like the writing in the language they are learning. It appears to move in the same direction as writing in their native language. That is, children who scribble in English tend to move from left to right (as seen in Figure 8–2), but children exposed to Arabic, for example, begin to scribble from right to left. Children's scribbling in Japanese tends to be vertical. Children's scribbles look like the language they are trying to represent much like babbling in infants begins to "sound like" the language it will eventually become.

When children see adults write in English, the adult writer is usually writing in cursive. So when children are pretending to write letters, lists, notes, or sign their names, their scribbling tends to reflect an impression of the cursive writing they have seen. It flows. It has few breaks between the "words" because the separation of words in talk is not obvious. They learn where the individual word boundaries are as they learn to read and write. When they are telling stories in scribble writing, they tend to use manuscript-like marks. Eventually, children realize their written inventions are not readable to others. This discovery influences them to attempt more conventional forms for their letters and words. As they continue to experiment with letter shapes and direction, they learn many of the standard features necessary for writing. They learn the physical, mechanical, and surface aspects of print, all necessary elements of learning for both writing and reading, but the "invention within convention" process remains at work throughout.

Emergent writing tends to be characterized by the recurrence of marks that begin to give the impression of letters in English (often in different combinations). Random marks begin to look like letters, and some recognizable letters or words may even be observable (see Figure 8–3). Continued explorations with print, in numerous and various reading and writing engagements, provide fodder for young learners as they move toward the writing we can actually read.

FIGURE 8–2
SCRIBBLE FROM LEFT TO RIGHT

FIGURE 8–3
SCRIBBLE WITH
RECOGNIZABLE WORD

Emergent Writing Many fortunate pre-schoolers have been read to. They have come to know that in their favorite books the print carries the message instead of the pictures. Perhaps their parents are showing them how to write their names and how to make the letters of the alphabet. Evidence of their learning is seen as letters begin to be visible in their messages (see Figure 8–4).

Children like to copy and to trace writing they see around them. They like to invent messages, too. They want to communicate with others because they understand that writing is supposed to convey meaning. It is not uncommon for children to "write" something and to proudly ask an adult to read it.

Emergent writing is characterized by experiments with some of the conventions of language. This is because children are learning more and more about the print in their environments, and they are coming to realize that letters and sounds have a relationship. Children first use idiosyncratic spellings such as the letters ONF to represent *cat*. But

FIGURE 8–4
PEOPLE PLAYING

this changes as they encounter more of the conventions of written language and as they learn more about letters and sounds.

Children in this phase tend to use all uppercase letters even though their parents have likely taught them to write their names with only the first letter capitalized. This is yet another example of the power of environmental print. Much of the print children observe around them—billboards, fast-food restaurants, advertisements, favorite cereal boxes—are written in all uppercase letters. Children readily generalize this concept to all their writing.

Children are influenced by the print around them. At this phase, demonstrations in letter making and models of good handwriting should be provided. Many classrooms have alphabet strips. However, that is only a small part of the print needed. They need to see and use models of teachers' handwriting on charts displayed in the room. Nursery rhymes, poems and songs, webs pertaining to children's interests and units of study, and messages displayed in the classroom not only provide models of what good handwriting looks like, they also contribute to the literate environment. Copying and tracing models of well-formed letters for handwriting provide children with opportunities to explore how letters work and to choose, to some extent, how they want their letters to look. The more interactions children have with print, the easier their transition into emergent writing.

Knowledgeable teachers provide many opportunities for their children to use print in meaningful experiences. A tablet in the kitchen center gives children an opportunity to write grocery lists. A journal adjacent to a science center allows students to record

their observations. Paper and writing implements placed at the block area can be used to label constructions. Even in the early writing phase, children need authentic and meaningful reasons to use print.

Early Writing   It is during this phase that children move into writing that can actually be read by others. Children go from random letters to using a combination of letters and words as their approximations grow toward adult forms. Having learned a great deal about spelling patterns in English, children experiment with them (Read, 1971). Learning more about the relationship between letters and sounds, they try new ways of communicating their intentions. Figure 8–5 is a love note to a student teacher. It says, "I like Miss Belissa and her mom." The author, a kindergartner, had trouble pronouncing the teacher's name, Miss Melissa, so she simply spelled it the way she said it. Look at what the child knows about the relationship between oral and written language. She does not have space to write the entire word *mom*, but she knows the sec-

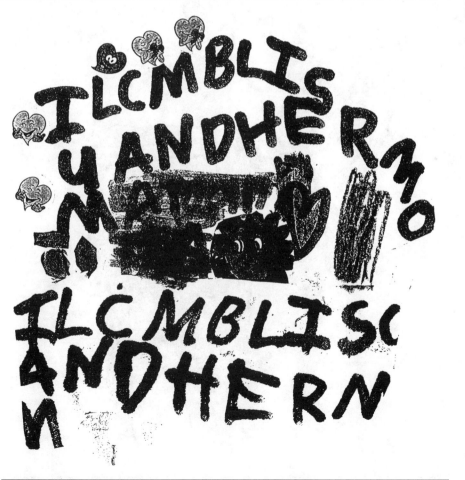

FIGURE 8–5
I LIKE MISS MELISSA

second M is part of that word, so on the next line, she gives the M a tail to connect it to the previous part.

As early writers, children also begin the composing process. Many children employ both drawing and writing in the same composition. For example, an emergent writer may draw a figure then label what the figure is doing, then draw another figure, label it, and so on until the page is filled (see Figure 8–6). Or the young writer may draw a picture first, then write about it. It is not uncommon for kindergartners and first graders to draw a picture and then write about it, but for second graders to write first

FIGURE 8–6
SIX FOOT(ED) BEAR

and then illustrate. With continued immersion in print, children gradually learn that not all pieces need to be illustrated, that illustrations are only necessary if they enhance the text.

Children also soon begin to realize the conventions of the letter-sound relationship. They use the initial letter to represent the entire word. *Cat* is represented by C. They begin to understand that letter names can be used to represent words. The letter U is not only a letter, but also a word. They write whole sentences using the initial letter of each word. "I love you" is represented as ILU. Then they begin to hear medial sound, for example, the V in love. ILU becomes ILVU. Their writing is more closely approximating traditional orthography. Their inventions become easier to read and reveal growth in knowledge of sound-letter relationships, as in Michael's menu (see Figure 8–7):

FIGURE 8–7
MICHAEL'S LUNCH
MENU:
PEACHES
SPAGHETTI
MILK
GREEN BEANS

As their writing develops, children learn to consider audience. As a result, their writing transitions, becoming more sophisticated. They move from narrative to exposition, learning that writing has multiple purposes and that a text can be depersonalized (see Figure 8–8). They explore description, argumentation, persuasion, and a wider variety of writing for other purposes (see Figure 8–9). Emotion in their writing begins to emerge as children realize they can make their audience laugh or cry. They expand their points of view, begin to write in third person, and from another's perspective. It is here that children begin to see the first glimmerings of an awareness of the transactional nature of writing (see Figure 8–10).

Fluent Writing　In this phase exposition and argumentation are developed. If the text shares information or explains something, it is expository. If it tries to persuade someone to do or believe something, it is argumentative. In both these modes, the writer stays in the background, and the topic of the piece is the focus; what is being explained, argued, or described is paramount.

Pattern is another element that characterizes transactional writing. The writing may start with the general and proceed to the specific or vice versa. Narratives or story material present a main point and support it with details. Expository or informational writing states a thesis and defends it with arguments. In any event, it is writing with a definite topic, a purpose or function, and a sense of audience. At this point, writers'

FIGURE 8–8
PLEASE KNOCK

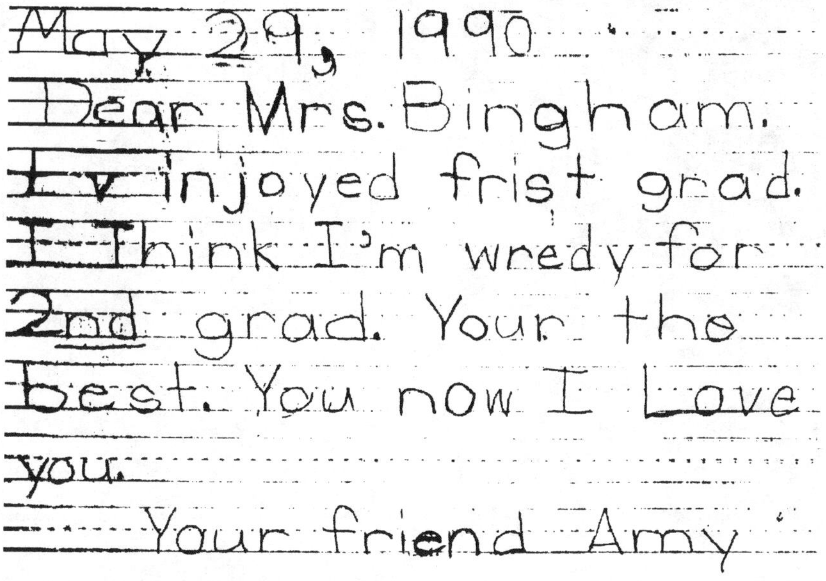

FIGURE 8–9
AMY'S LETTER

> May 29, 1990
> Dear Mrs. Bingham.
> Ev injoyed frist grad.
> I Think I'm wredy for
> 2nd grad. Your the
> best. You now I Love
> you.
> Your friend Amy

efforts reflect the maturity of their minds, the amount of practice they have had, their personal background of experiences, the number of examples and demonstrations they have seen, the opportunities available in the classroom, and their own drive to communicate (Calkins, 1990; Graves, 1994). Figure 8–11 presents a story Armondo wrote for his mother. It reflects his sense of both purpose and audience.

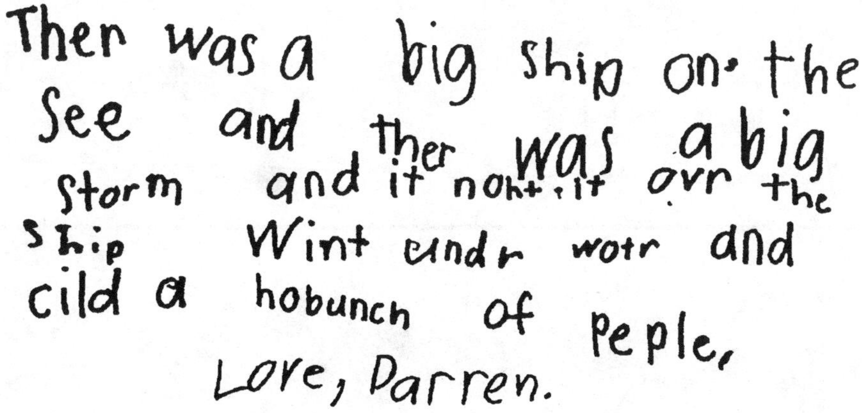

FIGURE 8–10
DARREN'S STORY

> Ther was a big ship on the See and ther was a big storm and it noht it ovr the ship Wint undr wotr and cild a hobunch of peple,
> Love, Darren.

FIGURE 8–11
ARMONDO'S STORY

FRANK AND The GHOST

On Halloween Frank went Trick-or Treating. He was dressed up like a ghost.

First he went to a yellow house He rang the doorbell. But no one answerd

He rang it again but still no one answered. So frank left the house. He looked all around. All the other kids seemed to be having fun.

FIGURE 8–11
CONTINUED

> He turned back around... the door to the yellow house opened A ghost came out and pushed the boy inside the house! They were having a party. Frank thougt he was in trouble But when he got home his mother just said,
>
> "Why where you out so late?" oh well you must of ha a lot of stuff do. "No, I got pulled into a place." what? A ghost pulled me in. And kept me in there. I tried

> to get out but I couldht. Util they were not looking. "well now your here and I'm happy. Now next time dont go trick-or-treating ever again with out me or your father. ok? ok. The end.

The writing phases—intentional play, emergent writing, early writing, and transitional and fluent writing—are not absolute. They are not steps. Children may skip a phase altogether or go back and forth between phases; certainly overlap occurs. Great variability also exists among children as to when these develop. The phases of writing development, as with oral language or reading development, are only general categories for learning that tend to describe what many children experience (McCarrier, Pinnell, and Fountas, 1999).

Writing, like reading, is a process. It is the synthesis of hundreds of complicated rules and elements that eventually flow together smoothly. Facility with writing comes with engagement—children learn to write by writing. Knowledgeable teachers set up conditions to engage students in great amounts of writing across the curriculum. Further, knowledgeable teachers expect children's writing to be different because they do not see real learning and language development as grade-level controlled or as a lockstep progression of discrete skills each child masters in the same sequence and at the same time. They look at what their students can do with writing more than they judge grammar, punctuation, or spelling and they celebrate writing together.

TRADITIONAL WRITING INSTRUCTION: A HISTORICAL PERSPECTIVE

In the 1700s and 1800s, it was important for people to be able to sign their names and engage in written correspondence. Schools in this country emphasized copying the letters of the alphabet, copying well-formed samples of correspondence, and calligraphy.

Literacy requirements were minimal for most people. Public elementary schools emphasized the recognition of a limited number of words and the ability to sign one's name. Legible penmanship was stressed (Burrows, 1977). "Educated" people used writing for letters, sermons, and legal and political documents.

The emphasis on copying and handwriting continued well into the twentieth century. Furthermore, it was believed that children had to be able to read before they could learn to write (Chomsky, 1971). Even as late as the 1970s, when children were asked to write, it was usually in the form of copying samples of poems, aphorisms, or brief essay-like texts. While much less prevalent, some teachers still require their students to copy a handwriting assignment from the board each morning. Fat pencils are still found in some kindergarten and first-grade classrooms, and wide-lined "first-grade" paper is still used.

Between the mid-1960s and late 1970s, "creative writing" appeared as a curricular subject because many students clearly were not being exposed to composition before high school. Some of you may remember "creative writing" with fondness; others, with dismay. Many teachers implemented "creative writing day" and everyone "wrote creatively" that day. Teachers assigned topics and children wrote. Topics became so creative that children were writing compositions called "My Life as a Sneaker" or "What the Rain Is Thinking." Usually the creative writing assignment was given to the teacher in first-draft form. Oftentimes the papers were returned with a smiley face or a sticker, having perhaps been read by the teacher but not really responded to. In other cases, papers were "corrected" and "graded" for mechanics. Many teachers had the children rewrite or otherwise correct all their spelling, grammar, and punctuation errors. Content was rarely addressed.

From this practice emerged two concerns. First, assigning the topic did not allow complete "creativity" on the children's part. Some teachers began allowing children to write about whatever they wished. Children who enjoyed writing prospered; those who didn't wrote little or nothing. To assist children in coming up with a topic, teachers developed lists from which the children could choose; some created picture files by mounting magazine photographs on construction paper and keeping them in a file. Second, teachers became concerned that correcting and grading the papers might diminish children's self-concepts, so papers were simply read aloud to the whole class, sometimes by the author, but usually by the teacher. Even with these innovations, creative writing never really caught on. As a result, well into the 1970s, writing instruction was still primarily penmanship.

But penmanship is only one aspect of writing. It is one of the mechanical aspects of writing. Skillful use of mechanics—grammar, spelling, punctuation—is important because they make the written piece readable; however, it is only a small part of effective writing. Historically, many have believed that if the mechanics of writing were first mastered, then students would eventually become effective writers (Solley, 2000). The product was what mattered, and it needed to be correct. Unfortunately, this practice is still common in many schools.

Perhaps many of you were taught this way. Did you find writing to be easy or difficult when you were required to produce your first paper? Is there a way to teach the process and mechanics of writing within the context of real writing? What can the tools of technology do to help us teach writing?

THE WRITING PROCESS: CURRENT PERSPECTIVES

The movement toward changing long-held traditional practices for teaching writing began in the early 1970s. Janet Emig (1971) studied high school students as they were actually engaged in the act of writing. She observed what they did as they wrote and discovered that they were not passive participants. They did not just sit quietly and write as many people thought writers did or should. In fact, many of Emig's high school students were observed asking themselves questions, talking to themselves, and even reading parts aloud to themselves and to others as they wrote. Her most significant finding was that writers actively thought about what they were writing when they were writing it. We realize today how ridiculous that sounds, but three decades ago, it was a revelation.

Emig's work led others to explore writing. Elbow (1973) postulated that teachers should respond to the meaning being conveyed in the writing, not just to the mechanics of the final product. He introduced the notion of writers' groups where discussions were led not by a teacher, but by the student writers themselves. It was via these studies that the idea of writing as a process rather than merely a product grew. However, these people studied high school students. Was it possible that elementary-age children engaged in writing as a process too? Many thought not.

In the late 1970s, Donald Graves (1983) began studying children's writing, and his findings revolutionized writing instruction for children. First, Graves described the three general stages children go through in writing: pre-writing, writing, and post-writing. Second, he discovered that children tend to write more for unassigned topics than they did on even the "cutest" of teacher assignments. However, the most important results of his research were that children's writing became viewed as a process and the elements of that process were made overt. The most serious upshot was the challenge to the old notion that it was good teaching to have children write and turn in a single draft on an assigned topic to be graded and corrected. No published author writes that way, and children authors shouldn't either.

Other researchers have helped explicate the writing process for classroom implementation (Atwell, 1998; Bissex, 1980; Calkins, 1983, 1990, 1994; Hansen, 1987; Harste, Woodward, and Burke, 1984; Lane, 1993: Short, Harste, and Burke, 1996). Sometimes called *the authoring cycle*, engaging children daily in authentic writing experiences for a variety of purposes is the focus in many classrooms today.

It is not possible to talk about the writing process or the authoring cycle without talking about each stage separately; however, it is imperative to understand that these elements are not steps. In writing this book, we did not rehearse one day, draft the next, revise on day three, edit on day four, and publish on day five. As writers write, they move in and out of different parts of the process. Let's examine the stages of the writing process. Calkins (1994) identifies six elements involved in the writing process: rehearsal, drafting, revising, conferencing, editing, and publishing.

Rehearsal   Rehearsing helps the writer, in this case the young writer, get started. In the authoring cycle, rehearsal begins with the children's lives, their oral language, their reading, and events in the daily life of the classroom. A number of activities can initiate writing. Chief among them is group discussion, usually stemming from children's experiences or pieces of literature that have been shared and enjoyed. Brainstorming, in which children participate in discussions, list their ideas, and organize the lists, is also a useful technique for initiating writing. Other ways to rehearse include storytelling, pantomiming, drawing, discussing, webbing, outlining, and reading.

Rehearsal helps writers immerse themselves in their own stories so they can begin to select and organize what they want to say. It is believed by some to be the most important part of the writing process because once the writer has a thorough understanding of what the piece is about and in what sequence it belongs, drafting comes more easily. Calkins (1994) believes this is especially true for children.

Drafting The purpose of drafting or composing is to get ideas on paper. Initial drafts give children and teachers something to work with and from. First drafts are the basis from which teachers plan authentic instructional events and provide collaborative evaluation of children's growth as writers.

With a first draft, students should not be overly concerned with spelling, capitalization, punctuation, or grammar, but they should be encouraged to pay attention to the conventions they already know (Atwell, 1998; Harwayne, 2001; Routman, 1999). The children are encouraged to get their words and ideas on paper and to attempt to spell whatever words they want to use. They are told that they will be helped with spelling and other aspects of mechanics during revision and editing. First drafts provide teachers with samples of the children's invented or developmental spellings, demonstrating what the learner knows about how words are spelled. These insights and observations can help teachers plan instruction in spelling. Or perhaps teachers see a need to help children write better titles, better beginnings, or better endings. Problems seen in first and subsequent drafts may be used for focus lessons.

Most children are unaccustomed to writing more than one draft. Today, many state-mandated writing assessments still require the students to turn in their first and only draft, so the notion of a second or third draft may be new to them as well. However, with teacher demonstration, children learn that the authors whose books and stories they have been reading do not submit their first drafts for publication. Writing for publication requires more than a first draft, and sometimes more than a second or third one. Hence, the blessings of word processing.

Sharing and Revising Some educators believe revision is the most crucial element of the writing process (*Dancing with the Pen*, 1992: Lane, 1993; Graves, 1994). The purpose of revision is to address the content of the piece. The author should ask, "Does the piece say what I want it to say?" The teacher should ask, "How can I help you?" Revision occurs as writers write, reread, receive comments, suggestions, criticisms, and rethink their intentions for the material. They may receive responses from their classmates and/or their teacher. Revisions rework the material, reflecting the writer's best thought and effort.

Children see the need for revising when they know someone outside the classroom is going to read their work. Revising can include text reorganization (perhaps by literally cutting and pasting or by using a word processor to do it), word choice, sentence structure changes, more description, more character development, better beginnings and endings, or any number of other additions and deletions. Revision ensures that the piece makes sense, that it has a good beginning, a well-developed middle, a logical end, and that it is the way the author wants it. Decisions regarding content revision belong to the author; the teacher or other students only make suggestions. The wealth of literature that has been shared and has become part of the classroom library and the literate environment available to the children serve as models to help young authors revise. That is, one cannot be a good writer without extensive writing, reading, and rewriting.

Conferencing   Ideally, conferencing occurs throughout the process. At any time during the authoring cycle, the teacher may ask, "How's it going?" The conference is the heart of instruction and evaluation. Through conferencing, the teacher asks questions, helps the author narrow the topic, makes suggestions for revising, models effective strategies for revising, helps with the editing, and makes notes on the child's progress.

Frequently, teachers find issues raised about writing that they can use as mini- or focus lessons for the larger group. Some common examples are where to put end marks and capital letters, how to check for misspelled words, how to write dialogue, how writers make characters come alive, and how to write good beginnings. With a writer's permission, the teacher may show the group what one of their classmates is working on and what they did, or are trying to do. Joanne Hindley (1996) identifies three categories of focus lessons on writing that she looks for during conferences with her students. They are: issues about literary techniques and devices, issues about organization, and issues about mechanics.

For example, one pair of second graders, during a conference with their teacher, was trying to figure out an operational definition for what a sentence is so they would know where to put end marks. The children came up with three possibilities. A sentence is: (1) all the words from the capital letter to the end of the biggest word, (2) on one line in the book, or (3) from the capital letter to the place where you stop to take a breath. The teacher presented these three hypotheses in a ten-minute focus lesson. Then she sent the whole group looking for examples in books until they decided which definition was best or until they could come up with a new and better one. The children searched and researched for days, trying new definitions and explanations. They finally decided they liked number three the best. They discovered for themselves, rather than being told, an operational definition of a sentence as a result of a pupil-teacher conference.

Editing   The purpose of editing is to produce a readable text, one that is as close to error-free as the learner can make it. Children quickly recognize that checking their writing for conventional usage will improve it so others can more easily read it. Teachers often push students into editing too many mechanical errors at one time. This is a mistake. Young writers can't work on all aspects of the language—spelling, grammar, punctuation, and capitalization—at once. A better strategy is for the teacher to choose one or two elements of written language to work on. More might reasonably be expected of older, more proficient writers.

Teachers may require that all pieces in final form be error-free or as error-free as the student can make them. However, the exception is first grade where the goal is to encourage risk taking. Even toward the end of first grade, many teachers demand essentially error-free final published products. It is well to remember that we cannot teach them to write if we can't get them to do it. Revising and correcting must be viewed as purposeful, important, and doable by the author. Assistance from the teacher during conference times and final checks by the teacher serving as the "final or Senior Editor" are important parts of the authoring cycle.

Some teachers have an editor's table in the classroom. When a piece of writing has undergone revision and self-editing, it may be placed in a box or folder for peer editors. Peer editors help the author correct spelling, punctuation, and grammar. This sequence of drafting, revising, and then editing signals young writers that conventions are important but that they are attended to only after meaning and content have been exhaustively addressed.

Children who serve as editors may have limited opportunities to write during the time they serve, usually for a week, but editing has a strong positive effect on their own writing. Editors are often anxious to return to their own writing, and the elements of writing they learned while in collaboration with other editors are incorporated into their work.

After peer editing, authors make the necessary changes before a final conference with the teacher. At this time, teachers listen to the authors read their final drafts. They talk about the piece; they may use this opportunity to teach or they may discuss publication options. Teachers record their observations of the work. To that end, simple checklists for the students are sometimes helpful. The guide in Figure 8–12 was developed by a group of second graders toward the end of the year. It became the booklet they used as a guide for proofreading and editing.

Knowledgeable teachers are careful that the finished work is the student's own, not the teacher's. Therefore, many teachers choose not to mark directly on children's drafts. They may encourage, question, suggest, and they may write notes to students about things to consider, but they do not require specific alterations. Drafts, revisions, and corrections must all belong to the students if they are to feel ownership of their work.

Publishing The purpose of publishing is to share and celebrate finished products. Some teachers refer to publishing as the opportunity for the children to "go public." Publication occurs in many forms. Simply presenting a finished work to a group is a form of publication. Formal, bound books include hardback books, softcover books, shape books, flip books, and accordion books (Johnson, 1992). Even finished pieces mounted on construction paper for display or letters ready to be mailed are examples of "published" work. Published pieces may be available in the classroom, placed in the school library, submitted for a Young Authors' celebration, or given as gifts. Audiences for published works include classmates, favorite children's authors, parents, grandparents, pen pals, children in lower grades, and school personnel. We have found that the most

FIGURE 8–12
CHILDREN'S EDITING
AND PROOFING
GUIDE

EDITING AND PROOFING GUIDE

Periods — At the end of a telling sentence.

Exclamation points — At the end of an exciting sentence or short sentence (ex., Boo! Hi! Yes!).

Commas — Go in dates, in addresses, to separate thoughts, before someone talks.

Quotation marks — Around what someone says (Jane said, "Hi!").

Upper case letters — Go at the beginning of a sentence, when using I, in story titles, for days of the week, months, things said in excitement, names of states, countries, other titles.

Reversals — Such as [b] for [d].

Spelling — Look it up. Ask someone. Skip it till later. Use another word.

Handwriting — Look at a good model.

Spacing — Make sure it's enough.

motivating ways to get children excited about writing is to have a classroom library made up of books the children have written themselves. (See Appendix B for book-binding instructions.)

As writers write, they move freely in and out of different phases of the authoring cycle. For example, while drafting, they may return to rehearsal if they get stuck. Or as they revise, they may find they need to add to their pieces by drafting a new part. Writers do not tend to move sequentially from one part of the process to the next.

Knowing now what the writing process or authoring cycle is all about, in Chapter Nine we look at how teachers engage learners in the writing process. Writers' workshop is one way to establish a process writing time in the classroom. The important thing to remember is that children learn to write by writing so they need many engagements in writing for a variety of reasons and purposes. They need to write every day. They need to know they have something to say that others want to read, and they have to believe that they will receive the help they need.

SUMMARY

In this chapter we have looked at what writing is and what it does for people. We have discussed why people write and the need humans have for writing. We have introduced the writing process or authoring cycle, as it is sometimes called. The focus on teaching writing increased dramatically over the last two decades of the twentieth century. Today, many states require their students to "pass" writing tests at various grade levels. Teaching writing—composing and revising— is difficult. Without some instruction, however, children will not learn what they are capable of and many will not perform adequately on state assessments.

In the next chapter, we describe how to establish a process writing classroom. We explore how to teach writing, how to show students revising and editing techniques, and how to improve their spelling. We discuss how to assess writing, and how to use assessment information to plan instruction.

THEORY-TO-PRACTICE CONNECTIONS

Writing Theory

1. Writing is a transactive process.

2. Writers learn that writing accomplishes the things they want to do.

3. Writers learn to write by writing.

4. Growth occurs in overlapping stages, which learners move in and out of.

5. Composing occurs in stages, which writers move in and out of.

6. Under the right conditions, writers learn to value revision.

Examples of Classroom Practice

1. Rehearsing, drafting, conferencing

2. Multiple and wide variety of functional writing opportunities available in the classroom

3. Daily sustained writing

4. Individual writing folders for works-in-progress and old drafts

5. Record-keeping forms for student writers to use that show at what stage each of their pieces is

6. Writers need an audience and authentic opportunities to write and publish

SUGGESTED READINGS

Calkins, L. 1983. *Lessons from a Child*. Portsmouth, NH: Heinemann.

Carr, J. 1999. *A Child Went Forth: Reflective Teaching with Young Readers and Writers*. Portsmouth, NH: Heinemann.

Dancing with the Pen: The Learner as a Writer. 1992. Wellington, NZ: Ministry of Education.

Graves, D. 1994. *A Fresh Look at Writing*. Portsmouth, NH: Heinemann.

Hindley, J. 1996. *In the Company of Children*. York, ME: Stenhouse.

EXTENDING YOUR DISCUSSION

1. For the next two days, keep a list of everything you use writing for in your life. Share your list with classmates. Add to your list anything anyone offers that you didn't already have. This will give you a reasonably good idea of what you can encourage your own students to "see" about the value and purposes of writing in our lives.

2. If possible, look at the writing products of one child across an academic year. Spread these writing samples out on a table from earliest attempt to most recent. Study them and then decide what stage or stages the writer is in. What evidence of growth can you detect across these samples? What kind of writing program is the child in? What relationships can you draw between instruction and growth? Share your findings with your classmates. What kind of rubric for evaluating them would you develop?

3. Write something on any subject, in any genre you want to use. It would be best to select a topic you know something about and a genre with which you are familiar, but it is not required. Share your drafts with your classmates and take turns. Do not criticize each other's writing. Rather, tell each student/writer one thing you like about their work. Be as specific as possible. Then ask one question that is not answered in the piece. How do your classmates' questions help you as a writer?

REFERENCES

Atwell, N. 1998. *In the Middle: Writing, Reading, and Learning with Adolescents*, 2nd ed. Portsmouth, NH: Heinemann.

Bridges, L. 1997. *Writing as a Way of Knowing*. York, ME: Stenhouse.

Bissex, G. 1980. *GYNS AT WRK: A Child Learns to Read and Write*. Cambridge, MA: Harvard University Press.

Burrows, A. 1977. "Composition: Prospect and Retrospect." In *Reading and Writing Instruction in the United States: Historical Trends*, ed. H. Robinson. Newark, DE: IRA.

Calkins, L. 1983. *Lessons from a Child*. Portsmouth, NH: Heinemann.

———. 1990. *Living Between the Lines*. Portsmouth, NH: Heinemann.

———. 1994. *The Art of Teaching Writing*, 2nd ed. Portsmouth, NH: Heinemann.

Chomsky, C. 1971. "Write First, Read Later." *Childhood Education* 47: 296–299.

Dancing with the Pen: The Learner as a Writer. (1992). Wellington, NZ: Ministry of Education.

Elbow, P. 1973. *Writing Without Teachers*. New York: Oxford University Press.

Emig, J. 1971. *The Composing Process of Twelfth Graders*. Urbana, IL: NCTE.

Graves, D. 1975. "An Examination of the Writing Processes of Seven-Year-Old Children." *Research in the Teaching of English* 9: 227–41.

———. 1983. *Writing: Teachers and Children at Work*. Portsmouth, NH: Heinemann.

———. 1994. *A Fresh Look at Writing*. Portsmouth, NH: Heinemann.

Hansen, J. 2001. *When Writers Read*, 2nd ed. Portsmouth, NH: Heinemann.

Harste, J., V. Woodward, and C. Burke. 1984. *Language Stories and Literacy Lessons*. Portsmouth, NH: Heinemann.

Hindley, J. 1996. *In the Company of Children*. York, ME: Stenhouse.

Johnson, P. 1992. *A Book of One's Own: Developing Literacy Through Book Making*. Portsmouth, NH: Heinemann.

King, S. 2000. *On Writing: A Memoir of the Craft*. New York: Scribner.

Lane, B. 1993. *After The End: Teaching and Learning Creative Revision*. Portsmouth, NH: Heinemann.

Leu, D. 2001. "Exploring Literacy on the Internet: Preparing Students for New Literacies in a Global Village." *The Reading Teacher* 54 (6): 568–72.

McCarrier, A., G. Pinnell, and I. Fountas. 1999. *Interactive Writing: How Language and Literacy Come Together, K–2*. Portsmouth, NH: Heinemann.

Miller, K. 2000. "Language, Learners, and Culture in an ESL Multi-Age Classroom." In *Teaching At-Risk Students in the K–4 Classroom: Language Literacy, and Learning*, eds. C. Stice and J. Bertrand. Norwood, MA: Christopher Gordon.

Newkirk, T., and N. Atwell. 1988. *Understanding Writing: Ways of Observing, Learning, and Teaching*. Portsmouth, NH: Heinemann.

Read, C. 1971. "Pre-school Children's Knowledge of English Phonemes. *Harvard Educational Review* 41: 1–34.

Short, K., J. Harste, and C. Burke. 1996. *Creating Classrooms for Authors and Inquirers*, 2nd ed. Portsmouth, NH: Heinemann.

Solley, B. 2000. "Writing: Past, Present, and Future." In *Writers' Workshop: Reflections of Elementary and Middle School Teachers*, ed. B. Solley. Boston: Allyn and Bacon.

Temple, C., R. Nathan, N. Burris, and F. Temple. 1988. *The Beginnings of Writing*. Boston: Allyn and Bacon.

CHILDREN'S LITERATURE

Surat, M. 1989. *Angel Child, Dragon Child*. New York: Scholastic.

Yep, L. 1991. *The Star Fisher*. New York: Scholastic.

CHAPTER NINE

"The quality of writing in our classrooms grows more from the tone, values, and relationships of our classroom communities than from anything else."

(Lucy Calkins, 1994, 142).

WRITING: REFLECTIVE EVALUATION, PLANNING, AND TEACHING

Julie entered Stacie Newton's third-grade classroom as a needy, dependent child; but by the end of a year, a different Julie emerged (Newton, 2000). Julie rarely chose to read a book when third grade began. A follower, she was largely influenced by her classmates. Rather than offer an opinion, Julie forfeited hers. However, during writers' workshop, Julie discovered the power of her own voice.

Stacie employed writers' workshop in her classroom for the first time in her five-year teaching career. Stacie had learned about writers' workshop and had engaged in it as part of her graduate course work. New to third grade and new to her school, Stacie was anxious to involve her children in the writing process.

She documented all her children's progress over the course of the year, but it was Julie who appeared to change the most. "It was a story about Julie's parents in January that began her transformation. From that point forward, she viewed herself as an author with much to share" (Newton, 2000, 56).

Stacie's classroom was a literate environment where Julie came to see the connections between reading and writing. The more Julie wrote, the more she read, drawing ideas for her own writing from the books Stacie read to the class and that Julie read independently. As Stacie noted, Julie's favorite authors became her teachers. She used dialect; she made characters stammer when they expressed emotion; she put quotations around sound effects. When Stacie asked Julie about all the different strategies she was experimenting with in her writing, Julie responded, "It's just something I saw in a book I was reading. I thought I would try it. It's the way it would be if the story was really happening" (Newton, 2000, 57).

By February other third graders sought Julie's advice with their writing. They valued her opinion. Julie gained academically; but moreover, she learned responsibility, gained independence, and discovered her own voice as she participated and became a writer. Choosing her own topics and audiences empowered Julie. She believed she was a good writer because she was given choice and people wanted to read what she wrote.

By the end of third grade, Julie stated that "she was 'an author' who wrote 'mostly about her life'" (Newton, 2000, 61). She had found her voice. She viewed her life as significant enough to write about. And she was only in the third grade.

Over the years, we have seen many children like Julie, children who are fortunate enough to find themselves in classrooms where teachers understand the importance of the composing process in the development of children's literacy and learning. From inner-city to rural classrooms across the United States, children are learning to like writing and that their writing helps inform the rest of their learning.

The purpose of this chapter is to present a theoretical framework for teaching writing parallel to that established for teaching reading. Here, we explore several ways to assess and document children's writing growth and how to use that knowledge in planning appropriate instruction. Children typically go through several identifiable stages as they develop into writers. Teachers who recognize these are able to evaluate children's writing, structure classroom events based on that evaluation, and help children evaluate their own progress. Knowledgeable teachers also recognize the strategies children use in their writing. They know what their children might be ready to learn next (Anderson, 2000; Atwell, 1998; Calkins, 1986, 1994; Hansen, 1987; Harwayne, 2000;

Newkirk and Atwell, 1988; Ray, 1999; Short, Harste, and Burke, 1996; Temple, Nathan, Burris, and Temple, 1988).

In this chapter, we present a practical view of teaching writing that more closely fits what is now known about language and learning in general and reading and writing more specifically. We believe that a major goal for teachers is to prepare their learners for the complex, highly technological information age of the twenty-first century, an era in which literacy is paramount.

The writing children do at school must be more than just copying or completing arbitrary activities on worksheets. Learners learn by doing; readers learn by reading; writers learn by writing. Children must practice the act of composing just as a reader must practice the act of reading. And, as in learning in general and reading in particular, learners perform inefficiently at first, learning from their mistakes, figuring out how to "do" it, as they engage in the activity being learned. When a knowledgeable teacher is present, helping, praising, demonstrating, informing, encouraging, suggesting, coaching, comforting, and assuring, learners learn more quickly and more surely.

Writing fulfills both a social and personal communicative need. Children need time each day to practice their writing. The traditional ways children have been taught to write—assigning topics, copying from a textbook, copying from the board, handwriting, and completing other types of seatwork—are not reflected in the purposes writers experience in adulthood. As adults, writers write from their own ideas, from an inner voice and drive, from need and want.

GETTING STARTED: WRITERS' WORKSHOP

As teachers' beliefs about writing and the role writing plays in their students' lives changed, they found it necessary to change their instructional practices. *Writers' workshop* emerged in the 1980s when teachers began exploring ways to implement the writing process in their classrooms (Atwell, 1998; Calkins, 1994; Graves, 1983; Short, Harste, and Burke, 1996; Turbill, 1984, 1985). Writers' workshop is a way of organizing the classroom that provides ample opportunity to engage children in the authoring cycle. It provides time for children to write, fosters writing for a variety of purposes, and enables children to learn about writing as they use writing for their own purposes and as they learn to write.

This curricular *component* is called writers' workshop for two obvious reasons. First, the word *workshop* refers to the place people go each day to work on their crafts. For example, furniture makers go to the workshop each day to design and build their chairs, tables, and cabinets. Second, note that the word *writers'* is possessive. That means it belongs to the writers. The writers' workshop is a place where authors (in this case, children and their teachers) go each day to work together or alone on their crafts (writing). Just as furniture makers mold and shape wood into furniture, writers mold and shape language into narratives and expositions. Both are processes; both require time, thought, and practice.

Workshops are also places where the tools for crafting are located. In the woodshop are such tools as lathes, planers, joiners, sandpaper, and stains. Authors need tools, too. The writers' workshop is equipped with paper (we recommend unlined paper in a variety of colors), pens, pencils (graphite and colored), markers, computers with word processors and publishing software, printers, dictionaries and other reference materials, and lots and lots of books.

The traditional thirty minutes usually allotted to teach "English" does not allow teachers or students enough time to craft their writing. Writers' workshop provides the time authors need. Typically sixty to seventy-five minutes of class time daily in self-contained classrooms is devoted to writers' workshop. Establishing a regular time is important so students can anticipate and plan (Anderson, 2000). Allotting enough time is important so authors can become invested and intensely involved in their work. Calkins (1994) asserts that it is nearly impossible to create an effective workshop if authors only write once or twice a week. Time is also a factor because the teacher needs time to incorporate all the components: focus lessons, work time for both writing and conferring, peer conferences, response groups, share sessions, and publications and celebrations.

Many teachers also like to employ readers' workshop in conjunction with writers' workshop. In that case, even more time is needed. Some teachers plan as much as two and one-half hours for combined writers' and readers' workshop time they call language workshop.

Space and Materials

Writers need storage facilities. While there are many ways to organize children's individual writing efforts, most teachers simply have children date their drafts and keep them in individual writing folders or portfolios. The children can decorate folders as an act of personalization that adds to their sense of ownership. Portfolios typically contain most, if not all, of the children's writing, both published and unpublished. The collection provides children with evidence of their own progress and allows teachers a means to engage in collaborative evaluation of children's work. Children select from their folders the piece they wish to work on. Sometimes teachers have a separate storage facility for works-in-progress, and another for other drafts and finished pieces. However accomplished, teachers must help children organize, date, label, and keep their written productions.

Make sure the children have access to lots of paper, lined and unlined, colored and plain, and a variety writing implements, pencils, pens, gel pens, and thin-line markers. Many teachers keep markers in tubs at a central location. Paper is stored on shelves for easy access. Publication materials include construction paper, wallpaper, glue, fasteners, yarn or string, and cardboard. Tubs, boxes, or plastic containers often hold such supplies. Some teachers create writing centers where materials are stored.

Nurturing Authors

The greatest difference between the traditional classroom and the language workshop is who is responsible for learning. In the traditional classroom the teacher teaches rules and definitions for children to memorize and then apply to assigned tasks. For the most part, this involves students copying from a textbook or the board or filling in worksheets. In the writers' workshop the children and their teacher become authors and "the tools of writing are taught in the context of 'real' writing" (Solley, 2000, 4).

Authors, especially children, must feel safe and secure if they are to take risks with their writing. Authors make mistakes; they must trust their peers when they share their works. They need to feel comfortable in seeking assistance from other members of their learning community. Establishing a sense of community in the classroom is crucial. Teachers accomplish this through modeling what is expected and by spending several weeks at the beginning of the year establishing routines, setting up a task management system, and taking it one step at a time.

Getting writers' workshop started is not always easy. Some children are reluctant to write, having been in classrooms where their work was marked with red ink, and they had to recopy to correct all their errors and turn their papers back in. Some children think they have nothing to say. Some think writing is too difficult. Graves (1983) cites four ways to motivate children to write: write every day, write with the students, allow students to select their own topics, and allow students to be responsible for making the decisions about what they say in the piece.

Some children are driven toward perfection and are initially uncomfortable with the notion of rough drafts. They want everything to be "perfect," each word spelled correctly, each letter perfectly formed. For these children, brainstorm with the class words they frequently need and post them around the room or on your class word wall. Word lists not only add to the literate environment, they provide confidence to children who are not good spellers. Continue to encourage drafting as a process every writer goes through; finished pieces take time. It takes time and authentic purposes for their writing before some young authors realize that the revising and editing parts of the writing process are both fun and profitable.

To establish a writing component in their classrooms, teachers typically demonstrate by writing their own first drafts. They show children through their own writing how writers cross out, attempt to spell, cut and paste, leave blank spaces till later, and so on. They allay students' fear by encouraging risk taking, and they support writing by suggesting their students write about what they know, what they are interested in, and allowing them to choose their own topics always.

Some Ways to Start the Process   Because nurturing a sense of authorship is delicate and the writing process is complex, implementing writers' workshop may take several weeks. Rehearsing, conferencing, peer editing, revising works in progress, final editing, and publishing finished pieces take time, but it also takes time to become comfortable with daily sustained silent writing (SSW). In the beginning, the class may engage in group, guided, or modeled writing. This may take place after a class event such as a field trip, be connected to something in which most of the children are interested such as an article in the local paper, or follow an especially good book read aloud.

After the first draft of the group story is complete, the children may be given copies and asked to work in pairs to revise it. They may work in small groups as well. After the revision suggestions are discussed and the best ones selected, the teacher may give the students a copy for editing, along with a list of basic mechanical errors to look for.

The piece can then be illustrated and bound into a class book. This process can be repeated. In the meantime, children may have started their own individual writing so that the demonstrations and individual SSW overlap. As soon as first drafts are well under way, student authors are rarely at the same place in the process. Be prepared to have some children rehearsing, some drafting, some revising, some editing, some publishing, and some stuck.

Personal narratives are a great place to start. All writers do best when writing what they know and feel strongly about. And the one thing we all know and feel strongly about is ourselves. Also, when asked questions about a particular episode in their personal stories, children can recall the event about which they are writing. If they are writing fiction, they may have trouble relating how it feels to be "in a spring storm," or what the details ought to be of "their life as a sneaker." So personal narrative is an easier genre to begin with.

However, personal narratives are but one of the genres children are acquainted with and when we as teachers force children to conform to only one genre, we are telling them that all writers begin here. By helping children discover what published authors do and the various styles of writing that are possible, we give learners a wider, fuller concept of what writing is and what it can do. That is yet another reason why reading several times each day from a variety of genres is so important.

Calkins (1994) points out, all writing begins as lifework rather than deskwork. She advocates showing students how to use a writer's notebook as a tool for collecting bits and pieces about their lives. A writer's notebook is a place in which writers can "jot down things they notice and wonder about, their memories and ideas, their favorite words and responses to reading" (24). They can record happenings in their lives, include pictures they find interesting, photographs that have meaning for them, items such as dried flowers, and other memorabilia. Writer's notebooks are small combinations of diaries and scrapbooks of things the writer may want to write about, remember, and use.

Writers' workshop is an ideal way to "teach" writing, for it is within the structure of the workshop that instruction takes place. And in that context, instruction is more meaningful because it has a real purpose. Authors must learn the conventions of language to effectively communicate their writings to other people. These include a sense of story, character and plot development, good beginnings, logical resolutions, not to mention following the rules of standard grammar, spelling, punctuation, and capitalization.

Rehearsing   Writing lessons are based in the writing process. In the beginning the teacher talks with the children about things that have happened to them, allowing them to tell stories of their own. They may discuss and list possible topics on the board or write topics on chart or butcher paper to display on a classroom wall. For some children, this is all the *rehearsal* they need; eager to write, they begin to draft. For others, acting out stories, pantomiming, puppetry, drawing, webbing, outlining, or telling their story to someone else are options.

Certainly, selecting a topic and starting a first draft are part of rehearsal. However, published authors cite that the topic is not as important as what the writer does with a topic. In this light, rehearsal takes on a new meaning. No longer just about finding a "perfect" topic, rehearsal is looking at possibilities and finding significance in all the things around us (Calkins, 1994). Katie Wood Ray (1999) talks about helping young authors "envision" possibilities. She suggests looking closely at how different texts are written: diaries, poems, alphabet and counting books, repeated lines and phrases, shifted perspectives in the middle, texts that hold one story inside another. By doing so, young writers are able to envision what their topics might look like written in all those ways. Ray (1999) suggests that envisioning "helps writers to see a single topic as having many different potentials . . . to see what isn't there yet" (59–60).

Rehearsal helps the writer form and organize the text. It helps with decisions such as character development, which episodes to include, and the order and sequence of the telling. Rehearsal may take some writers several days or even weeks, but if multiple rehearsals make drafting easier, the time is well spent.

Most experienced authors engage in many activities prior to beginning to draft. Some of these include research in the library or archives, interviewing people about events they experienced, imagining themselves as characters or perhaps pretending to be a character, and searching the Internet. Ray (1999) lists dozens of possibilities.

Drafting   Drafting becomes a continuation of rehearsal rather than another step in the process. For drafting, children need time. Some children prefer quiet time; others may wish to confer with classmates or the teacher. Anderson (2000) suggests a little of both. The point is to allow time for writers to write for an uninterrupted, sustained time. Sometimes young children, children who are learning English, and children who are struggling with literacy have difficulty with the act of writing. For those who need support in spelling, some teachers give their children small blank booklets to serve as personal dictionaries where children write the words they want and need. Some teachers use other students as scribes. The goal during SSW is for spelling, grammar, and punctuation not to interfere with the author's initial writing. Mechanics are worked on later.

When the author has completed the first draft, the teacher asks the author what he or she wants to do with it. Will it be published? If not, the teacher or student may file it in the student's portfolio, perhaps to be taken out and revised at a later time. However, if the author wishes to continue work on the piece toward publication, the teacher provides the time and the means.

Revising   Revising the piece ensures that it says what the author intends for it to say. Sometimes in drafting authors leave out pertinent information. Perhaps a character needs to be more refined, a setting more accurately described, the sequence of events more realistic, or a plot more fully developed. Perhaps dialogue needs to be added or expanded. Sometimes younger children are missing a piece in the middle or their stories end too abruptly. Helping authors rework their pieces so that the audience understands what is happening is the purpose of revising, not the succession of drafts. However, the final decision about what will be added or omitted during revision remains the writer's.

Author's circle is a strategy that helps authors communicate their intentions to an audience. In the author's circle, young writers move away from the solitary experience of writing to sharing, responding, and interacting with peers in either large or small groups. Author's circle is designed to facilitate sharing work in progress. A writer requests, or the teacher sets aside, time for a group of students to listen to an author read a draft of a piece of material to be published. After listening to the piece, members of the group respond to the author. First, they compliment the author about something specific in the piece—for example, what they liked best or how the piece made them feel. They are encouraged to use some of the language from the text in their remarks. This ensures that they really listen. Then they may question specific elements of the text they want clarified or amplified. In this setting, writers begin to refine their sense of audience. Authors direct the meeting, share their work, ask if it is clear, and respond to questions. They may request suggestions for improvement but they don't have to.

Editing   Frequently, as authors revise, they catch grammatical and spelling errors, and they fix them at those times. Sometimes, however, authors read what they intended to write rather than what they actually wrote. For that reason, to make the published piece readable to an audience and to help young writers learn the conventions of English, *editing* takes place. The author, a peer group, or the teacher may edit. However, if the teacher edits, it is not usually in the form of marking on the author's paper. Instead, editing allows teachers to ask their student authors to find problems in their drafts. For example, teachers might ask authors to circle all the words they think are misspelled (see Figure 9–1). They might ask them to check for capital letters, end marks,

FIGURE 9–1
FINDING MISSPELLED
WORDS

incomplete or run-on sentences, and so on. In most cases, especially if the piece is to be formally published, the teacher serves as a final editor. Typing or copying the text over in very neat handwriting usually occurs following the final edit. Typically, teachers ask writers to look for one type of convention at a time, rather than requiring them to focus on several at once.

Publishing   *Publishing* is sharing finished products. It may be as simple as a text displayed in the classroom or as complicated as a hardcover book. (See Appendix B for bookbinding ideas.) For many authors, publishing their first text is all the encouragement they need for publishing their next.

Author's chair is the standard venue for sharing finished work. At this point, children's work is enjoyed and celebrated. Much like shared book, author's chair is the time for writers to practice and then read their published products for the appreciation and applause of peers and teachers. Typically, author's chair is a large-group production, taking place at a regular time each week. Many teachers have a particular chair such as an old easy chair or a rocking chair that has been designated the read-aloud chair. This is where author's chair takes place.

A student with a finished piece of writing signs up for author's chair and reads his or her piece aloud to an enthusiastic teacher and classmates. Sharing writing that has undergone several revisions and final editing is itself one of the ways children "publish" their final drafts and if standards are maintained, one of the things that encourages young authors to write and revise their work. Author's chair may take place once or twice a week or as a special celebration marking the end of a unit of study or a grading period.

ONE TEACHER'S BEGINNING

Stacie, convinced her third graders would learn more about the skills they were being tested on if they applied them in their own writing instead of copying lessons and completing worksheets, embarked on establishing a writers' workshop in her classroom. While she expected to see her children writing more, she wondered if their skills with grammar would grow and if their attitudes toward writing would improve. She explored these wonderings in her master's thesis.

Stacie describes her classroom as one where students are invited to make choices. They choose writing topics, books they want to read, due dates for assignments, and in some instances, the ways assignments are assessed. She describes the classroom setting as painting a picture of the literate environment in which her learners participate. They engage in daily silent reading, and she reads aloud to them several times a day. They study published authors and their works. Critical to her success is that the children's writing is viewed as equally important to that of published authors and so it is displayed in the classroom and hallway.

Julie told Stacie that her ideas for stories came mostly from her life and the books she read. For example, Julie's story *Some House* was modeled after Patricia Polacco's *Some Birthday*. Stacie points out that Julie not only got ideas from her favorite authors, she also imitated their uses of conventions (Newton, 2000, 34).

> **Stacie:** You have used quotation marks around the words *click, click, click*. Was someone saying those words in your story?
>
> **Julie:** No. They're sounds. You know; someone was throwing rocks at the window. They're the sound the rocks made. So it's kind of like the rock is talking. Anyway, the quotation marks let you know it's different from the rest of the sentence.
>
> **Stacie:** Where did you get that idea?
>
> **Julie:** I see authors do it in the books I read all the time.

Julie's knowledge of the need to use conventions grew as her writing progressed. Stacie noticed that she not only attended to grammar and spelling but also to strategies that enabled her to more clearly communicate the meaning of her pieces to her audience (Newton, 2000, 40).

> **Julie:** I have to ask you if I'm using too many "Neptunes."
>
> **Stacie:** I see what you are talking about. Most of the sentences on the first page begin with the word Neptune. I see you have written a compound sentence. "Neptune is my favorite. . . , and you can not see it from Earth." That is one good way not to have to say Neptune twice in a row. You can combine two sentences.
>
> **Julie:** That's what I was trying to do.

Stacie: Do you see another place in your story where you could use a compound sentence?

Julie: Yes. I could use lots of them. That's easy.

All through the process, Stacie played an active role in helping Julie. She did so via conferences. *Writing conferences* are the heart of evaluation and instruction. Teachers confer with writers as they progress through the authoring cycle. Some teachers walk around the room as the children are writing, stopping by and simply asking, "How's it going?" Some teachers regularly schedule conferences so that they may ensure seeing everybody as often as possible. Some teachers do both.

THE WRITING CONFERENCE

Like reading conferences, writing conferences are one of the most important teacher-student interactions centering on reading and writing (Parry and Hornsby, 1988). Anderson (2000) describes conferences as conversations with authors, with one person taking the lead and then perhaps the other. Writing conferences provide the setting for both strategic teaching and evaluation. They may take two forms, the peer conference and the pupil-teacher conference. In peer conferences, children read their drafts to a single child or children in small-group settings.

Peer Conference   Author's circle may also be employed as a form of peer conference. Writers often come to the peer conference with requests for their peers: "What do you think of my beginning?" "Do I need more details?" "How can I make that part more clear?" "Can you think of a better ending?" The author instructs the peer group to specify what they like and then to ask any questions they actually thought of concerning the content of the piece they were listening to. In this way, authors have a chance to see what their potential audience thinks. They can then add information or make any changes to improve the text.

Pupil-Teacher Conferences   Pupil-teacher conferences provide writers opportunities to receive encouragement, support, and instruction from the teacher. In this risk-free environment, teachers may discuss problem areas and explore appropriate strategies with children. Conferences afford the teacher a way to assess and guide individual children's writing, as well as the opportunity to document children's growth as writers. Teachers encourage children to write freely without regard for mechanics on the first draft. When the children meet with the teacher to talk about their drafts, the focus is always on meaning first and then mechanics. Conferences also provide teachers with ideas for mini- or focus lessons.

Anderson (2000) cites four characteristics of the pupil-teacher conference. First, the point is to help students become better writers. One way to do this is to teach techniques their favorite authors use. Another way is to have them reflect on their writing. Second, in order to provide help, conferences must have structure. They are the time to talk about the type of writing the students are doing; to revise by ensuring the piece has a beginning, middle, and end; to develop the plot, to add a lead or a punch line; and to edit. They are the opportunity to talk specifically about what the writer wants and needs help doing and to provide examples to guide the writing. Third, the teacher pursues a line of thinking with the author, choosing only one line per conference. Fourth, both the student and the teacher have roles.

Anderson (2000) reminds us that the conference is a conversation, and as such, both the teacher and the student have roles. The student leads first and sets the agenda for the conference by describing the writing. The teacher's role is two-part. In the first part, the teacher invites the student to set the agenda by listening to the student read part or listening to the student tell what work is being done as a writer. The teacher uses this information to decide what to teach. In the second part of the conference, the teacher gives the student feedback about the writing, teaches the student something to make the writing better, encourages the student to "have-a-go," and links the conference to the student's independent work.

A conference may be requested by students who want help. Then students sign up or otherwise let the teacher know they want a conference. During these conferences, it is the student who takes the lead by describing the piece, asking for what he or she wants, and reading any or all of it aloud to the teacher as time permits. Perhaps the most helpful questions a teacher can ask are "What do you want to do with this piece?" and "How can I help you?" (This second question may be asked by the teacher of him- or herself.) Teachers take an active role in providing what the students ask for. Occasionally, perhaps they will offer one or two other things they see are also needed (Hindley, 1996).

With conferences the teacher has requested, the teacher takes the lead, asking questions, pointing out, and making suggestions. Questions are always open-ended. The teacher may begin by simply asking, "How's it going?" Anderson (2000) suggests establishing a routine question so that the authors know what to expect at the beginning of each conference. Finding out what the author is doing as a writer, what the author is working on during a specific period, or what the author wants and needs help doing are the key elements of the conference. In both types of conferences, the teacher shows care for the author and the work the author is doing. "The success of the conference often rests on the extent to which students sense that we are genuinely interested in their work, in them as writers—and as individuals" (Anderson, 2000, 21).

Conferences may occur at all stages of the writing process, but the focus varies according to where the writer is. During rehearsal, conferences may help the author find a topic, find a focus, or find out how to gather information. During drafting, they help the writer develop the idea and keep the writing flowing. As part of revision, they help improve the work of writing. During editing, conferences focus on helping students find their own problems with the mechanics so that they become better editors. Conferences even occur during publication to help the author determine pagination, where to put illustrations, and the style of the finished product.

The writers' workshop is a busy place. The wonderful thing is that a classroom filled with observing, talking, and planning is a splendid environment for literacy development (Calkins, 1994). Meant to run against the norm of the traditional fragmented daily schedule, language or writers' workshop is markedly different from the classroom where all learners move in unison through a set of prescribed steps and teacher-assigned worksheets designed to drill, skill, and kill young writers. Children fortunate enough to be members of writing workshop classrooms leave wanting to write, believing they are writers.

TEACHING APPROACHES: LESSONS WITHIN A LITERATE ENVIRONMENT

Unlike reading, few manuals or programs exist for teaching students how to write. Most language arts textbooks include a section on the writing process, but they treat it as a lockstep method with brainstorming the first day, drafting the second, and so on. Some books of story starters are available as are several rubrics and holistic scoring devices; but fortunately there are no commercially available basal programs as there are for reading. Therefore, teachers must match their learners with appropriate materials and strategies. The approaches for teaching writing are: *write-aloud*, *guided writing*, and *sustained silent writing (SSW)*, along with conferences and mini- or focus lessons.

Teachers choose different approaches with the whole class, within a small group, or individually. Student need dictates the choice. Knowing what the learner is doing and knowing what materials are available, the teacher selects the most appropriate approach. Like the approaches employed to teach reading, writing approaches offer instruction based on the amount of supports or challenges each offer the learner. Write-aloud offers more supports. It is used when the writing offers too many challenges for the young author. Guided writing offers some challenges and some supports. The teacher uses guided writing to show authors how to handle tough writing problems. Sustained silent writing provides the time needed for authors to successfully write texts of their own. Choosing the best approach does not supplant or replace writers' workshop; it complements it.

Write-Aloud   Write-aloud serves two important functions in the classroom. First, it provides demonstrations of how and why people write. Conventions such as where to begin writing, how to use spacing, how in English to write from left to right and return to the left for the next line, and how to approach spelling can be demonstrated when the teacher writes while the children watch. Children observe the teacher writing for different purposes: notes home to parents, newsletters, labels for the classroom, plans, and even reminder notes. Second, write-aloud provides an opportunity for the teacher to write or scribe for the children if what they are attempting to write has too many challenges for them. Both help young children come to understand that print can represent their talking and thinking. This insight is a fundamental part of learning how to read what others write and how to write for oneself.

Write-aloud can be a teacher demonstration to show strategies writers use or the teacher can share the pen and actively involve children in interactive writing. Some teachers use an overhead projector or the class computer to write a morning message to their class. This technique allows the children to watch as the teacher says what she is writing and writes it. Similarly, teachers may invite a child to the projector or computer, and the two may engage in a written conversation as the others watch. Chart stories may be used to demonstrate how writers cross out by drawing a single line through the word(s) they wish to change, spell the best they can, cut and paste, or leave blank spaces till later.

Write-aloud is a useful approach in the pre-school and primary years and especially for children who are just learning English. It may also be useful for teachers to demonstrate techniques for older students. Parent volunteers, older students, or any number of classroom helpers may print children's dictations. Authentic opportunities for children to engage in write-aloud abound: captions for their artwork, captions and labels for finished project displays, notes and messages, and signs posted around the room. These written products become part of the literate environment teachers are creating. Children read and reread them during the day or when the entire class takes a "reading walk" around the classroom, reading everything that is displayed.

All children love to tell stories and they usually have many to share; however, they may feel frustrated if their writing cannot be read by others. Teachers may sit with an individual child and write or "scribe" as the child dictates the story. While time-consuming, the demonstration is very powerful. It produces a text that can be read and reread by the child. It also produces a product that the child may take home to read and share. This process works well with group-dictated stories, too. During the composing process, the teacher demonstrates how writers "do it." They may negotiate with the group (or individual) about such things as spellings, sentence structure, and word choices. They might then use the text for further practice with reading or for additional teaching about the writing process.

Write-aloud provides opportunity for immersion and demonstration in the writing process. It assists those who need additional support in writing. When used in conjunction with writing workshop, write-aloud is a powerful approach for inexperienced writers and children whose native language is not English because it shows the connection between oral and written language.

Guided Writing   When children need help with specific aspects of the writing process or the mechanics of written language, teachers prepare strategic instruction in the form of demonstrations and think-aloud events. The goal is to make explicit and facilitate the development of all the strategies students need to become proficient writers. Guided writing instruction and guided practice may take place in formal one-on-one writing conferences, in informal on-the-spot interactions, and with planned instructional events for large groups. Guided writing is the equivalent of guided reading. Explorations and demonstrations of the writing process and the ways writers solve problems as they write give young writers information and help them develop insights and skills. As children explore how to make meaning with written language, demonstrations of various aspects of writing are extremely important instructional tactics and may be incorporated into any phase of the authoring cycle.

Look at Figure 9–2, "Lee is my friend." One of the skills this young writer appears ready to learn is paragraphing. She knew *when* she had completed a set of related sen-

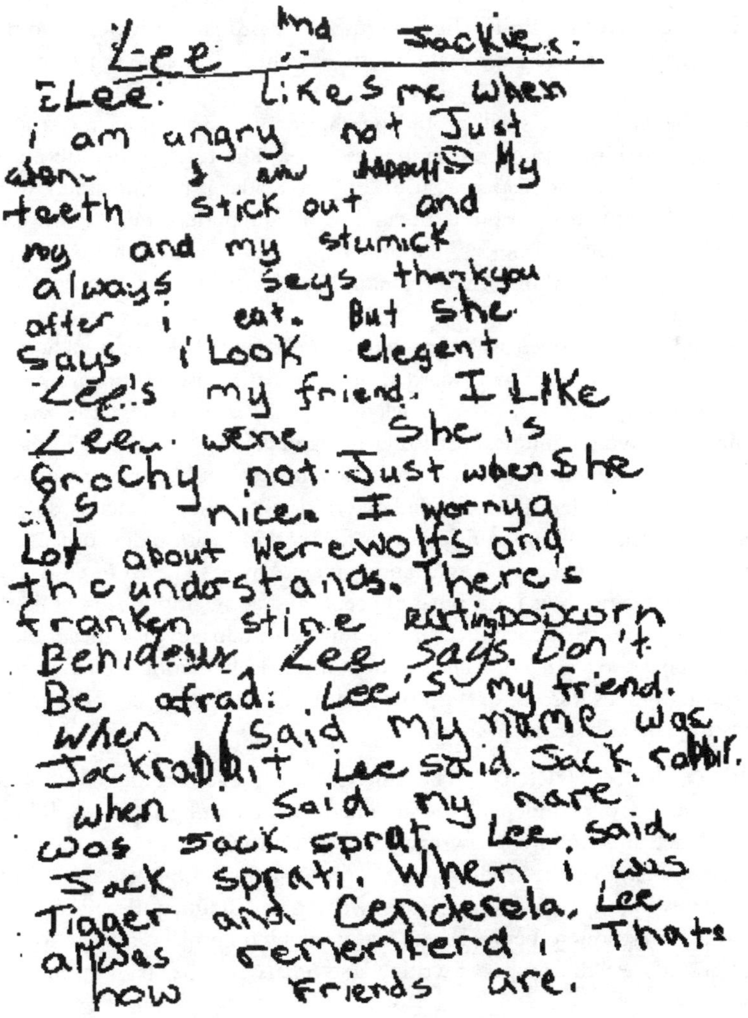

FIGURE 9–2
LEE IS MY FRIEND

Lee and Jackie

Lee likes me when i am angry not Just when i am happy My teeth stick out and my and my stumick always seys thankyou after i eat. But she says i look elegent Lee's my friend. I Like Lee wene She is grochy not Just when She is nice. I worry a Lot about Werewolfs and thc undorstands. There's franken stine eating popcorn Behidewr. Lee says. Don't Be afrad. Lee's my friend. When i said My name was Jackrabbit Lee said. Jack rabbit. when i said my nane was Jack sprat Lee said. Jack sprati. When i was Tigger and Cenderela. Lee alwas rememberd i That's how Friends are.

tences, but she did not know *how* to show the reader. The teacher recognized this and planned a guided writing session to explore paragraphing. She chose two books, *Koala Lou* by Mem Fox and *What Do You Do with a Kangaroo?* by Mercer Mayer. Both stories, which the child knew very well, provided models of what the teacher wanted to teach. She used these repeated-pattern books as demonstrations, allowing the child to explore how the author separated the text into paragraphs. Then using the child's text, the teacher and the child examined where and how to use the same technique to separate her story into paragraphs at the repeated line "Lee's my friend."

Guided writing may also be helpful with a small group of children who appear to be ready to explore the same concept. For example, many second graders discover compound sentences. As they write, they overuse the word *and*. It is not uncommon for children to write an entire page that consists of a single sentence wherein the simple sentences are joined by *and*.

The teacher may call a small group together or use the opportunity to show the whole class something about how sentences work. The teacher talks about how the author needs to allow the reader to stop, or if the reader is reading aloud, to breathe. The children help the teacher put in the end marks and perhaps even a new paragraph. They may look in several books while they explore how to do what they need to do with the example text. In this manner, children learn where and why to use end marks within a meaningful context.

Older students often need assistance with more advanced elements such as character development, plot development, word choice, and other aspects of their writing. All writers need to learn how and when to delete the unnecessary. One of the best resources for learning creative techniques that foster revision is Barry Lane's (1993) book, *After the End*. In it Lane describes dozens of ideas for how to get better beginnings, how to help students write richer, more detailed descriptions, livelier characters, surprise endings, and more. Other wonderful resources for working with older students are Tom Romano's (1995) *Writing with Passion* and Nancie Atwell's (1998) *In the Middle*.

Knowledgeable teachers learn what concepts and conventions their children need. They look for evidence of what their young authors can do and then they look for what their students need to learn next. They instruct individually during conferences, in small groups through focus lessons, or with the entire class as they guide their students into good writing and conventional usage.

Sustained Silent Writing   The third major approach teachers employ is scheduling time each day for independent sustained, silent writing (SSW). Children need time to practice and explore the writing process on their own just as they need time to practice and explore the reading process on their own. Opportunities for practice and self-expression include writing letters, writing in dialogue journals or observation logs, working on stories to be published, and working on projects arising from the current unit of study. All these types of writing, and others, may be taken through the writing process.

These three major instructional approaches are not steps. Rather, they are events that all may occur each day depending on the writing in which the children are engaged. Just as with reading, a balance is needed among these three approaches—all of which are fundamental to a classroom writing program. The teacher uses many strategies and techniques that encourage writing and help make it functional in the daily life of the classroom.

ASSESSING AND EVALUATING WRITING

While writing conferences provide a setting for instruction, they also offer teachers a means for evaluation. As they confer, teachers gain insights into children's understanding of the writing process, and they gain insights into themselves as teachers. Good teachers are accountable, to themselves and their students. They don't have to be told how or when to be accountable. They want their children to demonstrate proficiency in all skill areas related to reading and writing, including spelling, grammar, and punctuation. Often teachers develop a system for recording the information they learn during conferences, and they devise methods for systematically keeping track of rough drafts, sequential drafts, and final drafts. They create rubrics and checklists for at least some representative pieces of the children's writing (Calkins, 1994).

Assessment, like writing itself, is a process of developing meaning (Calkins, 1994). Knowledgeable teachers observe the strategies children use in their writing. Determining what children know and can do with writing allows teachers to document children's growing control over written language. It helps teachers plan instruction. However, no process-oriented instruments exist for evaluating writing as they do for evaluating reading—for example, miscue analysis. Good teachers create their own checklists, record-keeping devices, and evaluation procedures. What is paramount is that they develop these and use them systematically for documenting learner growth and planning instruction.

Checklists and More   It is important to evaluate children's progress and to report it to parents. Many teachers use checklists to keep track of their learners' progress. Many different checklists can be devised. Checklists are also needed that focus on the elements in more advanced pieces of writing. Figure 9–3 is an example of a checklist to track children's growth in writing. Figure 9–4 is an example of a checklist that looks for the elements in more advanced pieces of writing. Figure 9–5 is a holistic rubric for comparing children's final products.

Not only do checklists and rubrics provide a record-keeping system, they allow teachers to see strengths in their students' writing and to assess areas of need. Many teachers find checklists a quick way of identifying children with similar needs so that they may be grouped together for guided writing instruction. In addition, checklists and rubrics can provide information for assigning grades on report cards. And they provide tangible evidence of students' progress.

Child's Name: _____ Date: _____

FIGURE 9–3
A DEVELOPMENTAL
WRITING CHECKLIST

Pre-writing   N   S   F   C
Does the child . . .
1. know the difference between print and pictures
2. see multiple uses for print in the everyday life of the classroom
3. attend to print in the environment
4. draw to represent personal meaning
5. scribble to represent meaning
6. experiment with forms that begin to resemble either cursive
   or manuscript
7. realize that his/her scribbles are not really print?

FIGURE 9–3
CONTINUED

Early Writing   N   S   F   C

Does the child . . .

1. experiment with the conventions of written language
2. realize that letters and sounds have a relationship
3. employ idiosyncratic spelling
4. attempt approximations of conventional spellings
5. use tracing or copying to help him- or herself figure out
   how written language works
6. create words or grammatical structures that indicate the child
   is hypothesizing patterns
7. engage in natural writing during play, e.g., lists, signs
8. read own writing?

Emergent Writing   N   S   F   C

Does the child . . .

1. write so that others can read it
2. show closer approximations to adult forms
3. attempt spelling new words or new spellings of previous
   inventions
4. experiment with a variety of aspects of the mechanics of
   written language, e.g., commas, end marks, capitals
5. dictate logical and orderly stories, information, accounts
   of events
6. tell stories that have a beginning, middle, and end
7. attempt to self-edit or self-correct?

Transactional Writing   N   S   F   C

Does the child . . .

1. attempt to write information pieces, e.g., exposition
2. attempt to write to persuade, e.g., argumentation
3. begin with the general and move to the specific and
   vice versa
4. state a main point and then defend it
5. show a developing sense of audience
6. engage in writing willingly
7. explore the uses of more advanced mechanics,
   e.g., quotation marks, semi-colons
8. explore some of the literary devices e.g., flashback,
   metaphor, characterization
9. write with definite purpose?

Additional comments:

N = Not Yet   S = Sometimes   F = Frequently   C = Consistently

FIGURE 9–4
ADVANCED WRITING
CHECKLIST

Student's Name: _____ Date: _____

Organization   N   S   F   C
Does the writer . . .
1. write for various purposes
2. demonstrate sense of audience
3. write logical, well-ordered texts
4. develop generalizations with details
5. use appropriate transitions
6. maintain coherence within paragraphs?

Quality   N   S   F   C
Does the writer . . .
1. write original material
2. show developing sense of voice
3. experiment with various styles
4. experiment with various genres?

Vocabulary   N   S   F   C
Does the writer . . .
1. use correct word forms
2. avoid unnecessary repetition
3. use words appropriately
4. use descriptive words
5. show growth in vocabulary?

Sentence Structure   N   S   F   C
Does the writer . . .
1. write in complete sentences
2. write compound sentences
3. write complex sentences
4. use sentences of varied length and complexity?

Mechanics   N   S   F   C
Does the writer . . .
1. use capital letters correctly
2. use end marks correctly
3. have adequate spelling strategies
4. use internal sentence punctuation correctly
5. show improving handwriting?

Additional comments:

N = Not Yet   S = Sometimes   F = Frequently   C = Consistently

FIGURE 9–5
SAMPLE HOLISTIC
SCORING RUBRIC

	SE	EV	EM	NY

1. Story beginning grabs attention
2. Well-developed characters
3. Interesting plot
4. Resolution/climax
5. Evokes emotion
6. Evidence of editing
   words spelled correctly
   correct grammar
   correct punctuation
   correct capitalization
7. Evidence of proofreading
8. Illustrations add to text (optional)

SE = Strongly evident   EV = Evident   EM = Emerging   NY = Not Yet

Portfolios   Just as artists collect pieces of their work, authors collect pieces of their writing. Portfolios may be used simply as collections, or they may be used as learning tools, providing young authors opportunities to reflect upon their writings. Reviewing pieces and noting growth is an integral part of growing as a writer. Reflections are both oral and written. Teachers and students talk about their work as authors. They discuss what they discover about themselves as authors, what they note about other published authors. Then they pour over their own works, perhaps putting pieces in piles, and responding to the question, "Who am I as a writer?" (Short, Harste, and Burke, 1996). They choose pieces they believe best describe themselves as writers, and they share them with other class members. Then they return to write about their selections and why they chose the particular pieces they did. Portfolios offer opportunities for self-evaluation.

As more and more students are using computers and more computers are being found in classrooms, electronic portfolios are gaining popularity. Storing pieces on a disk simply offers an additional way of collecting artifacts that authors choose to represent themselves. And disks take up much less space. Electronic portfolios may also be used for self-evaluation in the same manner as hard copy ones.

Additional Record Keeping   Teachers may also wish to develop various recording forms for keeping track of what students have written, what they are currently working on, and what they have published. Forms may also be developed and kept by the students for this purpose. Figure 9–6 is an example of a student-developed log.

Evaluations of children's writing assess content, style, and mechanics. While some teachers may wish to develop more specific checklists, many teachers prefer open-ended anecdotal records, like the one in Figure 9–7. (See Appendix G)

FIGURE 9–6
STUDENT
DEVELOPMENTAL LOG

Name:
Date:
Title:

What I liked about my work:

What I plan to work on:

Comments:

Anecdotal Records   Teachers make and keep anecdotal records concerning the child's writing during formal and informal conferences. Anecdotal notes may include some or all of the following:

Student writes well-developed stories.

Student shows some application of the ideas and techniques discussed in previous conferences.

FIGURE 9–7
TEACHER'S WRITING
CONFERENCE LOG

Name:
Date:
Text Title:

First Draft Observations:

Second Draft Observations:

Final Draft Observations:

Publishing Plans:

Student perceives how stories are logically ordered.

Student uses literary devices: description, characterization, flashback, surprise, humor, etc.

Student's writings show development of sense of "voice."

Student shows sense of ownership in that _____.

Many teachers are beginning to use summary forms for evaluations of writing to demonstrate and document learner growth over time (see Figure 9–8).

Accountable teachers document growth in writing and plan appropriate instruction for both individuals and groups. Part of planning for classroom instruction includes implementing activities to encourage children's writing. These include, but are not limited to, author's chair, message boards, a classroom post office, observation logs, journals, and play writing. These and other classroom learning events establish an environment in which children come to view themselves as writers and authors.

FIGURE 9–8
WRITING EVALUATION
SUMMARY

Writer's Name: _____   Date: _____

Grade level: _____   Teacher: _____

Title of piece: _____

What percentage of the sentences are well developed?
  Total number of sentences written (TS): _____
  Number of well-developed sentences (WDS): _____
  (WDS/TS) × 100 = percentage of well-developed sentences: _____ %

What percentage of sentences are mechanically correct or nearly correct?
  Total number of sentences written (TS): _____
  Number of correct or nearly correct sentences (CS): _____
  (CS/TS) × 100 = percentage of mechanically correct sentences: _____ %

How does the writer go about constructing meaning?   N   S   U   A
  Writes for a purpose
  Logically orders writing
  Has beginning, middle, and end
  Self-corrects errors that disrupt meaning
  Uses resources to revise and edit
  Uses description and elaborates with details
  Writes complete simple and compound sentences
  Writes grammatically acceptable complex sentences
  Uses capitals and punctuation correctly
  Spells well for age and grade level
  Attempts to write for various purposes
  Has developed sense of own voice
  Writes with originality
  Has sense of audience

Writing narrative text   N   S   U   A   **FIGURE 9–8**
CONTINUED
   Character development
   Description
   Setting
   Relationship of events
   Plot
   Theme
   Overall rating

Writing non-fiction
   Major concepts
   Generalizations
   Specific information
   Logical order
   Vocabulary
   Overall rating

What the writer has learned since the last writing evaluation:

What the writer still needs help with:

The writer's major strengths:

What the writer appears ready to learn next:

N = Not Yet   S = Sometimes   U = Usually   A = Always

PLANNING FOCUSED INSTRUCTION

Mini- or focus lessons for improving writing can emphasize any aspect of authoring. For example, one teacher looks for focus lesson ideas in the following categories: (1) the writing itself—first drafts and revisions; (2) the editing phase whereby mechanics and usage are dealt with; and (3) publishing—where any aspect of books, the parts of books, and illustrations are examined.

   If, for instance, several young authors in your class want to write their own biographical sketches for the backs of their books, a nice focus lesson could be developed. In it, you might read two or three particular good bios from favorite authors, passing them around for the group to see. You might share one or two from books by students from previous years if you have them. The group could then discuss the elements they all have in common, which bios they like best and why. Your students might discover that most authors use the same one for all their books although they are published years apart. You might then encourage all your students to write their own bios for their next published book. These could be shared, revised, edited, and displayed together with individual photos even before they end up on the inside back cover.

When two or three children become interested in poetry, the time might be right for a focus lesson on books that are collections of poetry. Some poetry books are collections of poems by many authors on many different subjects. These are usually divided into concepts or themes. Others are collections by one author, sometimes about one subject. Several types of collections can be examined. The children can decide which type they like and for several weeks, work on poetry might follow. Some of the children might make collections of favorites and some might write their own poems about subjects in which they are interested.

Fodder for focus lessons comes primarily, though certainly not exclusively, from conferences with the children. It is through the conference that the teacher learns what elements of writing and publishing the children are having difficulty with, who has done a really good and interesting job with some piece of writing, what questions the students are having, and which authors they are using as models.

Focus lessons may be built by examining what a sentence is, how writers use commas, how we decide when to start a new paragraph, and more. Exploring dialogue in fiction can provide several focus lessons. You could look at how dialogue is punctuated, how much of it there tends to be before there is more narration/description, how many writers prefer "Bill said," as opposed to the adverbial, "Bill said, happily" type of dialog carrier, and so on. Dialogue is extremely important; and done well, it is not at all simple.

One particularly good focus lesson might be exploring what makes a writer's work identifiable. When second graders read Robert Munsch, what are the characteristics that identify that author's style? Could children who love his work recognize a new book of his without knowing the author? How? What are the common elements that allow us to recognize a Robert Munsch, or a Bill Peet, William Steig, Cynthia Rylant, James Marshall, Mem Fox, Tomie dePaola, or any of the many other wonderful children's writers? The children will know if you give them time to think about it and arrange for them to explore and examine several authors' works.

Spelling, Grammar, and Punctuation
Focus lessons and editing conferences provide the venue teachers need for working with and teaching the conventions of written English. The importance of conventional usage becomes evident to the children when a piece of their writing is to be read publicly by others, given to someone of importance, or otherwise published. Spelling, grammar, and punctuation are conventions we use to make reading a written piece easier; that is, they play a crucial role in aiding readers as they construct meaning from text. Therefore, to assist readers, it is important for the author to learn and conform to these conventions. If, for example,

too many words are misspelled, the audience will have difficulty reading the piece. Some members of the writer's audience may think the writer isn't very smart and will decide they don't want to read what he or she has written. Likewise, grammar, or syntax, is an important part of the reading process, so the author must also attend to grammar. Punctuation helps the reader know how to read the piece; it is especially crucial in showing the reader how to read aloud with appropriate expression.

Spelling   Teachers know that memorizing arbitrary words from the spelling list for the test on Friday does little to improve children's spelling. Creating an individualized spelling program produces better results. Because there is great emphasis on writing, revising, and editing in your classroom, there is a wide variety of print sources on display at all times. As a consequence, spelling tends to be one of the fastest growing of all children's abilities.

It is not the teacher's role to find all the misspelled words and correct them; rather, the author and the peer editors find as many words as they can, perhaps encouraged and guided by you. You might tell children to circle all the words they think are misspelled or to write the first letter and then draw a line for all the words they do not know how to spell. These techniques help children overcome their fear of making mistakes in spelling. Teachers may also give students a list of the words they need to begin looking up and looking for as they revise and edit. Over the course of the year as authors write more and readers read more, everybody learns to spell more words.

The students may be directed to make a list of ten to fifteen words they could not spell or read from the week before (fewer for struggling spellers). These can become the spelling words for the week. Teach them to practice the following steps as they learn to spell their own hard words and have them test each other on Friday: Read—spell—remember—reread—close your eyes and respell—write for practice—and learn.

Give the children simple spelling homework once or twice during the week if you must. Give them more points for long words to prevent them from selecting only short easy words. Record their scores from Friday's test and assign spelling grades accordingly. Give extra points if you see one of their spelling words spelled correctly later.

Usually during conferences, teachers collect and record information on children's spellings to help focus learners' attention on various aspects of their spelling and to document real growth in spelling over time. Gentry (2000) asserts that documenting children's spellings may also be used for literacy assessment. He points to invented spelling as being akin to miscues in reading, because they "allow the observer to assess and teach not only spelling, but also important aspects of phonemic awareness, phonics, writing, and other essential elements of literacy" (318). Figure 9–9 is a sample of the type of information a teacher might collect on a child's spelling.

A beginning teacher might also wish to use a checklist that evaluates growth in spelling. The development of spelling in children's writing is to some extent dependent on the amount of writing the child engages in, the amount of print in the environment and how it is used, and the amount of reading the child does. Many teachers teach spelling in an individualized manner without resorting to a textbook or lists of arbitrary words for students to memorize. Rather, they have children identify misspelled

FIGURE 9–9
GUIDE FOR SPELLING
EVALUATION: PRIMARY

Child's Name: _____ Date: _____

Approximate total number of words in child's story (TW): _____

Title: _____

Type of Strategy	Example	Percent of Sample
1. Phonetic (auditory memory/ sounded out)	eny/any (child knew word *enter*)	
2. Phonic (exaggerated sound)	Sbagede/spaghetti	
3. Known pattern (visual memory/homophone)	brix/bricks (child knew the word *next*)	
4. Synonym (generalizations)	brutren/brothers (child knew the word *children*)	
5. Transpositions (letter reversals)	lable/table	
6. Omissions (too few letters)	nit/night	
7. Additions (too many letters)	rooaze/rose	
8. Root word problem	incuraj/encourage	
9. Affix problems	goeg/going	
10. Scribbles (uses poor handwriting to cover up unknown word)		
11. Risk level (chooses easier word)	He felt good (child wanted *satisfied*)	
12. Other		

Summary:

Evidence of growth:

What the child is ready to learn next:

words in their writing, determine the correct spellings, practice the correct spelling in a variety of ways, and take self-tests at the end of each week. They look for evidence of the new correct spellings in their writing.

Developmental stages of spelling represent what the speller apparently knows about spelling and how the speller thinks about spelling. For example, if the child thinks that spelling is simply randomly writing letters with no attention to matching sounds, the child is still in the *precommunicative* stage. When the child uses letter names and some letters that correspond to matching sounds, the child is using *semi-phonetic* spellings. *Phonetic* spelling evolves as the child uses a strong sound-based strategy as the dominant way to spell. As the speller moves toward using letter patterns, letter sequences, and more morphologically and visually based strategies, the *transitional* stage is evidenced. *Conventional* spelling is attained as the speller adds to the store of words spelled correctly and adds knowledge about words and patterns (Gentry, 2000).

Many teachers find a word wall useful in aiding children's spelling. Word walls are arranged in alphabetical order. Each letter is represented. A 24″ × 36″ piece of construction paper can be divided down the middle and words beginning with two letters can be written on one piece of paper. Some teachers list words commonly used in writing; others expect that any word appearing on the word wall will be spelled correctly on all papers turned in. Another variation of a word wall is to list word families. Word walls are important features of the classroom because spelling is primarily a visual activity. The more learners have an opportunity to see the words, the more likely they are to remember how to spell them. For that reason, children should not be shown incorrect spellings. That spelling is primarily visual is yet another reason that reading is such a significant part of writing. Regardless of the purpose chosen for the word wall, it adds to the literate environment. (For more help with understanding spelling, see Gentry, 2000; Gentry and Gillet, 1993; Harwayne, 2001; Laminack and Wood, 1996; Wilde, 1992.)

Grammar

Grammar   Traditionally, grammar has been taught as separate from writing. Copying exercises from textbooks, completing worksheets, and memorizing rules have dominated the curriculum. Currently a program focusing on memorizing jingles about the parts of speech and identifying and labeling the parts of speech in sentences is popular.

Good teachers rarely use programs that isolate grammar from its actual use. Instead, they teach grammar as natural parts of oral and written language. For example, Stacie provided an excellent example of teaching grammar as part of writing when she encouraged Julie to use compound sentences in her writing (see pages 200–01). She then developed a wonderful focus lesson on sentence combining and sentence separating for the whole class using Julie's work.

Punctuation and Capitalization   Likewise, some teachers teach punctuation and capitalization as separate from writing. However, that is not necessary or particularly good. Stacie, our very knowledgeable writers' workshop teacher, helped Julie learn about using quotation marks in her writing (see page 200). Authors use punctuation to inform the audience where to pause, where to fully stop, where to raise or lower the voice, where to add excitement, and so on. They use sentence length—and in some cases sentence fragments, phrases, and even incomplete sentences—to cue the audience about how to read the passage. These help the reader construct meaning. Children who are exposed only to punctuation and capitalization exercises, who never experience learning to use punctuation and capital letters in real writing, or explore how real writers do it may not fully develop these conventions for their own writing.

Teaching spelling, grammar, punctuation, and capitalization in the context of real writing events offers children opportunities to not only study the conventions of language, but also to apply them in meaningful contexts. Application requires higher-level thinking. Spelling, grammar, punctuation, and capitalization are major parts of most state writing assessments. Children who have been denied the chance to explore and use these conventions as a regular part of writing instruction are disadvantaged. (For more help in understanding teaching mechanics, see Atwell, 1998.)

SUMMARY

Knowledgeable teachers know their students, the resources and materials available, and the approaches to writing. They know a great deal about literature. They write themselves. They employ conferences with their student writers. They immerse children in written language and in opportunities to write. They demonstrate how the writing process and the mechanics of written language work. This means that teachers are authors, too. They share their own writing with their students. They lead and encourage, and they set up authentic writing events. When children have the opportunity to write often, in low-risk environments, and when writing itself makes sense, they learn quickly.

Teachers promote the varied and authentic uses of writing, including communication. This means that they employ written language in functional ways in the classroom—for example, in lists for the children's information, charts of things the children are interested in, forms for children to keep track of their own work, forms for children to sign up for selected events, and messages to the children from the teacher as well as from other children.

Teachers provide daily writing experiences such as journals, which are not graded but which are responded to.

Journal writing without teacher response leaves students questioning its purpose. However, journals do give children a new and powerful means to process information and feelings, and they give the teacher a window into the minds and hearts of the children that may not be gained any other way. Teachers assist children in finding purpose in writing by allowing them to choose their own topics. For some, this may have to begin by encouraging the children to choose between two ideas offered by the teacher, then expanding the choices possible over a period of weeks until children are initiating their own work. Finally, teachers monitor and evaluate the writing process through observation and record keeping. The student-teacher conference is the key for planning, curriculum development, evaluation, and instruction.

This chapter has presented writing instruction based on authentic literacy events that serve the interests and purposes of the students. Children tend to learn to write faster, better, and more joyfully when they do so for their own purposes and when it is part of a process that is under the guidance and encouragement of a knowledgeable teacher.

THEORY-TO-PRACTICE CONNECTIONS

Theory of Writing

1. Writing is learned as it is used, in natural and functional ways.

2. Human beings write to remember, to help make sense of the world, and to express themselves aesthetically.

Examples of Classroom Practice

1. Journals, pen pals, sign-up forms, writing stories, messages

2. Reports from within units of study, personal narratives, poetry

Theory of Writing

3. Writing is a constructive process and children move through several phases in their development as writers.

4. Proficient writers engage in several procedures from first drafts to published works.

5. Writers write better when they choose their own topics.

Examples of Classroom Practice

3. Several opportunities to write daily for a variety of purposes

4. Rehearsals, rough drafts, revisions, etc.

5. Individual writing folders and free choice

SUGGESTED READINGS

Anderson, C. 2000. *How's It Going? A Practical Guide to Conferring with Student Writers*. Portsmouth, NH: Heinemann.

Atwell, N. 1998. *In the Middle: New Understandings About Writing, Reading, and Learning*, 2nd ed. Portsmouth, NH: Heinemann.

Calkins, L., with S. Harwayne. 1991. *Living Between the Lines*. Portsmouth, NH: Heinemann.

Gentry, R. 2000. "A Retrospective on Invented Spelling and a Look Forward." *The Reading Teacher* 54 (3): 318–32.

Lane, B. 1993. *After the End: Teaching and Learning Creative Revision*. Portsmouth, NH: Heinemann.

Ray, K. 1999. *Wondrous Words: Writers and Writing in the Elementary Classroom*. Urbana, IL: NCTE.

EXTENDING YOUR DISCUSSION

1. Discuss the theoretical basis for suggesting such classroom writing opportunities as message board, writer's notebook, individualized spelling program, or literature logs.

2. Collect several samples of children's self-initiated writing. Be sure to date the samples, label them with the child's name and age, and also include a description of the context in which the writing was produced. Arrange the samples by age or by type of writing. Examine the samples, and share and discuss with your classmates. What do these samples indicate about children's writing development?

3. Write a children's story or a personal narrative from your own childhood. Share it in draft form in a small-group setting. Each member of the group must tell what they like best about your text, and each may ask a question. Then revise your first draft. You may find that you want to work on it so that you actually pro-duce several versions before you consider the story complete. Perhaps you will want to type your final version and bind it into a hardback book.

4. Your instructor may wish to have you keep a journal of your observations and reflections on the course. You may be asked to respond in writing to the text, to any children's literature you are reading in conjunction with this course, or to a chapter book being read aloud to your class. Another option is to circulate a roving journal in which each member of your group writes on a regular basis, commenting on the class and on the text readings, as well as writing back in response to the entries made by other members of the group. This is a variation on dialogue journals.

5. Create your own writer's notebook. This is something you may keep going and use to model and share with the students in your own classroom when you ask them to begin their own writer's notebooks.

REFERENCES

Anderson, C. 2000. *How's It Going? A Practical Guide to Conferring with Student Writers*. Portsmouth, NH: Heinemann.

Atwell, N. 1998. *In the Middle, New Understandings About Writing, Reading, and Learning*, 2nd ed. Portsmouth, NH: Heinemann.

Bissex, G. 1980. *GNYS AT WRK: A Child Learns to Read and Write*. Cambridge, MA: Harvard University Press.

Britton, J., T. Burgess, N. Martin, A. McLeod, and H. Rosen. 1975. *The Development of Writing*. Urbana, IL: NCTE.

Burrows, A. 1977. "Composition: Prospect and retrospect." In *Reading and Writing Instruction in the United States: Historical Trends*, ed. H. Robinson. Newark, DE: IRA.

Calkins, L. 1986.

———. 1994. *The Art of Teaching Writing*. Portsmouth, NH: Heinemann.

Calkins, L., with S. Harwayne. 1991. *Living Between the Lines*. Portsmouth, NH: Heinemann.

Chomsky, C. 1971. "Write Now, Read Later." *Childhood Education* 47: 296–99.

Clay, M. 1975. *What Did I Write? Beginning Writing Behaviour*. Portsmouth, NH: Heinemann.

———. 1982. "Learning to Teach Writing: A Developmental Perspective." *Language Arts* 59: 65–70.

Fletcher, R., and J. Portalupi. 2001. *Writing Workshop: The Essential Guide*. Portsmouth, NH: Heinemann.

Fulwiler, T. 1987. *The Journal Book*. Portsmouth, NH: Heinemann.

Gentry, R. 2000. "A Retrospective on Invented Spelling and a Look Forward." *The Reading Teacher* 54 (3): 318–32.

Gentry, R., and J. Gillet. 1993. *Teaching Kids to Spell*. Portsmouth, NH: Heinemann.

Graves, D. 1983. *Writing: Teachers and Children at Work*. Portsmouth, NH: Heinemann.

———. 1991. *Build a Literate Classroom*. Portsmouth, NH: Heinemann.

Handwriting: Basic Skill and Application. 1987. Columbus, OH: Zaner-Bloser.

Hansen, J. 2001. *When Writers Read*, 2nd ed. Portsmouth, NH: Heinemann.

Harste, J., V. Woodward, and C. Burke. 1984. *Language Stories and Literacy Lessons*. Portsmouth, NH: Heinemann.

Harwayne, S. 2000.

———. 2001. *Writing Through Childhood*. Portsmouth, NH: Heinemann.

Hindley, J. 1996. *In the Company of Children*. York, ME: Stenhouse.

Johnson, P. 1992. *A Book of One's Own: Developing Literacy Through Book Making*. Portsmouth, NH: Heinemann.

Laminack, L., and K. Wood. 1996. *Spelling in Use*. Urbana, IL: NCTE.

Lane, B. 1993. *After the End: Teaching and Learning Creative Revision*. Portsmouth, NH: Heinemann.

Newkirk, T., and N. Atwell. 1988. *Understanding Writing: Ways of Observing, Learning, and Teaching*. Portsmouth, NH: Heinemann.

Newton, S. 2000. *Implementation of Writing Workshop: Empowering One Student with Literacy*. Unpublished thesis, Middle Tennessee State University.

Parry, J., and D. Hornsby. 1988. *Write On: A Conference Approach to Writing*. Portsmouth, NH: Heinemann.

Ray, K. 1999. *Wondrous Words: Writers and Writing in the Elementary Classroom*. Urbana, IL: NCTE.

Read, C. 1971. "Pre-school Children's Knowledge of English Phonemes." *Harvard Educational Review* 41: 134.

Reif, L. 1991. *Seeking Diversity: Language Arts with Adolescents*. Portsmouth, NH: Heinemann.

Romano, T. 1995. *Writing with Passion: Life Stories, Multiple Genres*. Portsmouth, NH: Heinemann.

Short, K., J. Harste, and C. Burke. 1996. *Creating Classrooms for Authors and Inquirers*, 2nd ed. Portsmouth, NH: Heinemann.

Solley, B. 2000. "Writing: Past, Present, and Future." In *Writers' Workshop: Reflections of Elementary and Middle School Teachers*, ed. B. Solley. Boston: Allyn and Bacon.

Temple, C., R. Nathan, N. Burris, and F. Temple. 1988. *The Beginnings of Writing*. Boston: Allyn and Bacon.

Thurber, D. 1987. *D'Nealian Handwriting*. Glenview, IL: Scott Foresman.

Turbill, J. 1984. *No Better Way to Teach Writing*. Portsmouth, NH: Heinemann.

———. 1985. *Now We Want to Write*. Portsmouth, NH: Heinemann.

Wilde, S. 1992. *You Kan Red This! Spelling and Punctuation for Whole Language Classrooms, K–6*. Portsmouth, NH: Heinemann.

CHILDREN'S LITERATURE

Fox, M. 1988. *Koala Lou*. New York: HBJ.

Mayer, M. 1973. *What Do You Do with a Kangaroo?* New York: Scholastic.

Polacco, P. 1991. *Some Birthday*. New York: Simon and Schuster.

CHAPTER TEN

"What children can do with the assistance of others [is] in some sense more indicative of their mental development than what they can do alone."

(Lev Vygotsky, 1978, 85)

TEACHING IDEAS AND TACTICAL INTERVENTIONS

The strategies that learners use take place in their minds as they employ their ever-growing network of processes for comprehending and producing language. The teacher's role is to make overt what good readers and writers do—how they make connections between the new and the known. When learners need strategies they have not yet figured out, teachers demonstrate, explain, and engage them in doing what proficient readers and writers do. Thus far, we have explored the power of demonstrations, the importance of teacher and learner expectations, the significance of approximations and the role of response, the need for learner engagement and practice, the meaningfulness of authentic events, the significance of learner choice, and the responsibility of the learner in the learning process. Now we probe specific ways teachers apply the conditions of learning in their classrooms.

Language workshop is one vehicle teachers use to accomplish much of the literacy instruction they need to provide. However, good teachers know that language is a tool, and as such, their children engage in reading and writing nearly the entire school day.

In this chapter, we offer a variety of effective literacy-based, kid-tested teaching ideas. Each technique is designed for a literature-rich classroom with language workshop as the central structuring element. These techniques may be employed as part of guided reading and writing or as extensions of them. They are meant as prototypes. Employ your own materials, adapting these suggestions to fit your situation and your students.

MAKING ORAL LANGUAGE CONNECTIONS TO PRINT

The amount and nature of children's early language and literacy experiences affect how well and how quickly children learn to read and write. Events that demonstrate how print works and the many and varied functions print serves help students learn to read and write and to use reading and writing for meaningful and interesting purposes. The following language and literacy events and activities help children make the connections between oral language and print.

Language Experience Approach   Language experience traditionally refers to stories dictated to the teacher, an individual child, or by a group of children (Allen, 1976). Although originally designed for beginning readers and for children having a difficult time making the connection between speaking and writing, Language Experience Approach (LEA) should not be limited to beginning readers. Variations on language experience stories extend into writing, especially for middle- and upper-grade students. Integrating subject areas within LEA is natural, as the heart of LEA is the experience. LEA is also excellent for English language learners. There are as many types of LEA as there are types of experiences.

Based on the theory that "what I think, I can say, what I say, I can write, and what I write, I can read and so can others," LEA begins with a shared experience. The classroom teacher and the children share or engage in the same experience. The experience may take place in the classroom or somewhere else. For example, the teacher and students may walk around the block looking for environmental print. They can take Polaroid photos, record observations in a journal or on an audiotape, or simply enjoy the walk.

Upon returning to the classroom, the children and the teacher *talk* about the experience, about the many pieces of print they saw on their walk, and about their observations and their musings. After talking about the experience, they *write* about it. They may choose to write a group story or individual stories. Dictated group stories provide opportunities for early literacy learners to match oral language with print. Conventions of written language are addressed as teacher and children negotiate spelling, phrasing and word choices, capitalization, and punctuation.

Individuals, especially older students, may choose to write on their own. Stories, poems, picture books, even alphabet or counting books are among the many genres from which children may choose. Another option is to write captions for the photos. When a written product is complete, it is *read* and shared.

Shared experiences also stem from chapter books that have been read aloud. For example, having read *The Devil's Arithmetic* by Yolen, a group was intrigued by the Seder. They explored Seders in other books. A Seder then became their shared experience. Together, the teacher and students planned, prepared, and enjoyed their meal. Then they talked about it, wrote about it, and read their written pieces. Written works become part of the classroom resources to be read and shared.

LEA provides opportunities for authentic talking, listening, writing, reading, and sharing. It also allows the teacher to demonstrate any number of aspects about reading and writing together. For early readers and writers and English language learners, LEA is a valuable approach. But don't discount its effectiveness for older learners.

Music   Music is another symbol system humans have invented to represent meaning. Some students find music a more comfortable form of self-expression than talking, drawing, or writing. Many teachers make music a regular part of their curriculum.

The most common way teachers employ music is through sing-along. Teachers frequently plan sing-along time using songs written on chart paper and stored on flip charts. In the early grades, the teacher or the morning leader "walks" the class through the song by pointing to the words with a pointer as they sing the song in unison. This demonstrates left-to-right tracking, voice-print matching, sound-letter associations, vocabulary, capital letters and end marks, rhyme and rhythm, and more.

Music as part of the curriculum takes many forms. For example, one kindergarten teacher we know, by using familiar tunes, puts all her big books to music if they don't already come that way. Her children learn a great deal about reading from singing their big books. One first-grade teacher helps the children turn some of their favorite stories into operas; another helps her students write letters to their favorite country music artists. Children in a local second grade write, illustrate, and publish raps, and a local third-grade teacher employs a "composer of the month" beginning with Chopin and ending with Doc Watson. A sixth-grade teacher in our region engages students in writing their own music and lyrics as part of a guided study of the history of rock and roll.

Music is an important part of all cultures. Allow children to share songs in their native languages and teach simple ones to the class. Write the lyrics on chart paper so children can see what another language looks like. Music as part of the daily routine leads to investigating different forms of musical expression. That, in turn, leads to exploring how music illustrates themes, why people love music, how music expresses human emotions, and creating lyrics and poetry.

Poetry   Children's poetry is fun and exciting. Children enjoy poems for the images and feelings they evoke. Poems for children have been written about every possible subject: families, animals, nightmares, nature, death, adventure. Part of the classroom routine might involve sharing the "poem for the week." Poems written on chart paper are readily available for reading and serve as prototypes for poetry writing. Young children who are learning to read as well as children who are just learning English can "read" poems they have memorized.

Children read and respond to poetry in several different ways. Some write and illustrate their own poetry books and create new collections of poems about any subject. To add to the growing classroom collection, ask children to bring their own favorites. Many poems can be sung, acted out, or pantomimed. In addition, many wonderful poems have been illustrated as picture books—for example, Robert Frost's *Stopping By Woods on a Snowy Evening* and Dylan Thomas' *A Child's Christmas in Wales*. And of course, several well-known children's authors like Dr. Seuss and Bill Peet write stories in rhyme.

Many wonderful collections of poems written especially for children are available. The following are but a few:

Selected Children's Poetry Collections

Baird, A. 2001. *Storm Coming!* Honesdale, PA: Boyds Mills Press.

Cisneros, S. 1991. *House on Mango Street.* New York: Vintage.

Cullinan, B. 1996. *A Jar of Tiny Stars: Poems by NCTE Award-Winning Poets.* Honesdale, PA: Boyds Mills Press.

Dunn, S. 2000. *All Together Now.* York, ME: Stenhouse.

Florian, D. 1998. *Insectlopedia.* San Diego, CA: Harcourt Brace.

Florian, D. 2000. *Lizards, Frogs and Poliwogs.* San Diego, CA: Harcourt Brace.

Frost, R. 1979. *Stopping by Woods on Snowy Evening.* New York: Dutton.

Greenfield, E. 1988. *Nathaniel Talking.* New York: Black Butterfly Children's Books.

Hopkins, L. 1994. *Hand in Hand: An American History Through Poetry.* New York: Simon and Schuster Books for Young Readers.

Johnston, R. 2000. *It's About Dogs.* San Diego, CA: Harcourt Brace.

Ohuigin, S. 1988. *Scary Poems for Rotten Kids.* Toronto: National Press.

Prelutsky, J. 1976. *Nightmares: Poems to Trouble Your Sleep.* New York: Greenwillow Books.

Prelutsky, J. 1983. *The Random House Book of Poetry for Children.* New York: Random House (and other poetry books by this author).

Rylant, C. 1996. *The Whales.* New York: Scholastic.

Rylant, C., and W. Evans. 1994. *Something Permanent.* New York: Harcourt Brace.

Seuling, B. 1998. *Winter Lullaby.* San Diego, CA: Harcourt Brace (and other poetry books by this author).

Sierra, J. 1998. *Antarctic Antics: A Book of Penguin Poems.* San Diego, CA: Harcourt Brace.

Silverstein, S. 1974. *Where the Sidewalk Ends.* New York: Harper and Row (and other poetry books by this author).

The Tall Book of Mother Goose. 1942. New York: Harper and Row.

Thomas, D. 1954. *A Child's Christmas in Wales.* New York: New Directions.

Yolen, J. 1993. *Welcome to the Green House.* New York: Putnam.

Alphabet and Counting Books   Primary-grade curriculum requires teaching the alphabetic principle and the names of the letters of the alphabet. Children need experiences with the letters of the alphabet, letter names, and the sounds most commonly associated with them. They do not need, nor do most children really understand, the "letter a week" technique. Children of all ages like and appreciate many of the beautiful alphabet books available. Alphabet books, used in a variety of meaningful and interesting ways, are a staple of the classroom. The rhyming and repeated patterns provide support for early readers and also for English language learners. Alphabet books are an important genre for older readers, too. Some may choose to turn their writing topics into alphabet books.

One interesting and fun alphabet book is *Q Is for Duck* by Elting and Folsom. In this book, "*A* is for zoo." Do you know why? Because . . . *animals* live in the zoo. *B* is for dog. Why? Because . . . dogs *bark*. Discuss with the children that the authors made choices, but their choices weren't the only words they could have used. They could have said "Because dogs eat *bones*," for instance. Sometimes the children predict words that are not in the text, but they may be just as good or even better than the ones the authors chose.

Using *Q Is for Duck* as a prototype, children may write a new alphabet book for their classroom. For example, *S* is for alligator. Why? Because . . . alligators *swim*. Children may work in pairs or small groups to complete their new book. An interesting variation is to match all class members with things they like to do. For example, *R* is for Carole. Why? Because . . . Carole likes to *read*.

Listed below are a few very good alphabet books. Each lends itself to expanding children's alphabet awareness, language, and thinking.

Selected Alphabet Books

Alpha-Bakery: Children's Cookbook. 1991. Minneapolis, MN: General Mills, Inc.

Base, G. 1986. *Animalia.* New York: Harry N. Abrams, Inc.

Bayer, J. 1984. *A My Name Is Alice.* New York: Dial.

Bridwell, N. 1983. *Clifford's ABC.* New York: Scholastic.

Cohen, I. 1997. *ABC Discovery: An Alphabet Book of Picture Puzzles.* New York: Mulberry Books.

Elting, M., and M. Folsom. 1980. *Q Is for Duck.* New York: Clarion Books.

Hepworth, C. 1992. *Antics! An Alphabetical **Ant**hology.* New York: G. P. Putnam.

Isadora, R. 1983. *City Seen from A to Z.* New York: Greenwillow Books.

Jonas, A. 1990. *Aardvarks, Disembark!* New York: Greenwillow Books.

Lear, E. 1983. *An Edward Lear Alphabet.* New York: Lothrop, Lee and Shephard Books.

Lobel, A. 1981. *On Market Street.* New York: Greenwillow Books.

Mayer, M. 1989. *The Unicorn Alphabet.* New York: Dial.

Musgrove, M. 1977. *Ashanti to Zulu: African Traditions.* New York: Dell.

Owens, M. 1988. *The Carabou Alphabet Book.* Brunswick, ME: The Dog Ear Press.

Pallotta, J. 1989. *The Yucky Reptile Alphabet Book.* Watertown, MA: Charlesbridge Publishing (and many more by this same author).

Seuss, Dr. 1963. *ABC*. New York: Random House.
Wildsmith, B. 1962. *Brian Wildsmith's ABC*. New York: Franklin Watts.

In addition to alphabet books, counting books also offer many supports for early readers and English language learners. Most languages use Arabic numerals to represent numbers. Counting books offer support in matching the English word to the corresponding numeral.

Selected Counting Books

Anno, M. 1975. *Anno's Counting Book*. New York: Thomas Y. Crowell.
Anno, M. 1983. *Anno's Mysterious Multiplying Jar*. New York: Philomel Books.
Bang, M. 1983. *Ten, Nine, Eight*. New York: Greenwillow Books.
Crews, D. 1986. *Ten Black Dots*. New York: Mulberry Books.
Frankel, A. 2000. *Joshua's Counting Book*. New York: Harper Festival Books.
Gerstein, M. 1984. *Roll Over!* New York: Crown.
Haskins, J. 1987. *Count Your Way Through Russia*. Minneapolis, MN: Carolrhoda
    Books Inc. (and other countries in this series).
Howe, C. 1983. *Counting Penguins, 0–9*. New York: Harper and Row.
Leedy, L. 1985. *A Number of Dragons*. New York: Holiday House.
Noll, S. 1984. *Off and Counting*. New York: Greenwillow Books.
Pomerantz, C. 1984. *One Duck, Another Duck*. New York: Greenwillow Books.
Tudor, T. 1956. *1 Is One*. Chicago: Rand McNally.
Wild, R., and J. Wild. 1978. *The Bears Counting Book*. New York: Harper and Row.

Predictable Books   Books that support children's reading with repeated language patterns, rhymes, rhythm patterns, easy language, picture support, and accumulated patters are called predictable books. They may be familiar or unfamiliar stories, fiction or non-fiction. Many predictable books employ combinations of patterns. Emberley's *Drummer Hoff* is a classic example of a rhyming book with an accumulated pattern.

Predictable books help children acquire knowledge about sound-letter cues. They provide successful early reading experiences for young children and demonstrate that written language is both manageable and enjoyable. As the teacher reads aloud, children often join in. Predictable books help children take risks in reading and experience immediate success.

Teachers use predictable books to demonstrate to children that they *can* read. They are especially appropriate for beginning and less proficient readers. Even on the first day of first grade, children can "read" an easy predictable book on their own. Familiar songs such as "Frog Went A'Courtin'" and "There Was an Old Lady Who Swallowed a Fly" are examples of highly readable predictable materials for older readers.

Predictable books make up a significant portion of the class library for K–2 classrooms but are important in the middle grades, too. In the primary grades, teachers typically read predictable books aloud during read-aloud and/or guided reading time. A book may be reread several times in one sitting. Teachers encourage the children to join in as the book is read aloud. Sometimes the teacher pauses to let the children fill in the next word or phrase in the story. This enables them to experience predicting, and it can be referred back to when children need to be reminded that they already know how to predict. In upper grades, predictable books serve as examples of that genre to be studied for the author's craft (Ray, 1999).

The simple repetitive text and colorful corresponding illustrations of predictable books provide many supports for early readers and English language learners. For example, after a book like Bill Martin Jr.'s *Brown Bear, Brown Bear* has been shared several times, most children can "read" it without help.

Selected Predictable Books

Carle, E. 1981. *The Very Hungry Caterpiller*. New York: Philomel Books.
Carle, E. 1990. *The Very Quiet Cricket*. New York: Philomel Books.
Carle, E. 1999. *The Very Noisy Click Beetle*. New York: Philomel Books.
Cowley, J. 1980. *Mrs. Wishy Washy*. Auckland, NZ: Shortland Pub. Ltd.
dePaola, T. 1986. *Teeny Tiny*. New York: Putnam.
Emberly, B. 1967. *Drummer Hoff*. Englewood Cliffs, NJ: Prentice-Hall.
Kellog, S. 1974. *There Was an Old Woman*. New York: Parents' Magazine Press.
Martin, B. 1967. *Brown Bear, Brown Bear, What Do You See?* New York: Henry Holt.
Martin, B. 1991. *Polar Bear, Polar Bear, What Do You Hear?* New York: Henry Holt.
Nelson, J. 1989. *Peanut Butter and Jelly*. Cleveland, OH: Modern Curriculum Press.
Nelson, J. 1989. *There's a Dragon in My Wagon*. Cleveland, OH: Modern
    Curriculum Press.
Shulevitz, U. 1967. *One Monday Morning*. New York: Charles Scribner's Sons.
Wildsmith, B. 1983. *All Fall Down*. Oxford, England: Oxford University Press.
Woods, A. 1998. *Quick as a Cricket*. Swindon, England: Child's Play International.
Woods, D., and A. Woods. 1984. *The Napping House*. San Diego, CA: Harcourt,
    Brace.

Paired Reading   Paired reading and the "Say Something" activity (Short, Harste, and Burke, 1996) tend to happen naturally in classrooms where students are reading a lot. Of course, paired reading simply means two students selecting a book and reading it together. In the "Say Something" technique, the partners examine their selected book and predict what it is likely to be about. Then one softly reads a section aloud to the other. When the reader stops, the listener leads the discussion. Students discuss their favorite part or the questions they had during the reading. They are encouraged to relate what they already know to the story.

When they have finished talking about the section, they predict what they think the next part will be about and why. Then the other partner reads the next section. This strategy, employed with appropriate materials and demonstration, may even be used in kindergarten and first grade. Paired reading lays the foundation for literature study groups in succeeding grades.

ENGAGING STRUGGLING READERS AND WRITERS IN COMPREHENDING AND PRODUCING TEXT

So far, we have discussed comprehending in terms of strategic reading, retelling what has been read, and talking about it. We want our readers to read with an awareness of the processes they use to construct meaning and the processes writers use to make texts potentially meaningful. To do so, we demonstrate useful strategies in guided reading and focus lessons. But some children need additional assistance. What follows are several teaching ideas that engage students with texts in ways that enable them to use their prior knowledge about how texts work along with all three cueing systems to construct meaning.

Assisted Reading   One of the most effective techniques specifically designed for children who are having serious difficulty learning to read is assisted reading. Assisted reading is a variation of a technique developed for severely disabled adolescent readers called the neurological impress method (Rhodes and Dudley-Marling, 1996), but it is effective for helping younger readers gain fluency as well. The method is designed to simulate lap reading. The teacher and reader sit side-by-side with the teacher to the right of the reader if the reader is right-handed. Employed as little as five minutes, three times a week, assisted reading yields measurable results.

Assisted reading works best with an entire text or story that the reader has heard before and likes. However, it is not imperative that a familiar text be chosen. If the reader has not heard the story before, the teacher reads the story to the child. In this way, the child hears the text read fluently and begins to build knowledge of the text in its entirety. The teacher then repeats the reading, this time inviting the child to read along.

As they read aloud the text simultaneously, the teacher reads smoothly and with expression. As the child shows evidence of controlling the text, the teacher's voice softens so that the child's voice is louder. If the child falters, the teacher reads louder to provide the reader more help. As the child again gains control, the teacher's voice again diminishes, and so on. The reading of the text is never interrupted. If discussion of individual words is needed, it is done after the entire text has been read.

When employing this technique, the teacher must know the needs of the learner. For example, if the child needs help with voice-print matching, the teacher points to the words in the text as they are read. Initially, word-by-word pointing by the reader may be encouraged to ensure voice-print match. However, as the reader becomes more proficient in voice-print matching, pointing should no longer occur on a word-by-word basis but as a sweep. If the child needs help self-correcting, troublesome words are explored after the reading.

Clozure Variations   The terms *cloze* and *clozure* come from the same root as *close* and *closet*, meaning "to shut." Clozure relies on our natural tendency to complete something we perceive as an incomplete pattern. For example, do re mi fa so la ti _____. When used for instruction in reading, clozure requires the reader to employ the non-graphophonic cueing systems to fill in the blanks; that is, readers must rely on prior knowledge, grammar, and meaning to complete the patterns and produce a reasonable and meaningful text.

Clozure activities are easy to create, and they encourage the use of syntactic and semantic cues in reading. Well-written stories and information materials may be used for developing clozure activities. Predictable books are an excellent source for early readers. Stories from old basal readers, discarded library books, or magazines can also be used.

Full clozure activities are at least three hundred to five hundred words long. Typically, every *nth* word in the text is omitted and replaced with a blank. For younger and less experienced readers, omit every tenth word; omit every fifth word for more difficulty. The text may be typed or copied and White-Out used. Always leave the first paragraph intact. When typed, the blank should consist of at least six to ten spaces to give readers sufficient space to write in their words. Be sure to keep a list of the omitted words.

Clozure may be oral or written. Clozure passages may be placed on chart paper or used with the overhead for a group demonstration experience. Together the students and the teacher decide how best to fill in the blanks with words that both make sense and sound right. They discuss how a reader goes about deciding what word to put in each blank.

Occasional clozure activities are used for children who do not understand what they read and who rely too heavily on sounding out every letter in every word without reference to what makes sense and sounds right. Clozure helps them understand that what sounds right must also make sense.

Sketch to Stretch   The brain is all about divergent thinking, but all too often, schooling is about convergent thinking. Sketch to stretch is a way to expand a learner's ideas about what has been read. Proficient readers integrate new material into their own backgrounds of experiences, enabling them to view the world from more than one perspective. Engaging learners in generating new insights and meanings gained from readings gives them experience looking at "the world" in new and perhaps unusual ways. Their learning is expanded. Good teachers invite learners to express their understandings in a variety of sign/symbol systems.

Select a piece of literature with a lesson or moral. Merriam's *The Wise Woman and Her Secret*, Silverstein's *The Giving Tree*, Oberman's *The Always Prayer Shawl*, Steptoe's *Mufaro's Beautiful Daughters*, Bunting's *Smoky Night*, Fox's *Feathers and Fools*, and Altman's *Amelia's Road* are but a few examples of the type of story that works well with this activity. Students may read the text for themselves or teachers may read it to them. Reread the text if necessary.

Following the reading, give each student a sheet of paper on which to sketch or draw what the story meant. Try not to give students any more information; encourage them to do whatever they think best. Provide crayons, markers, watercolors, chalks, and any other available art supplies from which to choose. Accept any graphic display.

When the drawings are finished, everyone walks around looking at each other's sketches. Students share, explain, and discuss their sketches. This allows students to set the parameters on their attempts and makes the activity essentially risk-free. Some students may include writing on their sketches. Some student sketches will be more concrete than others. A few students may not have an idea for what to do at first, and a few

may produce rather abstract representations. Each time sketch to stretch is employed, students express their understandings in graphic ways, and they "see" aspects of the story they did not think of on their own. (Adapted from an idea by Jerry Harste.)

Schema or Identifying Macro-Structures   English uses cohesive ties such as pronouns and their referents to weave the thread of the language into meaningful wholes. Readers and writers need to know and explore how written text does this. The value of this idea lies in talking about what they are doing as readers and writers and what they discover.

Select well-written stories from children's books or magazines. *Weekly Reader, Cricket, Highlights for Children, Ladybug, Ranger Rick, Scope,* and *World* usually contain many possibilities; however, this idea may be employed with fiction as well. Selections from social studies and science textbooks, newspaper articles, and magazines provide rich experiences for the students. Stories from basal readers may not be a viable source because if "formula written," they lack the natural organizing structures found in good literature.

Copy the selected text, cut it into sections, and mount it on pieces of heavy construction paper or cut poster board. Give one piece of the story to each child or pair of children. As they read their section silently, ask them to think about what happened before or after it.

Discussion begins by asking the student who has the beginning to read it aloud. The teacher asks the class how they know it is the first part. The second section is identified and read aloud, and the children are asked what makes them sure it is the second part. Continuing in this fashion, the children figure out how the rest of the text goes together. Keep the original text to check after they have reassembled it or if there is controversy. Students will begin to see how texts work and what cues authors provide.

When working with younger readers or English language learners, a no-bake recipe like marshmallow cereal treats or mud pies works well. Copy the ingredients list on a sheet of paper, then write the directions one statement at a time. Give the children the name of the dish, the ingredients, and each piece of the directions to figure out how the dish is made.

Older students enjoy reconstructing a particularly good story or chapter from an information book. Everyone is given the entire text, the pieces shuffled, and they are asked to reconstruct the text. Students compare their results and discuss any differences they find. (Adapted from an idea by Dorothy Watson.)

Webbing and Story Mapping
This technique allows students to explore how story elements interrelate and how they connect to other subject areas. It provides for the development of a wide variety of activities that extend children's language, thinking, and learning and uses good books in the process.

Teachers read a story with a variety of aspects to it. After the story has been read at least twice, brainstorm with the children and draw a web of the story's elements and categories. The children learn a great deal about the story as they think about how to display its key components and the relationships among them (See D'Angelo, 1996). Figure 10–1 is a web of Stanley's book *Raising Sweetness*.

Some books lend themselves to expanded pursuits. Figure 10–2 is a web of Tomie dePaola's *Michael Bird Boy* and some of the areas of investigation that one second-grade teacher and his students developed together.

Each identified area led to activities in reading, writing, art, drama, math, science, music, health, and social studies. Project ideas were developed jointly by the teacher and the children, then the children chose what they wanted to work on.

Communication

1. Children planned a "taste of honey" party and served things made of honey. They wrote invitations to their guests.

2. Children conducted a telephone poll to see how many factories in their community have women bosses. They needed to find out how many factories there were, how many "bosses" were in each factory, and how many were women. They practiced asking questions and decided how to record and present their findings.

Food

1. Children collected food labels and studied the ingredients to find examples of artificial and natural ingredients, to learn what food additives are supposed to do, and to

FIGURE 10–1
RAISING SWEETNESS
WEB

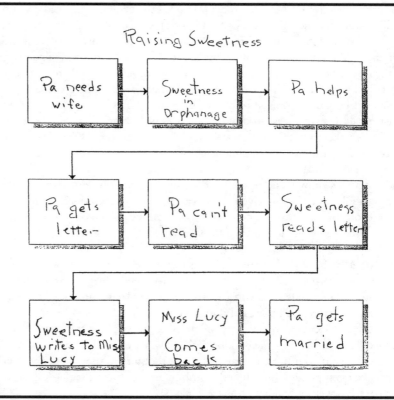

determine which ones may be harmful. They had to decide how to collect this information—libraries, guest speakers, etc.—and how to present their findings.

Science/Nature

1. Children learned how bees make honey. To do so, they contacted a local wildlife agent and located a film and other materials in the library.
2. They collected information on air and water pollution to determine how much better/worse things are now than they were one hundred years ago. They wanted to find out what causes pollution and what is being done about it, so they read about pollution and invited someone from a nearby university to visit their classroom.

Music

1. Children listened to a recording of "Flight of the Bumblebee" by Ippolitov-Ivanov. They drew pictures of several stinging insects, labeling the insects and their parts. This became a wall display for their classroom.

As you can easily see, books rich in ideas, content, settings, and actions lead to interesting extension projects, thereby connecting the story to the larger world.

FIGURE 10–2
MICHAEL BIRD BOY
WEB

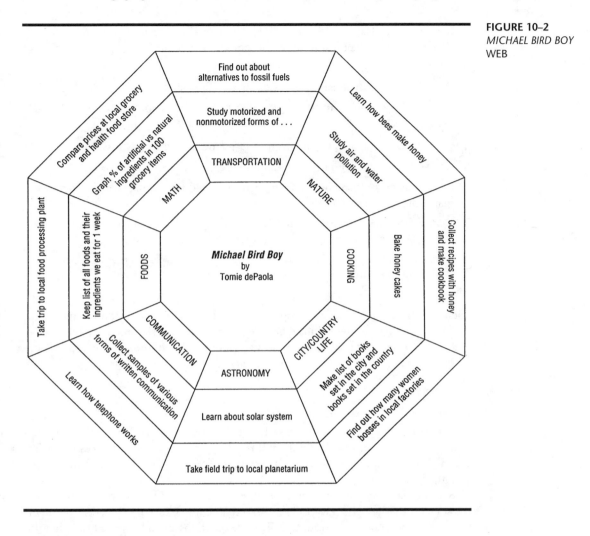

Concept Mapping

Learning is described as building cognitive schema, creating knowledge structures, and making connections—as in scaffolding. Concept mapping is a technique teachers use to make internal knowledge structures, or scaffolds, overt so learners can explore them in metacognitive ways.

Concept maps are word diagrams. They differ from webs in two ways. First, concept maps are more structured; they form a hierarchy from most general to most specific. Second, the links between words are labeled to show what the connections are. Concept maps help students organize, categorize, and visualize the relationships between and among concepts. They are frequently used for increasing comprehension of complex stories and for studying textbooks. However, they are most powerful for examining whole concept areas, the ways knowledge is structured, and the ways knowledge structures interrelate.

Key terms (nouns) and relational words (conjunctions, prepositions, and verbs) are used in forming concept maps. One procedure for developing concept maps is to have the students:

1. *Read* the text or material related to topic to be mapped.
2. *Select* the most important or broadest idea to which all concepts are related.
3. *Write* the main idea and a list of words related to the main idea.
4. *Rank* the words hierarchically from most inclusive to least inclusive.
5. *Arrange* the words from the hierarchical list to form relationships.
6. *Link* concepts by drawing lines between them and label using words or phrases that explain the relationship.
7. *Review* the maps, adding information as it is acquired. Maps may be revised or completely restructured to better represent the topic.
8. *Summarize* in paragraphs to accompany their maps. Display as part of the information and resources in the classroom.

The example in Figure 10–3 is a concept map created by fifth graders as part of a science/social studies unit on transportation. Vehicles are forms of transportation. In this map, vehicles are divided into the categories of commercial and non-commercial. Those categories are further broken down to show different modes of transportation. (More information on concept mapping may be found in Novak and Gowin, 1984, and Alvarez, 1989.)

Reciprocal Questioning

Proficient readers ask themselves questions as they read. Encouraging less able readers to ask themselves questions as they read and demonstrating how proficient readers employ this strategy helps struggling readers better understand the reading process. Students having difficulty comprehending benefit from this strategy.

Select a piece of material with fairly long sentences and little or no dialogue. Tell the students they are going to read this story differently. Explain that readers ask themselves questions when they read. Usually these questions are only in our heads, but this time they will be asked out loud.

For example, in Rafe Martin's *Foolish Rabbit's Big Mistake*, the first sentence is, "Early one morning a foolish little rabbit lay sleeping under a tree in the forest." The teacher reads this sentence aloud then says, "When I read that, I asked myself, 'Who was sleeping in the forest?' I answered, 'A foolish little rabbit.' Then I asked myself, 'What was he doing?' and I thought to myself, 'He was sleeping.' What did you ask yourself?"

Reciprocal questioning provides an opportunity for the teacher to demonstrate internal questioning and other thought processes that go into understanding text. This thinking-aloud, question-answer pattern continues until the group provides reasonable hypotheses about what happens in the remainder of the story. This strategy also works well as a written conversation between teacher and students or between pairs of students. (Developed from an idea originated by Anthony Manzo.)

FIGURE 10–3
TRANSPORTATION
CONCEPT MAP

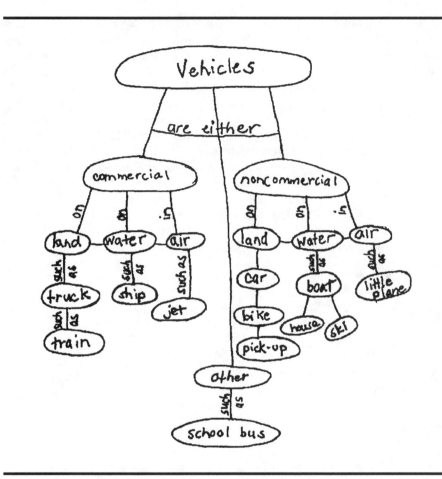

BEYOND COMPREHENDING SINGLE TEXTS

While comprehending single texts is crucial to reading, the ability to make connections between and among texts requires higher-order thinking. Proficient readers often read several books that are related in some manner. Therefore, engaging readers in comparing texts is a good way to encourage reading. The more students read, the better readers they become. And the more teachers read, the better readers they become.

Text Sets   Conceptually related texts assembled for students to read and discuss in order to explore the commonalities and related features among them are called text sets. They consist of both narrative and expository materials from a variety of genres: books, magazine articles, newspaper articles, poems, or any combination. Appropriate for all students, and especially helpful to learners who do not relate what they read to themselves or to other information, text sets offer the added benefit of exposing learners to a variety of texts. Types of text sets are as varied as the teacher can think of: same theme, same problem, opposite problem, similar characters, same setting, same author, or same illustrator.

Text sets are read by everyone in the group, read aloud by the teacher, or read by the small groups of students taking turns. After all the texts in the set have been read, they are discussed. Teachers may ask one or two questions to initiate discussion, or they may find they achieve better results by simply encouraging the children to talk about how the texts are alike and how they are different.

After discussing similarities and differences among texts, students may rank their findings from most to least important. They are encouraged to locate other texts to add to the original set, or they can produce a group or individual story that "fits" into their set. If desired, stories are shared, revised, edited, and bound to add to the classroom library. (Developed from an idea originated by Lynn Rhodes, 1987.)

The following books are but a few examples of possible text sets:

Multiple Versions

Blegvad, E. 1980. *The Three Little Pigs*. Hartford, CT: Antheneum.
Brenner, B. 1972. *The Three Little Pigs*. New York: Random House.
Galdone, P. 1970. *The Three Little Pigs*. New York: Scholastic.

Retold Tales

Briggs, R. 1970. *Jim and the Beanstalk*. New York: Coward, McCann and Geoghegan.
Howe, J. 1989. *Jack and the Beanstalk*. Boston: Little, Brown and Co.

Contrasting Theme

McDonald, J. 1991. *Homebody*. New York: G. P. Putnam's Sons.
Moore, I. 1991. *Six Dinner Sid*. New York: Simon and Schuster.

Same Story, Different Culture

Edens, C. 1989. *Little Red Riding Hood*. San Diego, CA: Green Tiger Press.
Young, E. 1989. *Lon Po Po*. New York: Philomel Books.

Climo, S. 1989. *The Egyptian Cinderella*. New York: Harper Trophy.
Ehrlich, A. 1985. *Cinderella*. New York: Dial.
Martin, R. 1992. *The Rough-Faced Girl*. New York: G. P. Putnam.

Similar Information

Jordan, H. 1960. *How a Seed Grows*. New York: Thomas Y. Crowell.
Krauss, R. 1945. *The Carrot Seed*. New York: Harper and Row.

Cherry, L. 1990. *The Great Kapok Tree*. San Diego, CA: Harcourt, Brace, Jovanovich.
Cowcher, H. 1988. *Rain Forest*. New York: Farrar, Straus and Giroux.

Godkin, C. 1989. *Wolf Island*. New York: W. H. Freeman.
Greene, C. 1991. *The Old Ladies Who Liked Cats*. New York: HarperCollins.

Similar Theme

Fox, M. 1988. *Koala Lou*. San Diego, CA: Gulliver Books.
Penn, A. 1993. *The Kissing Hand*. Washington, DC: Child and Family Press.

Baker, J. 1991. *The Window*. London: Julia MacRae Books.
Burton, V. 1942. *The Little House*. Boston: Houghton Mifflin Co.
Waddell, M. 1989. *Once There Were Giants*. New York: Delacorte Press.
Wheatley, N., and D. Rawlins. 1987. *My Place*. Long Beach, CA: Australia in Print.

Pinkwater, D. 1977. *The Big Orange Splot*. New York: Scholastic.
Yashime, T. 1955. *Crow Boy*. New York: Viking Press.

Carrier, L. 1985. *There Was a Hill*. Natick, MA: Alphabet Press.
Clement, C. 1986. *The Painter and the Wild Swans*. New York: Dial.
Yoshi, 1987. *Who's Hiding Here*. Natick, MA: Picture Book Studio.

MacGill-Callahan, S. 1991. *And Still the Turtle Watched*. New York: Dial.
Wood, D. 1992. *Old Turtle*. Duluth, MN: Pfeifer-Hamilton, Inc.

Bourgeois, P. 1986. *Franklin in the Dark*. New York: Scholastic.
Crowe, R. 1976. *Clyde Monster*. New York: Dutton.
Hoban, R. 1960. *Bedtime for Frances*. New York: Harper and Row.
Mayer, M. 1965. *There's a Nightmare in My Closet*. New York: Dutton.
Mayer, M. 1987. *There's an Alligator Under My Bed*. New York: Dial.
Waber, B. 1972. *Ira Sleeps Over*. Boston, MA: Houghton Mifflin.

Bailey, C. 1988. *The Little Rabbit Who Wanted Red Wings*. New York: Putnam.
McDermott, G. 1975. *The Stone Cutter*. New York: Viking.

Eduar, G. 2000. *Dream Journey*. New York: Orchard Books.
Osofsky, M. 1992. *Dream Catcher*. New York: Orchard Books.

Fiction/Non-fiction Sets

Bland, C. 1997. *Bats: Eyes on Nature*. Chicago: Kidsbooks, Inc.
Cannon, J. 1993. *Stellaluna*. San Diego, CA: Harcourt Brace.

Same Author

Herriot, J. 1986. *The Christmas Day Kitten*. New York: St. Martin's Press.
Herriot, J. 1990. *Oscar, Cat-About-Town*. New York: St. Martin's Press.

Point of View

Brett, J. 1989. *Beauty and the Beast*. New York: Clarion Books.
Hastings, S. 1985. *Sir Gowain and the Loathly Lady*. New York: Mulberry Books.

The benefits of using text sets are many. Freeman and Freeman (2000) point out that text sets are also an excellent activity for English language learners. First, they include books with different levels of difficulty. As such, more proficient English users can assist English learners. Second, because the texts are organized around themes, the vocabulary is often repeated. The natural repetition of important words helps English language learners and less proficient readers learn words in context. Third, text sets develop concepts in depth and help learners broaden perspectives. Last, text sets required higher-level thinking skills as learners must compare and contrast the texts.

Text sets are challenging, engaging, and enjoyable ways to introduce learners of all abilities to a wide variety of texts. They enable learners to naturally make connections between the new and the known.

Book Baskets, Bags, and Backpacks   Different families practice different types of literate behaviors in the home that can be extended with books. Book Baskets, Bags, and Backpacks (BBB) is designed to put books and other literature into children's hands at home and to provide parents with a few ideas for using these materials with their children. BBB promotes children's familiarity with books as well as positive experiences with books in the home. This enjoyment may in turn foster an interest in reading and a love of books. Organized around a concept or theme, an author, or a genre, an assortment of books and other related materials are collected and put into baskets, canvas bags, backpacks, or even decorated boxes. A list of the materials, along with a few ideas for parents and children to do together, are included on a card and inserted along with the books. Teachers may even add audiotapes, videotapes, maps, pictures, a toy, and other materials appropriate to the collection. Each basket or pack is given a title: Bedtime Books and Stories, The Rain Forest, Humorous Poems, Bear Books, Dr. Seuss Books, American Folktales, Stories About Cats, Stories About Pigs, Intergenerational Stories, etc.

Prepare BBBs to be checked out by the children from Thursday to Monday. Label each basket, bag, or backpack with the name and address of the school and classroom to which it belongs in case it is lost. When every child has taken them home, they can be changed and other sets developed. BBBs are checked out and returned along with a note from the parents stating how they liked the set and what they did with it. Some teachers arrange for older students to check the contents of the baskets and straighten them up on Tuesday or Wednesday, getting them ready to be checked out again the next day.

While not an inexpensive project for classroom teachers to undertake, BBB is extremely effective. Many teachers secure small grants to fund the creation of BBBs. Student book clubs, yard and garage sales, and flea markets are excellent places to find bargain books. In addition, teachers sometimes include audiocassette players with rechargeable batteries. This is especially helpful for children whose parents cannot read or whose first language is not English. Books written in languages other than English may also be included for English language learners or students interested in learning another language.

INTERRELATING ALL THE LANGUAGE MODES

Becoming literate is more than learning to read and write. Therefore, employing activities that encourage students' using all the language modes is important. What follows are several ideas for integrating and interrelating oral and written language and productive and receptive language.

Readers Theater   Designed to expand students' language and creativity and to help them understand dialogue as it develops characters and moves the plot along, readers theater is a technique for students in grades 2–8. Students having trouble comprehending or who don't relate personally to the characters and situations in stories may benefit from readers theater. Notice that there is no apostrophe in readers theater. That is because it is plural but not possessive. A group of readers engage in the production; but in readers theater, there is no movement or acting. Students read a script as if they were the characters talking.

Select a story that deals with important concepts. Read the story together or individually, discuss the characters, what is said in the story, and how the plot develops and is resolved. Invite students to rewrite the story like a play.

To do so, students must make decisions about how the story might be arranged if it were a play. Bring copies of several plays into the classroom to be examined. The teacher may help by asking, "What would happen next?" "What would that character say?" "What does the audience have to know to understand?" The students write their script like a play complete with dialogue, stage directions, props, and scene descriptions. However, they may decide that while most of the script can be delivered in dialogue, a narrator is needed to read some.

The script is shared, revised, and edited until everyone is satisfied with the final product. Then the script is cast, and the readers practice their parts. What little scenery is called for is created, and the few props that are needed are gathered. When everything is ready, stools or chairs are arranged on the "stage," and the readers present their production.

Recast the script so that more than one group has a chance to perform and present to more than one audience. The production can be one of several for a week-long drama festival in the classroom or school. Several favorite stories can be turned into readers theater productions, one by each of the groups in the classroom, or one by each participating classroom (Sloyer, 1982).

Non-fiction works well, too. If students decide they like this form of expression, have them select an interesting event in history. After they have read about the event in several texts and reference books, they write the script for a readers theater presentation. Some classes might wish to make readers theater a regular event for presentation to younger classes.

Literature and Author Studies   Talking about good books leads to literature and author studies (Peterson and Eeds, 1990; Short and Pierce, 1990). When books become personally meaningful, people learn to love reading. For some, this happens at an early age; sadly for others, never. Good literature transcends time. It combines both information and ideas about the world with feelings and attitudes that help children grow. Good literature educates. It stretches the imagination and assists people in bringing meaning to their worlds. To benefit fully from the reading experience, children need good books, time to read and reflect, and time to share.

Literature and author studies are appropriate at all grade levels. In kindergarten, they usually consist of a group of children looking at, reading, and talking about the same picture book. In later grades, literature and author study groups are in-depth studies of books with similar themes or of several books written by the same author.

Just as some adults tend to read everything written by a certain favorite author, so do children. Fortunately many authors have provided a plethora of good works. In the primary grades, Eric Carle, Robert Munsch, Bill Martin, Jr., and Mercer Mayer have numerous books from which to choose. In the elementary grades, Bill Peet, Tomie dePaola, William Steig, and Cynthia Rylant are among our favorites. Some authors also illustrate their own books as in the case of Eric Carle, Bill Peet, and Cynthia Rylant, in her more recent books.

Cynthia Rylant provides an interesting author/illustrator study. Two of her early works, *When I Was Young in the Mountains* and *The Relatives Came*, are both reminiscent of her childhood in West Virginia; however, her writing style differs greatly between the two. As a result, different illustrators were chosen. Rylant has also written chapter books for older readers, *Missing May* and *A Fine White Dust* are perhaps the best known. How is the writing among her books the same? How does her style differ? What techniques does she employ to show emotion? Can students use some of her techniques in their writing (Ray, 1999)?

Literature and author studies provide readers authentic opportunities to read by allowing young readers to emulate the behaviors of real readers. People who read for pleasure frequently read all the works by their favorite authors; they talk about the books they are reading; they recommend them to friends. They do not answer comprehension questions on a computer screen or complete worksheets.

Selected Chapter Books

Armstrong, W. 1969. *Sounder*. New York: Harper and Row.
Babbitt, N. 1975. *Tuck Everlasting*. Toronto, CA: Collins Pub.
Barrett, T. 1999. *Anna of Byzantium*. New York: Delacorte Press.
Byers, B. 1985. *Cracker Jackson*. New York: Viking.
Blackwood, G. 1998. *The Shakespeare Stealer*. New York: Dutton Children's Books.
Blume, J. 1970. *Are You There God? It's Me Margaret*. New York: Dell.
Blume, J. 1972. *Tales of a Fourth Grade Nothing*. New York: Dell.
Blume, J. 1974. *Blubber*. New York: Dell.
Blume, J. 1977. *Starring Sally J. Freedman as Herself*. New York: Dell.
Bosse, M. 1993. *Ordinary Magic*. New York: Sunburst Books.
Buchanan, J. 1997. *Gratefully Yours*. New York: Puffin.
Childress, A. 1973. *A Hero Ain't Nothin' But a Sandwich*. New York: Putnam.
Cleary, B. 1983. *Dear Mr. Henshaw*. New York: Dell.
Collier, J., and C. Collier. 1981. *Jump Ship to Freedom*. New York: Dell.
Collier, J., and C. Collier. 1987. *Who Is Carrie?* New York: Dell.
Creech, S. 1994. *Walk Two Moons*. New York: HarperCollins.
Creech, S. 2000. *The Wanderer*. New York: HarperCollins.
Cushman, K. 1995. *The Midwife's Apprentice*. New York: HarperCollins.
Curtis, C. 1999. *Bud, Not Buddy*. New York: Delacorte Press.

Curtis, P. 1995. *The Watsons Go to Birmingham, 1963*. New York: Bantam Doubleday Dell.

Dahl, R. 1975. *Danny, the Champion of the World*. New York: Bantam.

Dahl, R. 1982. *The BFG*. New York: Viking Penguin.

Fleischman, S. 1986. *The Whipping Boy*. Mahwah, NJ: Troll Books.

Fox, P. 1973. *The Slave Dancer*. New York: Dell.

Fox, P. 1984. *One-Eyed Cat*. New York: Dell.

Gardiner, J. 1980. *Stone Fox*. New York: Harper and Row.

Haddix, M. 1995. *Running Out of Time*. New York: Aladdin.

Haddix, M. 1997. *Don't You Dare Read This, Mrs. Dunphrey*. New York: Aladdin.

Hansen, J. 1986. *Which Way Freedom?* New York: Avon Books.

Highwater, J. 1985. *Eyes of Darkness*. New York: Lothrop, Lee and Shepherd.

Hinton, S. 1967. *The Outsiders*. New York: Viking.

Howe, D., and J. Howe. 1979. *Bunnicula*. New York: Avon Books (and others in the Bunnicula series).

Hunt, I. 1976. *The Lottery Rose*. New York: Charles Scribner's Sons.

King-Smith, D. 1986. *Pigs Might Fly*. New York: Puffin.

Konigsburg, J. 1967. *From the Mixed-up Files of Mrs. Basil E. Frankweiler*. New York: Bantam Doubleday Dell.

Kretzer-Malvehy, T. 1999. *Passage to Little Bighorn*. Bismark, ND: First Impressions.

Lowry, L. 1990. *Number the Stars*. New York: Dell.

Lowry, L. 1994. *The Giver*. New York: Dell.

MacLachlan, P. 1985. *Sarah, Plain and Tall*. New York: Harper and Row.

MacLachlan, P. 1992. *Journey*. New York: Delacourt Press.

Mathis, S. 1975. *The Hundred Penny Box*. New York: Scholastic.

Merrill, J. 1986. *The Pushcart War*. New York: Dell.

Meyer, C. 1997. *Jubilee Journey*. San Diego, CA: Harcourt Brace.

Montgomery, L. 1985. *Anne of Green Gables*. New York: Bantam.

Murphy, R. 2000. *Night Flying*. New York: Delacorte.

Naidoo, B. 1985. *Journey to Jo'burg*. New York: Alfred A. Knopf.

Nolan, H. 1997. *Dancing on the Edge*. New York: Puffin Books.

Paterson, K. 1977. *Bridge to Terabithia*. New York: Harper and Row.

Paterson, K. 1978. *The Great Gilly Hopkins*. New York: Harper and Row.

Paterson, K. 1985. *Come Sing, Jimmy Jo*. New York: Dutton.

Paulsen, G. 1987. *The Crossing*. New York: Orchard Books.

Paulsen, G. 1987. *Hatchet*. New York: Penguin.

Paulsen, G. 1991. *The Monument*. New York: Dell.

Richter, C. 1953. *The Light in the Forest*. New York: Alfred A. Knopf.

Rockwell, T. 1973. *How to Eat Fried Worms*. New York: Dell.

Rowling, J. 1997. *Harry Potter and the Sorcerer's Stone*. Scholastic (and others in this series).

Rylant, C. 1986. *A Fine White Dust*. New York: Dell.

Rylant, C. 1992. *Missing May*. New York: Orchard.

Sachar, L. 1987. *There's a Boy in the Girls Bathroom*. New York: Alfred A. Knopf.

Sachar, L. 1999. *Holes*. New York: Alfred A. Knopf.

Smith, M. 1973. *A Taste of Blackberries*. New York: Thomas Y. Crowell.

Speare, E. 1983. *Sign of the Beaver*. Boston: Houghton Mifflin.

Spinelli, J. 1990. *Maniac Magee*. New York: Scholastic.

Taylor, M. 1975. *Roll of Thunder, Hear My Cry*. New York: Dial.

Taylor, M. 1990. *The Road to Memphis*. New York: Puffin.

Yep, L. 1975. *Dragonwings*. New York: Harper and Row.

Yolen, J. 1988. *The Devil's Arithmetic*. New York: Puffin Books.

White, E. B. 1952. *Charlotte's Web*. New York: Scholastic.

Wilder, L. I. 1935. *Little House on the Prairie*. New York: Harper and Brothers.

Wojciechowska, M. 1964. *Shadow of a Bull*. New York: Macmillan.

Zindel, P. 1968. *The Pigman*. New York: Bantam Books.

READING, WRITING, LISTENING, AND TALKING IDEAS FOR THE UPPER GRADES

Too often students in the upper grades are not given the same opportunities to engage in literacy events that naturally integrate the language arts. Most often, they are seated in rows with little or no chance even to converse with one another. Then when asked to participate in language and literacy events requiring group work, collaboration, and co-operation, they do not know how to respond. What follows are some ways to engage upper-grade learners in experiences that involve using more than one language mode. The text cited in the following section is especially suitable for older readers.

Critical Literacy   This experience asks the reader to become a text analyst. Critical literacy can be started in the early grades and more fully developed at the upper grades. It involves asking the reader to look critically at a text. For example, ask the students what kinds of things prompt authors to write as they do. Using a book such as Rylant's *A Fine White Dust* (1986), ask why they think she wrote that story and why she wrote as she did.

Look at specific elements of style and voice. With *A Fine White Dust,* explore the reasons the author chose that particular title. Discuss what the boy in the story could have done differently and how the story would have turned out if he had chosen differently. Critical literacy goes well beyond comprehending a selection.

All writing is social construction—writers have values, and they make decisions. A critical literacy stance invites readers to consider these issues. It asks them to think about the text from the writer's perspective as well as how and why it has the impact it does. Reflections include how the author shapes our understanding of the situation, the character(s), and the event(s); how readers feel about the situations, character(s), and event(s); whose voice is heard, whose is silent, and why. Thinking like a writer enables students to improve their own writing (Ray, 1999).

Study Guides and Methods   Students rarely become so proficient that they need no organizers for their work. Study guides can be valuable aids. Probably the most widely known study method is SQ3R and its variations SQ4R and SQ5R: Survey, Question, Read, Recite, Review (Reread, Respond). Most study methods, including these, actually help if students employ them. We are going to share two more with you.

The E-Z Study Guide   After the teacher has introduced the material, which might include examining the title, the pictures, and/or scanning the text, students work in pairs or small groups. As they read, they make a list of key words, terms, or phrases encountered. They write them on the inside, left column of a folded piece of paper. When the students are ready, each term or phrase is turned into a question and written down the right column. Working together, the students answer each of the questions. Answers may be written on the back of the folded paper or on another sheet. The students help each other study by using the questions and answers. Study methods for non-fiction information material include outlining, note taking, and summarizing. Studying fiction requires a somewhat different approach. (Adapted from an idea by C. M. Santa.)

Estimate, Read, React, Question   Students who like to read are usually more able to connect new information and experiences with information and experiences they already have. They are more likely to comprehend. Students who have not had intense personal relationships with text and who do not read willingly benefit from experiences that engage them in making connections between a text and their own thinking and feelings. ERRQ (Estimate, Read, React, Question) is one way to do this.

This comprehension and study tactic is meant to show students how to relate to narrative, but it can be applied to non-fiction as well. Students preview a piece of material they have selected to estimate how far they can read with complete understanding. A sticky note or light pencil mark identifies the stopping place. Students are reminded to be aware of their feelings, any images and memories that come to mind, and the thoughts that flash through their minds as they read the passage. After reading, students react to the material and share their feelings, thoughts, and other experiences sparked by the text. Finally, students ask at least two questions about the text. These questions may be used to begin the next session or they may be discussed at the time. ERRQ might be employed as preparation for more in-depth literature studies. (Developed by D. Watson and C. Gilles, 1988.)

Advance Organizers
Advance Organizers are designed for reading longer stories and for learning content material. By activating students' thinking *before* they read a selection, learners are ready to react to the text at a personal level and make the connections necessary to comprehend it.

Anticipation Guides   Well-written chapter books, ones with important concepts about which students can relate emotionally, are excellent sources for the development of anticipation guides. The following, arranged from younger to older readers, are examples of texts that work well: *Stone Fox* by Gardiner, *Number the Stars* by Lowry, *Bridge to Terabithia* by Paterson, *Holes* by Sachar, *Tuck Everlasting* by Babbitt, *The Giver* by Lowry, *Jacob Have I Loved* by Paterson, and *The Lottery Rose* by Hunt.

The anticipation guide is a set of assertions about the book. Assertions are stated in direct and absolute terms, either in the negative—for example, "Students should never. . . ," or in the positive—"Families should always. . . ." Assertions do not necessarily reflect the teacher's beliefs and values. Rather, they are designed to make the students take a stand and reasonably defend their beliefs. The list should probably contain no fewer than four and no more than ten statements.

If there are enough copies for everyone in class to read the same book, prepare one anticipation guide. If, however, groups are going to read a different books—either because of the number of copies or because the children have a choice—then prepare one guide for each selection.

Below is a set of assertions one teacher prepared as an anticipation guide for use with Hunt's *The Lottery Rose:*

1. Parents, by law, should not be allowed to spank children.

2. Children should stay with their natural parents no matter what.

3. Every teacher should have to visit every child's home and meet the parents.

4. Sometimes teachers are justified when they are mean to students.

5. If someone is mean to you, it's okay for you to get even any way you can.

6. People usually deserve what they get in life.

Before they preview or read the story, students read the guide statements and discuss them one at a time. Controversies occasionally ensue. Each student states in writing if they agree or disagree (and why) with each assertion. Then they predict what the book is likely about. As they read, they consider if, when, and why they changed their minds about any of the stands they took before reading.

Each group presents the book in some form to the rest of the class. Students might research and develop a "kangaroo court" where they indict and bring to trial one of the characters in a story, or they might stage a panel discussion or debate of one or more of the issues raised. Anticipation guides are useful techniques for fostering higher-level thinking skills.

Post Organizers   After reading, students are encouraged to respond to what they have read. This can be accomplished through art, drama, movement, dance, or by writing in literature response logs, retelling the story to the teacher or a peer, or talking about it during literature study discussion group meetings. These types of activities are especially helpful for English language learners and struggling readers because they allow for more than oral recall of story events. Comprehension is making connections—connecting the new to the known. Knowledgeable teachers provide many and varied opportunities for their students to demonstrate their comprehension.

SUMMARY

Instructional approaches appropriate for primary-, middle-, and upper-grade students help develop their oral language and literacy abilities. Through student choice, they grow in skill and confidence; they take control of their own learning and come to have deeper understandings.

Teachers also become more empowered; they control their own teaching. They begin to see new ways of helping children make sense of the world. They stay engaged and tend to suffer lower burnout rates than teachers in classrooms where they feel they are being told what and how to teach.

These instructional ideas are but a few designed to support specific aspects of the listening, speaking, reading, writing, and thinking processes. As a teacher, you will know your children, what their strengths are, and what they need to learn. These instructional ideas will need to be adapted to fit your learners and the resources available. Use them as prototypes for developing other ideas.

THEORY-TO-PRACTICE CONNECTIONS

Learning Theory	*Examples of Classroom Practice*
1. Learners learn to read and write by really reading and really writing.	1. Classroom post office
2. Learning best takes place in a low-risk environment of cooperation rather than competition.	2. Paired reading, assisted reading
3. Learning best occurs as learners explore making meaning with a purpose.	3. Using and making alphabet books
4. Part of strategic teaching involves immersion, demonstration, and approximation.	4. Shared and guided reading and writing
5. Classrooms invite learners' language and culture to become part of the curriculum.	5. Critical literacy
6. One tenet is that learners need to explore self-expression in a variety of media, with a variety of symbol systems.	6. Sketch to stretch
7. Helping learners have personal experiences with book and make connections across texts and across content.	7. Exploring text sets
8. Learning as exploration.	8. Anticipation guides
9. Learning a scaffolding and making connections.	9. Concept mapping, peer teaching

SUGGESTED READINGS

Flynn, N., and S. McPhillips. 2000. *A Note Slipped Under the Door: Teaching from Poems We Love*. York, ME: Stenhouse.

McClure, A., and J. Kristo. 1996. *Books That Invite Talk, Wonder, and Play*. Urbana, IL: NCTE.

Sloyer, S. 1982. *Readers Theater: Dramatization in the Classroom*. Urbana, IL: NCTE.

EXTENDING YOUR DISCUSSION

1. Discuss how each activity described in this chapter reflects constructivist theory.

2. If you are involved in an elementary classroom, try out some of the suggested practices with your children. Share you experiences and observations.

3. Using the instructional ideas in this chapter as samples, develop your own strategy idea—either from a piece of children's literature or a child's miscue pattern. Share among your classmates. Critique each other's ideas for theoretical fit by asking such questions as, Will this help children become more independent learners and thinkers? Does this present the actual reading process?

REFERENCES

Allen, R. 1976. *Language Experiences in Communication.* Boston: Houghton Mifflin.

Alvarez, M. 1989. "Using Hierarchical Concept Maps." In *How to Study in College,* ed. W. Pauk. Boston: Houghton Mifflin.

Atwell, N. 1990. *Coming to Know: Writing to Learn in the Intermediate Grades.* Portsmouth, NH: Heinemann.

———. 1998. *In the Middle: Writing, Reading, and Learning with Adolescents,* 2nd ed. Portsmouth, NH: Heinemann.

Cullinan, B. 1987. *Children's Literature in the Reading Program.* Newark, DE: IRA.

D'Angelo, K. 1996. *Webbing with Literature: Creating Story Maps with Children's Books,* 2nd ed. New York: Simon and Schuster.

Flynn, N., and S. McPhillips. 2000. *A Note Slipped Under the Door: Teaching from Poems We Love.* York, ME: Stenhouse.

Freeman, D., and Y. Freeman. 2000. *Teaching Reading in Multilingual Classrooms.* Portsmouth, NH: Heinemann.

Goodman, Y., and A. Marek. 1996. *Retrospective Miscue Analysis.* Katonah, NY: Richard C. Owen.

Goodman, Y., D. Watson, and C. Burke. 1987. *Reading Miscue Inventory: Alternative Procedures.* Katonah, NY: Richard C. Owen.

Meier, D. 1995. *The Power of Their Ideas.* Boston: Beacon Press.

Novak, J., and D. Gowin. 1984. *Learning How to Learn.* New York: Cambridge University Press.

Peterson, R. 1992. *Life in a Crowded Place: Making a Learning Community.* Portsmouth, NH: Heinemann.

Peterson, R., and M. Eeds. 1990. *Grand Conversations: Literature Groups in Action.* Ontario, CA: Scholastic-TAB.

Ray, K. 1999. *Wondrous Words: Writers and Writing in the Elementary Classroom.* Urbana, IL: NCTE.

Reif, L. 1992. *Seeking Diversity: Language Arts with Adolescents.* Portsmouth, NH: Heinemann.

Rhodes, L. 1987. "Text Sets." In *Ideas and Insights,* ed. D. Watson. Urbana, IL: NCTE.

Rhodes, L., and C. Dudley-Marling. 1996. *Readers and Writers with a Difference: A Holistic Approach to Teaching Struggling and Remedial Readers and Writers,* 2nd ed. Portsmouth, NH: Heinemann.

Short, K., and C. Burke. 1991. *Creating Curriculum: Teachers and Students as Community of Learners.* Portsmouth, NH: Heinemann.

Short, K., J. Harste, and C. Burke. 1996. *Creating Classrooms for Authors and Inquirers,* 2nd ed. Portsmouth, NH: Heinemann.

Short, K., and K. Pierce. 1990. *Talking About Books: Literature Discussion Groups in K–8 Classrooms.* Portsmouth, NH: Heinemann.

Sloyer, S. 1982. *Readers Theater: Dramatization in the Classroom.* Urbana, IL: NCTE.

Watson, D., and C. Gilles. 1988. "ERRQ." In *Whole Language Strategies for Secondary Students,* eds. C. Gilles, M. Bixby, P. Crowley, S. Crenshaw, M. Henrichs, F. Reynolds, and D. Pyle. Katonah, NY: Richard C. Owen.

Vygotsky, L. 1978. *Mind in Society: The Development of Higher Psychological Processes.* Cambridge, MA: Harvard University Press.

CHILDREN'S LITERATURE

Altman, L. 1993. *Amelia's Road.* New York: Lee and Low Books.

Babbitt, N. 1975. *Tuck Everlasting.* New York: Farrar, Straus and Giroux.

Bunting, E. 1994. *Smoky Night.* New York: Harcourt Brace.

dePaola, T. 1975. *Michael Bird Boy.* Englewood Cliffs, NJ: Prentice-Hall.

Fox, M. 1989. *Feathers and Fools.* San Diego, CA: Harcourt Brace.

Gardiner, J. 1980. *Stone Fox.* New York: Harper and Row.

Gilles, E. 1998. *Dream Journey.* New York: Orchard Books.

Hunt, I. 1976. *The Lottery Rose.* New York: Berkley Books.

Lowry, L. 1989. *Number the Stars.* New York: Dell.

———. 1993. *The Giver.* Boston: Houghton Mifflin.

Martin, R. 1985. *Foolish Rabbit's Big Mistake.* New York: Putnam.

Merriam, E. 1991. *The Wise Woman and Her Secret.* New York: Simon and Schuster.

Oberman, S. 1994. *The Always Prayer Shawl*. Honesdale, PA: Boyds Mills Press.

Paterson, K. 1977. *Bridge to Terabithia*. New York: Harper and Row.

———. 1980. *Jacob Have I Loved*. New York: Avon Books.

Rylant, C. 1982. *When I Was Young in the Mountains*. New York: Dutton.

———. 1985. *The Relatives Came*. Scarsdale, NY: Bradbury.

Sachar, L. 1998. *Holes*. New York: Farrar, Strauss and Giroux.

Silverstein, S. 1964. *The Giving Tree*. New York: Harper and Row.

Stanley, D. 1999. *Raising Sweetness*. New York: Penguin Putnam.

Steptoe, J. 1987. *Mufaro's Beautiful Daughters*. New York: Lothrop, Lee and Shepard.

Waddell, M. 1989. *Once There Were Giants*. New York: Delacorte Press.

Yolen, J. 1988. *The Devil's Arithmetic*. New York: Puffin Books.

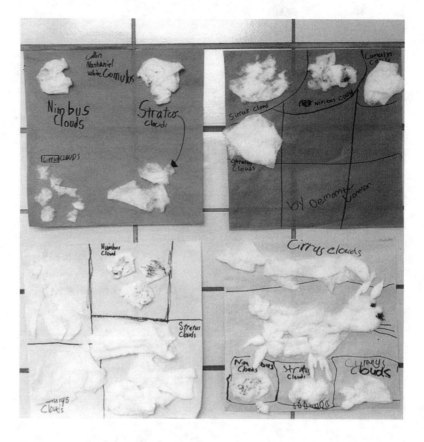

CHAPTER ELEVEN

"Instead of making what is not worth teaching into interesting activities, we need to change our teaching to focus on what is signifi-cant in children's lives."

(Kathy Short, Jerome Harste, and Carolyn Burke, 1996, 350)

INTEGRATING CURRICULUM IN ELEMENTARY CLASSROOMS

Authentic language and literacy experiences are what people do when they listen, speak, read, and write in the "real world." People listen for many reasons—for entertainment, for information, and for conversa-tion. They talk for many reasons—to inform, to entertain, to converse, and sometimes even to rehearse. They read for many reasons—for entertainment, for information, to pass the time, and because they love the inner journey reading provides. And people write for many reasons—to remember, to inform, to persuade, and because they love to express themselves in print.

Classrooms rich in content and opportunities for authentic language and literacy experiences require a multitude of human and print resources including a wide variety of books, magazines, and catalogues, audio- and videotapes, and access to the Internet. Teachers provide demonstrations, examples, organization, engaging experiences, direction, support, and standards. Children bring their wonderful ideas, their sense of helpfulness and fair play, and their boundless curiosities. Knowledgeable teachers use these resources as the basis for advancing their skills as educators. (Appendix C offers a list of Internet sites for children and Appendix D lists sites to help teachers learn to navigate the Web.)

Classrooms like these are excellent environments for the diverse student populations in today's schools. Because they are cooperative and collaborative, they allow for students of all abilities and ethnicities. All students are able to participate and contribute.

We have outlined the conditions for natural learning and described how they can be realized in classrooms regardless of the grade level or abilities of the learners. We have established the underlying framework for learning and teaching and provided detailed descriptions the basic approaches to instruction, the major resources needed, and the ways teachers come to know their students.

In this chapter, we explore how teachers use language and literacy across the curriculum. Specifically, we examine utilizing the project approach, creating thematic units, and assisting learners' inquiry pursuits. In the project approach (Katz, 1994), children explore narrow topics. In thematic units and inquiry, learners explore broader concepts. All three are natural ways to integrate the curriculum. For example, a study of dinosaurs naturally involves children in several science areas as well as history, geography, archeology, reading, writing, math, and art.

DEVELOPING AN INTEGRATED CURRICULUM

Educators define curriculum as all those actions and programs within the school setting, formal and informal, that are intended to achieve one of a number of desired outcomes. Integration is the intentional correlation of what have heretofore been viewed as separate subjects in such a way that the internal connections become evident to the learner. In a truly integrated curriculum, all the actions and programs of the school—all subject areas, after school programs, clubs, intramural activities, etc.—are connected, not just the subject areas.

Through integrating the curriculum, all the seemingly disparate elements of the curriculum come together. After all, we do not live history apart from biology, biology apart from health, health apart from economics, economics apart from arithmetic, or arithmetic apart from language. In an integrated curriculum, teachers provide an environment in which learners use their natural proclivities to make and represent meaning in ways that are most productive for them. Teachers provide resources and information, suggest activities, demonstrate strategies, set standards, and help students self-assess.

They direct, inform, organize, orchestrate, empower, and more. (See Wells and Chang-Wells, 1992.)

THE PROJECT APPROACH

The project approach is one way teachers, especially those of young children, organize their classrooms. Whereas themes tend to be arranged around broad concepts and topics, projects are in-depth investigations of smaller topics. For example, the theme fire fighting encompasses several areas of exploration: firefighters, fire equipment, fire prevention, and fire safety. However, the topic fire trucks is much narrower. Helm and Katz (2001) support the project approach for very young children, even three-year-olds.

The key feature of the project approach is that it is "a research effort deliberately focused on finding answers to questions about a topic posed either by the children, the teacher, or the teacher working with the children" (Katz, 1994, 1). Katz argues that projects involve children in richer intellectual experiences because they engage learners in a variety of problem-solving activities. In projects children learn to use tools like language, math, and scientific thinking to investigate problems of interest to themselves. They do not spend time completing worksheets or doing the same art activity.

Helm and Katz (2001) cite three phases of the project approach. In the first phase, a possible topic emerges either from the children, the teacher, or both. Helm and Katz point out that "there is no substitute for being a good listener and knowing (the) children, their families, their cultures, and their interests" (16). Once a possible topic is identified, the teacher poses anticipatory questions, webs curricular opportunities, and explores resources to determine if the topic is suitable. If the topic is appropriate and doable, the teacher and the children web current understandings and concepts from which to generate a list of questions. Displaying the list in the classroom contributes to the literate environment. Using graphic representations alongside the words helps children who are not yet reading or who may not speak English recall the concepts depicted on the web and match concepts with their written words.

Success of the project is highly dependent on the appropriateness of the topic. Young children need concrete topics, ones that provide lots of hands-on opportunities with real objects that can be manipulated, touched, moved, carried, tasted, heard, and looked at more closely. That is why a topic such as fire trucks is more suitable than the theme of fire fighting. The topic must also be related to what young children already know. Topics that require minimal assistance from adults are preferable; therefore, the use of secondary resources such as encyclopedias and videos is not recommended.

For very young children finding a topic that is represented in developmentally appropriate ways is important. In general, the potential for dramatic play and constructions with blocks, models, and clay makes a topic more suitable. Cultural relevance is also an important consideration. For example, if many of the children's parents are employed by the same local industry, children's interest and background knowledge is likely greater.

Phase two of the project approach is developing the project. At this point the teacher re-examines the children's web to see where skills and concepts fit in and should be taught. Integral to the project approach is fieldwork. The field site is where the investigators go to do their fieldwork—to examine materials and equipment, to interview experts, to draw, photograph, or videotape daily events at the field site, and to borrow artifacts. Unlike a field trip, which usually is a culminating event with a broad focus, the field site visit provides opportunities for the learners to explore answers to the questions they have posed. Preparing for fieldwork requires careful planning. The children have to know what they are to do, and the experts at the site have to know what to expect from the children.

As the investigation continues, children represent their learning in a variety of ways. They draw, label, write, count, build, role-play, dance, and talk about their growing knowledge. If new questions arise, the whole process to this point may be repeated. Following fieldwork, debriefing or sharing occurs. What do the children remember? Were there any surprises? Data and artifacts are collected and discussed. At this point, a chart story may be drafted and words added to the word wall in English and perhaps in another language.

Phase three is concluding the project. Together, the teacher and children plan a culminating event to tell the story of the project. This event allows the children and the teacher to review skills and consolidate knowledge. The event itself may provide an opportunity for sharing the results of their work with a wider audience. Following the event, the teacher reviews the children's progress and assesses attainment of goals.

It is here that documentation occurs. Throughout the project the teacher collects evidence of the children's learning. Now the evidence is analyzed and interpreted. Helm and Katz (2001, 57) suggest five ways to accomplish this:

1. Individual portfolio—a collection of specific content items obtained at specified intervals—for example, writing samples and/or sketches that show the learner's interests and style

2. Products children made—signs, labels, captions, drawings, constructions (or photographs of them), videotapes of children's musical or movement expressions

3. Observations including checklists, anecdotal records, and behavioral indices

4. Statements of children's self-reflections—statements of preferred activities, enjoyment and interest in content areas, and pride in their accomplishments

5. Narratives of learning experiences including teacher journal, newsletters, explanations for parents, lists of books and stories read to children and/or composed by children

An interesting idea for documenting children's continuing growth posed by Helm and Katz (2001) that is generalizable to other contexts is that of photocopying works in progress in order to capture sequence—how their learning progressed. Labels can be placed on photocopies without putting them directly on the original. And photocopies can be reduced so that the entire product fits on a single page.

Experiential hands-on learning is more easily remembered than passive teacher-directed teaching. The project approach works well in pre-school, kindergarten, the primary grades, multiage settings, and classrooms with English language learners because children get meaning from the experiences as well as from language. In addition, if graphic representations are used in addition to English, children pick up on relationships they might have missed if only written language is used. In this respect, the project approach develops literacy in more than just English.

THEMATIC UNITS

Sadly, by second or third grade, some children are no longer in self-contained classrooms. Instead they find themselves in departmentalized situations where they change classes and go to different teachers for different subjects. This type of structure is designed to fragment the curriculum. Too often it leads to instruction that focuses narrowly on teaching to tests. In contrast, thematic units integrate all that is being studied and present content through related concepts. Integrating language, thinking, and content produces learners who have more synergistic understandings of the world. Thematic teaching tends to be teacher planned, implemented, and directed.

One wonderful third-grade teacher began a thematic unit by reading aloud two versions of "The Three Little Pigs" to her students. They compared the two stories. Then she suggested that there were other versions and invited the children to look for them. Several children knew *The True Story of the Three Little Pigs* (1989), by A. Wolf (as told to Jon Scieszka), and the teacher shared that version. The next day a child brought in *The Fourth Little Pig* (1990), by Celsi, and another child shared *The Three Little Javelinas* (1992), by Lowell. The children wanted more, so the teacher brought in more versions of this archetypal fairy tale and some information books about pigs as well. Reading, sharing and discussing those resources led to a field trip to a pig farm. The teacher also took this opportunity to begin reading aloud the chapter book, *Charlotte's Web* (1952), by E. B. White, while the children continued reading, writing, and learning about pigs.

Many activities and projects developed as the teacher guided the theme. The children read many stories that involved pigs. They wrote information books about pigs and wolves. They surveyed students to determine who favored the pigs' version versus those who believed the wolf, and they presented their findings both orally and in graph form. They wrote and dramatized stories about pigs and wolves. The teacher arranged for someone to bring a pet potbellied pig to school for one day. This thematic unit ended with the children creating a wall display with their captioned artwork around stories of pigs and wolves.

Selected Books about Pigs

Brown, M. 1983. *Perfect Pigs: An Introduction to Manners*. Boston: Little, Brown.
Celsi, T. 1990. *The Fourth Little Pig*. Austin, TX: Steck-Vaughn.
Claverie, J. 1989. *The Three Little Pigs*. New York: North-South Books.
Galdone, P. 1970. *The Three Little Pigs*. New York: Scholastic.
Jeschke, S. 1980. *Perfect, the Pig*. New York: Scholastic.
Lowell, S. 1992. *The Three Little Javelinas*. Flagstaff, AZ: Northland Publishers.
Munsch, R. 1989. *Pigs*. Toronto: Annick Press.

Peet, B. 1965. *Chester, the Worldly Pig*. Boston: Houghton Mifflin.

Marshall, J. 1989. *The Three Little Pigs*. New York: Dial.

Saul, C. 1992. *Peter's Song*. New York: Simon and Schuster.

Scieszka, J. 1989. *The True Story of the Three Little Pigs!* New York: Viking Kestrel.

Steig, W. 1968. *Roland, the Minstrel Pig*. New York: Simon and Schuster.

Trivizsa, E. 1993. *The Three Little Wolves and the Big Bad Pig*. New York: Margaret K. McElderberry.

White, E. B. 1952. *Charlotte's Web*. New York: Harper and Row.

Interest in this genre led the class to other versions of standard tales. They read multiple versions of such tales as Jack in the Beanstalk, Little Red Riding Hood, The Gingerbread Boy, Cinderella, Puss in Boots, The Three Billy Goats Gruff, and The Steadfast Tin Soldier. They wrote their own versions in which the teacher encouraged them to experiment with "point of view." Some children wrote versions of the Three Billy Goats Gruff from the Troll's viewpoint. Ultimately, the thematic unit involved many subject areas: reading and writing, cooking, art, music, geography, health, and math.

The teacher suggested several writing activities from which the children could choose. Some created a newspaper they called "Grimm Facts" with articles on the characters they were reading about. Others produced a fairy tale cookbook with recipes for such tempting treats as "Wolf Burgers," "Spaghetti and Wolf Balls," "No-Lumps Porridge," and "Grandma's Goodies." Their thematic unit culminated with a project that combined characters, plots, settings, and story problems from several fairy tales into one play that the children wrote, revised, edited, cast, practiced, and performed for the entire school.

Sources of Ideas for Thematic Units

Thematic units usually spring from one of four basic sources. But in all cases, the ideas are big ones. Usually, thematic unit ideas come from the teacher and/or the prescribed curriculum. Some teachers develop units because they think children at that age need and want to study about certain topics, for example, the solar system for fourth graders or dinosaurs in the second grade. Indeed, some topics are part of the curriculum because the school system requires them at given levels. Simple machines tends to be part of the third-grade science curriculum, and geography and state history are typically part of the seventh-grade curriculum.

A second source for thematic ideas is the wealth of high-quality children's literature. For example, reading folktales and fables may lead to exploring how they vary across cultures. Some teachers encourage the study of books by the same author, and so they begin each school year with their favorite children's author. Then the children vote for each author to be studied thereafter.

Sometimes a teacher may read a book for one reason only to find the students expressing interest in an entirely different concept from the story. For example, one teacher shared several books about giants with her first graders beginning with *Fin M'Coul* (1981), by Tomie dePaola. She had planned on its leading to exploring more fairy tales. The children, however, became interested in the whole notion of giant things and tiny things, and a theme emerged.

Other examples include a teacher who read *Dragonwings*, (1975), by Yep to her junior high school students to encourage their exploration of China and the history of Chinese Americans. However, during the course of their study, some students expressed an interest in aerodynamics, planes and kites, and the history of powered flight. As a result, the theme of aviation evolved and expanded in a variety of significant ways. And after reading Laura Ingalls Wilder's *Little House on the Prairie* (1935) to his fifth graders, the teacher planned a thematic unit exploring what is known about the lives of the Plains Indians before and after the arrival of Europeans.

A third area from which thematic ideas are generated is objects and events occurring in the school or classroom. When the local science and nature museum hosted an exhibit on dinosaurs, one class scheduled a field trip to see it. This proved a perfect time to embark on a unit that tapped children's natural fascination with creatures from Earth's distant past. On another occasion, a child brought an "abandoned" hornet's nest to class one winter day, only to discover as it heated up in the warm classroom that it was not empty at all. After the exterminators left and calm was restored to the room, the theme "Insects, Their Habits and Habitats" seemed unavoidable.

Many themes produce threads of varied topics from which students can pursue their own interests. The teacher guides the learning in a manner that enables the children to scaffold, spiral, and weave the fabric of what they are learning in one area into learning in several other areas. Themes blend into one another; for example, what begins as a unit on pioneers leads into a study of Native Americans, which, in turn, ends as a study of celebrations and rituals around the world.

Finally, current events lead to the creation of thematic units. Many teachers subscribe to a daily newspaper for their classrooms, and the children spend some part of each day gathering and sharing news items. Local, state, national, and world events provide fertile ground for thematic units. Examples of newsworthy events that have led to units of study include attempts to save a stranded whale in the North Atlantic, global warming, the greenhouse effect, the destruction of tropical rain forests, an adoption plan to save wild horses and burros, the adoption of greyhounds after they can no longer race, local concerns with and attempts to get people to recycle, and the national election.

Thematic teaching is nothing new. Many good teachers have used thematic teaching for years. At various times in our history, education, in general, has emphasized teaching by some sort of integrated unit. However, the actual implementation of guided teaching by thematic unit has never been widespread, and it often still tends to reflect the organization of the adopted textbook.

Furthermore, in many schools, one teacher may teach both math and science in a large block of time, while another teacher handles social studies and language arts during the same block. Theoretically, the blocked subjects could and should be combined. In reality, however, the subjects are usually divided with lessons in each that are unrelated to the others. This is a shame since it misses opportunities to help children see for themselves how things interrelate and connect—the basis of being educated.

Basic Elements of Appropriate Themes
Teachers judge the appropriateness of potential themes by several criteria. Thematic concepts or topics should be of interest to the children. They must be broad enough so that they can be divided into

subtopics—into the knowledge structures that make them up—and the relationship of the subtopics to the broader theme must be clear. Appropriate themes lend themselves to comparing and contrasting ideas, allow for extensive investigation of concrete situations, materials, and resources, and permit learners to use the surrounding world as a laboratory for part of their study (Gamberg, Kwak, Hutchings, and Altheim, 1988).

Since student interest is key to the success of any thematic unit, the subject must be flexible enough to allow for a great deal of student choice and creativity. Whatever the theme, it must be rich enough so that all of the children can manipulate the central concept(s) in various ways as they try to make sense of what they are learning. Resource materials must be plentiful and cover a wide range of age and ability levels. Even the inclusion of adult-level reference or non-fiction materials is acceptable if there are pictures and/or if the teacher helps the students read, understand, and use them.

There are at least ten things to remember when selecting a theme:

1. personal interest
2. suitability for age group
3. resource availability—print and other
4. relevance
5. potential for concept development
6. potential for exploring knowledge structures
7. potential for developing independence
8. adequate time
9. potential for helping children make connections
10. worthiness of the concepts and issues

Planning and Organizing the Theme   Thematic teaching requires blocks of time. Students need time to explore content materials, to read and write, and to discuss and plan. The conditions for natural learning are more readily established in classrooms that employ thematic teaching.

The steps involved in planning a unit are selecting the theme, brainstorming and webbing, and listing the resources. Although the teacher is largely responsible for selecting the theme, themes that are requested by the students are likely to be the most successful. After a topic for study has been decided upon, children and their teacher brainstorm and web (Corwin, Hein, and Levin, 1976) the theme for possible subtopics. The web includes questions the children have, interesting learning activity ideas, ways to compare and contrast ideas, and the availability of known and needed resources. As the theme grows, a framework will begin to take shape.

Figure 11–1 is an example of a web designed by Holli Keith and her third-grade class as they explored information about the world's oceans. The web shows the knowledge structure "Oceans." It is a visual display to aid understanding the vocabulary, concepts and the relationships that constitute oceans. It is also used as a guide to subdivide the theme into topics to be studied.

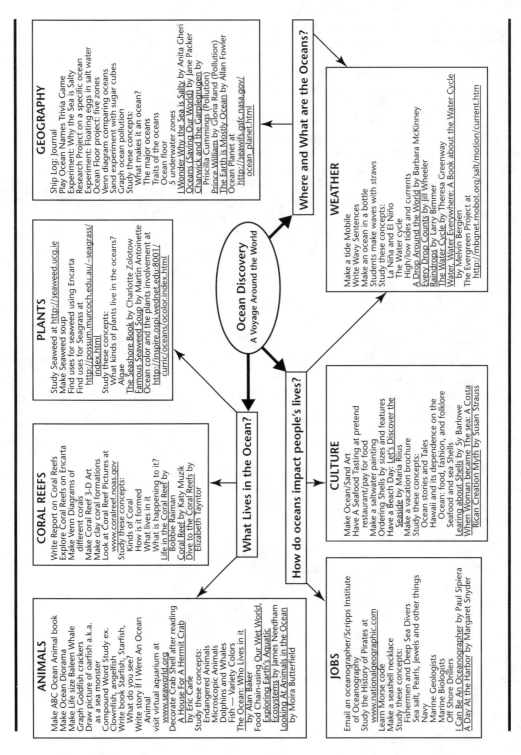

FIGURE 11–1
THE WORLD'S OCEANS

Listing resources by category including books and other printed materials, artifacts, community resources, media, the children themselves, and their parents provides an organizational structure. The school library and the school system's resource and media center (if one exists) are checked for additional materials, equipment, "props," and other aids that might be helpful and interesting. Comb local public libraries and consult pertinent information clearing houses or other resources—for example, local or state historical societies, tourist bureaus, government offices, and chambers of commerce, etc.

Another category of possible resources for inclusion in a thematic unit is the arts. Paintings, music, drama, and dance offer another form of self-expression relative to the thematic unit. Local art galleries and museums as well as local colleges and universities provide resources in the area of the graphic and performing arts. In addition, children ask their parents for any experiences, expertise, or artifacts relative to the theme that they might share. Family involvement supports children's learning and encourages their enthusiasm for the unit.

As materials are collected and activity and project ideas developed, these lead to other materials and project or activity ideas. The unit soon appears to have a life of its own, a sign that the theme has "taken off." If this doesn't happen within the first few days, then the unit was not really of interest to the children or was developed in such a way that the children felt no sense of ownership. At that point, the teacher may decide to choose another topic.

In the unit on the world's oceans, the students were intensely interested in reading, writing, looking at pictures, and other resources about oceans. What follows is a partial list of resources they found:

Fiction

Carle, E. 1987. *A House for a Hermit Crab*. New York: Scholastic.
Levinson, R. 1988. *Our Home Is the Sea*. New York: Dutton Children's Books.
Lionni, L. 1968. *Swimmy*. New York: Random House.
Peet, B. 1965. *Kermit the Hermit*. Boston: Houghton Mifflin.
Pfister, M. 1992. *Rainbow Fish*. New York: North South Books.
Rand, G. 1995. *Prince William*. New York: Henry Holt.
Sheldon, D. 1990. *The Whale's Song*. New York: Dial.
Steig, W. 1971. *Amos and Boris*. New York: Puffin Books
Tokuda, W., and R. Hall. 1992. *Humphery, the Lost Whale*. Torrence, CA: Heian.

Non-fiction

Baker, A. 1999. *The Ocean (Look Who Lives in It)*. New York: Peter Bedrick Books.
Butterfield, M. 1999. *Looking at Animals in the Oceans*. Orlando, FL: Steck Vaughn.
Cooper, A. 1997. *Along the Seashore*. New York: Roberts Rhinehart.
Dunbier, S. 2000. *Sea Turtles*. Hauppauge, NY: Barrons Juvenile.
Fowler, K. 1995. *The Earth Is Mostly Oceans*. New York: Little Simon.
Ganeri, A. 1997. *I Wonder Why the Sea Is Salty: And Other Questions About the Ocean*. New York: Kingfisher Books.
Gibbons, G. 1999. *Exploring the Deep, Dark Sea*. Boston: Little Brown and Co.

MacQuitty, M. 1995. *Oceans: Eyewitness Books*. New York: DK Publishing.

Muzik, K. 1995. *At Home in the Coral Reef*. Watertown, MA: Charlesbridge.

Parker, S. 2000. *Fish: Eyewitness Books*. New York: DK Publishing.

Sipiera, P. 1987. *I Can Be an Oceanographer*. Chicago, IL: Children's Press.

Smith, S. 1995. *Exploring Saltwater Habitats*. New York: Mondo.

Walker-Hodge, J. 1999. *Seals, Sea Lions, and Walruses*. Hauppauge, NY: Barrons Juvenile.

Others

About sharks: http://www.netzone.com:80/~drewgrgich/picshark.html

About pirates: http://www.filmzone.com/cutthroat/highseas.html

About saving the world's oceans: http://www.greenpeace.org

About exploring the world's oceans:
http://school.discovery.com/spring97/themes/h2oceans.index.html

Implementing Thematic Units   Some teachers introduce the thematic unit by reading aloud a book, poem, or article related to the theme. Others begin by finding out what their students already know (K) about the topic, what they want to find out (W) about the topic, and how they can go about finding out (L) what they want to know. Teachers list these on charts or butcher paper to display in the classroom. KWL discussion charts provide an early goal-setting opportunity and contribute to the literate environment.

Figure 11–2 is an example of a KWL chart copied from one designed by a group of second graders preparing to learn about the earth's oceans. Their teacher helped them create a chart that could accommodate additional questions as they arose.

Day two might involve browsing the Internet for more information and beginning to categorize what the unit should cover. The teacher may develop a web and/or begin a "word wall" from the books and resources already obtained. Toward the end of the week, students are ready to select the subtopics they will study, complete activities, form groups, and develop projects.

One teacher we know calls the groups into which the children divide "clubs." The children name their clubs and decide what their clubs will do. Another teacher calls her groups "special interest groups" (SIGs), and another teacher refers to the groups as "Research and Development Committees" or R and Ds. Whatever the designation, the students choose the part or parts of the unit with which they wish to be involved. Some teachers encourage the children to select two groups. This is an excellent idea, but it does carry with it additional organization and record-keeping requirements for both the students and teacher. Some teachers allow children who like to work alone to do so for at least part of the unit.

Each day, sometimes several times a day, the teacher and children enjoy shared book time with resources related to the unit of study. Materials to be read aloud are selected carefully. Instruction in reading and writing occur through materials employed as part of the unit. Some teachers plan activities around the subject areas; others find that subject areas naturally emerge as the unit progresses. Teachers make games and activities involving subject areas. For example, math games employing counting, sequencing,

FIGURE 11–2
KWL CHART

K-W-L CHART
(OCEANS OF THE WORLD)

K . . .	W . . .	L . . .
They are salty.	How many oceans are there?	
Sharks live in oceans.	What is the difference between an ocean and a sea?	
Whales live in oceans.	How salty are they?	
There are lots of other fish in the oceans.	What do they do for us?	
The biggest ocean is the Pacific.	How were the oceans made?	
There are big storms on oceans.	What is the difference between fish and mammals that live in the ocean?	
People like to go to beaches on an ocean.	Are there other life forms in the ocean? What are they?	
Plants live in oceans, too.	How cold does it have to get to freeze salt water?	
	Where are all the oceans?	
	What is the biggest animal in the ocean?	
	What is the smallest?	
	How much water is in an ocean?	

estimating, or measuring can be created, and games requiring the recall of information learned as part of the unit can be made.

Teachers provide the materials for hands-on projects—making something in art, music, science, even cooking. Map or globe study is another suggested learning event. The list of options is long and widely varied. Students learn content and at the same time, they improve their reading, writing, talking, listening, synthesizing, information seeking, and problem-solving abilities.

The overall "goal" of thematic units is to open for children the many possibilities and connections that exist in even the simplest of ideas. Thoughtful, reflective teachers working with children who are encouraged to think for themselves, ask questions, find and share answers, and explore their own amazing ideas usually accomplish these and a great deal more.

Evaluating Thematic Units   Perhaps one of the most troublesome aspects of thematic teaching is determining how to evaluate the students' work and their learning. For the most part, the teacher designs the assessment tools to be used. Asking students to choose what they want to have graded helps learners evaluate their own progress. Developing checklists and rubrics for finished products, referring back to the original goals and purposes of the unit, testing such things as vocabulary learned and used, and determining whether the students have answered their own questions provide avenues of evaluation.

One Classroom's Thematic Unit   Joy Cole, a wonderful fifth-grade teacher, developed and implemented a thematic unit on Australia with her inner-city class. The children became interested in koalas and kangaroos after a field trip to the city's new zoo. The children and the teacher began by collecting a variety of pictures, music, storybooks, maps, and other printed materials about animals from Australia. The school library, local public libraries, and The Australian Book Source in Davis, California, provided most of the resources. The teacher received money from a mini-grant she had written to purchase support materials for thematic units. The study of Australia ultimately led to studying about explorers and colonization around the world, strange and amazing animals, and eventually the American Wild West.

When the unit began, the teacher and the students created a web of what they already knew and wanted to learn. Figure 11–3 shows the initial web they constructed to get started on their "Exploring Down Under" thematic unit. Below is a list of the resources they used.

Non-fiction

Arnold, H. 1996. *Postcards from Australia*. Austin, TX: Steck Vaughn.

Clarke, H., C. Burgess, and R. Braddon. 1988. *Prisoners of War*. N. Sydney, NSW, Australia: Time-Life Books.

Clark, M. 1983. *A Short History of Australia*. Ringwood, Victoria, Australia: Penguin Books, Australia.

Condreu, K. 1987. *The Ridge Didge Guidebook to Australia*. Queensland, Australia: New Brighton Press.

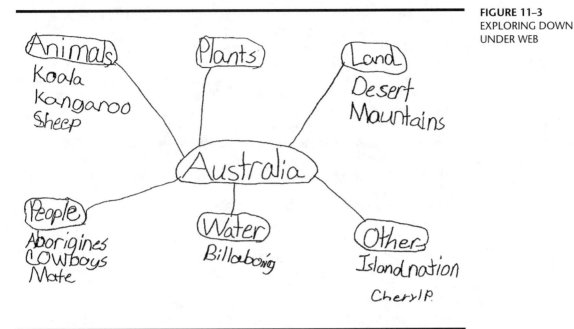

FIGURE 11–3
EXPLORING DOWN
UNDER WEB

Davis, K. 1999. *Look What Came from Australia*. New York: Franklin Watts.

Dixon, M. 1976. *The Real Matilda*. Victoria, Australia: Penguin Books, Australia.

Gelman, R. 1986. *A Koala Grows Up*. New York: Scholastic.

Grant, T. *The Platypus: A Unique Animal*. Kensington, NSW: Union Press.

Grunwald, H. 1986. *Australia*. Alexandria, VA: Time-Life Books.

Grupper, J. 2000. *Destination Australia*. Washington, DC: National Geographic
    Society.

Haddon, F., and T. Oliver. 1986. *Living Australia, Animals and Their Homes*. Lane
    Cove, NSW, Australia: Hodder and Stoughton, Ltd.

Hughes, R. 1966. *The Art of Australia*. Victoria, Australia: Penguin Books of
    Australia.

Lee, A., and R. Martin. 1988. *The Koala, A Natural History*. Kensington, NSW,
    Australia: New South Wales University Press.

Martin, D. 1987. *Australians Say G'Day*. Melbourne, Australia: Ozmarket, Ltd.
    (includes cassettes).

Miller, J. 1985. *Koori: A Will to Win*. North Ryde, NSW: Angus and Robertson,
    Pub.

Moffat, A. 1985. *Handbook of Australian Animals*. Sydney, Australia: Bay Books.

Neidjie, B. 1986. *Australia's Kakadu Man*. Darwin, N. Territory: Resource
    Managers Ltd.

Newman, G. 1987. *The Down Under Cookbook*. New York: Harrow and Heston.

Peterson, D. 1998. *A True Book: Australia*. New York: Children's Press.

Pride, M. 1989. *Australian Dinosaurs*. San Diego, CA: Mad Hatter Books.

Reader's Digest Services. 1988. *Reader's Digest Visitor's Guide to the Great Barrier Reef*. Surry Hills, NSW: Australia.

Reader's Digest Services. 1989. *Reader's Digest Motoring Guide to Australia*. Surry Hills, NSW: Australia.

Roberts, M. 1988. *Echoes of the Dreamtime: Australian Aboriginal Myths in the Paintings of Ainslie Roberts*. Melbourne, Australia: J. M. Dent Pty Ltd.

Schouten, P. 1987. *The Antipodean Ark*. N. Ryde, NSW: Angus and Robertson, Pub.

Terrill, R. 1978. *Australians*. New York: Simon and Schuster.

Tourist Map: Australia. Australian Surveying and Land Information Group. 1988. Cairns, Australia: Tropical Publications, Ltd.

Treborlang, R. 1985. *How to Survive Australia*. Potts Point, Australia: Major Mitchell Press.

Vandenbeld, J. 1988. *Nature of Australia: A Portrait of the Island Continent*. New York: Australian Broadcasting Company.

Wilkes, G. 1978. *A Dictionary of Australian Colloquialisms*. Sydney, Australia: Collins.

Wilkes, G. 1988. *You Can Draw a Kangaroo*. Canberra, Australia: Australian Government Publishing Service.

Audiocassettes

Larrikin Records. 1982. *Seven Creeks Run: Songs of the Australian Bush*.

Mackness, B. *Fossil Rock and Other Prehistoric Hits*. Larrikin/Rascal Records.

Maza, B. *Music of My People: Australian Aboriginal Music*. Twintrack Productions.

Fiction

Baker, J. 1991. *Window*. Sydney, Australia: Julia MacRae Books.

Base, G. 1983. *My Grandma Lives in Gooligulch*. Davis, CA: The Australian Book Source.

Brennan, J. 1984. *A Is for Australia*. Baronia, Victoria: J. M. Dent Ltd.

Burt, D. 1984. *I'm Not a Bear*. Asuburton, Victoria: Buttercup Books Ltd.

Factor, J. 1985. *All Right, Vegemite!* Kew Victoria, Australia: Oxford University Press.

Cobb, V. 1991. *Imagine Living Here: This Place Is Lonely*. New York: Walker and Co.

Cox, D. 1985. *Bossyboots*. New York: Crown Pub., Inc.

Factor, J. 1983. *Far Out, Brussel Sprout!* South Melbourne, Australia: Oxford University Press.

Factor, J. 1986. *Unreal, Banana Peel!* South Melbourne, Australia: Oxford University Press.

Fox, M. 1983. *Possum Magic*. Nashville, TN: Abingdon Press.

Fox, M. 1989. *Koala Lou*. San Diego, CA: Gulliver Books.

Generowicz, W. 1982. *The Train*. Ringwood, Victoria: Penguin Books Ltd.

Green, M. 1984. *The Echidna and the Shade Tree*. San Diego, CA: Mad Hatter Books.

Heseltine, H. 1972. *The Penguin Book of Australian Verse*. Victoria, Australia: Penguin Books of Australia.

Heseltine, H. 1976. *The Penguin Book of Australian Short Stories*. Victoria, Australia: Penguin Books of Australia.

Knowles, S. 1988. *Edward the Emu*. Sydney, Australia: Angus and Robertson.

Lavery, H. 1985. *The Kangaroo Keepers*. Queensland, Australia: University of Queensland Press.

Mowalijarlal, D. 1984. *When the Snake Bites the Sun*. Gosford NSW, Australia: Mad Hatter Books.

Pugh, J. 1985. *Wombalong*. San Diego, CA: Mad Hatter Books.

Small, M. 1986. *The Lizard of Oz*. Ashburton, Victoria: Buttercup Books Ltd.

Steele, M. 1985. *Arkwright*. Melbourne, Australia: Hyland House Publishing Ltd.

Trinca, R., and K. Argent. 1982. *One Woolly Wombat*. Brooklyn, NY: Kane/Miller Books.

Utemorrah, D. 1983. *Dunbi the Owl*. Sydney, Australia: Mad Hatter Books.

Wheatley, N. and D. Rawlins. 1987. *My Place*. Long Beach, CA: Australia In Print, Inc.

Wilson, B. 1987. *Australian Stories and Verse for Children*. Melbourne, Australia: Thomas Nelson of Australia.

Winch, G. 1986. *Enoch, the Emu*. Adelaide, Australia: Childerset, Ltd.

On the first day, Joy read *Possum Magic* (1983) by Mem Fox aloud to the class. They talked about the unusual vocabulary; the strange animals, place names, and foods in the story. Joy asked the children what they thought vegemite tasted like, and they talked about that. She brought out a jar of Marmite, which is identical to vegemite and gave each child a half slice of bread spread with "Vegemite." Everyone tasted, then they wrote or drew their reactions to vegemite. That afternoon, Joy read *My Grandma Lives in Gooligulch* (1983) by Graeme Base. Following that, the children talked about both books, and they listed all the animals mentioned in the two. Then each child selected an animal from the list to study.

Joy's goals for her students included learning about the similarities and differences between Australia and the United States, coming to appreciate another place and culture, and adding to the children's understanding of the size and makeup of the earth. Each child in the classroom could locate Australia and its major cities on a globe. Actually, they all wanted to go to Australia (fair dinkum), even if they didn't like vegemite very much.

Products of the Thematic Unit   The following are activity and project ideas that the children developed with Joy's support and expert guidance.

Art

Display of crafts indigenous to Australia

Presentation about aboriginal art

Presentation about Australian art and famous Australian artists

Paintings with oral explanations of "Dreamtime"

Calendar of Australian animals

Calendar of Australian birds

Illustrated information book of favorite Australian animals

Captioned drawings of what aboriginal music made the group think of

Topographical map of Australia with printed labels for the wall

Primitive, homemade musical instruments using wood, metal, and rubber bands

Picture postcards from places of interest such as Ayres Rock and Sydney Harbor

Literature

Discussed similarities and differences of Australian and American stories and poems

Wrote "Dreamtime" stories

Made Australian alphabet book for the kindergartners

Made Australian counting book for younger children

Presented comparison of Australian humor to American humor

Wrote story using Aussie slang language and presented as readers theater production

Turned favorite Australian children's story into a puppet show

Interviewed an Australian about the country and the way they talk

Made a "Fictionary" game of Australian terms and plausible definitions

Created "new" Australian animal, described and drew it

Health (foods and recreation)

Planned trip into the outback to hunt opals—what needed to survive and why

Tasted some foods mentioned in *Possum Magic*

Math

Surveyed students who liked vegemite (Marmite) versus peanut butter on crackers

Constructed bar graph to report poll results

Prepared demographic report comparing Australia to the United States: size, population, miles of roads, miles of coast, annual rainfall, highest point, lowest point, cities over 100,000, etc.

Prepared charts, graphs, and diagrams to illustrate comparisons

Constructed word problems using demographic findings constructed, illustrated, and placed on the wall outside of the classroom for passersby to solve

Social Studies (peoples, history, prehistory, geography)

Compared European settling of Australia to settling North America

Made clay prehistoric relief map of Australia with plastic dinosaurs

Planned motoring trip around Australia—included estimate of the time trip would take, cost of fuel, food, and lodging, and itinerary

Created, wrote, and "sent" picture postcards from the places they studied to classmates and family members back home

Science (ocean, land, plants, and animals)

Learned about the Great Barrier Reef—painted giant underwater mural labeling plants and animals for their classmates

Created display of poisonous animals and insects

Vocabulary (games using words from the unit)

Teacher created vocabulary game with beach ball—small note card with words taped to ball—when the ball tossed, catcher spelled, defined, used in a sentence, or gave synonym for the word closest to the index finger right hand—words changed as needed

The unit came to a close after several weeks with students singing Australian songs, talking in "Aussie," eating Lamington (chocolate over sponge caked rolled in coconut) and sharing their favorite thing about Australia. Joy asked them a few questions to determine their understanding: Where is the Great Barrier Reef? What is the Great Barrier Reef? How is Australia like the United States? How is it different? She developed a checklist for assessing finished products. Accuracy, clarity, spelling, and neatness were included.

Thematic teaching helps all learners make sense of daily lessons (Freeman and Freeman, 2000). In addition, they cite six reasons that organizing the curriculum around themes is especially important for English language learners. First, it enables learners to see the big picture, thereby helping them make sense of English language instruction. Second, the content areas are interrelated. Third, vocabulary is introduced naturally and often repeated. Fourth, themes that are based on big questions enable teachers to connect to learners' lives. Fifth, because the curriculum makes sense, English language learners engage more fully and experience more success. And last, since themes deal with universal human topics, they are appealing to all students. The lessons and activities can be adjusted to meet the needs and levels of all learners.

Thematic teaching provides continuity. It provides authentic purposes for speaking and listening and for reading and writing. All learners, including teachers, profit from thematic teaching.

INQUIRY

Inquiry has a rich history dating all the way back to Socrates. He believed that learning was enhanced through questioning. Indeed, the Socratic method consisted of asking a series of questions carefully crafted to lead the student to discover the intended lesson.

As a way of engaging learners, inquiry has evolved through the years. The focus has shifted from one of the teacher asking carefully crafted questions to the learners asking questions that genuinely concern them. "Children are natural inquirers. When something interests them or causes them tension, they immerse themselves in it;

they systematically pursue it" (Short, 2000, np). Today, inquiry is viewed as a philosophical stance rather than just an instructional approach.

Some educators believe that inquiry is the same as research; after all, learners immerse themselves in a topic that interests them, they study it by gathering as much information about it as they can, and they present their findings in a formal fashion. Others view inquiry is synonymous with thematic teaching, that teachers who employ thematic units are by definition also employing inquiry. However, if inquiry is viewed as a philosophical stance, it is substantively different from thematic teaching for several reasons.

First is the question of who is in charge. Thematic units may be in the hands of the children but most often the teacher directs them. The learner always directs inquiry. As such, learning is not limited by teacher knowledge.

Second is what constitutes curriculum. Thematic units frequently include all the subject areas, but are they truly integrated? Many thematic units do include activities that cut across all content areas, but too often they are merely correlated, not integrated. As a result, content areas remain the heart of the curriculum.

Third, not all thematic units lead to further study. True, some themes do naturally cycle into other studies, but many do not. In thematic teaching, learners often have the notion of being finished once the unit is completed because time frames tend to dictate how long the units last. On the other hand, inquiry is never "done." It may even continue after the school year is over.

Fourth, in thematic units the idea of "covering" topics sometimes outweighs the importance of the topics. While it is true that learners are more engaged in learning through thematic teaching and more hands-on activities than traditional drill and skill models, they still may feel that they are simply doing activities. Real learning results from prolonged engagements. Activities, no matter how cute or creative, at the expense of "coming to know" are not very different from collecting facts for the purpose of memorizing them. Inquiry provides opportunity to know deeply.

In attempting to explain what inquiry is, Short (1997) poses four statements. "Children are both problem posers and problem solvers" (55). This means that learners are capable of asking their own questions and exploring them. They do not have to depend on someone else—the teacher or a curriculum guide—to do this for them. Short suggests that teachers who employ the KWL charts as a beginning point may actually be doing so too early in the process. As Smith (1990) asserts, you can't think critically about something you don't know much about. Therefore, learners have to know something about their topic before they are sophisticated enough to know what they already know, don't know, and want to learn about. Inquiry serves as the vehicle.

"Inquiry involves different types of learning" (Short, 1997, 55). What really differentiates inquiry from thematic teaching is that in inquiry the content areas are the tools learners use to explore their questions. In thematic teaching, the theme is the tool. As such, integration of the knowledge systems—the subject areas humans use to organize their knowledge—occurs more naturally. Since inquiry begins with the background knowledge of the learner, which may or may not be pretaught knowledge, the social and personal knowledge of the learner is utilized. Inquiry offers learners multiple ways of communicating knowledge rather than a series of activities.

"Inquiry is a never-ending cycle" (Short, 1997, 56). When a learner is really invested in something of interest, new understandings are reached, but not necessarily final answers. And new understandings lead to new questions. Answers are always temporary.

Finally, Short (1997) points out that inquiry occurs in democratic classrooms, classrooms where negotiation and participation among equals are required. Teachers cannot just give choices from predetermined options. Instead, learners come up with their own choices. Learning is a social-collaborative process. In an inquiry classroom, the curriculum is learning centered. Curriculum is built *with* the learners, not just *from* them.

Where Ideas for Inquiry Come From

Inquiry ideas come from the questions and curiosity of the learners. The students develop inquiry with the teacher acting as supporter, facilitator, resource, standard setter, and guide. "Children's inquiry acts provide a window to their thinking, allowing us to glimpse what they are making sense of and how they are doing it" (Lindfors, 1999, 16).

Inquiry provides a framework through which learners successfully tackle complex issues in the classroom. As such, it is designed to accomplish several educational goals:

1. to reflect how children naturally learn
2. to help children explore and discover the ways in which knowledge is structured and interrelated
3. to help children become independent learners
4. to simultaneously expand and refine children's language development, vocabularies, and problem solving as they explore and extend their worldview
5. to help them gain confidence as they make their way in this complex world

Inquiry allows children to construct their own understandings, to ask and answer their own questions, to pose and solve their own problems by generating and testing their own hypotheses, and to present and evaluate their own learning. The best learning comes from "the having of wonderful ideas" (Duckworth, 1987). This means that classroom content comes partly from what the children already know and are interested in. The more they know about an area and the more interested they are in it, the more ideas they will generate and the more complex and detailed their personal, internal schemas are likely to become (Pappas, Kiefer, and Levstik, 1998).

A local teacher, when encouraged in a graduate class to ask his fourth graders what they wanted to learn about during their year in his classroom, made an interesting discovery. His students didn't immediately know. So he allowed them time to think and to talk among themselves. He encouraged them to ask important questions. He invited them to feel free to inquire into any subject that was interesting to them and affected them. Little did he realize how literally they would take him.

He divided his class into groups. Each group, after three days of thinking, talking, and listing, presented their top five ideas or questions to the larger group. From those suggestions, a master list was created. From the master list, the students voted for their favorite five in order of preference. The teacher was amazed, not only at how well this worked, but also how thoughtful his students were. However, he was a bit disconcerted when their number one choice was to begin the year studying religions around the world. Their second choice, death and dying, bowled him over, too!

We don't really know what our children are thinking and what they want to learn about until we ask them and give them time to consider.

SUMMARY

Education at the elementary level should be as broad and as deep as possible, with the goal of producing students who know a great deal, understand relationships, make connections, and enjoy learning. Children are constantly trying to make sense of their world. That's their job. They naturally do it through play and social interactions. Unfortunately, however, too many students conclude that school learning is too difficult, boring, and meaningless to be worthwhile—that it is something you do only to please others. And sadly, others conclude that school is too easy—that it is silly, frivolous, irrelevant, and unimportant. Good teachers prevent these from happening.

Over the years, many educators have pointed out that young children enter school successful learners of language,

eager to learn more, and curious about the world around them. Yet, by middle grades, or even earlier, all too many of these same children appear to have learning difficulties. They are bored and dislike school. An integrated curriculum employing the project approach, thematic units, and/or inquiry is one way to change schools and keep students engaged.

Such a change sometimes feels risky. It requires support and transition time. However, teachers who are interested in developing integrated classrooms may find that thematic teaching and inquiry keep them, as well as their students, engaged.

THEORY-TO-PRACTICE CONNECTIONS

Learning Theory

1. Learning as inquiry

2. Learners as active constructors of their own knowledge

3. Learning as generative, as in figuring out how the world works

4. Self-assessment, teacher ongoing assessment, and learner responsibility are all key elements

Examples of Classroom Practice

1. Inquiry selected by students in pursuit of their own interests within the unit as much as possible.

2. Themes evolve as learners become interested and as they find and share information and resources, make connections, and get deeper and deeper into the subject(s).

3. Learners pursue their own questions, and the theme expands to encompass the entire curriculum.

4. Learners create their own rubrics, and teacher measures learning against standards as well as goals.

SUGGESTED READINGS

Allington, R. 1994. "The Schools We Have. The Schools We Need." *The Reading Teacher* 48: 14–29.

Lindfors, J. 1999. *Children's Inquiry: Using Language to Make Sense of the World*. New York: Teachers College Press.

Meier, D. 1995. *The Power of Their Ideas*. Boston: Beacon Press.

Short, K., J. Harste, and C. Burke. 1996. *Creating Classrooms for Authors and Inquirers,* 2nd ed. Portsmouth, NH: Heinemann.

Short, K., J. Schroeder, J. Laird, G. Kauffman, M. Ferguson, and K. Crawford. 1996. *Learning Together Through Inquiry: From Columbus to Integrated Curriculum.* York, ME: Stenhouse.

Wells, G., and G. Chang-Wells. 1992. *Constructing Knowledge Together: Classrooms as Centers of Inquiry and Literacy.* Portsmouth, NH: Heinemann.

EXTENDING YOUR DISCUSSION

1. If you were teaching the unit on Australia, what would *you* do with the children on the first day? Why? Share and discuss.

2. Select a high-quality piece of adolescent literature such as Babbitt's *Tuck Everlasting,* or Lowry's *The Giver,* and read it thoroughly. Discuss the story in small groups. Then web the story by categories and begin to create project ideas that you might set up and/or suggest to students if you were using this book in classrooms as a literature study. Think about how such books might lead into several guided inquiries.

3. Select a favorite author. Collect and read several of his or her books. Repeat the process outlined in #2.

4. Examine content area textbooks at your favorite grade level. Select a theme topic required to be covered in science or social studies and begin to create a thematic unit. Consider how knowledge relative to that concept is structured. (That is, how might a unit on animals be subdivided?) Begin to identify resources: books, human, audio, video, the Internet, etc. Web the unit, develop a few project ideas, think about how to incorporate math, art, and music. Describe what you would do on the first day with the children to "kick off" your thematic unit. Exchange theme ideas with classmates.

5. Interview at least ten children at a given age or grade level. Ask them what they would most like to learn about or most like to study in school if they could. Arrange it so that you and your classmates cover children of all the elementary grades. Compile a list of children's top ten inquiry interests by age groups.

6. The pluralistic, diverse, multicultural reality of today's classrooms and communities can become the foundation for much of your curriculum. Children need to develop a sense of themselves in the world they live in. However, multicultural education should not be programs or workbook exercises where students learn about "others." Multicultural and diversity education should be a part of everything that happens. Viewed as one of the essential underpinnings of the integrated curriculum, diversity education reflects the society in which it exists. Theme teaching is well suited to developing deeper and broader understandings of the diverse nature of twenty-first century world. Describe the kind of thematic teaching unit you would develop at Thanksgiving after sharing Yolen's *Encounter* with your fourth graders. One question everyone ought to ask is, "How can someone 'discover' a place that already has people living in it?"

REFERENCES

Armstrong, T. 2000. *Information Transformation: Teaching Strategies for Authentic Research, Projects, and Activities.* York, ME: Stenhouse.

Chatton, B., and N. Collins. 1999. *Blurring the Edges.* Portsmouth, NH: Heinemann.

Corwin, R., G. Hein, and D. Levin. 1976. "Weaving Curriculum Webs: The Structure of Non-linear Curriculum." *Childhood Education* 52 (5): 248–51.

Duckworth, E. 1987. *The Having of Wonderful Ideas and Other Essays on Teaching and Learning.* New York: Teachers College Press.

Gamberg, R., W. Kwak, M. Hutchings, and J. Altheim. 1988. *Learning and Loving It: Theme Studies in the Classroom.* Portsmouth, NH: Heinemann.

Graves, D. 1999. *Bring Life into Learning: Creating a Lasting Literacy.* Portsmouth, NH: Heinemann.

Helm, J., and L. Katz. 2001. *Young Investigators: The Project Approach in the Early Years.* New York: Teachers College Press.

Katz, L. 1994. *The Project Approach.* Champaign, IL: ERIC Clearinghouse in Elementary and Early Childhood Education.

Lindfors, J. 1999. *Children's Inquiry: Using Language to Make Sense of the World.* New York: Teachers College Press.

Pappas, C., B. Kiefer, and L. Levstik. 1998. *An Integrated Language Arts Perspective in the Elementary Classroom*, 3rd ed. New York: Longman.

Rogovin, P. 2001. *The Research Workshop: Bringing the World into Your Classroom.* Portsmouth, NH: Heinemann.

Short, K. 1997. "Inquiring into Inquiry." *Learning.* May/June: 55–57.

———. 2000. "Inquiry." Special Topic presented at the Winter Workshop, Tucson, AZ.

Smith, F. 1990. *To Think.* New York: Teachers College Press.

Wells, G., and G. Chang-Wells. 1992. *Constructing Knowledge Together: Classrooms as Centers of Inquiry and Literacy.* Portsmouth, NH: Heinemann.

Wilhelm, J., and P. Friedemann. 1998. *Hyperlearning: Where Projects, Inquiry, and Technology Meet.* York: ME: Stenhouse.

CHILDREN'S LITERATURE

dePaola, T. 1981. *Fin M'Coul.* New York: Holiday House.

Wilder, L. I. 1935. *Little House on the Prairie.* New York: Harper and Row.

Yep, L. 1975. *Dragonwings.* New York: Harper and Row.

Yolen, J. 1992. *Encounter.* San Diego, CA: Harcourt Brace.

CHAPTER TWELVE

"Teachers need to trust in children's learning and in their own ability to learn along with their children. When teachers believe in their own professional judgments and respect children's abilities, success occurs as a part of curricular experience."

(Yetta Goodman, 1996 227.)

GETTING STARTED: LIFE IN TODAY'S CLASSROOM

Do you remember when you were in elementary school? Have you visited an elementary classroom lately? Chances are it looks quite different from the ones you remember. Did you have classmates who did not speak English? Were there children with physical- and/or health-related challenges? Today's classrooms are unlike those many of us remember.

Certainly, one of the most frustrating issues classroom teachers face is the diversity among learners. And one of the most confounding issues is related to children's difficulty in learning to read and write. Children who have problems learning to read and write have concerned educators for many years, dating back to the time when the systematic teaching of reading and writing began in our schools (Lipa, 1983).

In this chapter, we discuss the ways these seemingly disparate learners are alike and how they really are different. We talk about today's changing classrooms and what engaging classrooms look and sound like. We believe good beginnings are essential, so we suggest ways teachers get off to a good start and the rituals and ceremonies that make their classrooms distinctive. We try to answer frequently asked questions about the issues of inclusion, discipline, test scores, scheduling, room arrangement, and planning. We discuss goal setting and self-evaluation for both the children and the teacher, and, finally, we address some of the ways teachers have found to keep their passion for teaching alive.

As we discussed in Chapter One, human learning is social. Human beings don't learn best in contrived settings where they are isolated from their peers. They learn in environments that contain a wide and rich variety of factors—including other people (Rhodes and Dudley-Marling, 1996). What and how they learn is affected by what they already know. Likewise, what human beings know is affected by what they learn. This is because, "all knowledge is 'embedded' in other knowledge" (Caine and Caine, 1991, 36). Therefore, learning cannot be understood by focusing on the learning task in isolation.

Traditionally, and even today, American classrooms are designed around individual learning tasks and fragmented bits of information. Learning is defined as a measurable outcome, and standardized test scores are used to measure what has been "learned" in these situations. This view of how learning occurs is called behaviorism or "reductionism" because learning is broken down or reduced to small parts that are presumably easier to learn and to access than larger, more complex, connected learnings. For example, it is easier to assess the accuracy of playing musical scales than it is to assign a numerical grade for performing a concerto. Teachers "teach" isolated learning activities because they are easier to measure and grade than are processes and more complex products. When teachers "teach" aspects of language in isolation, learners are left to reassemble the parts to form the whole again. This is accomplished usually with great difficulty. To justify this type of instruction, learning is viewed as being additive.

Most human learning occurs in context. Learning to talk, for example, is natural and happens because children are in situations that facilitate learning to talk, and where they use talk to get what they want and need. Under the right conditions, learning to read and write occur as naturally as learning to talk. When learners are actively engaged with the demonstrations of print and how print works, they make sense of the reading and writing processes for themselves. They are on their way to full literacy development. Since learning involves learners in constructing their own understandings, it is possible that schools that employ a reductionist view of learning actually cause some of the problems children have when learning to read and write. At the best, they fail to provide what the children really need.

However, many legitimate questions and concerns are raised about classrooms that do not follow a prescribed curriculum: What commonalities do these classrooms share? How can changes in practice be justified to parents and principals? Where will the additional materials come from? Will the children learn the "skills" they need? Can novice teachers provide adequate structure and direction? How will standardized test scores be affected? What is the best way to start the year? How do teachers build community in their classrooms?

INSIDE TODAY'S CLASSROOMS

Regular education, inclusive classrooms are heterogeneous places made up of groups of children with varied experiences, from varied ethnic backgrounds, and with varied abilities. Teachers cannot really teach one child at a time with methods customized for a particular type of learner (Caine and Caine, 1991).

How Learners Are the Same and Different

Some children do come to school with problems that are deep-seated and difficult to deal with. However, the majority of children who are labeled in need of special or remedial education are not distinguishable from their peers when they enter school (Cartwright, Cartwright, and Ward, 1995; Goodman, 1991; Smith, 1986). As Smith (1986, 1990) points out, it is ironic and tragic that many children have no recognizable problems at all until they actually enter school. Cambourne (2001, 784) suggests six reasons why seemingly normal students sometimes fail to learn to read and write:

1. Learners receive faulty demonstrations of how to read and write or of how to use reading and writing.
2. Although the demonstrations are effective, the learners' engagements are shallow or not present.
3. Learners don't expect to learn to read and write so their engagements are too shallow.
4. The responses learners receive to their approximations or developing understandings carry the wrong message.
5. They do not or cannot take the responsibility for their learning.
6. All of the above.

Often, these are children from homes where there are too few adults to talk to, where no one reads to them, where there are no books or magazines to look through, where little experimentation with writing occurs, or where English is not spoken. When they enter school, the children are tested with a variety of diagnostic instruments to identify their deficits. Some are pulled out of their regular classrooms and taken to special or remedial classrooms where they receive intensive levels of drill and practice on isolated skills. While pullout programs do enable teachers to work more easily with the rest of class, overall they have not proven very effective for children they are designed to serve.

On the other hand, many special needs children find themselves in inclusive classrooms where a special teacher comes to the regular classroom to provide extra support. But in almost all cases, instruction focuses on what the tests show that children can *not* do. Rarely do children find themselves in programs that allow them to use their previous learning. Neither do most special programs focus on what students do well or encourage them to pursue their own interests. The singular exception to that phenomenon is the Reading Recovery Program.

The commonly used reductionist approach provides few opportunities for children to engage in real literacy events. This continual barrage of practice with non-mastered, abstract skills focusing on their deficits treats learners as deficient and defective and serves as a constant reminder to them of their own perceived inadequacies and shortcomings. These instructional methods often have lasting, devastating effects on children's learning lives (Rhodes and Dudley-Marling, 1996; Taylor, 1991). Many special students become passive learners because drill and practice is boring, meaningless, and it does not require them to be active constructors of their own knowledge (Rhodes and Dudley-Marling, 1996).

Many teachers have been taught that they must wait until children are able to read and write before giving them opportunities to actually read and write. Many teachers have been taught that unless children can read and write error-free, they are not learning to read and write well. This practice places children in general, and special needs children in particular, at a decided disadvantage. What would happen if we thought children should be able to walk well before we gave them opportunities to actually do it? What sense does that make?

Many argue that special needs children do not learn the same way as regular education learners. As a result, many special and remedial programs focus on "multi-sensory" learning activities to compensate for regular programs that tend to favor learners whose primary mode is visual. True, tactile and kinesthetic modes are commonly ignored in traditional classrooms. Special multi-sensory programs have been developed to involve these two modalities because it was believed they are more successful with labeled learners. Labeled children may require more time and more support, but little need exists to design special learning programs that are markedly different from programs found in integrated classrooms.

Knowledgeable teachers establish classrooms that are multi-sensory by definition. While reading is certainly visual, nothing is more tactile or kinesthetic than writing. Learners are constantly engaged in using all their senses and their different modes of learning as they construct meaning. They are not confined to a single mode of learning or to a single mode of presenting their learning.

Take, for instance, Laura Klugg's first-grade classroom. After a field trip to a major airport where the children toured a jet, they decided to make a replica of the airport ticket counter in their classroom. With cardboard boxes, markers, scissors, tape, and butcher paper, the ticket counter came to life. The children made paper tickets, suitcases, and clothes. They created an airplane cabin with rows of seats. They role-played taking a vacation to Disneyland. They created posters that advertised their destination.

Laura's children were not confined to a set of isolated skills, a single mode of learning, or a single mode of presenting their learning. Few people viewing this classroom would be able to spot her so-called "special needs" learners.

Regardless of the type of classroom or special program, children's progress is based on the extent to which they engage with the demonstrations and opportunities provided. Unfortunately, learning will likely be assessed by scores on tests that are designed more to measure their recognition of and knowledge about isolated skills than their application of them. Furthermore, teachers', and even parents', expectations for special learners tend to be lower than for their regular education counterparts.

Teachers cannot prevent every problem. Some children have obvious sensory, physical, and/or neurological conditions and are best served in special education classrooms. While most special education and remedial classrooms are still reductionist, many are moving toward more constructivist practice. But these special and remedial classrooms cannot solve all the problems of labeled children.

Some students may still have reading difficulties and problems learning in certain subject areas. If they are separated from their peers for much of the day, they may experience difficulties with social relationships. Their learning may be slowed and their progress intermittent. Nevertheless, what classroom teachers can do, whether they are regular, special, or remedial education teachers, is to help special learners experience success. When children's confidence is enhanced through interesting and successful experiences, they are likely to try harder and improve more rapidly.

What Good Classrooms Look Like

Classrooms that support exploration, integration, and inquiry are good places for all children to have successful learning experiences. These classrooms are busy, collaborative places with children working in pairs, small groups, and large groups. They are rich in materials and may even appear cluttered at times. How children work in these environments is determined by the nature of what is being accomplished. Consequently, these classrooms provide opportunities for active, imaginative, exciting, and sometimes noisy learning to occur. Students read and are read to; they write, learn about science, use computers, develop math skills, and employ information from social studies as they engage in projects that integrate content, including music, art, and movement. As a result, learning in these classrooms comes more naturally and easily, and all children excel whether they have special needs, are English language learners, or are not labeled.

Desks are rarely lined up in straight rows, nor do the children work in silent isolation on workbooks, copying from the chalkboard, or reading an assigned section of a textbook. The work, movement, and noise in these classrooms are not chaotic (Cambourne and Turbill, 1987). A difference exists between chaos and the bustle of purposeful learning, of children going in different directions to accomplish various tasks. The classroom may buzz with the noise of students engaged in collaborative problem solving, group discussions, creative projects, and working with teachers. Of course, some children do work independently at times, and many children are found reading silently for long periods, so at other times these classrooms are absolutely quiet.

Instead of directives such as: "Everyone, please open your books to page 33," teachers do a great deal of listening, guiding, suggesting, negotiating, and encouraging. "Good thinking!" "Tell me what you were imaging when you wrote this." "What do you plan to do next?" "How can I help?"

Today's classrooms have a distinctive look. They are filled with print. Children's written work, art, lists, labels, charts, webs, and messages are abundant and prominently displayed. Poems, songs, and group stories are among the many examples of teacher print also available in the room. Trade books, reference books, newspapers, magazines, catalogues, student-published books, and many other resources line the walls, shelves, and tabletops. The furniture is arranged for flexible grouping and may reflect what is going on that day. Some rooms have no desks at all, only tables and perhaps one larger surface for projects. Some rooms have areas where children can read and write in comfort.

Space may be generic—for example, where projects are conducted—or specific, for example, where centers are located. Work materials, paper, pencils, markers, scissors, and paint, are stored openly for easy access. Some teachers keep many of these items in small containers at each table. This relieves the occasional student disagreement over availability of supplies, and it alleviates the need for shelf or drawer storage space in already crowded space.

Storage is always a problem in classrooms. Many schools were built when classrooms housed only a few sets of texts workbooks, and desks for thirty students. Nevertheless, materials and other resources must be plentiful. Textbooks are used as a resource. Science and social studies equipment such as magnifying glasses, magnets, microscopes, globes, and maps are ideally available in every room. Functional and environmental print are prominent: lists of class activities, sign-up forms, observation logs, product labels, newspapers, advertisements, and a written record of the class field trips are but a few of the possibilities.

For very young children, classroom articles are often labeled in phrases or sentences, such as "our front door," "the east windows," "This is Ms. Smith's desk." Other materials include math manipulatives, art supplies, shelving for a wide range of children's literature, animal cages, and items supporting the current unit of study.

Much of the literature needed in classrooms is expensive and has to be accumulated over years. Teachers obtain small grants, use bonus points from children's book clubs, and spend money from their own pockets. However, some of the printed materials needed in classrooms are cheap if not free. As fluent adult readers, we read a variety of materials on a daily basis. Catalogues, junk mail, bus schedules, phone books, product packages, bills, and other household reading materials can be brought in for children to read. White paper, colored paper, construction paper, butcher paper, chart paper, and a variety of pens, pencils, paints, and the like are also necessary. Discarded computer paper is good for rough drafts and children's artwork.

The backdrop for all the literacy learning is an environment rich in print and content. The list in Figure 12–1 includes types of resources needed to create a literate classroom.

FIGURE 12–1
CREATING THE CHILD-CENTERED CLASSROOM

fiction books	wordless books	novel sets	bus schedules
predictable books	poetry	counting books	menus
picture books	anthologies	big books	songs on charts
books on tape	non-fiction books	lists	poems on charts
records	audiovisual material	student author displays	job applications
student writing	vocabulary cards	recipe books	junk mail
message boards	encyclopedias	felt boards	webs
dictionaries	word walls	thesauri	magnetic boards with letters and numbers
mailboxes	magazines	writing center supplies	
newspapers	telephone directories	alphabet books	computers with word processors
drama area	television guides	advertisements	
library corner	catalogues	sign-up forms	grocery items
puppets	signs	directions	
labels	posters	maps	

ROUTINES, RITUALS, AND CELEBRATIONS

Unfortunately, school is not the dominant reality in children's lives. Teachers face the challenge of creating classrooms where students want to spend their time and where they feel a sense of belonging (Peterson, 1992). Most teachers find their year easier if they get off to the right start. For many, this means establishing a sense of community from day one. Remember, children learn best if they want to learn, and part of wanting to learn involves their relationship with the teacher and their sense of ownership of the classroom. From the first day, teachers should want their classrooms to be different, and they want their students to feel that the classroom belongs to them.

To accomplish community building, creating a sense of ownership, developing caring relationships, and the attitude that this classroom *is* different, knowledgeable teachers employ routines, rituals, and celebrations. For example, Linda begins on the first day by having her kindergartners who recognize their names in print help those who can't. She follows that experience by showing the children how to help each other find classroom materials or solve a simple problem, and so it goes.

Tina begins on the first day by having her second graders write the one thing they most hope to learn in her classroom. They put their "hopes" in boxes, decorate their boxes, and store them on a shelf to be looked at again and added to later in the year. Making a "hope" box becomes a part of the welcoming ceremony for new students. New students make their hope boxes on their first day and place them on the shelf next to the others.

Debbie shows her fifth graders how rubrics work by having them list the elements that make for the world's best chocolate chip cookies: warm, chewy, big, lots of chocolate chips. They use their rubric to assess various examples of cookies. Finally, after two or three days, she shows the students how to use the rubric format to think about what elements make for the very best fifth-grade year.

Routines are important, too. As Melanie begins each school year in her inner-city first or second grade, she spends a great deal of time showing the children how to negotiate her classroom. Together they plan the morning routine. She gives the children choices: when to take attendance, check the calendar, check the weather, plan the day's schedule, read the poem and song for the day, and check the time line from the first day of school. They read and edit the daily message, and so on. Finally, they have group "check-in" time where each child speaks briefly about whatever he or she wants to talk about, sharing important events in each other's lives. A group hug and a moment of silent "being together" follow check-in time. Melanie knows morning routines are extremely important every morning; this is how Melanie helps her students make the transition from the street into their learning day.

At the start of the year, Melanie and the children spend a lot of time talking about how to become a family of learners, and the children offer wonderful suggestions. As the year progresses, they set up various routines such as time to write in their journals and time to talk to each other. Selected children lead the rest of the class through established morning routines. In no time, her classroom coalesces into a learning family or community where children cooperate and help each other. They engage in what is happening, their questions driving the development of the curriculum from the first day.

Melanie also spends time teaching the children conflict resolution. She focuses her efforts at the start on getting to know each child in her room individually. She does so by talking to each one, being a good listener, and trusting.

Lynn came to Melanie's classroom two weeks after school started. She was terrified, shaking and crying when they brought her from the office. Melanie had to sit down and hold her for a long time and talk to her, just to calm her enough to get on with class. Afraid to take risks, Lynn never wanted to write; and when she did write, she'd become so frustrated she'd almost cry. Everything she wrote was repetitive with short choppy sentences. "I like my Mom. Do you like my Mom?" "I like school. Do you like school?" Lynn wouldn't use a word she couldn't spell.

Melanie said she was beginning to think Lynn never would get beyond those short, nearly meaningless sentences that sounded like pre-primer and primer texts. But she decided that Lynn needed time to feel safe. She was, Melanie reasoned, writing predictable, repetitive language texts just like the ones that help children first learn to act like readers. Melanie was patient. Then in early March, Lynn wrote the story in Figure 12–2 (Ricks, 2000, 52.).

Lynn didn't realize that her story was really about herself and her year in Melanie's classroom, but Melanie knew. With Lynn's permission, Melanie read Lynn's story aloud to the class. All the children enjoyed it. They congratulated Lynn with pats on the back and much clapping and cheering.

Personal engagement, supportive responses, time, multiple demonstrations, a safe community, celebrations of children's successful approximations, and a teacher who trusts and values what each child is capable of doing are the key elements in a successful classroom. The teacher can set up the learning environment and offer guidance, encouragement, instruction, direction, and support, but the teacher cannot do the learning for the students. Learning takes place in the mind of each learner. To learn, learners have to engage—that is how they make the necessary connections between what they are doing and what they already know. They have to believe that the classroom is theirs, that they have a voice in what is happening, and that they are respected and listened to. Teachers provide the environmental conditions to make that happen.

The sights, sounds, and materials of the classroom reflect the theoretical base of the teacher (Stice and Bertrand, 1992). Teachers who believe in the collaborative nature

---

FIGURE 12–2
LYNN'S STORY

A KITE ON A ROPE
BY LYNN

I fly my kite. I like to fly my kite. I fly my kite and it gets so high. It gets on top of Mrs. Childress' portable and I have to bring it back. My kites says, "Get me down, I am scared." Sometimes I say, "I can't get you down," and my kite starts crying. Then I say, "Stop crying kite. If you can't get down by yourself, I will come and help you. And I will talk to you until you get down." Then my kite isn't sad any more.

The End

of learning, in immersing children in good literature and rich content, in allowing learner choices, and in giving learners responsibility demonstrate the strategies and processes they employ. They engage children in active, authentic, purposeful learning.

Teachers not only demonstrate what they want children to be able to do, they also demonstrate positive attitudes about their students and their students' abilities to learn. They value knowledge, thinking, and cooperative problem solving. They treat learners with respect and kindness and receive those same behaviors from them. They expect students to do their best and maintain high but reachable standards for learning.

Teachers who are curious and eager learners themselves find it easier to engage children in intellectual activity. Teachers who keep clean, organized, neat, and tastefully decorated classrooms provide low-risk and predictable environments. When the students' work is mounted on colorful paper and carefully displayed, teachers demonstrate to them that they value their work and their workplace.

Students spend most of their time engaged in pursuits that require them to find information, interact with others, reflect on what they are learning, and present or share their learning in some way. Teachers spend most of their time explaining, facilitating, encouraging, counseling, demonstrating, attending, observing, documenting, evaluating, gathering materials, and collaborating. Activities revolve around the use of language, thinking, and content.

The classroom reflects the teacher's belief that learning is engaging, continuous, useful, and important. As a result, most students enjoy learning. Teachers do not spend hours preparing the classroom; they believe the room belongs to the students. The walls are typically bare at the beginning of the year and bare again at the start of each new unit of study. They quickly fill up with children's plans, written work, lists, notes, artwork, new words, and materials for the unit. For example, the learners may create an airport in one corner or turn the whole room into a rain forest. They are classrooms where teachers talk to students about ideas and books, discuss individual pieces of writing, topics of interest, and current events, and where they share information and talk about each other's lives. They are highly literate places, ever renewing and changing places, where children and their teachers celebrate learning and the world around them.

Teachers encourage learners to explore and take risks with language and learning; they negotiate with the students what they will study and how they will be evaluated. To be successful, teachers must have a thorough knowledge of language and language learning. They must know the learners, know the resources, and know the approaches. In these classrooms, authentic oral language and literacy events occur.

GETTING STARTED AND MOVING AHEAD

First-year teaching is a challenge. While there is no single way to get started, some commonalities do exist among teachers who want their practice to more closely reflect their philosophy. Many teachers start with an assessment of their own educational beliefs and philosophy. What teachers believe is the key. The following suggestions are only that—suggestions—that have been gleaned from what many teachers say worked for them.

1. Enlist the support of your principal. Tell the principal what you are doing and why. Invite the principal to your classroom to observe, to take part in authors' celebrations, and to listen to children read aloud.

2. Educate parents. Explain what you are doing and ask for their help.

3. Keep a teaching log or journal. As you reflect on each day, each week, record your observations, insights, and frustrations. What worked? Why? What didn't? Why? Be aware that teaching, like learning, is inquiry-based, and what you are trying to do is answer the questions that naturally arise. A teaching journal will be invaluable to you over time.

4. Find a classroom or two to visit. Talk to teachers about how they got started. Join a support group if one is near. If not, link up with a teacher from another school. Phone, write, or Email to share your questions, celebrations, and frustrations.

5. Pick an area you feel comfortable with: writing, literature studies, or using the basal reader in a more natural way, and try it. Decide what to try next—create a rubric, use a holistic checklist to assess spelling or writing, add some literature, or conduct a miscue analysis of your less proficient readers. Then decide what you want to omit from your existing program—ditto sheets, the suggested reading lesson format, or workbooks. See how it goes. Focus on how your practice fits your theory,

6. Read professional literature. For a comprehensive list, see Appendix E. Becoming a proficient teacher means reading a wealth of professional literature. Some teachers read a book a month. Some read one professional journal (see Appendix F) every month and several professional books over the summer. However you do it, professional reading is the only way to grow as a teacher.

7. Take a university course if one is available; attend workshops and conferences.

8. GIVE YOURSELF TIME. Like all other learning, becoming a teacher is an active, constructive process.

Many teachers we know begin each year with a ritual that sets the tone for their classroom. For example, write letters to each of your students introducing yourself. Ask that they write back introducing themselves and telling what they hope to learn about in your classroom. (This also works well when you student-teach or intern.)

Whatever types of suggestions you try, the more you are able to integrate them with content, the better. Determine your goals, decide what you want your classroom to look and sound like, and be confident in your choices of resources and approaches but continue to self-assess.

Emerging Teachers' Questions
Obviously, we cannot answer every question here. That's why joining a support group, reading professional books, and attending conferences and workshops is so important. However, we address some of the more typical issues encountered by novice teachers. These include such concerns as scheduling, communicating with parents and administrators, standardized testing, discipline, evaluating, planning, and assigning grades.

Scheduling and Room Arrangement Scheduling plays an important part in every teacher's classroom. Larger blocks of time are needed to provide ample time for students to attend to activities such as shared books, independent reading and writing, and author's chair. Scheduling in this manner allows learners opportunities to become involved in the content and concepts of a book, to practice being an author, and to explore using language and other forms of self-expression for their own purposes. Large blocks of time are necessary since the curriculum is integrated through themes.

When scheduling, conference time or instructional time—as in guided reading or guided writing—must be worked into the day. Figure 12–3 shows a general schedule to consider. It will likely need to be altered to accommodate the needs of the group or the school schedule.

The presence of the written schedule, the presence of daily routines and ceremonies, and the fact that the children learn to be in charge of much of the governance of the classroom provide them with a sense of ownership.

Just as time frames are altered, so must the physical arrangement of the classroom reflect the teacher's philosophy. The physical arrangement must be flexible enough to support a variety of working conditions. Classroom setup is very important. It should allow students opportunities to communicate with each other. Desks, if they are present, are pushed together to form groups. Accessibility to materials is crucial, as is accessibility to the many different forms of print displayed in the room. Also, students must be

FIGURE 12–3
SAMPLE ORAL DAILY SCHEDULE

8:00–8:30	Journal writing or read aloud to children
8:30–8:45	Community meeting or rug time (What's going on, assignments, create projects, follow-up, family matters)
8:45–10:00	Language workshop
10:00–10:15	Break
10:15–10:50	Physical education/music/art/library/special explorations
10:50–11:35	Math (may be separate time for practice)
11:35–12:30	Lunch, break, mailbox, talk with adults, etc.
12:30–2:00	Quiet time with soft music; read aloud, followed by projects; theme study; inquiry
2:00–2:30	Read aloud to children/author's chair/peer conferences
2:30–2:50	Community meeting (review day, solve problems; discuss/plan next day; assign any homework, etc.)
2:50–3:00	Cleanup
3:00	Dismissal

able to pursue various types of projects, so centers must be easy to get to. Figure 12–4 shows a general diagram of a workable classroom arrangement.

Communicating with Parents   Communicating with parents about their child's learning is an essential element of classrooms. Typically, parents only hear from schools when there is a problem (Epstein, 1988). However, most parents really want to know what is going on in the classroom and how their children are doing. When teachers communicate with parents on a regular basis, about the good things as well as the problems, parents typically are very pleased. While most schools schedule regular parent-teacher conferences, there are countless ways to inform parents. Consider some of the following:

1. Invite parents to review portfolios that stress the child's progress and strengths.
2. Send newsletters, class newspapers, and flyers that explain coming events, etc.
3. Send notes home that stress good things children do so that the occasional note that regards something negative does not stand out so strongly.
4. Employ report card schemes that include anecdotes as well as grades. The report card should reflect how the teacher sees the child and invite parents to come in if their views differ.
5. Begin parent volunteer programs.
6. Send invitations several times a year to parents to observe the classroom at work.
7. Schedule home visits.
8. Instigate home reading programs (parents reading to children).
9. Telephone or Email parents on a regular basis.
10. Explore projects (community service, for example) that involve both students and parents.

Communicating with Principals and Other Administrators   Communicating with principals and other administrators is equally important. Administrators set the tone for the entire school. Provide information about how the children are progressing and invite the principal into the classroom to see children's work on a regular basis. Keeping the principal informed about what is happening in your classroom increases the potential for support and reduces the possibility of misunderstanding. When problems do arise, principals who know what their teachers are doing and why they are doing it, tend to be more supportive.

Standardized Testing   In today's schools, everyone is concerned about standardized test scores. Everyone recognizes their influence. Students in integrated classrooms nearly always score at least as well, if not better, than children in traditional classrooms (Gunderson and Shapiro, 1987; Hagerty, Hiebert, and Owens, 1989; Kohn, 2000; Stice and Bertrand, 1990). Frequently, in the area of reading, the comprehension scores of children in these classrooms are higher than their word identification scores. This is because of the nature of the tests and the nature of instruction. The standardized tests used in most public schools tend to assess subskill types of knowledge and tend to focus

FIGURE 12–4
SAMPLE FLOOR PLAN

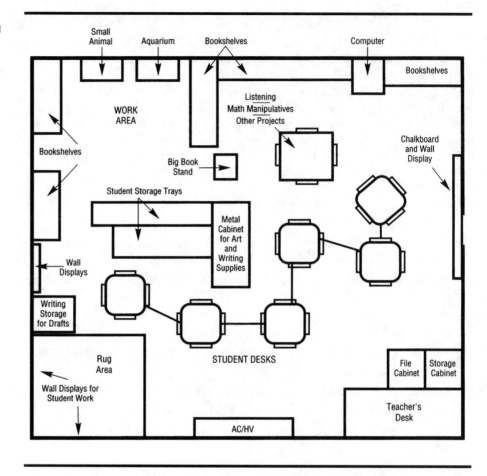

on assessing factual information. For these reasons, many teachers do not risk lowered test scores in adopting an integrated curriculum. However, the fact is that scores will likely increase because students' learning is broader.

Disciplining   The issue new teachers bring up most often is discipline. What will happen, they ask, when students, especially young ones, have all these choices and opportunities? Talking and collaboration are legitimate ways of coming to know. When learners have a voice in what happens to them in school, they become empowered. Students do better in cooperative and low–risk environments than in competitive classrooms (Harwayne, 1999; Peterson, 1992; Rogovin, 2001). They do better when they are learning about things in which they are interested. A growing sense of ownership and responsibility reduces behavior problems. Students learn that power is not only what they can do, but also what they should do for their own welfare and the welfare of others.

Wasicsko and Ross (1994) suggest ten ways to reduce discipline problems. They begin by saying to expect the best from learners. Then tell the students exactly what is expected of them. Offer rewards rather than punishments, but if punishment is needed, make sure it fits the crime. Offer privileges. Be careful not to reward or draw attention to negative behaviors. Be consistent. Use schoolwork as reward, not as punishment. And know each student well, and treat each student with love and respect.

BECOMING A REFLECTIVE PRACTITIONER

As teachers develop from novice teachers to expert ones, they find that they are increasingly able to look at what is happening in their classrooms and assess it objectively. They ask questions such as, "What is happening here?" What are the children really doing and learning?" "What do the children really need and want that can be provided?"

One of the activities many teachers find beneficial as they begin is selecting one element of the curriculum, one instructional strategy to observe as the students engage in it over a long period of time. These teachers write a log of what they see happening. They reread what they've written from time to time and reflect on what they think they are learning based on their reflections. They look deeply into what they think went well and why, and they explore possible reasons some plans did not go as well as expected.

For example, a teacher might choose to implement and then observe a technique called Paired Reading Peer Tutors (Allington, 2001). In this technique less proficient, struggling readers are paired with a tutor. The tutor—a classmate; another, older student; a parent volunteer—is trained to Preview-Pause-Prompt-Praise (PPPP). For Preview, the tutor engages the child in a brief discussion of the title and cover illustrations, asking, "What do you think the story will be about?" The pair begins reading aloud together. When the tutee wishes to read alone, he or she taps the table and the tutor allows the tutee to continue unaided. If the tutee stumbles, the tutor will Pause (or say "pause") allowing the tutee to self-correct. The tutee then applies the self-correction strategies he or she is being taught—reread, look at the pictures, decode to sound, read on and come back, try again, or substitute something that makes sense and go on. If the difficulty cannot be figured out or a reasonable substitution made, the tutor may Prompt or tell. When the tutee figures out the difficulty, Praise if offered.

Careful observation and reflection of this technique provides the classroom teacher with both a viable tool and time to learn about the students, how they are using the reading process, how they are developing their abilities to use multiple strategies, and how they go about learning.

Evaluating   The area that reportedly causes emerging teachers the greatest difficulty is evaluation. Teachers evaluate to document growth, plan for instruction, and assign grades. To be a good evaluator for purposes of planning and grading, teachers have to develop their abilities to observe and reflect on their practice and on what their learners are doing.

The word *evaluation* has as its root the word *value*. What *evaluation* ought to be is a systematic means of showing what we value in children's school experiences (Harwayne, 1999; Wong-Kam and Kimura, 2001). A theoretically sound view of evaluation involves activities wherein the teacher and students collect, analyze, and interpret several types of data to judge how well learners are reaching educational goals. This is called "process evaluation." The gathering of quantitative data only, from measures such as testing, is "product assessment."

Teachers need both types of information about students. However, product assessments are of little practical value in the actual planning of students' learning experiences. For one thing, they typically address lower-order thinking and lower-order analysis in ways that are meaningless outside schools (Smith, 1990). Product assessments separate students into categories based on scores. Process evaluations, on the other hand, allow teachers to make informed judgments about their students' growth and capabilities.

Many forms of performance do not lend themselves to product assessment (Harwayne, 1999). It is difficult to evaluate real knowledge and skills. Teachers realize that often the test scores that go home and grades they assign reflect students' abilities to take tests as much or more as underlying knowledge and/or real competence.

Individual assessment by objective measures—teaching the test—limits the curriculum. It reduces opportunities for children to learn and places artificial constraints on the amount and rate at which teachers introduce information into the classroom. One justifiable criticism of traditional testing is that it provides too small and artificial a sample of what children know. These constraints also act as levels through which children have to pass. In other words, tests can control the curriculum; and when that happens, education ceases to exist. Schools where the curriculum is driven by standardized tests pay little or no attention to such processes as synthesis, summary, observation, analysis, classification, self-expression, application, creativity, diverse thinking, and critical thinking. They rob learners of their potential and of the real abilities they will need outside of school (Kohn, 2000; Smith, 1990).

In process-oriented classrooms, evaluation is based on a different philosophy—that of empowering learners and teachers. Since the purposes of evaluation are different from traditional assessment, the practices are also different. Evaluation procedures reflect what is known about learning, language learning, and literacy. They require informed teacher judgment, documentation of the strategies learners are developing, and a focus on learner growth over time. Because they serve to encourage learners, they become an integral part of the classroom.

Teacher-informed judgment stems from two sources, what teachers know and what children "tell" them. First, teachers look at children through their knowledge of child development, language, learning, and world knowledge. Second, teacher judgment is informed by the children's responses to classroom events. Informed teachers come to know each child intimately. They do this by closely observing what the children are doing, what their interests and intentions are, and what they are learning. This type of evaluation involves both literacy and content learning (Graves and Sunstein, 1992; Harwayne, 1999; Wong-Kam and Kimura, 2001).

Good teachers ask, "What have the students learned?" "What are they ready to learn next?" The following principles are suggested:

1. Evaluation of performance should be over time using regular observation and informed perspectives.

2. Evaluation is non-punitive.

3. Evaluation does not control teachers; teachers control evaluation.

4. Evaluation is reliable and valid.

5. Evaluation is a dual agenda encompassing both evaluation of the learners and evaluation of instruction.

6. Evaluation is carried out using forms and instruments that resemble those learners may encounter outside of school.

7. Evaluation includes learners' collaborative efforts.

8. Good evaluation brings the child into the process.

9. Evaluation reflects what the teacher knows and has observed and serves as the basis for assigning grades.

10. Evaluation is holistic and does not fragment language or learning.

Evaluative data are the source for teacher reflection and decision making. Reflective teachers carry on an internal dialogue that constantly questions what students are accomplishing (Goodman, 1985). Teachers want to know if what is happening fits their theory of learning. They want to know if what they are doing is good for learners—if it promotes independence, if it broadens rather than narrows children's thinking.

In general, evaluation revolves around six activities: goal setting, observing, reflective observation, record keeping, planning, and assigning grades.

Goal Setting   Teachers are actually the final arbiters of the goals and values for their classrooms. Teachers' goals derive from their philosophy and from what they value for learners. However, this is not a responsibility held solely by teachers. Parents, school officials, the wider community, and children are partners in goal setting and evaluation. Teachers are the professionals. They are the only ones in the classroom milieu who have the opportunity to truly know the children and their needs, to serve as the advocate for parents' desires, and to protect children from inappropriate demands. Setting attainable, meaningful, and realistic goals is one of the main the purposes of observing or "kid-watching."

Observing   Excellent teachers become sensitive, reflective "kidwatchers" (Goodman, 1985). Learning what to look *for* and what to look *at* take time and experience. Learning what to listen for and what to focus on also require time and experience. Looking for children's learning strategies and identifying their strengths is the main goal. The following guidelines were developed by Yetta Goodman to help teachers become better kidwatchers.

Figure 12–5 summarizes the major options available to teachers for gathering observational evaluation information. It includes what types of activities to observe as the children are engaged with print. The numerous settings in which reading and writing occur are identified. Teachers inform themselves about children's reading and writing

FIGURE 12–5
SETTINGS AND
LITERACY EVENTS FOR
KIDWATCHING

SETTINGS AND LITERACY EVENTS TEACHERS MAY USE FOR KIDWATCHING AND EVALUATION

To Be Observed and Evaluated	On the Spot	Regular, Formal	Continual Informal
Use of reading cues and strategies	Paired reading SSR Running record	Taped readings Miscue analysis Reading conferences	Shared book Author's chair
Reading	Paired reading	Taped retellings	Lit study groups
Comprehension	Group discussion	Reading conferences	
Writing process	Paired writing SSW	Writing conferences Journal entries	Author's chair Drafts
Mechanics of written language	SSW Message board Notes	Initial writing conference Final editing conference	Journal entries
Attitudes, values, self-concepts of books	Self-selections Difficulty levels	Interest inventories Interviews and contributions Porfolio presentations Projects attempted	Child's comments
Other	Work in progress	Tests	Projects

development through on-the-spot observations; formal, planned observations; and continual, informal "kidwatching" opportunities.

The list in Figure 12–6 suggests what kidwatching is for and what teachers keep in mind as they engage in it.

Reflective Observation   Reflective observation is at the heart of what knowledgeable teachers do. Only through intimate knowledge of the learners can a teacher structure classroom programs to truly meet children's needs, interests, and intentions. Teachers "kidwatch" in a variety of ways and settings. Conferences, shared work, journals, letters, and conversations are some of the ways children reveal what is in their heads and hearts. Teachers engage in continuous evaluation and set up situations that allow them to observe students' responses to the learning events.

For instance, when teachers hear two children reading together, they focus on the strategies the children use. They watch as the children select books. They listen to see if the children predict based on meaning. They determine if retellings show evidence that

FIGURE 12–6
KIDWATCHING

1. Know what, how, and when to observe.
2. Know how language and learning operate in order to observe.
3. Observe in a variety of social/cultural settings: streets, homes, and/or libraries and relate to interest.
4. Observe reading by watching and listening to kids read things usually read. Base evaluation on what is known about reading.
5. Observe writing by watching kids write. Base evaluation on what is known about writing.
6. Explore the nature of miscues (errors)—miscues are indicators of all language developmental processes.
   a. Everyone makes miscues, has misconceptions.
   b. Miscues reveal interpretative differences.
   c. Miscues reveal editing process, change process, version process, folk process.
   d. Focus on high-level miscues that indicate reading effectiveness and efficiency.
7. Listen and observe what many different adults do.
8. Understand responses in relation to social/cultural view of learner.
9. View "right" answers with care.
10. Ask "Why is this happening? What does this tell me about the intellectual functioning of the learner?"

Developed by Yetta Goodman, 1989. Reprinted with permission of the Society for Developmental Education.

readers are constructing meaning. They record their observations anecdotally or on a form or checklist. What will the teacher do with this information?

As teachers study the notes they have made about students' learning and the materials they have collected, a coherent, overall picture of the students emerges. No single, right way exists to explain how teachers reflect. Some peruse all the anecdotes, papers, samples of work, and/or published books, looking for evidence of learning. Others log events in a journal to document evidence of student growth. Others use a tape recorder to record rough notes that are later organized and transcribed, adding reflections as they transcribe. Whichever techniques teachers use, the act of making sense out of the events and artifacts from the classroom is the key to evaluation.

Record Keeping Accurate, up-to-date record keeping is essential for all teachers, but teachers are set apart by the kinds of records they keep. Most teachers keep at least three kinds of records. (Additional sample record-keeping devices are found in Appendix G.)

First, *representative samples* of each child's work are dated and retained to provide teachers with examples of growth over time. This allows teachers to gauge both learners' overall ability to get and make meaning and their developing control over the conventions of language.

Second, teachers keep informal observation records. These include quick notes to oneself, checklists, observation summary forms, and charts or graphs of learners' progress. Checklists and other systematic recording devices can be developed or adapted for children's creative projects, their oral reading, and writings. Many teachers prepare narrative summaries of students' experiences every week or two. Sometimes teachers write anecdotal notes to remind themselves of seminal events in the lives of their learners.

The third type of data is formal observations. These include miscue analyses, running records, finished products such as published books, records of conferences, and other activities that lend themselves to end product types of evaluation.

A benefit of good record keeping is that it not only fulfills a purpose in evaluation, but it models the behaviors that teachers want children to learn. Record keeping is a real and contextual use for literacy.

All records, anecdotal or more quantitative ones, are summarized periodically, and the bits and pieces of paper used to record informal, anecdotal notes are discarded. Many teachers prefer to collect these bits and pieces during the week, dropping them into each student's folder once or twice a day. Then they are compiled on a simple summary once a week. Summary forms, checklists, and graphs are dated and kept in the learners' folders. Good record keeping is a secondary "memory" for teachers. It gives them an accurate picture of what has transpired over time. Documentation of children's growth is the teacher's best tool. It enables teachers to determine what students need to learn next and to plan for that learning.

Planning   Classroom instruction is planned to help learners, not to penalize them. It starts with what they know and what they appear to need. Planning is not a separate, artificial system in the classroom. Rather, it is a continuous, integral part of the daily activities used to inform and guide teachers as they select materials and develop programs (Harwayne, 1999).

The most meaningful planning is individual, but it is not always practical. Planning is aimed at identifying what each learner can do, what each learner knows, and what each learner may be ready to work on next. Teachers use both qualitative and quantitative information to help plan guided reading, guided writing, and teacher/pupil conferences. Evaluation data inform teachers. Teachers use these data to work with individuals and to bring together ad hoc groups of children with common needs. The knowledge and understandings that students possess inform teachers and determine the direction the classroom curriculum will take.

The daily lesson plans by experienced classroom teachers look rather like short notations. Substitute teachers typically need only follow the daily schedule because the students know what they are working on. But the plans that beginning teachers need to keep are more detailed. They focus on the choices learners have within the framework of the daily schedule. They include short-term events: conduct the experiment with the popcorn during language workshop time, meet with Billy, Marcus, and Fran to help them with their letter to the editor. Plans also include activities based on long-term goals: set up the art project for painting scenery for the play, read the new book on dinosaurs, encourage writing about favorite dinosaur.

Daily lessons are typically written in large blocks by time frames from the daily schedule. They may cover a page in the plan book for each day because of the amount of information and materials that need to be kept track of. Figure 12–7 shows a sample block plan format.

Assigning Grades Assigning grades is a responsibility most teachers have. Grading with test scores is easy. Turning anecdotal notes, narrative data, checklists, and other, more qualitative, process evaluations into letter or numerical grades is more difficult. Grades reflect work and progress, and the reporting form of choice for many teachers is a narrative with work samples attached.

However, most school systems still require teachers to report children's progress in the form of a grade on a report card. In some cases, progress in the primary grades is reported as E for Excellent, S for Satisfactory, N for Needs Improvement, and U for Unsatisfactory. In the middle and upper grades, progress is usually reported by the traditional A, B, C, D, F scheme, or percentage scores that mean the same thing. Regardless of the scheme used to report grades, teacher-developed techniques for determining grades abound. The following are examples of how teachers may accomplish this task for reading and writing and are guides that teachers may adapt for turning observations into letter or even percentage grades. A similar format can be applied to grading in other subject areas (adapted from Kemp, 1987).

Note that Figures 12–8 and 12–9 are set up on a base of ten so that conversion to percentages is simple since letter grades usually reflect percentages. An A might be from 90–100. Assigning letter grades is simplified in this manner.

FIGURE 12–7
SAMPLE BLOCK PLAN FORMAT

PERIODS	MONDAY	TUESDAY		WEDNESDAY	THURSDAY	FRIDAY
8:30 AM to 10:45 AM	language workshop	language workshop		language workshop	language workshop	language workshop
10:45 AM to 12:00 PM	guided reading	unit study		guided reading	unit study	guided reading

FIGURE 12–8
GUIDE FOR GRADING
READING

GUIDE FOR GRADING READING

Name: _____ Date: _____

OBSERVING	Always	Often	Occasionally	Not yet
The learner:	10	9/8	7 or fewer	

1. Views reading as language
   Expects reading to make sense
   Reads for pleasure, information
   Makes reading sound like language
     instead of word calling

2. Uses prior knowledge
   Demonstrates personal experience
     and information aid
     understanding

3. Makes predictions based on
     prior knowledge
   Previews material
   Reads title, looks at pictures,
     uses picture clues during reading

4. Makes predictions while reading
     based on grammar and meaning
   Confirms or disconfirms predictions

5. Self-corrects
     when does not make sense
     when does not sound like language
     rereads and attempts corrections

6. Reads with fluency
   Oral reading demonstrates natural
     intonation, speed, and rhythm
   Reader adjusts to various materials

7. Reader produces grammatically
     acceptable sentences within own
     dialect

8. Reader produces meaningful
     sentences within story context

9. Reader uses letter-sound
     relationships to identify unknown
     words

10. Reader's retellings include
      important information directly
      stated and inferred

GUIDE FOR GRADING WRITING

FIGURE 12–9
GUIDE FOR GRADING
WRITING

OBSERVING The learner:	Always 10	Often 9/8	Occasionally 7 or fewer	Not yet
1. Writes a complete story with beginning, middle, and end				
2. Selects and revises drafts, Works on content				
3. Edits drafts Works on mechanics				
4. Attempts to use "best" word				
5. Uses appropriate suggestions				
6. Uses multiple resources for drafts and editing				
7. Exhibits growing control of conventional spelling				
8. Writes willingly on a daily basis				
9. Writes for a variety of purposes				
10. Shows sense of different audiences				
11. Shows originality and imagination				
12. Develops own "voice"				

ASSISTING STUDENTS' SELF-EVALUATION

Good evaluation brings the learner into the process. It encourages independence. Teachers serve learners well when they find ways to help them take responsibility for their own learning and their own evaluation. A large part of all classroom evaluation should be self-evaluation. A realistic appraisal of one's own work, aided by the teacher, is often the most perceptive. Teacher-pupil conferencing, peer conferencing, portfolios, and three-way conferencing (with parent, teacher, and student) are among the techniques that promote realistic self-evaluation.

Good evaluation concerns both literacy and subject matter learning. It is structured in such as way as to address both as they interact with each other. Evaluation is most informative when it occurs as students work on authentic events of their own choosing. Learners need to reflect on and evaluate their own learning. This enables them to become more consciously aware of the processes they go through in their own learning. Therefore, learning is enhanced. For example, as we examine our own reading behavior and that of others, our reading tends to improve. When we examine our own writing processes and strategies, as well as how other authors write, we find new avenues for improving our own writing. It is important for students to really know how they are doing. Identifying evidence of their own learning, and their use of skills and knowledge, improves learners' self-concepts and offers them a purpose for continued learning.

Portfolios   A popular form for self-evaluation in many classrooms is the portfolio (Graves and Sunstein, 1992; Tierney, Carter, and Desai, 1991). Portfolios are collections. Artists use portfolios to represent their best work. Models, architects, and some preservice teachers keep them to impress prospective employers. Even professors are developing portfolios. They are not scrapbooks. They represent highly selective artifacts that have meaning for the individual. Because of the emphasis on self-evaluation, authenticity, and the personal-social nature of learning, portfolios are promising additions to classrooms where the process of learning is valued as well as the products.

Portfolios are *not* used in grading. Rather, they allow students to present themselves through their learning—they are self-evaluative. Teachers use portfolios in a variety of ways. For instance, children may select to develop portfolio presentations for the end of each unit of study, for every six-week grading period, one per semester, or throughout the year. After examining different types of portfolios, children may list some of the categories they want for their own portfolio collections. They decide how to make their portfolios best present their work and their learning. These could include any of the following:

1. letters written at the beginning of the school year describing what they think the year will be like and what they hope to learn
2. examples of their best artwork, dated and arranged by topics
3. early drafts and finished products of their favorite writing: stories, informative pieces, poems, raps, or free verse
4. lists and samples of all their published work
5. lists of books they read during SSR
6. copies of any formal letters or favorite pen pal letters
7. copies of tests, both formal and informal
8. lists of all the words they learned to spell or lists of favorite vocabulary words
9. projects accompanied by photos or written descriptions
10. copies of any math games or other products they created
11. letters describing what the learner thought she or he had learned
12. photographs that represent important class events, field trips, displays

Portfolios are organized by the presenter to reflect a purpose. Some of the more obvious organizational structures include time, events, and concepts. Many teachers require their students develop a table of contents and number the pages. Portfolios are both a culminating event and a time to show off. While they are the property of the learner and are the learner's personal expression, they may also provide teachers with information and insight. Again, the key is knowing what to look for.

The same summer that Jenny learned to water-ski, she attended summer camp. While there, she wrote a letter to her parents (Figure 12–10). Can you read it? Not very many of the words are spelled correctly. Some of the letters are made backward. She doesn't have a very strong sense of leaving space between words. Can she write or not? What can she do as a writer?

Jenny's letter says:

Dear mom dad
   A snake almost climbed up
   my leg! Girls were screaming
   I went away fast! How is Katy?
good bad
   ◯   ◯

   I love you!
      Love,
      Jenny
      P.S.
      I need a backpack.
look down.

FIGURE 12–10
JENNY'S LETTER

Below the letter, Jenny created a word search for her parents. She included words from the letter in the puzzle. She listed the ones she had included so they would be easier to find. One supposes she didn't want her parents to be bored in her absence, so she provided them with an activity she thought they might enjoy.

Jenny is an extremely competent child and an excellent problem solver. She has above average intelligence and an extensive speaking vocabulary. Her self-image was bolstered by learning to water-ski. However, because her ability to use conventions of written language has not developed as quickly as some other children her age, she has found her traditional-style school a punitive place. How do you think she would respond in an integrated classroom full of reading and writing opportunities?

The world is full of children like Jenny.

KEEPING YOUR PASSION FOR TEACHING ALIVE AND WELL

School is not always fair. It is often not a nice place. Teachers who value children, who care about their mental, physical, social, and psychological development, and who themselves love learning, sometimes struggle against less enlightened bureaucratic constraints and requirements.

Traditionally, educational talk is about skills, skills mastery, commercial products and programs—panaceas, as they were—and test scores. Rarely is it about heart, trust, beliefs, feelings, respect, curiosity, or connections. The intent has been to educate the intellect and treat it as if it exists apart from the living child. Schools remove learners from their lived experiences and march them through a sequence of activities. Then the children are judged for mastery and labeled according to their "weaknesses" (Peterson, 1992). Traditional education is cold and mechanistic. Because of that, it can be damaging to warm-blooded creatures like children and teachers.

How can we resist the mindlessness and heartlessness so often found in traditional education while protecting our students and ourselves? We can find like-minded colleagues from whom receive and give support. We can read carefully selected professional literature. We can make a conscious effort to stay in touch with what it means to be a child. We can study the success stories we have each year, focusing on what has gone well and how we know, sharing them with colleagues, and encouraging them to do the same. By so doing, we work to create a ritual within the school community in which we live.

We can keep slogans, sayings, and quotations that are particularly meaningful to us, post them, and read them on a daily basis. An example is, "Our classroom is a safe place for all learners. Each person in it will be cared for by his or her peers and by me. Expressions of caring strengthen us and our community."

Most teachers we know keep their passion alive because they love learning and they love children. They know their students are their best teachers, so they look to them to inform their practice. They get "booster shots" when they need them by talking with other teachers, reading professionally, attending conferences, and taking graduate courses. Keep your passion for teaching alive!

SUMMARY

Integrated classrooms based on the constructivist theory of learning are places full of children's books, their writings, and their imaginations. They do not sound or look like traditional classrooms. Students learn to read and write, to use reading and writing to further their learning, and to open a multitude of worlds. Learners explore the physical world, the world of computers, literature, math, history, geography, and so much more. These classrooms are learner-centered and risk-free. They are places children want to be.

Teachers must first set goals for themselves and their students. They do so by acquiring current information about learning, child development, and language. They decide what they believe and make decisions based on what they know and value. They decide where to begin, and they give themselves time. Becoming a teacher is a process of inquiry.

Evaluation is an integral part of the process. Teachers use evaluation to make informed judgments about their children and to tailor their programs to the needs, interests, and intentions of their learners. But most important, they use evaluation to learn about themselves as teachers.

THEORY-TO-PRACTICE CONNECTIONS

Language and Learning Theory

1. Special needs learners are more like regular education students than they are different.

2. Good teachers are good kid watchers.

3. Getting off to a good start.

4. Learning is social.

5. Learning is best when it involves inquiry in which the learner is interested.

Examples of Classroom Practice

1. Group projects; class discussions; multiple ways of learning and sharing

2. Observations include learners' collaborative efforts

3. Writing advance letter, hope box, establishing routines

4. Peer tutoring; collaboration, dialogues, negotiated meanings, rituals and ceremonies

5. Integrated themes

SUGGESTED READINGS

Allington, R. 2001. *What Really Matters for Struggling Readers: Designing Research-Based Programs.* New York: Addison Wesley Longman.

Peterson, R. 1992. *Life in a Crowded Place: Making a Learning Community.* Portsmouth, NH: Heinemann.

Rhodes, L., and Dudley-Marling, C. 1996. *Readers and Writers with a Difference: A Holistic Approach to Teaching Learning Disabled and Remedial Students,* 2nd ed. Portsmouth, NH: Heinemann.

EXTENDING YOUR DISCUSSION

1. Read about and share your findings on what one or more experts say about how to teach reading and writing to children who are variously labeled: ESL, LD, AD/HD (select one).

2. Read about and share your findings on the success of teaching literacy with such programs and techniques as the Fernald Approach, Doman-Delacatto, Slingerland, DISTAR, Wilson, Shurley, Accelerated Readers, Success for All, or Reading Recovery, among others (select one).

3. Design your ideal classroom. How would you arrange student desks/tables? What materials would you want?

Where would you put the various elements needed? Present your design to the class. Discuss.

4. Write a letter to parents and students explaining the new curriculum you are implementing in the upcoming school year. Share your letters.

5. Prepare a persuasive statement for your principal explaining to him or her what changes you want to make in your classroom program and WHY. Share your statements with classmates and add any ideas from others that you think you should include in your request.

6. Many teaching applications ask for a brief statement of your philosophy of teaching. What could you say about your philosophy of teaching and learning?

7. How have you been evaluated in schools up to now? Have you ever had input into your own evaluations? If so, to what extent or under what circumstances? What was the purpose? How did it work? What do you believe to be the purpose of evaluation? In school settings, who has the right and the obligation to evaluate?

REFERENCES

Allington, R. 2001. *What Really Matters for Struggling Readers: Designing Research-Based Programs*. New York: Addison Wesley Longman.

Au, K. 1993. *Literacy in Multicultural Settings*. Fort Worth, TX: HBJ.

Barr, M., D. Craig, D. Fisette, and M. Syverson. 1999. *Assessing Literacy with the Learning Record: A Handbook for Teachers, Grades K–6*. Portsmouth, NH: Heinemann.

Bridges, L. 1995. *Assessment: Continuous Learning*. York, ME: Stenhouse.

Brownlie, F., and J. King. 2000. *Learning in Safe Schools*. York, ME: Stenhouse.

Caine, R., and Caine, G. 1991. *Making Connections: Teaching and the Human Brain*. Alexandria, VA: Association for Supervision and Curriculum Development.

Cambourne, B., and J. Turbill. 1987. *Coping with Chaos*. Portsmouth, NH: Heinemann.

———. 2001. "Why Do Some Students Fail to Learn to Read? Ockham's Razor and the Conditions of Learning." *The Reading Teacher* 54 (8): 784–86.

Cartwright, G., C. Cartwright, and M. Ward. 1995. *Educating Special Learners*, 4th ed. Belmont, CA: Wadsworth.

Dewey, J. 1930. *Construction and Criticism*. New York: Columbia University Press.

Epstein, J. 1988. "How Do We Improve Programs for Parent Involvement?" *Education Horizons* 66: 58–59.

Fisher, B. 2001. *The Teacher Book: Finding Personal and Professional Balance*. Portsmouth, NH: Heinemann.

Freeman, D., and Y. Freeman. 2000. *Teaching Reading in Multilingual Classrooms*. Portsmouth, NH: Heinemann.

Goodman, K. 1991. "Revaluing Readers and Reading." In *With Promise: Redefining Reading and Writing for "Special" Students*, ed. S. Stires. Portsmouth, NH: Heinemann.

Goodman, Y. 1985. "Kidwatching: Observing Children in the Classroom." In *Observing the Language Learner*, eds. A. Jaggar and M. Smith-Burke. Newark, DE: IRA.

———. 1996. "Observing Children in the Classroom." In *Notes from a Kidwatcher: Selected Writings of Yetta Goodman*. Portsmouth, NH: Heinemann.

Graves, D., and B. Sunstein, eds. 1992. *Portfolio Portraits*. Portsmouth, NH: Heinemann.

Gunderson, L., and J. Shapiro. 1987. "Some Findings on Instruction." *Reading Canada Lecture* 5: 22–26.

Hagerty, P., E. Hiebert, and M. Owens. 1989. "Students' Comprehension, Writing and Perceptions in Two Approaches to Literacy Instruction." In *National Reading Conference Yearbook*, eds. S. McCormick and J. Zutell.

Harwayne, S. 1999. *Going Public: Priorities and Practice at The Manhattan New School*. Portsmouth, NH: Heinemann.

Johnston, P. 1997. *Knowing Literacy: Constructive Literacy Assessment*. York, ME: Stenhouse.

Kemp, M. 1987. *Watching Children Read and Write: Observational Records for Children with Special Needs*. Portsmouth, NH: Heinemann.

Kitagawa, M. 2001. *Enter Teaching: The Essential Guide for Teachers New to Grades 3–6*. Portsmouth, NH: Heinemann.

Kohn, A. 2000. *The Case Against Standardized Testing: Raising the Scores, Ruining the Schools*. Portsmouth, NH: Heinemann.

Lipa, S. 1983. "Reading Disability: A New Look at an Old Issue." *Journal of Learning Disabilities* 16: 453–57.

Ohanion, S. 2001. *Caught in the Middle: Nonstandard Kids and a Killing Curriculum.* Portsmouth, NH: Heinemann.

Peterson, R. 1992. *Life in a Crowded Place: Making a Learning Community.* Portsmouth, NH: Heinemann.

Rhodes, L., and C. Dudley-Marling. 1996. *Readers and Writers with a Difference: A Holistic Approach to Teaching Learning Disabled and Remedial Students*, 2nd ed. Portsmouth, NH: Heinemann.

Ricks, M. 2000. "I Can Read So Good 'Cause I Write So Much." In *Teaching At-Risk Students in the K–4 Classroom: Language, Literacy, Learning*, eds. C. Stice and J. Bertrand. Norwood, MA: Christopher Gordon.

Rigg, P., and V. Allen. 1989. *When They Don't All Speak English: Integrating the ESL Student into the Regular Classroom.* Urbana, IL: NCTE.

Robb, L. 2000. *Redefining Staff Development: A Collaborative Model for Teachers and Administrators.* Portsmouth, NH: Heinemann.

Rogovin, P. 2001. *The Research Workshop: Bringing the World into Your Classroom.* Portsmouth, NH: Heinemann.

Schwartz, S., and M. Pollishuke. 1991. *Creating the Child-Centered Classroom.* Katonah, NY: Richard C. Owen.

Smith, F. 1986. *Insult to Intelligence: The Bureaucratic Invasion of Our Classrooms.* Portsmouth, NH: Heinemann.

———. 1990. *To Think.* New York: Teachers College Press.

Stice, C., and N. Bertrand. 1992. "Grouping For Reading Instruction: The 'Sights' of the Round Table." *Holistic Education Review* 5 (1): 37–42.

Taylor, D. 1991. *Learning Denied.* Portsmouth, NH: Heinemann.

Tierney, R., M. Carter, and L. Desai. 1991. *Portfolio Assessment in the Reading-Writing Classroom.* Norwood, MA: Christopher Gordon.

Topping, K., and S. Ehly 1998. *Peer Assisted Learning.* Mahwah, NJ: Lawrence Erlbaum.

Wasicsko, M., and S. Ross. 1994. "How to Create Discipline Problems." *The Clearing House* 67 (5): 248–51.

Wong-Kam, J., and A. Kimura. 2001. *Elevating Expectations: A New Take on Accountability, Achievement, and Evaluation.* Portsmouth, NH: Heinemann.

PHONICS PATTERNS

As an alphabetic system, the patterns of letter-sound relationships are one of the three cue systems readers must become aware of and use when reading and writing. This store of information is most usable to learners who have developed their phonemic awareness *as* they engaged in real reading and writing. Merely memorizing the multitude of letter-sound associations in drills and on worksheets causes many children to misunderstand the reading process and fail to fully develop their ability to read.

The alphabetic code for English is complex. For instance, there are more than ten alternative spellings for the long /a/ sound—the first vowel sound you hear in the word b*a*by. These include:

a as in l*a*dy

ay as in d*ay*

a + silent e as in g*a*me (as well as silent e with at least two other patterns, ai as in pr*ai*se, and au as is g*au*ge)

ai as in m*ai*l

ey as in th*ey*

ea as in br*ea*k

ei as in r*ei*n

eigh as in n*eigh*bor

aigh as in str*aigh*t

et as in bouqu*et*

ee as in matin*ee*

This complicates things for the young writer. The young reader has a slightly different concern. That is, every time one of these patterns appears in a word, does it always represent the same sound? The answer is no. For example, every time the letter [a] appears in a word (for example, machine), how does the reader know what sound is being represented? The letter [a] by itself represents at least seven different sounds.

They are:

[a] as in ide*a*

[a] as in mount*a*in

[a] as in s*a*id or *a*ny

[a] as in sw*a*llow or f*a*ther

[a] as in spin*a*ch or vill*a*ge

[a] as in talk or draw

[a] as in apple

The following is a list of most of the common alternative spelling patterns in fairly common words for both the vowel and consonant sounds.

Vowels

/a/ as in date

a	shady	au-(e)	gauge
ay	lay	ee	matinee
a-(e)	late	ea	steak
ey	prey	ei	rein
ai	tail	et	bouquet
eigh	eight		
aigh	straight		
ai-(e)	raise		

/e/ as in be

e	me	i	ski
ea	mean	ae	algae
y	happy	e-(e)	these
ee-(e)	freeze	ey	key
ie	field	eo	people
ee	seen	ei-(e)	seize
ie-(e)	achieve	i-(e)	machine
ea-(e)	peace		

/i/ as in kind

i	mild	ey	geyser
i-(e)	time	ay	bayou
igh	night	ei	stein
y	sky	eigh	height
ie	pie	ai-(e)	aisle
y-(e)	type	oy	coyote

/o/ as in go

o	gold	oe	toe
o-(e)	those	ough	though
ow	know	eau	plateau
oa	coal	ew	sew
ou	soul	oa-(e)	loathe

/u/ as in to

o	who	o-(e)	whose
oo	noon	oe	shoe
ou	you	ou-(e)	rouge
ew	threw	ough	through
u-(e)	rule	ui-(e)	bruise
ue	blue	oo-(e)	choose

/a/ as in at

a	cat
ai	plaid
au	laugh

/oi/ as in boil

oi	coil
oy	toy
oi-(e)	noise

/a/ as in hot

o	odd
a	father
o-(e)	dodge

/au/ as in hour

ou	out	ou-(e)	house
ow	owl	ow-(e)	browse
ough	drought		

/e/ as in yes

e	get	e-(e)	edge
ea	head	ea-(e)	cleanse
a	many	ei	heifer
u	bury	eo	leopard
ai	said	ie	friend

/ə/ as in about (schwa)

a	around
i	happily
e	listen
e + (e)	sentence
o	lemon
o + (e)	purpose
ou	famous
u	study
ai	certain
ie	ancient
eo	pigeon
ie-(e)	patience

/u/ as in look

oo	book
u	put
o	wolf⎯

/o/ as in off

aw	draw
o	off
a	walk
au	author
oa	broad
augh	daughter
ough	thought
a-(e)	false
au-(e)	cause

/i/ as in if

i	in	e-(e)	privilege	o	women
y	system	ui	build	ee	been
a	spinach	ie-(e)	sieve	u	busy
i-(e)	give	a-(e)	village		

Consonants

/b/ as in bib

b	bib
bb	ebb

/ch/ as in church

ch	churn
tch	pitch
t	nature

/h/ as in high

h	home
wh	whole

/f/ as in for

f	for
ff	effort
ph	graph
gh	laugh

/j/ as in judge

j	project	dg	edge
g	digest	d	educate

/m/ as in mom

m	some	lm	calm
mm	summer	mn	condemn
mb	climb		

/p/ as in pop

p	pup
pp	puppy

/r/ as in rear

r	roar
rr	correct
rh	rhyme
wr	wrap

/d/ as in did

d	do
dd	add
ld	could

/g/ as in gag

g	go
gg	egg
gh	ghost
x	example

/k/ as in king

c	cap	ch	chorus
k	keep	lk	chalk
ck	crack	que	antique
cc	occur		

/l/ as in lull

l	low
ll	allow

/n/ as in none

n	no	nn	announce
kn	knee	gn	gnat

/th/ as in this and thin

th	bathe
th	bath

/s/ as in sass

s	so	st	whistle
ss	pass	ps	psychology
c	cent	sw	sword
sc	scent		

/t/ as in tot

t	to	bt	debt
tt	better	ct	indict
ed	cracked	pt	receipt
cht	yacht		

/sh/ as in shush

sh	rush	s	sure
t	action	sc	conscious
ch	chef	ss	tissue
c	ocean		

/v/ as in vote

v	valve
f	of
lv	calves

/w/ as in wow

w	water
u	aqua

/ng/ as in ring

ng	singer
n	sink

/y/ as in yet

y	yet
i	senior

/z/ as in zero

z	zeal
ss	dessert
zz	buzz
cz	czar
s	poison

/zh/ as in vision

s	usual
g	beige

ADDITIONAL PHONICS INFORMATION

Other phonics information teachers need includes the numbers of sounds that any one spelling pattern reflects. We already provided that for long /a/. Here is another example. An [e] by itself in a syllable may represent long /e/ as in penal and fetal, or it may represent short /e/ as in metal and petal. Phonics knowledge also includes an understanding that some single vowel sounds are spelled with two letters. These are called *vowel digraphs* (for example, /ea/ as in each, /oa/ as in oak, /ie/ as in friend). Some single consonant sounds are spelled with two letters. These are called *consonant digraphs* (for example, /ch/ as in perch, /ph/ as in phone, /ng/ as in sing). Some vowel sounds are actually two sounds blended together. These are called *diphthongs* (for example, /oi/ as in boil, /ai/ as in al). The *schwa* is an unstressed neutral vowel sound (for example, a as in about, e as in listen, o as in lemon).

Some consonants are blended in words as well. These are called *consonant blends*. English has three basic varieties of consonant blends:

consonant + r as in brick or drop

consonant + l as in blow or flip

s + consonant as in stick or spot

Three letter blends are combinations of the above (s + consonant + l, as in splash, or s + consonant + r as in stripe). A few consonant blends occur in final position within words and syllables. These are exceptions to the three patterns described above. For example, the [ld] in fold, and the [nk] as in drink. Past tense markers, such as in the word slapped, are spelled with one, two, or three letters and often represent another form of consonant blending. In slapped, the final consonants are pronounced as though the word were spelled SLAPT.

Other sound-letter patterns include: (1) double consonants—for example, [dd] as in middle, [gg] as in wiggle, [bb] as in bubble, [tt] as in butter; (2) silent letters—for example, *k*n as in know, *mb* as in thumb, *pt* as in receipt; and (3) the letter [c] sounded like /s/ before e, i, and y—for example, cent, city, and cycle, or sounded like /k/ everywhere else—for example, cat, cot, and cut—the letter /x/ sounded like /gz/ in words such as exaggerate, and like /ks/ in words such as exit.

Finally, phonics "rules" have been attempted in an effort to identify highly consistent letter-sound patterns. These include little rhymes such as, "When two vowels go walking, the first one does the talking"—as in goal and bean. Or, simply stated observations such as "When the letter [r] follows a vowel, the vowel is neither long nor short"—as in burn or fir. Actually only a few generalizations with sufficiently high utility to be useful exist, and children's reading ability is not enhanced by their memorizing the "rules" anyway (Rosso and Emans, 1981).

HIGHLY PREDICTIVE PHONIC GENERALIZATIONS

The following sound-letter patterns or phonic generalizations are applicable in at least three out of four occurrences, or roughly 75 percent of the time.

1. A single vowel in the middle of a one-syllable word is usually short; for example, cat.

2. The [r] causes the preceding vowel to be neither short nor long; for example, jerk.

3. In words having an [oa] the long sound of the /o/ is heard and the /a/ is unvoiced; for example, soap.

4. In words with [ee] the long sound of /e/ is usually heard; for example, flee.

5. In words with an [ay], the y is unvoiced and the long sound of /a/ is usually heard; for example, may.

6. When the letter [i] is followed by the letters gh, the long sound of /i/ is usually heard and the [gh] is unvoiced; for example, flight.

7. When the letter [y] is the final letter in a word, it usually represents a vowel sound; for example, long /i/ as in sky; long /e/ as in berry.

8. When the letters [ch] are next to each other in a word, they represent only one sound, for example, church.

9. When a word begins with the letters [wr] the w is unvoiced; for example, wrong.

10. When two of the same consonants are next to each other in a word, only one sound is voiced; for example, marry.

11. When a word ends with [ck] only the /k/ is voiced; for example, stick.

12. In most two-syllable words, the first syllable is stressed, for example, only.

13. The syllables [ture] and [tion] appearing as second syllables in two syllable words are unaccented; for example, nature and nation.

14. In words that end in [le] the consonant preceding the [le] usually begins the syllable, for example, stable.

15. When the last syllable in a word is the sound /r/, the syllable is unaccented; for example, wonder.

BASIC RIMES OR "WORD FAMILIES"

The following are several basic rime patterns. If students can read the word *bad*, they can also read all the other [-ad] words. Practice, play, and exploring onset and rimes or word patterns are important for early readers and writers. Remember rimes don't always rhyme!

-ad	-ag	-all	-ap(e)	-at
bad	bag	all	ap(e)	at
cad	gag	ball	cap(e)	bat
dad	hag	call	gap(e)	cat
fad	jag	fall	lap	fat
gad	lag	gall	map	hat
had	nag	hall	nap	mat
lad	rag	mall	tap	pat
mad	sag	pall	tap(e)	rat
pad	tag	wall	clap	sat
sad	wag		flap	brat
tad			drap(e)	flat
			grap(e)	
			scrape	

-ed	-eg	-en	-ep	-et
bed	beg	Ben	pep	bet
fed	keg	den	yep	get
led	leg	hen		jet
Ned	Meg	men		let
red	peg	pen		met
set		ten		net
Ted		when		pet
wed		yen		set
				wet
				yet

-ib	-id	-in	-ip	-it
bib	bid	bin	dip	bit
fib	did	din	hip	fit
jib	hid	fin	lip	hit
rib	kid	gin	nip	kit
	lid	kin	pip	lit
	rid	pin	rip	pit
	Sid	sin	sip	quit
		tin	tip	sit
		win	whip	

-ob	-og	-on	-op	-ot
Bob	bog	Don	bop	cot
cob	cog	non	cop	dot
fob	dog	Ron	hop	got
gob	fog	son	lop	hot
job	hog	ton	mop	lot
mob	jog	won	pop	not
nob			sop	pot
rob			top	rot
sob				sot

-ub	-ug	-um	-up	-ut
bub	bug	bum	cup	but
cub	dug	gum	pup	cut
dub	hug	hum	sup	gut
hub	jug	mum		hut
nub	lug	rum		mut(t)
pub	mug	sum		nut
rub	pug			put(t)
sub	rug			rut
tub	tug			

Somewhat more complex patterns and examples:

-and	-ash	-ent	-ild	-ong
band	ash	bent	child	along
demand	bash	cent	mild	belong
grand	brash	dent	wild	dong
hand	cash	gent		gong
land	clash	lent		long
sand	crash	pent		prong
	dash	rent		song
	gash	sent		strong
	hash	tent		throng
	lash	vent		wrong
	mash	went		
	rash			
	sash			
	slash			
	stash			
	trash			

Add to this list. There are many more word family patterns to explore: "ent, able, ess, ell, as, ame, ake, ide," and so on. Adding initial consonants (onsets) in alphabetical order to determine how many real words we can make is both fun and interesting. Substituting initial consonant blends and consonant digraphs or adding final silent /e/ to the words you have—as in the case of the "ap(e)" examples listed above—also produce new words.

Avoid drilling students or trying to have them memorize the patterns. Enjoy these word patterns. Create games and puzzles with them. Have the students keep their own lists as they encounter words in writing and reading. Create word walls that provide lists of these patterns for the student to see, read, and use. It will help students feel more confident, improve their spelling and their willingness to write, and increase their vocabularies. However, reading is not word calling, and we do not want to present it as if it were merely a matter of calling words. Reading is constructing *meaning* from print. As students become aware of word patterns, they begin to understand two things: the fact that they are learning letter names and sounds, and that once they can read one of the words in a pattern they pretty much can read them all. Your students might also choose to keep lists of such words in their journals and add to them for easy reference. This list can be kept alphabetically by the pattern much like rhyming dictionaries.

Make your own. . . .

–ab	–ice	–od	–ide	–ug	–age (etc.)
cab					
dab					
fab					
gab					
jab					
lab					
nab					
blab					
grab					
stab					

Create word ladders and display them on your word wall. Show students how word forms build upon the base or root part of the word. They can use what elements of a word they know and recognize to help them read and write longer words.

pen	it	do	net	an	up	end
open	hit	dog	next	and	pup	bend
opens	hits	dogs	nest	band	puppy	blend
opened	hitter	digs	nesting	brand	puppies	
opening	hitting	dig		bland		
reopening		digger		band		
		digging				

bed	is	or	ebb	at	sum	
beds	his	nor	web	bat	sums	
bedding	history	more	webs	bats	summer	
	historic	bore	webbing	battle		
	historical	boring		batter		
				batting		
				battery		

Word study and word play are important for developing proficient readers and writers. The following ar examples of the kinds of words that compose the English language and pose problems for learners.

Compound words	baseball
Contractions	didn't should've
Synonyms	glad, happy
Homophones	there, their, they're
Antonyms	good, bad
Homographs	*pre* sent pre *sent*
Roots	dict– (to tell)
	dictionary
	dictate
	predict
Root words	dress
	dresser
	redress
	address

REFERENCES

Dahl, K., P. Scharer, L. Lawson, and P. Grogan. 2001. *Rethinking Phonics: Making the Best Teaching Decisions.* Portsmouth, NH: Heinemann.

Goodman, K. 1993. *Phonics Phacts.* Portsmouth, NH: Heinemann.

Moustafa, M. 1997. *Beyond Traditional Phonics: Research Discoveries and Reading Instruction.* Portsmouth, NH: Heinemann.

Opitz, M. 2000. *Rhymes and Reasons: Literature for Language Play and Phonological Awareness.* Portsmouth, NH: Heinemann.

Rosso, B., and R. Emans. 1981. "Do Children Use Phonic Generalizations and How?" *The Reading Teacher* 34: 653–58.

BOOKBINDING

DIRECTIONS FOR MAKING A BOOK

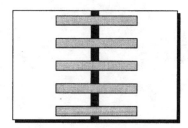

1. Using pattern on next page, place backboards 5/8" apart. Leave center space open.

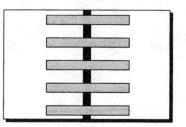

2. Place five pieces of masking tape (4" strips) horizontally, starting at top and bottom, then in between. Note: Boards must be at least 5/8" apart for taping.

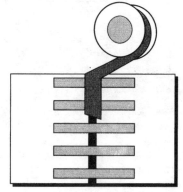

3. Turn boards over and repeat taping on reverse side.

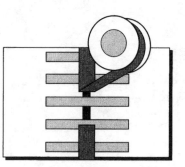

4. Using 36" length of masking tape, cover spine vertically from front to back. Continue wrapping until tape is used up.

Developed by Dr. Elizabeth Brashears, Profesor Emeritus, Middle Tennessee State University. Reprinted with permission.

Pattern

5. Spread glue smoothly on wrong side of cloth. Cover surface completely with glue. Dip fingers in water to spread smoothly if using white glue. Rubber cement may be used instead of white glue, but should be used over surface of boards.

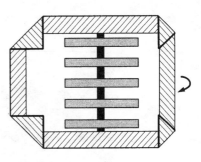

On back of cloth, spread glue evenly with fingers that have been dipped in water. Keeping fingers damp, spread glue into corners.

6. Center taped backboards on glued side of cloth. Fold corners of cloth down first, pressing carefully to glue corners to backboards.

7. Fold sides of cloth and press to backboard to complete cover.

8. Lay this aside to dry. A heavy book placed on it may be used to help flatten out bookback, but be sure to place wax paper between to keep book from sticking.

9. Fold six sheets of 8½"-x-11" paper to make writing pages.

10. Fold two sheets of construction paper in half to make endpapers and flyleaf. Place writing pages inside endpapers as in illustration.

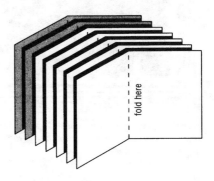

fold here

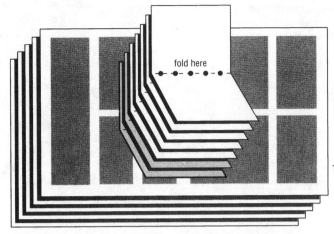

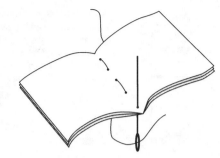

12. Thread large needle with 30" of waxed dental floss. Push needle through first hole from back side. Tape end of thread to back side of construction paper or knot end to secure it.

11. Using large needle, punch five holes on fold using pattern on previous page. Punch through writing pages and construction paper.

Place pages on pad of old newspapers to protect table. *Note:* Holes are shown greatly enlarged in picture.

13. Stitch through all holes in both directions, leaving end of thread on back side. Tape or tie ends to secure stitches.

14. Cover inside of bookbacks completely with white glue or rubber cement. Smooth glue with just a few drops of water.

15. Glue fold into spine of cover, pressing hard with ruler to bond. Smooth endpapers onto backboards. Open and close book gently while drying to prevent creases.

**These are some special effects that may be included when designing books.
The use of these enhances the feeling of ownership.**

1. Write an original personal narrative or a story in draft.

2. Design a title page on the first writing page.

3. Design a dedication page.

4. Design and make a bookplate to glue on the inside front cover.

5. Design and make a bookmark.

6. Design the signature including the endpapers and flyleaf.

7. Design and make an "About the Author" (photo if possible).

8. Copy the story from your draft into the book.

9. Design a library pocket and library checkout card to place in the back of the book.

10. Place your copyright in your book.

11. Design the front cover (title and author).

12. Design chapters or the beginning of the story.

13. Plan a logical ending for the story.

14. Design illustrations, if any (photos, if appropriate).

15. Design a table of contents if appropriate.

16. Design an "Other Books by This Author" page.

**When writing with young authors,
the following kinds of activities should be going on in the classroom:**

17. Examining various trade books for ideas to use in designing books.

18. Sharing ideas for topics, word choices, writing styles, sentence patterns, characters, spelling, grammar, and other considerations.

19. Participating in an author's chair.

20. Editing and proofreading each other's drafts.

21. Bringing materials and making the book in class.

Designing the Title Page

The title page contains the title of the book and the name of the author. This information is usually found on the right side of the first writing page in the book.

Designing the Copyright

A piece of writing is copyrighted the moment it is put to paper and you indicate your authorship with the word "Copyright," the year, and your name. Children enjoy using this privilege and may also write in the name of their own personal publishing company. This information is usually found on the reverse side of the title page.

Designing a Dedication Page

The dedication statement is written by the author to dedicate the book to some very special person or persons. This information is usually placed on the right page facing the copyright page. Bookstores and libraries are excellent sources for books to examine for ideas concerning the expressions of dedication.

Designing the "About the Author" Page

A short autobiography of a few sentences is usually written by the author in third person. Sometimes a photograph is included. Also a list of other publications by the author is often included. This information is usually found on the last page of the book excluding the flyleaf.

Designing an "Other Books by This Author" Page

A list of other books and publications by the author is given either in the back or the front of the book.

MAKING LIBRARY CARDS AND POCKET FOR BOOK

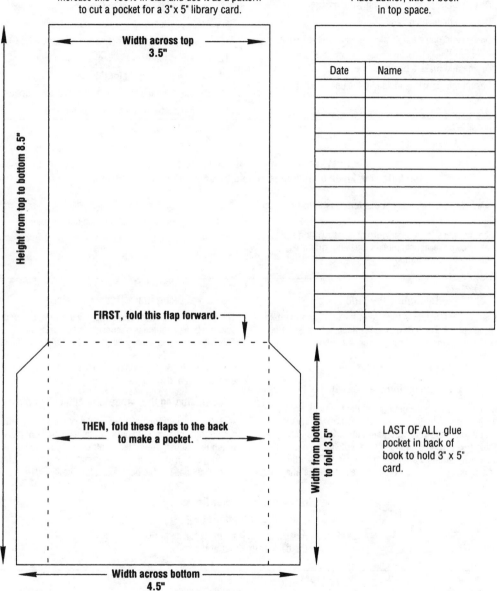

Increase this 150% in size and use it as a pattern
to cut a pocket for a 3"x 5" library card.

Place author, title of book
in top space.

Width across top
3.5"

Height from top to bottom 8.5"

FIRST, fold this flap forward.

THEN, fold these flaps to the back
to make a pocket.

Width from bottom
to fold 3.5"

Width across bottom
4.5"

Date	Name

LAST OF ALL, glue
pocket in back of
book to hold 3" x 5"
card.

This Book Belongs To

A good book is the best
of friends, the same
to-day and for ever.

—Martin Tupper

This Book Belongs To

No entertainment is so cheap as reading:
nor any pleasure so lasting.

—Lady Mary Wartley Montagu

This Book Belongs To

The desire to read grows with reading.

—Erasmus

This Book Belongs To

What we read with pleasure we never forget.

—Alfred Mercier

Examples of Bookplates

ONE WAY TO MAKE A "BIG BOOK"

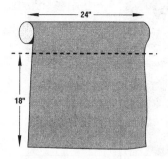

Step 1. Cut two pieces the same size from a roll of brown wrapping paper. A good size is 24" wide and 18" deep.

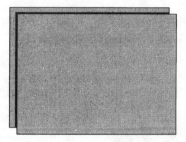

Step 2. Place the two pieces together so that the edges are exactly matching all the way around.

Step 3. Put masking tape around all four edges so that the two sheets are taped together. This makes one sheet double thick. Decorative tape may be used if desired.

Tape is folded in half and finished on the reverse side.

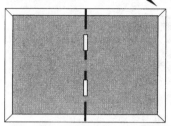

Fold here and place 2 or 3 ACCO fasteners through all thicknesses to finish the book.

Step 4. Make several more double-thickness pages until you have enough for your book. Stack them up neatly and fold all of them in half to make the spine for the book. Secure all thicknesses along the fold with ACCO paper fasteners.

GUIDELINES FOR MAKING "BIG BOOKS"

1. The story of a big book needs to be predictable—that is, children must be able to predict the language patterns as well as the story itself so they will know how to "join in" with the reading.

2. The print needs to be large so children may see words from a distance.

3. The pictures need to be large so children may see them from a distance.

4. The book needs to be easily manipulated. It needs to be heavy enough to hold pages in place when turning but not so heavy that it is difficult to pick it up. A big book does not need to be awkward to store and use naturally. It does not need to be so big that it loses its effectiveness.

5. Predictable themes may be divided into these (and other) broad categories:

   a. repetitive
   b. cumulative
   c. cause and effect
   d. rhyme and rhythm
   e. opposites
   f. numbers
   g. alphabet
   h. time sequence
      time of day
      days of week
      months
   i. familiar story formats
      fairy tales
      fables
      sequels for popular stories
      wordless stories

HOW TO MAKE AN ALBUM-STYLE BOOK

Step 1. Obtain two sheets of **very** heavy 9" x 12" cardboard. Triple-weight illustration board is best, but use whatever is available. *Note:* Corrugated cardboard is **not** recommended as it "breaks" too easily. Cut a 1" strip off the left edge of each board. These dimensions, 9" x 12", are suggested because they fit standard-size paper. Other sizes and shapes may be used, but all other materials must be scaled to size.

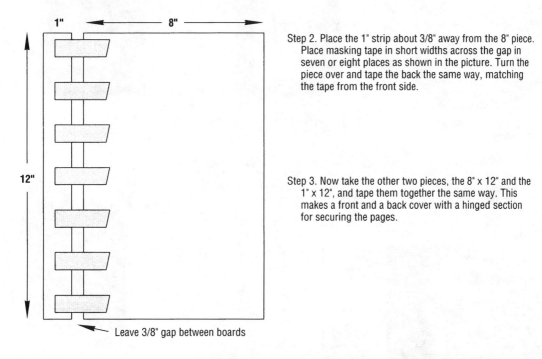

Leave 3/8" gap between boards

Step 2. Place the 1" strip about 3/8" away from the 8" piece. Place masking tape in short widths across the gap in seven or eight places as shown in the picture. Turn the piece over and tape the back the same way, matching the tape from the front side.

Step 3. Now take the other two pieces, the 8" x 12" and the 1" x 12", and tape them together the same way. This makes a front and a back cover with a hinged section for securing the pages.

Step 4. Cover the front first with a piece of cloth or wallcovering that is about 12" x 15". Use glue or rubber cement. After covering the front, complete the back by covering the same way.

Inside front cover

Inside back cover

Turn the corners of the material down and glue as in the sequence of the pictures below.

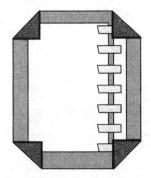

Step 5. Glue corners down inside both covers.

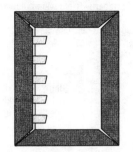

Step 6. Glue edges of cover material inside both covers.

Step 7. Glue endpaper inside covers of both front and back.

Step 8. Collate both front and back covers, the flyleaves, and all of the writing pages to form the book. Punch three holes in the 1" strip, the flyleaves, and all pages. Tie together by putting one end of the tie through each outside hole on the **front**. Pull tight to the back. Now push both ends back through the middle hole and secure them by tying a bow.

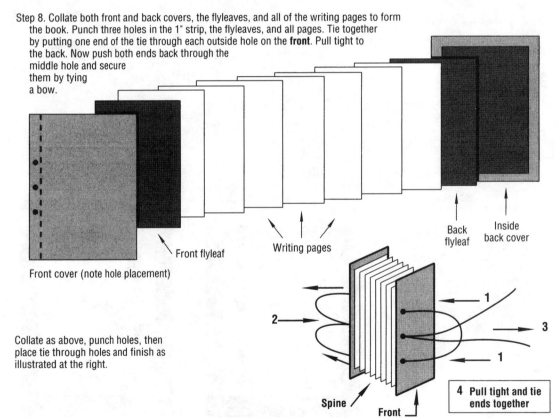

Front flyleaf

Writing pages

Back flyleaf

Inside back cover

Front cover (note hole placement)

Collate as above, punch holes, then place tie through holes and finish as illustrated at the right.

Spine

Front

4 Pull tight and tie ends together

SAFE WEBSITES THAT KIDS LIKE

http://frog.simplenet.com/froggy/

This page has been on the Web for a long time, and kids seem to really like it, maybe because they tend to like frogs.

http://coloring.com/

This used to be called Carlos' Coloring book. It is very interactive.

http://www.kidscom.com/

There's a chat room for kids and one for parents here. There are games, contests, and rules. It's colorful and lively.

http://sln.fi.edu/tfi/hotlists/kids.html

Kids did this one. Come see what kids can do.

http://www.kids-space.org/

International—kids and space information.

http://www.yucky.com/

The Yucky Home page is gross, but kids seem to love it.

http://www.nwf.org/nwf/rrick/

Here's the website for Ranger Rick, with lots of great information and insights.

http://www.wvaworldschool.org/html/lesson/lesson.htm

This one is for teachers too.

http://pbskids.org/

Public Broadcasting does this one and it's very good. There are lots of interactive choices here.

http://sunsite.berkeley.edu/KidsClick!/

This is a search engine with fifteen categories including art, literature, and science all leading to safe websites for kids.

APPENDIX D

TECHNOLOGY IN THE CLASSROOM

Anderson, R., and B. Speck, 2001. *Using Technology in K–8 Literacy Classrooms*. Upper Saddle River, NJ: Merrill.

Churma, M. 1999. *A Guide to Integrating Technology Standards into the Curriculum*. Upper Saddle River, NJ: Merrill.

Cotton, E. 2000. *The Online Classroom: Teaching with the Internet*. Bloomington, IN: ERIC and EDINFO Press.

Ertmer, P., C. Hruskocy, and D. Woods. 2000. *Education on the Internet: The Worldwide Classroom*. Upper Saddle River, NJ: Merrill.

Jody, M., and M. Sccardi. 1998. *Using Computers to Teach Literature: A Teacher's Guide*. Urbana, IL: NCTS Press.

Websites for Learning About the Internet

http://www.screen.com/start

http://www.vmedia.com/hpia.html

http://www.bookshop.co.uk

http://www.gcase.org/gcase.org–LearnInternet.htm

The International Reading Association Web site for using technology in the classroom

http://www.reading.org/positions/technology.html

APPENDIX E

PROFESSIONAL BOOKS FOR NOVICE TEACHERS

Anderson, C. 2000. *How's It Going? A Practical Guide to Conferring with Student Writers.* Portsmouth, NH: Heinemann.

Atwell, N. 1998. *In the Middle: New Understandings About Writing, Reading, and Learning,* 2nd ed. Portsmouth, NH: Heinemann.

Cambourne, B., and J. Turbill. 1987. *Coping with Chaos.* Portsmouth, NH: Heinemann.

Daniel, A. 1992. *Activities Integrating Oral Communication Skills for Students Grades K–8.* Annandale, VA: Speech Communication Association.

Fisher, B. 1998. *Joyful Learning in Kindergarten,* 2nd ed. Portsmouth, NH: Heinemann.

Fletcher, R., and J. Portalupi. 2001. *Writing Workshop: The Essential Guide.* Portsmouth, NH: Heinemann.

Fountas, I., and G. Pinnell. 1996. *Guided Reading: Good First Teaching for All Children.* Portsmouth, NH: Heinemann.

———. 2000. *Guiding Readers and Writers (Grades 3–6).* Portsmouth, NH: Heinemann.

Freeman, D., and Y. Freeman. 2000. *Teaching Reading in Multilingual Classrooms.* Portsmouth, NH: Heinemann.

Gentry, R. 2000. "A Retrospective on Invented Spelling and a Look Forward." *The Reading Teacher* 54 (3): 318–32.

Hindley, J. 1996. *In the Company of Children.* York, ME: Stenhouse.

Jensen, E. 1998. *Teaching with the Brain in Mind.* Washington, DC: ASCD.

Johnston, P. 2000. *Running Records: A Self-Tutoring Guide.* York, ME: Stenhouse.

Lindfors, J. 1999. *Children's Inquiry: Using Language to Make Sense of the World.* New York: Teachers College Press.

Opitz, M. 2000. *Rhymes and Reasons: Literature for Language Play and Phonological Awareness.* Portsmouth, NH: Heinemann.

Opitz, M., and M. Ford. 2001. *Reaching Readers: Flexible and Innovative Strategies for Guided Reading.* Portsmouth, NH: Heinemann.

Owocki, G. 2001. *Make Way for Literacy! Teaching the Way Young Children Learn.* Portsmouth, NH: Heinemann.

Peterson, R. 1992. *Life in a Crowded Place: Making a Learning Community.* Portsmouth, NH: Heinemann.

Ray, K. W. 1999. *Wondrous Words.* Urbana, IL: NCTE.

Rief, L. 1992. *Seeking Diversity: Language Arts with Adolescents.* Portsmouth, NH: Heinemann.

Routman, R. 1999. *Conversations: Strategies for Teaching, Learning, and Evaluating.* Portsmouth, NH: Heinemann.

Stice, C., and J. Bertrand. 2000. *Teaching At-Risk Students in the K–4 Classroom.* Norwood, MA: Christopher Gordon.

Wilde, S. 2000. *Miscue Analysis Made Easy: Building on Student Strengths.* Portsmouth, NH: Heinemann.

JOURNALS IN READING AND LANGUAGE ARTS EDUCATION

Elementary School Journal
5 issues per year

This journal covers all subject areas, reports research, and presents think pieces for and by teachers, researchers, administrators, and teacher educators.

Holistic Education Review
2 issues per year

This is a forum for innovative, experimental, leading-edge ideas in education. It explores and challenges traditional assumptions and methods of mainstream education. The journal seeks to explain humanistic alternative approaches to education.

The Horn Book
6 issues per year

This journal presents announcements of forthcoming works and reviews of children's literature. Covering both fiction and non-fictional genres, the magazine also offers articles on using literature in the classroom.

Language Arts
8 issues per year

This journal is the elementary language arts journal for the National Council of Teachers of English. Each monthly issue is themed. The journal contains articles dealing with issues in language arts and literacy development.

The New Advocate
4 issues per year

This journal promotes children's literature in the classroom and issues related to more humanistic instruction. Reviews of children's literature are also included.

The Reading Teacher
9 issues per year

This journal focuses on practical application articles. It is the elementary journal of the International Reading Association. Included in this publication is "Children's Choices," a list of books chosen by children as their favorites.

Primary Voices
4 issues per year

Published by the National Council of Teacher of English, *Primary Voices* provides a forum for discussion of issues and ideas concerning teaching the English language arts in the early grades.

Voices from the Middle
4 issues per year

Published by the National Council of Teacher of English, *Voices from the Middle* provides a forum for discussion of issues and ideas concerning teaching the English language arts in the middle grades.

Talking Points
2 issues per year

Published jointly by the Whole Language Umbrella and the National Council of Teachers of English, its mission is to provide a forum for discussion of ideas concerning the teaching of the language arts in open education classrooms.

Young Children
6 issues per year

Covering the ages from pre-school through the primary grades, this journal offers articles dealing with critical issues of early childhood education.

Childhood Education
4 issues per year

This journal focuses on practical application articles for teachers K–8. It is the elementary journal of the Association for Childhood Education International. Feature articles include teacher strategies, classroom idea-sparkers, and other books for children.

EXAMPLES OF ADDITIONAL RECORD-KEEPING DEVICES

Child Record-Keeping Form

THINGS I DID THIS WEEK

Name: _____ Week: _____

	Mon.	Tues.	Wed.	Thurs.	Fri.

Writing _____

Books Read _____

Projects _____

Art _____

Science _____

Other _____

Teacher Comments: _____

_____

_____

READING SUMMARY FORM

Student's name: _____   Date: _____

Examiner: _____

Name of Text(s)

1. No. RW = _____   No. errors = _____   No. SC = _____

   Error ratio = 1: _____   SC ratio = 1: _____   Percent Read Accuracy = _____%

2. Out of _____ errors, percent based on:

   % Meaning (m) _____
   % Syntax (s) _____
   % Visual (v) _____

3. Out of _____ errors, percent self-corrections based on:

   % Meaning (m) _____
   % Syntax (s) _____
   % Visual (v) _____

4. What was the reader's score on retelling:

   Very High 100–90% _____   High 89–80% _____   Moderate 79–70% _____
   Low 69–50% _____   Very Low –49% _____

Comments:

5. Major elements in retelling: _____

   Elements missing: _____

6. Reader's strengths: _____

7. Reader's needs: _____

8. Improvement since last assessment: _____

9. Recommendations: _____

CLASS WRITING RECORD   Date:

Children's Names	Nonwriting	Emergent	Early	Fluent	Spelling	Mechanics	Style	Variation	Audience

STUDENT READING RECORD

Name: _____ Date: _____

A. Before reading

What is the subject? _____
_____
_____

What do I know about this topic? _____
_____
_____

What does this remind me of? _____
_____
_____

What do I want to find out about this topic? _____
_____
_____

B. During reading

Things I want to remember and discuss later _____
_____
_____
_____

C. After reading

What new information do I know now? _____
_____
_____

What else would I like to know? _____
_____
_____

What was the most interesting part? _____
_____
_____

How can I best represent what I like best about this book? (For instance, artwork, play, science project)
_____
_____
_____

Author Index

SUBJECT INDEX